Official Catholic Teachings

worship & liturgy

James J. Megivern

 A Consortium Book
from McGrath Publishing Company
Wilmington, North Carolina   1978

262.6

M

(OCT)

VI

The publisher gratefully acknowledges permission to quote from the following
copyrighted publications.

AMERICA PRESS
MEDIATOR DEI, © 1947.
AMERICAN CATHOLIC QUARTERLY REVIEW
MIRAE CARITATIS, Volume XXVII, 1902.

THE CATHOLIC MIND
ADDRESS OF POPE PAUL VI TO THE SECRET CONSISTORY, 1977.

DAUGHTERS OF ST. PAUL
*DECREE RESTORING EASTER VIGIL; DIVINI CULTUS; CODE OF
CANON LAW, BOOK III; ABHINC DUOS ANNOS; QUAM SINGULARI,*
"The Liturgy", ©1962.

B. HERDER BOOK COMPANY
*CHRISTUS DOMINUS; DECREE ON RESTORATION OF THE HOLY WEEK
ORDER; MOTU PROPRIO OF POPE JOHN XXIII ON THE NEW RUBRI-
CAL CODE; ADDRESS OF POPE JOHN XXIII TO A GATHERING OF
YOUNG CHORISTERS; SACRAM LITURGIAM; U. S. BISHOPS' COM-
MISSION ON THE LITURGICAL APOSTOLATE; ECCLESIAE SEMPER,*
"The New Liturgy", ©1966.

INTERNATIONAL COMMITTEE ON ENGLISH IN THE LITURGY, INC:
GENERAL INSTRUCTION OF THE ROMAN MISSAL, © 1973 as printed
by the United States Catholic Conference.
DECREE AND RITE OF PENANCE, © 1974 as printed by the United States
Catholic Conference.

OUR SUNDAY VISITOR
MUSICAE SACRAE, "The Pope Speaks", Volume 3, No. 1, ©1956.
*ADDRESS OF POPE PIUS XI TO THE INTERNATIONAL CONGRESS ON
PASTORAL LITURGY,* "The Pope Speaks", Volume 3, No. 3, ©1956.
SACRAM COMMUNIONEM, "The Pope Speaks", Volume 4, No. 1, ©1957.
INSTRUCTION ON SACRED MUSIC AND SACRED LITURGY, "The Pope
Speaks", Volume 5, No. 2, ©1959.
SACROSANCTUM CONCILIUM, "The Pope Speaks", Volume 9, No. 3,
© 1964.
INTER OECUMENICI, "The Pope Speaks", Volume 10, No. 2, ©1965.

ADDRESS OF POPE PAUL VI TO PASTORS & LENTEN PREACHERS OF ROME, "The Pope Speaks", Volume 10, No. 3, ©1965.

ADDRESS OF POPE PAUL VI TO A GENERAL AUDIENCE, MARCH 17, 1965, "The Pope Speaks", Volume 10, No. 4, ©1965.

ADDRESS OF POPE PAUL VI TO THE COMMISSION FOR IMPLEMENTING THE CONSTITUTION ON THE SACRED LITURGY; LITURGICAL EXPERIMENTS, "The Pope Speaks", Volume 12, No. 1, ©1967.

MUSICAM SACRAM; ADDRESS OF POPE PAUL VI TO THE COMMISSION FOR IMPLEMENTING THE CONSTITUTION ON THE SACRED LITURGY, "The Pope Speaks", Volume 12, No. 2, ©1967.

TRES ABHINC ANNOS, "The Pope Speaks", Volume 12, No. 3, ©1967.

MISSALE ROMANUM; SACRA RITUUM CONGREGATIO, "The Pope Speaks", Volume 14, No. 2, ©1969.

INSTRUCTION ON APPLICATION OF THE ROMAN MISSAL; ADDRESS OF POPE PAUL VI TO A GENERAL AUDIENCE, NOVEMBER19, 1969, "The Pope Speaks", Volume 14, No. 4, ©1970.

SACRAMENTALI COMMUNIONE, "The Pope Speaks", Volume 15, No. 3, ©1970.

LITURGICAE INSTAURATIONES, "The Pope Speaks", Volume 15, No. 4, ©1971.

LAUDIS CANTICUM, "The Pope Speaks", Volume 16, No. 2, ©1971.

AD PASCENDUM; MINISTERIA QUAEDAM, "The Pope Speaks", Volume 17, No. 3, ©1972.

SACRAM UNCTIONEM INFIRMORUM, "The Pope Speaks", Volume 17, No. 4, ©1973.

IMMENSAE CARITATIS, "The Pope Speaks", Volume 18, No. 1, 1973.

EUCHARISTIAE PARTICIPATIONEM, "The Pope Speaks", Volume 18, No. 2, ©1973.

PUEROS BAPTIZATOS, "The Pope Speaks", Volume 18, No. 4, ©1974.

LETTER FROM CARDINAL VILLOT TO A LATIN AMERICAN LITURGICAL CONFERENCE, "The Pope Speaks", Volume 22, No. 4, ©1977.

TIPOGIAFIA POLIGLOTTA VATICANA
MYSTICI CORPORIS, ©1943, as printed by National Catholic Welfare Conference.

UNITED STATES CATHOLIC CONFERENCE
EUCHARISTICUM MYSTERIUM, 1967.
SACRUM DIACONATUS ORDINEM, 1967.
INSTRUCTION ON THE TRANSLATION OF LITURGICAL TEXTS, National Conference of Catholic Bishops, 1969.
IN CELEBRATIONE MISSAE, 1972.

VINCENT A YZERMANS
SACRA TRIDENTINA; TRA LE SOLLECITUDINA, "All Things in Christ", ©1952.

Table of Contents

Introduction

Among all the areas of change in Catholic life in our century that of the Liturgy is the most dramatic. For four centuries a policy of tightly controlled uniformity had been pursued as the appropriate response to the challenge of the Protestant Reformation. The limited reform initiated by the Council of Trent was carried out by Rome, especially by the Sacred Congregation of Rites, the agency founded in 1588 to act as the central regulatory instrument of the Roman Liturgy. For the millions of Catholics of nearly four centuries, the most visible characteristic of the Liturgy was its stability. It did not change. The accent might vary as one moved from Rome to Munich, or from Dublin to Baltimore, but the Latin was the same, the gestures and the vestments were the same. This uniformity in worship was often invoked as symbolic of the Church's unity in Christ.

The nostalgia which many feel for the dignity, the distinctiveness, and the simplicity of the Tridentine era (from the Council of Trent to Vatican Council II) is understandable. The uniform Roman Liturgy was a large component in Catholic identity. It fostered an awareness that transcended national barriers. It engendered a mystique of universality that had much to commend it. At the same time, however, it had growing liabilities in a rapidly changing world. The two realms of greatest deficiency were intelligibility and participation. Because of the use of Latin and the proliferation of rubrical rules, the Liturgy had become overly clericalized. Any talk about lay people taking greater part in Church life had a hollow ring as long as their place in the Liturgy was on the periphery.

Another profound complication of this Tridentine period had even deeper roots. Concern with the regulation of the externals of worship became something of a touchstone of loyalty to Rome. The more closely one observed the rubrics, the more faithful and obedient one was. Despite the commendable motives behind such an approach, it involved a general tendency to separate the externals from the inner meaning, to reduce the Liturgy to rubrics. This "rubricism" and how to eliminate it became a chief target of the 20th century Liturgical Movement. The intention was to restore the theological understanding of Liturgy as the central activity of the Church. "Matters Liturgical" had become the designation for "matters rubrical." A wholesale restructuring of theology would be called for if proper perspective were to be recovered.

The present volume appears as the 75th anniversary is being marked of Pius X's initiation of the Liturgical Renewal with his Motu Proprio *Tra Le Sollecitudini* of November 22, 1903. It is meant to serve as a documentary reflection of what has happened in those three-quarters of a century. It is safe to say that there has never been a parallel period in the history of the Christian Liturgy. It is also necessary to admit that it is not yet over. The commitment to reform made by Vatican Council II continues to bear fruit. But it is certainly an appropriate moment to pull things together and try to put some perspective on what has thus far been done. The 44th anniversary of Pius X's beginnings saw the appearance of Pius XII's great Encyclical *Mediator Dei*; the 60th anniversary saw the promulgation of the Vatican II Constitution on the Liturgy; now, 15 years removed from the Council, the changes have been enormous, sometimes traumatic, often insufficiently prepared for, but decidedly remarkable.

Deciding what to include in this volume was not always easy. My first idea was to start with the Council of Trent and sample the relevant documents of four centuries of liturgical uniformity. This quickly proved to be too antiquarian. In the first 300 years of its existence the Sacred Congregation of Rites, entrusted with deciding all manner of questions and cases submitted to it, issued nearly 6,000 decrees. The vast majority of them were of limited application, were never translated into English, and are now of only historical interest in the narrowest sense. Their publication might serve some useful purpose, but not that for which this volume is intended—i.e., to provide insight on the present by consulting the documents of the time of change.

The first decision thus was to stay with the documents of the 20th century. The first item is the 1902 Encyclical *Mirae Caritatis* of Leo XIII. As the first Papal Encyclical ever devoted entirely to the subject of the Eucharist, it deserves a place here. But also, as the last work issued before the pastoral impact of Pius X, it is an interesting witness to some of the problems which the Liturgical Movement was going to have to struggle with. What needed to be changed was not so much the content as the context. The Eucharist would have to be placed in a different framework if renewal were to occur. It would have to be seen in a more dynamic way. It would take long years of controversy and adjustment to make it clear that what was happening was not a repudiation but a recovery of authentic tradition.

A second decision had to be made once the collection was restricted to the 20th century documents, and that concerned a principle of selection. Once more, an obvious possibility was to print everything that had been issued in the past 78 years. But in examining the feasibility of such an approach, new questions arose. For instance, when Annibale (now Archbishop) Bugnini assembled and published all the Latin documents of the first half-century of the renewal (1903-1953), he found 57 that filled a total of 200 pages of small print.[1] When he returned to update that collection only six years later, there were already another 32 new ones, filling another 100 pages.[2] And those 89 documents are from the preconciliar phase! The real explosion was yet to come.

When Reiner Kaczynski, under Bugnini's guidance, brought out in 1976 a collection of the first ten years of post-conciliar documents (1963-1973), he discovered no less than 180 on hand.[3] The pace in the intervening five years has slowed somewhat, but there are at least 300 Roman documents dealing with the Liturgy in this century alone, and some of them are extremely lengthy. When you add to this the products of the U.S. Bishops and their Committee on the Liturgy, and then include less formal items like Papal addresses, the bulk is prohibitive. There is no way in which complete documentation could be published except in a series of volumes.

Before deciding on the principle of selection of documents, however, it was necessary to check present availability. The collections of Bugnini and Kaczynski are in the original Latin. When English translations are desired, the obvious place to go is to *The Pope Speaks*, which has rendered such commendable service in making a wealth of documentation available.[4] But naturally documents on the Liturgy are there mixed in with all other subjects throughout each of the annual volumes. As for previous collections, the most extensive effort to gather the more important documents and present them in English translation was that of Kevin Seasoltz, *The New Liturgy*, which included 95 items from the years 1903 to 1965.[5] Only 12 of these were from the post-conciliar period, which obviously was only getting under way at the time he published.

In view of the fact that mere bulk continues to be a prohibitive factor in any attempt to present the documentation of the 20th century Liturgical Renewal between the covers of one book, the principle of selection adopted in the present volume was the primacy of the theological. The book is envisioned as promoting insight more than providing regulations. The intention is to show the thinking behind renewal more than the "house-keeping details" of its implementation. This principle was applied especially where documents have been excerpted. The focus is on the rationale rather than the rules of the new Liturgy.

So much has happened in so relatively short a time that it is difficult to retain an accurate perspective. Even at the end of the Council there were those who were still convinced that at least the Roman Canon would certainly never be "tampered with."

The gradual introduction of change after change in subsequent years has brought home all too convincingly how serious the intentions of Vatican II were. As long as the reform was in the "talking" stage, most Catholics were unaffected by it. But once its worldwide implementation got under way, it was a different story. There was, as it were, "no place to hide." Parish life everywhere and on every level was deeply altered. Even the most avid advocates had to admit to at least an occasional jolt as a long cherished mode was replaced.

This volume, it seems to me, is quite different from the others in this series. All of them show the evolution of Catholic theological thought in some particular domain over the last century or more. But in none of the other areas has there been so much change in thinking accompanied by so much reform in practice in so short a period. Biblical scholars are aware of the important advances made in Church understanding of the Bible in recent years, but (unfortunately) this awareness has not really reached the "grass roots." Whereas, with the Liturgy, the case is otherwise. The reform has forced upon all church-goers at least the basic fact that things are different, that changes have been made, that a new style has been adopted, even if the reasons are not always understood.

One of the things which the collection tries to do is to capture the atmosphere, the spirit of the reform, with all its vicissitudes. That is the reason for sprinkling Papal addresses throughout. Very often they provide a "feel" for how things were progressing at the time. For instance, Pope Pius XII, in his 1956 address to the Assisi Congress, revealed more of his own assessment of the Liturgical Movement and its importance than in anything else on record. So too Pope John XXIII in his New Year's Day address of 1961 expressed to a group of children the heart of the matter in simplest terms. But the real work of reform, as the record now shows, was to take place, as called for by Vatican II, under the direction of Paul VI in the hectic decade from 1963 to 1973. Thus, some of his addresses during those years provide an invaluable commentary on the development.

Even though some of the changes came earlier and others came later, the period from 1963 to 1973 is already insured an unparalleled place in history as the decade of the basic Liturgical Reform of Vatican II. Who could fail to be impressed with the intensity with which Paul VI entered into the promotion of the reform at the very beginning? Listen to his plea to the Lenten preachers in 1965: "Devote the greatest care, especially during this first year, to knowing, explaining and applying the new norms that the Church intends to use from now on in celebrating divine worship. This is not an easy thing to do; it is a delicate thing. It demands direct and systematic interest. It calls for your personal, patient, loving, truly pastoral help. It means changing many, many habits that are, from many points of view, respectable and dear. It means upsetting good and devout faithful to offer them new forms of prayer that they won't understand right away; it means winning over many, many people, who pray or don't pray in church as they please, to a personal and collective expression of prayer. It means fostering a more active school of prayer and worship in every assembly of the faithful, introducing into it aspects, gestures, usages, formulas, sentiments that are new; what we might call a religious activism that many people are not used to . . . this is something difficult and delicate; but it is also necessary, obligatory, providential, revivifying and, We hope, consoling." (¶1108)

It is difficult to decide which is the cause for greater marvel: his idealism or his realism. He knew all too well that he was speaking to men of deep conservative inclination, but he also had confidence in their basic good will, their willingness to do what they were convinced was required of them. So he went on to try to stir that fund of good will into action: "You have to be convinced that this is a great event; that there are very lofty ideas at stake; that there are divine truths, divine realities involved; that the aim is to use this method . . . to reach the heart of modern man and re-enkindle in it the flame of love for God and neighbor." (¶1109)

Throughout the intervening years it is that perspective which has been most troublesome to maintain. Pope Paul made it clear that he was aware of the petty annoyances some experienced. Just two weeks after the address just quoted he returned to the subject in a General Audience and painted what some had felt: "Previously everything was peaceful; everyone could pray as he wished; we understood all about the way in which the ceremony was carried on. Now, every-

thing is new, surprising, changed; even the ringing of the bells
at the Sanctus has been done away with! And then those
prayers that one doesn't know where to find; Communion
being received standing up; and Mass ending cut short with a
blessing. . . In short, there is no longer any peace, and we
understand less than we did before."

While expressing sympathy with those who felt this way,
he let them know in no uncertain terms where the fault was
principally to be found. Such petty criticisms "reveal very little penetration into the meaning of the religious rites and give
evidence not of true devotion and a true sense of the meaning
and value of holy Mass, but rather of a certain spiritual laziness. . ." (¶ 1134-35)

If one looked only at the documents and revisions that were
appearing in systematic sequence throughout this period, this
human dimension would be missed. The task of leading an
institution like the Roman Catholic Church through a total
Liturgical Reform is mind-boggling. The Pope had to push
and pull, persuade and cajole, goad the slowpokes and rein in
the eager beavers. This aspect of his Pontificate has not received the attention it deserves and which history will surely
provide it. Besides the two instances given above, where he
pleaded with the Lenten preachers to preach the Reform and
with the General Audience to accept and adopt the Reform,
we see another dimension when he addressed the scholars
involved in revising the documents for use in the Reform. In
October 1966 he spoke to them of "the great work you are
doing. We must thank you for your efforts. Nothing can serve
the Church better in these post-conciliar days; nothing can do
more to awaken her love for God, win for her the Holy Spirit's
help and enable her to draw men to her, teach them and make
them holy. . . . It is a complex task which can be mishandled."
He then gives them practical advice on how to approach it.
"Your inquiry must not be conducted in an excessively radical spirit, as if you were iconoclasts, with a fury to put everything right and leave nothing as it was. No, you must judge
maturely, on sound principles, aware that you are dealing with
a religious matter that demands respect. The best thing, not
the newest fashion, is what we must have in view. . ." (¶ 1145-
46)

But if he knew how to admonish mildly, he also knew how to support staunchly. When an Italian publication issued a vicious attack against Cardinal Lercaro over the question of preserving Latin in the Liturgy, he labeled it "unjust and irreverent," noting that "it does not edify anyone, nor does it help the cause it purports to advance." (¶ 1218) He goes on in the same address to "urge the clergy and all the faithful not to give in to unbridled and free-wheeling experimentation, but rather to perfect and execute the rites prescribed by the Church." (¶ 1223) The very tone shows that by this time (April 1967) the ultraconservative backlash was mounting.

Ten years later (April 1977) Pope Paul's assessment of the Reform was mixed. "The course of these recent years shows that we were on the right path." But painful departures from that path took place on the left and on the right. On the left, "abuses have been committed and liberties have been taken in applying the liturgical reform." On the right are "those who take an unbending attitude of non-acceptance in the name of a tradition that proves to be more a banner for contumacious insubordination than a sign of authentic fidelity." (¶ 1947) One can sense a certain weariness as he requests all to banish "from within the ecclesial community those sources of corrosive criticism, division of minds, insubordination to authority and mutual suspicion that have occasionally succeeded in paralyzing abundant spiritual energies and in holding up the Church's conquering advance on behalf of the kingdom of God." (¶ 1951)

The reason for the doleful mood becomes clear a bit later in the same address when the Pope refers to the disobedience of Archbishop Lefebvre. "We ask this brother of ours to be mindful of the breach he is producing, the disorientation which he is causing, the division which he is introducing with the gravest responsibility." (¶ 1957)

This is all part of the record. By inserting these addresses in their chronological positions in the midst of the Reform, the intention is to provide a living dimension, a taste of the atmosphere as the revised prayers and rites trickled out. The book is thereby meant to serve as a one-volume testimony to the monumental achievement of the Liturgical Renewal of the 20th century Catholic Church.

In saying this, the objection can readily be raised that this is too "Papalist" a view. Objection sustained. If there is a major obvious defect in presenting the enclosed as proof of the Liturgical Movement, it is that it leaves out of sight the influences that account for the Roman developments. Yet, our excuse is that all interested parties should by now know this story which has been well told elsewhere. As Charles Davis put it nearly two decades ago, "Papal decrees do not constitute a movement, and for the beginning of the movement properly so called we must turn to Belgium and the work of Dom Lambert Beauduin."[6] Ildefons Herwegen and Odo Casel of Maria Laach in Germany and Pius Parsch in Austria would also have to be credited, along with Virgil Michel, H. A. Reinhold and Godfrey Diekmann in this country.

But where would one draw the line? The Liturgical Movement with its small beginnings was blessed with some noteworthy talent in its development. Josef Jungmann, Dom Botte, Pere Gy, Clifford Howell, Cipriano Vagaggini, William O'Shea, Gerard Sloyan, Robert Hovda, Balthasar Fischer, Frederick McManus, Annibale Bugnini, and A. G. Martimort, to name a random dozen. But in terms of ultimate effectiveness, the work of all of them would have to be termed preliminary. The groundwork was indispensable but would have come to nought if it had not been adopted into an actual program of official Church reform. Therein lies the significance of Pius X, of Pius XII, of Vatican II, and of Paul VI.

One document included here gives an unusual glimpse behind the scenes as the reform was in progress. The January 1969 Instruction of the Consilium deals with "the trials of a translator" of the Liturgy. (¶ 1510) Anyone inclined to be dissatisfied with or critical of the new English Liturgy would do well to mull over the points of this Instruction. Because Americans are, as a people, so notoriously unfamiliar with other languages, we often fail to appreciate what a host of difficulties confronts the translator. This Instruction, studded

with examples, calls attention to some of the frequently overlooked problems that must be solved before a trustworthy
translation can be produced. It makes one aware of why translation is truly a fine art that requires abundant talent and
expertise, and even then will provoke reactions as varied as
those prompted by any other work of art.

If the amount of documentation seems somewhat over-
whelming, even though it is already only a selection from the
full material, it may be useful to make some recommendations
for someone who would want to pick his way through the
more important ones. For such purposes a case could be made
for the following seven:

1) 1903—The November 22 Motu Proprio of Pius X, *Tra
Le Sollecitudini,* is still looked back to as the doorway to a
new era. Its chief aim, of course, was the restoration of Church
music, but this is so intimately tied in with the whole question
of active participation that the key issue was thereupon
raised. One statement in particular became the slogan for the
Liturgical Movement for the rest of the century: that active
participation in the Liturgy is "the foremost and indispensable
fount" of the true Christian spirit. (¶ 28)

2) 1947—The November 30 Encyclical of Pius XII, *Mediator
Dei,* became the Magna Charta of the Liturgical Movement.
Like his earlier encyclical on Biblical studies (*Divino Afflante
Spiritu* - 1943), it came as an unexpected leap forward that
left many behind, bewildered by its appearance. It vindicated
what many had considered a fringe movement, clearing the
way for the Church to make that movement its own, making
its insights and values accessible to all.

3) 1963—The December 4 Constitution on the Liturgy
appropriately bears the title *Sacrosanctum Concilium,* for it
was the first document of Vatican II, setting the tone for all
the rest. The renewed vision of the Church embraced therein
forced the abandonment of the static ecclesiology of the
preparatory schemata. The later Constitution *Lumen Gentium*
and *Gaudium Et Spes* represent the further fruit of this renewal, and would have been quite impossible without the
Liturgy Constitution.

4) 1964—The September 26 Instruction *Inter Oecumenici* of the Congregation of Rites was the first document of implementation of the Liturgy Constitution (incorporating the directives of Pope Paul's January 25, letter *Sacram Liturgiam*).

5) 1967—The May 4 Instruction *Tres Abhinc Annos* of the Congregation of Rites was the second document of implementation of Vatican II, introducing the next series of changes in the gradual reform.

6) 1967—The May 25 Instruction *Eucharisticum Mysterium* of the Congregation of Rites, even though somewhat excerpted, is the third largest document in this book (after *Mediator Dei* and the Vatican Constitution on the Liturgy). It is a comprehensive review of how far things had changed and what the overview of the situation was midway in this decade of reform.

7) 1970—The September 5 Instruction *Liturgicae Instaurationes* of the Congregation for Divine Worship. It was the third major document implementing the reform initiated by Vatican II. It conveys more of a confidence that things were going well despite the many obstacles to renewal. The perennial effort to avoid letting minutiae blind one to the real significance of the change was prominent. "The present reform, drawing upon an ancient yet living spiritual tradition, has sought to create a liturgical prayer which is visibly the work of the whole People of God, structured in its variety of orders and ministries. This unity of the whole body of the Church is the guarantee of the liturgy's efficacy and authenticity." (¶ 1706)

When all the rationale and rhetoric have been reviewed, however, one may still ask what difference all these changes have really made. Human ignorance, malice and weakness have ever been equal to the task of scuttling ideals. No reform in history has ever been more than partially successful. Finitude implies failure and frustration. Yet the fact remains that there are ups and downs, degrees of advance as well as retreat; and in order to illustrate from another angle the general contention that the 20th century Liturgical Movement has borne considerable fruit, the final document included in this collection is of another kind. It is a letter of Cardinal Villot to the Latin

American Liturgical Conference, written July 21, 1977. It is placed last here since that is its appropriate chronological position, but also because it serves as something of a fitting finale. Such a letter would simply have been unthinkable and impossible in earlier eras. It reflects the integral view recovered by the modern liturgical, theological, biblical renewals. It acknowledges that Christian faith cannot be restricted to the sacristy but must be "dedicated to the work of evangelization and human progress. The Church is endeavoring to help men discover their dignity and their faith and to live these in a more authentic way. In this task the liturgy is the summit toward which pastoral work should tend, as being the way of full participation in the Christian mystery of salvation." (¶ 1963-64)

The pervasive problem of formalism is not ignored. "At least for some . . . the reform has meant a purely external change. They have not grasped with sufficient depth the spiritual life-giving content which the liturgical reform seeks to bring to faith and to the development of the various ecclesial communities. . . Where necessary we must begin anew. . . All must move forward and pass from reform to renewal, from ritual change to the perception and assimilation of the content of the reform. In the process there will also be a renewal of consciences and of commitment to the Christian life, for these spring from the experience of the mystery of Christ in the liturgy. . ." (¶ 1966-68)

Nor is the existence of an unliturgical "popular" religion viewed in merely negative terms as an obstacle to any kind of renewal. "It would be a mistake to try to eliminate it from the life of the people, especially the more simple, without providing an adequate substitute. On the contrary, it should be studied, understood, appreciated and purified of all that is incorrect. It should be . . . enriched with elements from the liturgy which will help it to develop. . ." (¶ 1999)

The massive problems of Latin America are not thereby assured of solution. But at least the whole question of Christian faith is brought back to the center. Traditional institutional involvement in the political power-structure and relationship to the grinding poverty of the masses will inevitably be altered when such directives as the following are heeded: "Let the bishops guide their fellow-workers and be an example and inspiration to them, by showing how the liturgy can, when its possibilities are prudently exploited and when it has its proper place in the overall pastoral plan, be a vital force for the accomplishment of the Church's mission." (¶ 2011)

This is, as the saying goes, "the bottom line." It has been the contention of the advocates of liturgical reform from the very start that this was their ultimate motivation. Clifford Howell said it years ago: "During the past half century there has been a growing number of people, both clergy and laity, who have realised that we cannot afford to treat as mere ritual that which enshrines the very life of the Church herself, namely, the liturgy. The liturgical movement of modern times is filled with a spirit of sincerity. It strives to make dead ritual into living and meaningful worship, to live the life of the Church according to the mind of the Church as expressed in the words of the liturgy, to pray the Church's prayers in sincerity and truth."[7] An unreformed liturgy in an unfamiliar language used to drive Catholics to the adoption of other forms of piety in their research for meaningful spirituality. This book presents the historical documents that resulted when the Church undertook the colossal task of bringing the Liturgy back from the periphery to the center of Catholic life, of altering general consciousness from thinking of Liturgy as rubrics to understanding Liturgy as worship.

1   A. Bugnini, C. M., *Documenta Pontificia ad Instaurationem Liturgicam Spectantia (1903-1953)*, (Bibliotheca "Ephemerides Liturgicae," Sectio Practica 6), Roma: Edizioni Liturgiche, 1953.

2   A. Bugnini, C. M., *Documenta Pontificia ad Instaurationem Liturgicam Spectantia II (1953-1959)*, (Bibliotheca "Ephemerides Liturgicae," Sectio Practica 9), Roma: Edizioni Liturgiche, 1959.

3   Reiner Kaczynski, *Enchiridion Documentorum Instaurationis Liturgicae I (1963-1973)*, Roma: Marietti, 1976.

4   *The Pope Speaks*, Our Sunday Visitor Incorporated, Noll Plaza, Huntington, Indiana 46750.

5   R. Kevin Seasoltz, *The New Liturgy*, N. Y. Herder & Herder, 1966.

6   Charles Davis, *Liturgy and Doctrine*, N. Y.: Sheed & Ward, 1960.

7   C. Howell, *Preparing for Easter*, London: Burns & Oates, 1957, rev. ed., p. 53.

Subject Index

MIRAE CARITATIS
Encyclical Letter of Pope Leo XIII
on the Most Holy Eucharist
May 23, 1902

The wonderful zeal for the salvation of men of which Jesus Christ has given us so bright an example we, in accordance with the sanctity of our office, strive to study and imitate unceasingly, and, with His help, we shall continue to follow the same Divine model as long as life remains in us. As it is our lot to live in times bitterly hostile to truth and justice, we have endeavored to supply abundantly as far as lay in our power, by teaching, admonishing and working, whatsoever might seem likely to avert the contagion of error in its various forms or strengthen the energies of Christian life. In this connection there are two things within the memory of the faithful, intimately connecting one with the other, the accomplishment of which fills us with consolation in the midst of so many sorrows. One is that we declared it most desirable that the whole human race should be consecrated in a special manner to the Sacred Heart of Jesus Christ the Redeemer; the other that we most earnestly exhorted all bearing the Christian name to adhere steadfastly to Him who by divine authority is for all men the Way, the Truth and the Life.

And now, in truth, watching with vigilance over the fortunes of the Church in these evil days, we are impelled by the same apostolic love to add something which will crown and finish the project we had in mind; namely, to recommend

to the Christian world by a special act of our authority the
Most Holy Eucharist.

3　　　The Blessed Eucharist is the most divine gift, given to us
clearly from the inmost heart of the Redeemer, with the desire of one desiring this singular union with man and instituted
chiefly for the generous disposal of the fruits of His redemption. In this matter we have hitherto manifested by our authority and zeal not a little solicitude. And it is pleasant to
remember, among other things, that we, by legitimate approval and privileges, largely increased the number of institutes and sodalities devoted to the perpetual adoration of the
Divine Host: that we also took care to have Eucharistic congresses held with suitable splendor and corresponding usefulness, and that we made patron of those and similar works,
the heavenly Paschal Baylon, who stood out in his day as a
most devout worshiper of the Eucharistic mystery.

4　　　Therefore, venerable brethren, it is well to fix our minds
on certain features of this mystery in defending and illustrating which the zeal of the Church has constantly been manifested and not infrequently crowned by the palm of martyrdom, whilst the doctrine itself has called forth the learning
and eloquence of the greatest men and the most noble
masterpieces in various arts. Here it will be our duty to point
out clearly and expressly the power that is in this mystery
to cure the evils and meet the necessities of the present age.
And surely, as Christ, at the close of His mortal life, left
this sacrament as the great monument of His love for men,
as the greatest support "for the life of the world" *(St. John
vi., 52)*, so we, who are likewise soon to depart, can desire
nothing more eagerly than to excite and nourish in the minds
of all men feelings of grateful love and religious devotion
towards this most wonderful sacrament, in which, we believe,
are to be found the hope and assurance of salvation and peace.

5　　　It may be a cause of surpirse to some that we should think
this age, so universally disturbed and groaning under so great
a burden, should be best aided by such remedies and helps,
and persons shall not be wanting, perhaps, who will treat our
utterances with fastidious indifference. This comes, chiefly
from pride, and pride is a vice which weakens Christian faith

and produces such a terrible darkness about divine things that of many it is said: "Whatever things they know not, they blaspheme." (*Jude* x.) But so far are we from being averted from the purpose we have in view that we believe more firmly than ever that it will bring light to those who are well disposed and obtain, by the brotherly intercession of the devout, pardon from God for those who revile holy things.

To know with full and perfect faith what is the virtue of   6
the Most Holy Eucharist is to know what God, made Man, accomplished for the salvation of the human race in His infinite mercy. For as it is a duty of true faith to proclaim our belief in Christ and worship the Supreme Author of our salvation, who by His wisdom, laws, example and the shedding of His blood renewed all things, it is a duty of equal obligation to worship Him who is really present in the Eucharist, that so He may abide among men to the end of the world, and by the perennial communication of Himself make them sharers in the blessings of His redemption.

Now, he who studiously and religiously considers the bless-   7
ings flowing from the Holy Eucharist sees at once that in it are contained in the most eminent degree all other blessings of every kind; for from it that life flows which is truly life: "The bread which I will give is My flesh for the life of the world." Not in one way alone is Christ the life— Christ, who assigned as the cause of His coming among men that He might bring them a sure fullness of life that was more than human: "I come that they may have life, and have it more abundantly." For as soon as "the goodness and compassion of God our Saviour" appeared upon earth, a power at once came forth that almost created a new order of things and influenced every department of civil and domestic society. Thence new relations between man and man; new rights, public and private; new duties; a new direction given to institutions, laws, arts and sciences. The thoughts and studies of men were drawn towards the truth of religion and the sanctity of morals, and hence a life given to men truly heavenly and divine. All this is frequently commemorated in the sacred

writings; the tree of life, the word of life, the book of life, the crown of life, and, expressly, the bread of life.

8   But this life about which we are speaking bears an express resemblance to the natural life of men, and so, just as the one is nourished by food and grows strong, so does the other likewise require to be supported and strengthened by food. And here it is well to recall the time and manner in which Christ moved the minds of men and excited them to receive suitably and righteously the living bread which He was about to give them. For where the fame had spread abroad of the miracle of the multiplication of the loaves which He had wrought on the shore of Tiberias, many people followed Him so that their hunger, too, might be appeased. Then Jesus, seizing the opportunity, just as when He infused into the Samaritan woman at the well a thirst for the water "springing up into life everlasting," similarly disposes the minds of the eager multitude to desire more eagerly another bread, the bread "which endureth unto life everlasting." But this bread, as Jesus continues to show, is not that heavenly manna given to their fathers wandering through the desert, nor is it that which they themselves had lately received from Him in astonishment; but He Himself is the true bread which He gives: "I am the bread of life." He inculcates still further the same lesson both by council and by precept: "If any man eat of this bread, he shall live forever; and the bread that I will give is My flesh for the life of the world." And the gravity of the command He thus shows clearly: "Amen, amen, I say unto you: Except you eat the flesh of the Son of Man and drink His blood, you shall not have life in you." Away, therefore, with that common and most pernicious error of those who believe that the Holy Eucharist is only for those who, free from business and troubled in mind, resolve to seek repose in some design of a more religious life. For the Holy Eucharist, than which there is nothing more excellent or salutary, is for all, whatsoever their employment or dignity, who wish (and there is no one who should not wish) to nourish in themselves the life of Divine Grace, of which the ultimate end is the attainment of life eternal.

Would that those whose genius or industry or authority   9
could do so much to guide the men and affairs of the age
would think rightly of eternal life and impart the knowledge
of it to others. But, alas! we see with regret that most of these
arrogantly believe that they have given to the world a life
prosperous and almost new, because they urge it forward to
strive in its excited course for utilitarian objects and the mere
gratification of curiosity. Look where you will, human society, alien though it is from God, far from enjoying that tran-
quility of affairs which it seeks, labors in great anguish and
trepidation like one tossing in a fever; it strives vainly to obtain that prosperity in which alone it puts its trust, ever vainly pursuing it and clinging desperately to what is slipping from
its grasp. For men and states come necessarily from God, and
therefore in no other can they live or move or do good but
in God through Jesus Christ, from whom men have received
and still receive the best and choicest gifts. But the chief
source and fountain head of all these gifts is the Holy Eucharist, which, while it nourishes and supports that life for which
we strive so ardently, exalts in the highest degree that dignity
of human nature which seems to be so highly valued in these
days. For what can be greater or more desirable than to be
made as far as possible participators and partners in the Divine
nature? But this is what Christ does in the Eucharist, raising
man up to divine things by the aid of grace and uniting Himself to him by bonds so close. For there is this difference between the food of the body and the food of the soul, that
the former is converted into us, but the latter converts us
into itself, and it is to this that Augustine refers when he puts
the words into the mouth of Christ: "You shall not change
Me into thee as food of thy flesh, but thou shalt be changed
into Me."

But this most excellent sacrament, which renders men par-   10
ticipators of the Divine nature, also enables the soul of man
to advance in every class of the higher virtues. And first in
faith. At all times faith has had its assailants; for although
it exalts the minds of men with knowledge of the most lofty
things, yet, while it has revealed that there exist things above

nature, it conceals their precise character, and so seems to depress the human mind. Formerly only this or that article of faith was attacked; afterwards war was waged much more widely, until it finally came to be affirmed that there was nothing at all above nature. Now, for renewing in the mind the vigor and fervor of faith there is nothing more suitable than the mystery of the Eucharist, which is properly called the mystery of faith; for truly in this one mystery, by reason of its wonderful abundance and variety of miracles, is contained the whole supernatural order. "He has made a remembrance of His wonderful works, being a merciful and gracious Lord. He hath given food to them that fear Him." For if God acknowledged what He wrought above nature as due to the incarnation of the word, through whom the salvation of the human race was restored, according to that word of the Apostle: "He hath purposed . . . to reestablish all things in Christ, that are in heaven and on earth, in Him;" the Eucharist, according to the testimony of the Holy Fathers, is a continuation and an expansion of the incarnation. For by it the substance of the incarnate word is united to men, and the supreme sacrifice of Calvary is renewed in a manner that is full of mystery. This the prophet Malachy signified in the words: "In every place there is sacrifice, and there is offered to My name a clean oblation." And this miracle, the greatest of all, is accompanied by innumerable others, for here all the laws of nature are suspended; the whole substance of the bread and wine is changed into the Body and Blood of Christ; the species of bread and wine are sustained without a subject by Divine power; the Body of Christ dwells at the same time in as many places as the sacrament is consecrated. But human reason is enabled the better to reverence so great a mystery by the prodigies which have been performed in its glory in past ages and in our own days, of which, indeed, there still exist renowned and public proofs, and that not in one place merely. We see, therefore, that by this sacrament faith is fostered, the soul nourished, the falsehoods of rationalists dissipated and the whole order of the supernatural made clear to our eyes.

But it is not pride alone, but depravity of mind as well,   11
that makes faith in Divine things grow weak. For if it happens
that the better the morals the clearer the intelligence, if even
the prudence of the Gentiles perceived that the mind is
blunted by the pleasures of the body, as Divine wisdom has
already borne testimony, then so much more in Divine things
do the pleasures of the body obscure the light of faith, and
even extinguish it altogether in God's just punishment. And
for these pleasures there is burning in those days an insatiable
cupidity, a cupidity which, like the contagion of disease,
widely infects all even from their first tender years. There is
a remedy for this terrible evil in the Divine Eucharist. For,
first of all, by increasing charity it checks voluptuous desire;
as Augustine says: "The nourishment (of charity) is the lessening of lust; perfection, no lust." Besides, the most chaste
flesh of Jesus restrains the luxury of our flesh, as Cyril of
Alexandria has said: "For Christ existing in us calms the law
of the flesh raging in our members." But even more the peculiar and most precious fruit of the Eucharist is that signified
in the saying of the prophet: "What is the good thing of Him
(Christ), and what is His beautiful thing but the corn of the
elect, and wine springing forth virgins?"—namely, the strong
and constant resolve of sacred virginity, which, while the age
slips away in pleasures, flourishes in the Catholic Church
more widely and more fruitfully from day to day, and, indeed, what a great advantage and ornament this is everywhere
to religion and even to ordinary human intercourse is well
known. Moreover, this sacrament strengthens beyond conception the hope of immortal blessings and the confidence of
Divine aid. For the desire of happiness which is in the minds
of all is more and more sharpened and strengthened by the
emptiness of all earthly goods, by the unjust violence of
wicked men and by all the other troubles of mind and body.

Now the august Sacrament of the Eucharist is at once the   12
cause and pledge of happiness and glory not only for the soul,
but also for the body. For while it enriches the soul with an
abundance of heavenly gifts, it also fills it with joys so sweet
that they far surpass every thought and hope of man; in ad-

versity it sustains; in strife of virtue it confirms; it leads to everlasting life as by an open pathway. But to the frail and perishable body that Divine Host gives a future resurrection, for the immortal Body of Christ implants the seed of immortality which is some time to bud forth. This advantage, both to soul and body, the Church has at all times taught, following Christ, who said: "He that eateth My flesh and drinketh My blood hath everlasting life; and I will raise him up on the last day." And here it is of great importance to consider that the Eucharist, being instituted by Christ as a "perennial memorial of His passion," declares to all Christian men the necessity of mortifying themselves. For Jesus said to His first priests: "Do this for a commemoration of Me," that is, do this to commemorate My sorrows, griefs, tortures and death on the cross. Hence this sacrament, which is also a sacrifice, is a ceaseless exhortation, for all time, to penance and every spiritual effort; it is also a solemn and severe reproof of those pleasures which shameless men praise and exalt so highly. "As often as you shall eat this bread, and drink this chalice, you shall show the death of the Lord until He come."

13   Moreover, if you diligently examine into the causes of the present evils, you will find that they arise from the fact that the charity of men towards one another has grown faint according as the love of God grew cold. They have forgotten that they were sons of God and brothers in Jesus Christ; they think of nothing but themselves; the rights of others they not only disregard, but attack and invade. Hence the frequent quarrels and contentions among the various classes of citizens; the arrogance, harshness, dishonesty among the more powerful; the misery, envy and spirit of revolt among the weaker. For these evils it is vain to seek a remedy from the enactments of law, the fear of punishment or the plans of human prudence. What must be aimed at, as we ourselves have more than once recommended, is to reconcile the various orders of citizens by a mutual union of duties, a union which would come from God and give birth to works stamped with the true spirit and charity of Christ. This union Christ brought upon earth; by it He wished all things to be inspired, as being

the one thing that could bring some happiness, even in the present, not only to the soul, but also to the body, restraining as it does man's immoderate love of himself, and repressing the passion for riches, which is "the root of all evils."

But although it is necessary that all just rights should be well protected, it is nevertheless lawful to establish and preserve in society that salutary "equality" which St. Paul recommended. This, therefore, is what Christ wished in instituting this august sacrament—to excite love toward God and to foster charity among men. For the one flows, as is evident, of its very nature and almost spontaneously, from the other; nor can men live without it at all; nay, it must even burn and flourish in their hearts, if they consider the charity of His marvelous power and wisdom, and also "poured forth the riches of His divine love for men." And as Christ has given as such an example of love, how we should love and help each other, bound together as we are still more closely by the needs of our common brotherhood! Moreover, the outward symbols of this sacrament are in a special manner calculated to incite us to union. For St. Cyprian says: "The very sacrifices of redemption themselves proclaim the necessity of Christian concord in the firm and inseparable bonds of charity. For when the Lord calls His body bread which is made up of the union of many grains, He indicates the union of that people whose sins He bore; and when He calls His blood wine which is drawn from many ripe grapes, again He signifies a flock made one by the union of the multitude." Similarly the Angelic Doctor following St. Augustine says: "Our Lord commended His body and blood in those things which are moulded in unity; for the first, the bread, namely, is made one from many grains, and the other, the wine also becomes one from many grapes." And therefore Augustine elsewhere says: "O Sacrament of piety, O sign of unity, O bond of charity."

All this is confirmed by the declaration of the Council of Trent, that Christ left the Eucharist to the Church "as a symbol of that union and love with which He wished all Christians to be bound together—a symbol of that body of which He is head, and to which He wished us to be united

14

15

as members by the most firm bonds of faith and hope and charity." And this St. Paul himself had declared: "For we, being many, are one bread, one body, all that partake of one bread." Yes, truly, here is a most beautiful example of Christian brotherhood and of social equality, that all should approach the same altars without distinction; the nobility and the people, the rich and the poor, the learned and the unlearned, are equally sharers in the same heavenly banquet. And if it has been the glory of the Church that, in the first ages, "the multitude of believers had but one heart and one soul," it cannot be doubted that such a wonderful blessing was due to the custom of approaching the holy table; for of them we find it recorded, "And they were persevering in the doctrine of the Apostles, and in the communication of the breaking of bread." Moreover, the grace of mutual charity among the living, so much strengthened and increased as it is by the Sacrament of the Eucharist, flows out unto all who are in the communion of saints particularly through the power of the Holy Sacrifice. For the communion of saints, as all know, is nothing else than the mutual communication of aid, expiation, prayer and benefits among the faithful, whether in heaven or enduring the expiatory fires of Purgatory, or still abiding upon earth, but all forming one state, whose head is Christ, and whose life-giving principle is love. It is also a matter of faith that while to God alone the Holy Sacrifice may be offered, yet it can also be celebrated in honor of the saints reigning in heaven with God "Who crowned them," to obtain their patronage and protection, and also to blot out the stains of the brethren who had died in the Lord, but who had not yet made full atonement. That true charity, therefore, which is wont to do and endure all things for the salvation and utility of all, leaps and burns into life from the Most Holy Eucharist, in which Christ is really present, in which He gives way to His love for us in the highest form, and under the impulse of His divine love, perpetually renews His sacrifice. It is from this that the arduous labors of apostolic men, as well as the various institutions that have had their origin among Catholics and deserve so well of the human race, derive their influence, strength, constancy and successful results.

These few things written by us on a great subject will, we doubt not, produce much fruit if you, venerable brethren, seasonably expound and commend them to the faithful.   16

At the same time this sacrament is so great and so abound-   17
ing in virtue that no one has ever yet adequately praised it by his eloquence or worshiped it by his adoration. Whether you meditate upon it or rightly worship it, or better still, purely and worthily receive it, it is to be regarded as the great centre round which turns the whole Christian life; to it all other forms of piety lead; in it they end. In the self-same mystery that gracious invitation and still more gracious promise of Christ: "Come to Me all you that labor and are burdened, and I will refresh you," are renewed and daily fulfilled. Lastly, it is, as it were, the soul of the Church, towards which is directed the fulness of sacerdotal grace through the various grades of orders. From the very same source does the Church draw all her power and glory, all the ornaments of her Divine ritual, and all the efficacy of her blessings. Therefore, she takes the greatest care to instruct the faithful and lead them to this intimate union with Christ by the Sacrament of His Body and Blood; and for the same reason she adorns it and makes it more worthy of reverence by means of the most sacred ceremonies. The constant care of our Holy Mother the Church in this matter is summed up in the exhortation of the Council of Trent; an exhortation breathing forth wonderful charity and piety, and worthy of being entirely recalled again by us to the Christian world: "With paternal affection the Holy Synod admonishes, exhorts, demands and, by the bowels of God's mercy, entreats all, without exception, who are called Christians, to sometimes meet and find peace in this sign of unity, in this bond of charity, in this symbol of concord; to be mindful of that immense majesty and of that wonderful love of Jesus Christ, our Lord, who gave His life as price of our salvation, and His flesh to be our food; to believe and venerate those sacred mysteries of His Body and Blood with such constancy and

firmness of faith, such devotion of mind and piety and zeal, that they may be able to frequently receive that supersubstantial bread, so that He may be truly to them the life of their soul and the perpetual health of their mind, and thus that strengthened by its vigor, they may be able, after the journey of this miserable exile, to reach their heavenly country and eat without any veil upon their eyes the very same bread of angels which they now eat concealed under the sacred species."

18   Now, history bears witness that Christian life flourished better in the times when the reception of the Blessed Eucharist was more frequent. On the other hand, it is not less certain that when men began to neglect and almost depise this heavenly bread the vigor of the Christian profession sensibly diminished. Lest it should some time pass away altogether, Innocent III., in the Council of Lateran, imposed the most solemn precept that, at the very least, no Christian should abstain at Paschal time from receiving the Body of the Lord. This precept, however, was imposed with reluctance, and, it is clear, only as the last remedy; for it has been always the wish of the Church that the faithful should approach the holy table at every sacrifice. "The most Holy Synod would wish the faithful attending each Mass to communicate not only spiritually, but even sacramentally, so that they might receive more abundantly the fruits of the sacrifice."

19   And this most sacred mystery contains as a sacrifice the plenitude of salvation not only for individuals, but for all men; hence the Church is accustomed to offer it unceasingly "for the salvation of the whole world." It is fitting, therefore, that by the common zeal of the devout there should be greater love and esteem for this sacrifice; in this age particularly there is no more pressing necessity. Accordingly, we desire that its efficacy and power should be remembered more widely and even more diligently proclaimed. Principles evident from the very light of reason tell us that God, the creator and preserver of all things, has a supreme and absolute dominion over men, both privately and publicly; that all that we have and are in every sphere has come from His bounty; and that we, in turn, are bound to give Him the highest rever-

ence as our Master and the greatest gratitude as our most generous benefactor. And yet how few are there to-day who fulfil those duties with suitable piety.

This age, if any, surely manifests the spirit of rebellion 20 against God; in it that impious cry against Christ again grows strong: "We will not have this man to reign over us," and that impious resolve, "Let us cut Him off." Nor, indeed, is anything urged more vehemently by very many than this, that they should banish and separate God from all intercourse with men. This criminal madness is not universal, we joyfully admit; yet it is lamentable how many have forgotten the Divine Majesty and His benefits, and the salvation that was obtained chiefly through Christ. Now, this wickedness and folly must be resisted by an increase of general devotion and zeal in the worship of the Eucharistic Sacrifice. Nothing could of itself be more full of sweetness and consolation to the Christian soul. For the Victim that is immolated is Divine, and, accordingly, the honor that we render through it to the Holy Trinity is in proportion to its infinite dignity; we offer also to the Father His only-begotten Son—an offering that is infinite in value and infinitely acceptable; hence it is that we not only give Him thanks for His goodness, but even make Him a return. There is also another twofold and wonderful fruit which may and ought to be derived from this great sacrifice.

The mind grows sad when it reflects on the fearful multi- 21 tude of crimes which abounds on all sides, God, as we have said, being neglected and the Divine Majesty despised. The human race in great part seems to call upon the Divine anger, although indeed that harvest of evil which has been reaped contains in itself the ripeness of a just punishment. The zeal of the faithful should be roused to appease God, the avenging Judge of crime, and obtain from Him the reform of a sinful age. This is to be done chiefly by the aid of this holy sacrifice. For it is by virtue alone of Christ's death that men can fully satisfy the demand of Divine justice, and abundantly obtain mercy and pardon. But this power of expiation or of entreaty Christ wished to remain wholly in the Eucharist, which is not a mere commemoration of His death, but a real and wonderful, although unbloody and mystic, renewal of it.

22   At the same time let us confess we have not a little joy knowing that in those last years the minds of the faithful seem to have been renewed in love and reverence for the Sacrament of the Eucharist; and this gives us a better hope for the future. For, as we said in the beginning, ingenious piety has done much in this direction, especially in sodalities; either by increasing the splendor of our Eucharistic rites, or worshiping the Holy Sacrament constantly by day and night, and making atonement for the insults and injuries it receives. But, venerable brethren, it is not lawful for us or for you to stop here; for yet many more things remain to be done or undertaken, so that this, the most Divine work of all, may be put in a clearer light and held in greater honor among those who practice the duties of the Christian religion, that so great a mystery may be honored in a manner worthy of its greatness. Hence the works that have been undertaken are to be urged on more vigorously from day to day; old institutions, where they have disappeared, are to be renewed, as, for example, the Sodalities of the Eucharist, the supplications poured forth to the holy sacraments exposed for adoration, all the solemnity of pomp with which it was surrounded, the pious salutations before the tabernacles, and other holy and most profitable practices of the same nature; in fine, everything is to be done that prudence and piety could dictate. But, above all, endeavor should be made to revive widely again among Catholic nations the frequent use of the Holy Eucharist. To this the example of the early Church, the decrees of councils, the authority of the fathers and of the holy men in every age exhort us; for as the body needs its own food, so does the soul, and the most life-giving nourishment is given by the Holy Eucharist. To this the example of the early Church, the decrees of councils, the authority of the fathers and of the holy men in every age exhort us; for as the body needs its own food, so does the soul, and the most life-giving nourishment is given by the Holy Eucharist. Therefore, condemn beforehand the opinions of those who oppose such frequent communions. Banish the idle fears of many and the specious excuses or reasons for

abstaining from the Body of the Lord; for nothing could be more effective in rescuing the world from its anxiety about perishable things, and in bringing back and perpetually preserving the Christian spirit. Here the exhortations and examples of the higher orders, and still more the zeal and industry of the clergy, will be of great value. For priests to whom Christ, the Redeemer, has given the office of consecrating and administering the mysteries of His Body and Blood, can surely make no greater return for the high honor they have received than to do all in their power to promote His glory in the Eucharist, and by following the desire of His Most Sacred Heart to invite and draw the souls of all to the saving fountains of so great a sacrament and sacrifice.

Thus may the surpassing fruits of the Eucharist become, as   **23** we ardently desire, more fruitful from day to day, with abundant growth, also, in faith, hope, charity, and in every virtue; may this revival of piety tend to the peace and advantage of the State, and may the designs of God's most provident love in instituting such a perpetual mystery for the life of the world be made manifest to all men.

Buoyed up with such a hope, venerable brethren, and as a   **24** pledge of Divine gifts as well as of our affection, we lovingly impart to each one of you, and to your clergy and people, our Apostolic Benediction.

Given at Rome, near St. Peter's, on this 23rd day of May,   **25** on the approach of the solemnity of Corpus Christi, in the year 1902, the twenty-fifth of our Pontificate.

TRA LE SOLLECITUDINI
Motu Proprio of Pope Pius X
on the Restoration of Church Music
November 22, 1903

Chief amongst the anxieties of the pastoral office, not only of this Supreme Chair, which we, although unworthy, occupy through the inscrutable disposition of Providence, but of every local church, is without doubt that of maintaining and promoting the decorum of the house of God where the august mysteries of religion are celebrated, and where the Christian people assemble to receive the grace of the sacraments, to be present at the Holy Sacrifice of the Altar, to adore the august Sacrament of the Lord's Body and to join in the common prayer of the Church in the public and solemn liturgical offices. Nothing then should take place in the temple calculated to disturb or even merely to diminish the piety and devotion of the faithful, nothing that may give reasonable cause for disgust or scandal, nothing, above all, which directly offends the decorum and the sanctity of the sacred function and is thus unworthy of the house of prayer and of the majesty of God.

27   We do not deal separately with the abuses which may occur in this matter. Today our attention is directed to one of the most common of them, one of the most difficult to eradicate and the existence of which is sometimes to be deplored even where everything else is deserving of the highest praise--the beauty and sumptuousness of the temple, the splendor and the accurate order of the ceremonies, the attendance of the clergy, the gravity and piety of the officiating

ministers. Such is the abuse in connection with sacred chant and music. And, indeed, whether it is owing to the nature of this art, fluctuating and variable as it is in itself, or to the successive changes in tastes and habits in the course of time, or the sad influence exercised on sacred art by profane and theatrical art, or the pleasure that music directly produces, and that is not always easily kept within the proper limits, or finally to the many prejudices on the matter so lightly introduced and so tenaciously maintained even among responsible and pious persons, there is a continual tendency to deviate from the right rule, fixed by the end for which art is admitted to the service of worship and laid down very clearly in the ecclesiastical canons, in the ordinances of the general and provincial councils, in the prescriptions which have on various occasions emanated from the Sacred Roman Congregations, and from our predecessors, the Sovereign Pontiffs.

It is pleasing to us to be able to acknowledge with real satisfaction the large amount of good that has been done in this respect during the last decades in this our fair city of Rome, and in many churches in our country, but in a more especial way among some nations in which excellent men, full of zeal for the worship of God, have, with the approval of this Holy See and under the direction of the Bishops, united in flourishing societies and restored sacred music to the fullest honor in nearly all their churches and chapels. Still the good work that has been done is very far indeed from being common to all, and when we consult our own personal experience and take into account the great number of complaints that have reached us from all quarters during the short time that has elapsed since it pleased the Lord to elevate our humble person to the summit of the Roman Pontificate, we consider it our first duty, without further delay, to raise our voice at once in reproof and condemnation of all that is out of harmony with the right rule above indicated, in the functions of worship and in the performance of the ecclesiastical offices. It being our ardent desire to see the true Christian spirit restored in every respect and be preserved by all the faithful, we deem it necessary to provide before everything else for the sanctity and dignity of the temple,

28

in which the faithful assemble for the object of acquiring this spirit from its foremost and indispensable fount, which is the active participation in the holy mysteries and in the public and solemn prayer of the Church. And it is vain to hope that the blessing of heaven will descend abundantly upon us for this purpose when our homage to the Most High, instead of ascending in the odor of sweetness, puts into the hand of the Lord the scourges with which the Divine Redeemer once drove the unworthy profaners from the temple.

29   Wherefore, in order that no one in the future may be able to plead in excuse that he did not clearly understand his duty, and that all vagueness may be removed from the interpretation of some things which have already been commanded, we have deemed it expedient to point out briefly the principles regulating sacred music in the functions of public worship, and to gather together in a general survey the principal prescriptions of the Church against the more common abuses in this matter. We, therefore, publish, "motu proprio" and with sure knowledge, our present "Instruction" to which, as "to a juridical code of sacred music," we desire with the fullness of our Apostolic authority that the force of law be given, and we impose its scrupulous observance on all by this document in our own handwriting.

INSTRUCTION ON SACRED MUSIC

I. General Principles

30   1. Sacred music, as an integral part of the solemn liturgy participates in its general object, which is the glory of God and the sanctification and edification of the faithful. It tends to increase the decorum and the splendor of the ecclesiastical ceremonies, and since its principal office is to clothe with befitting melody the liturgical text proposed for the understanding of the faithful its proper end is to add greater efficacy to the text, in order that by means of it the faithful may be the more easily moved to devotion and better disposed to receive the fruits of grace associated with the celebration of the most holy mysteries.

2. Sacred music should consequently possess, in the highest   31
degree, the qualities proper to the liturgy, and precisely
sanctity and goodness of form, from which spontaneously
springs its other character, universality.

It must be holy, and must, accordingly, exclude all pro-   32
fanity not only in itself, but in the manner in which it is
presented by those who execute it.

It must be true art, for otherwise it will be impossible for   33
it to exercise on the minds of those who hear it that efficacy
which the Church aims at obtaining in admitting into her
liturgy the art of musical sounds.

But it must, at the same time, be universal in this sense,   34
that while every nation is permitted to admit into its ecclesiastical compositions those special forms which in a certain
manner constitute the specific character of its native music,
still these forms must be subordinated in such a manner to
the general characteristics of sacred music that nobody of
another nation may receive, on hearing them, an impression
other than good.

II. The Kinds of Sacred Music

3. These qualities are possessed in the highest degree by   35
the Gregorian Chant, which is, consequently, the Chant proper to the Roman Church, the only Chant she has inherited
from the ancient fathers, which she has jealously guarded for
centuries in her liturgical codices, which she directly proposes
to the faithful as her own, which she prescribes exclusively
for some parts of the liturgy, and which the most recent
studies have so happily restored to their integrity and purity.

Upon these grounds the Gregorian Chant has always been   36
regarded as the supreme model for sacred music, so that the
following rule may be safely laid down: The more closely a
composition for church approaches in its movement, inspiration and savor the Gregorian form, the more sacred and
liturgical it is; and the more out of harmony it is with that
supreme model, the less worthy it is of the temple.

The ancient traditional Gregorian Chant must, therefore,   37
be largely restored in the functions of public worship, and

everybody must take for certain that an ecclesiastical function loses nothing of its solemnity when it is accompanied by no other music except them.

38   Efforts must especially be made to restore the use of the Gregorian Chant by the people, so that the faithful may again take a more active part in the ecclesiastical offices, as they were wont to do in ancient times.

39   4. The qualities mentioned are also possessed in an excellent degree by the classic polyphony, especially of the Roman school, which reached its greatest perfection in the fifteenth century, owing to the works of Pierluigi da Palestrina, and continued subsequently to produce compositions of excellent quality from the liturgical and musical standpoint. The classic polyphony approaches pretty closely to the Gregorian Chant, the supreme model of all sacred music, and hence it has been found worthy of a place side by side with the Gregorian Chant in the more solemn functions of the Church, such as those of the Pontifical Chapel. This, too, must therefore be restored largely in ecclesiastical functions, especially in the more important basilicas, in cathedrals and in the churches and chapels of seminaries and other ecclesiastical institutions in which the necessary means are usually not lacking.

40   5. The Church has always recognized and favored the progress of the arts, admitting to the service of worship everything good and beautiful discovered by genius in the course of ages--always, however, with due regard to the liturgical laws. Consequently modern music is also admitted in the Church, since it, too, furnishes compositions of such excellence, sobriety and gravity that they are in no way unworthy of the liturgical functions.

41   But as modern music has come to be devoted mainly to profane uses, greater care must be taken with regard to it, in order that the musical compositions of modern style which are admitted in the Church may contain nothing profane, be free from reminiscences of motifs adopted in the theatres and be not fashioned even in their external forms after the manner of profane pieces.

42   6. Amongst the various kinds of modern music that which appears less suitable for accompanying the functions of public

worship is the theatrical style, which was in the greatest vogue, especially in Italy, during the last century. This of its very nature is diametrically opposed to the Gregorian Chant and the classic polyphony, and therefore to the most important law of all good music. Besides the intrinsic structure, the rhythm and what is known as the "conventionalism" of this style adapt themselves but badly to the exigencies of true liturgical music.

III. The Liturgical Text

7. The language of the Roman Church is Latin. It is there- 43
fore forbidden to sing anything whatever in the vernacular in solemn liturgical functions--much more to sing in the vernacular the variable or common parts of the Mass and Office.

8. The texts that may be rendered in music, and the order 44
in which they are to be rendered, being determined for every liturgical function, it is not lawful to confuse this order or to change the prescribed texts for others, selected at will, or to omit them either entirely or even in part, unless when the rubrics allow that some versicles are simply recited in choir. However it is permissible, according to the custom of the Roman Church, to sing a motet to the Blessed Sacrament after the "Benedictus" in a Solemn Mass. It is also permitted, after the offertory prescribed for the Mass has been sung, to execute during the time that remains a brief motet to words approved by the Church.

9. The liturgical text must be sung as it is in the books 45
without alteration or inversion of the words, without undue repetition, without breaking syllables and always in a manner intelligible to the faithful who listen.

IV. External Form of the Sacred Compositions

10. The different parts of the Mass and the Office must re- 46
tain, even musically, that particular concept and form which ecclesiastical tradition has assigned to them, and which is admirably expressed in the Gregorian Chant. Different, therefore, must be the method of composing an Introit, a Gradual, an antiphon, a psalm, a hymn, a "Gloria in Excelsis".

47   11. In particular the following rules are to be observed:

48   (a) The "Kyrie," "Gloria," "Credo," etc., of the Mass must preserve the unity of composition proper to their text. It is not lawful, therefore, to compose them in separate pieces, in such a way as that each of such pieces may form a complete composition in itself, and be capable of being detached from the rest and substituted by another.

49   (b) In the Office of Vespers it should be the rule to follow the "Caerimoniale Episcoporum," which prescribes the Gregorian Chant for the psalmody and permits figured music for the versicles of the "Gloria Patri" and the hymn.

50   It will nevertheless be lawful on the greater solemnities to alternate the Gregorian Chant of the choir with the so-called "falsibordoni" or with verses similarly composed in a proper manner.

51   It may be also allowed sometimes to render the single psalms in their entirety in music, provided the form proper to psalmody be preserved in such compositions; that is to say, provided the singers seem to be psalmodising among themselves, either with new motifs or with those taken from the Gregorian Chant, or based upon it.

52   The psalms known as "di concerto" are, therefore, forever excluded and prohibited.

53   (c) In the hymns of the Church the traditional form of the hymn is preserved. It is not lawful, therefore, to compose, for instance a "Tantum Ergo" in such wise that the first strophe presents a romanza, a cavatina, an adagio and the "Genitori" an allegro.

54   (d) The antiphons of the Vespers must be as a rule rendered with the Gregorian melody proper to each. Should they, however, in some special case be sung in figured music, they must never have either the form of a concert melody or the fullness of a motet or a cantata.

V. The Singers

55   12. With the exception of the melodies proper to the celebrant at the altar and to the ministers, which must be always sung only in Gregorian Chant, and without the accompa-

niment of the organ, all the rest of the liturgical chant belongs to the choir of levites, and, therefore, singers in church,
even when they are laymen, are really taking the place of the
ecclesiastical choir. Hence the music rendered by them must,
at least for the greater part, retain the character of choral
music.

By this it is not to be understood that solos are entirely   56
excluded. But solo singing should never predominate in
such a way as to have the greater part of the liturgical chant
executed in that manner; rather should it have the character
of hint or a melodic projection, and be strictly bound up
with the rest of the choral composition.

13. On the same principle it follows that singers in church   57
have a real liturgical office, and that therefore women, as
being incapable of exercising such an office, cannot be admitted to form part of the choir or of the musical chapel.
Whenever, then, it is desired to employ the acute voice of
sopranos or contraltos, these parts must be taken by boys,
according to the most ancient usage of the Church.

14. Finally, only those are to be admitted to form part of   58
the musical chapel of a church who are men of known piety
and probity of life, and these should by their modest and
devout bearing during the liturgical functions show that they
are worthy of the holy office they exercise. It will also be
fitting that singers while singing in church wear the ecclesiastical habit and surplice, and that they be hidden behind
grating when the choir is excessively open to the public gaze.

VI. Organ and Instruments

15. Although the music proper to the Church is purely   59
vocal music, music with the accompaniment of the organ is
also permitted. In some special cases, within due limits and
within the proper regards, other instruments may be allowed,
but never without the special license of the ordinary,
according to the prescriptions of the "Caerimoniale
Episcoporum."

16. As the chant school should always have the principal   60
place, the organ or instruments should merely sustain and
never overwhelm it.

61   17. It is not permitted to have the chant preceded by long preludes or to interrupt it with intermezzo pieces.

62   18. The sound of the organ as an accompaniment to the chant in preludes, interludes and the like must be not only governed by the special nature of the instruments, but must participate in all the qualities proper to sacred music as above enumerated.

63   19. The employment of the piano is forbidden in church, as is also that of noisy or frivolous instruments such as drums, cymbals, bells and the like.

64   20. It is strictly forbidden to have bands play in church, and only in a special case and with the consent of the ordinary will it be permissible to admit a number of wind instruments, limited, judicious and proportioned to the size of the place-- provided the composition and accompaniment to be executed be written in a grave and suitable style, and similar in all respects to that proper to the organ.

65   21. In processions outside the church the ordinary may give permission for a band, provided no profane pieces are executed. It would be desirable in such cases that the band confine itself to accompanying some spiritual canticle sung in Latin or in the vernacular by the singers and the pious associations which take part in the procession.

VII. The Length of the Liturgical Chant

66   22. It is not lawful to keep the priest at the altar waiting on account of the chant or the music for a length of time not allowed by the liturgy. According to the ecclesiastical pre- scriptions the "Sanctus" of the Mass should be over before the elevation, and therefore the priest must here have regard to the singers. The "Gloria" and the "Credo" ought, according to the Gregorian tradition, to be relatively short.

67   23. In general, it must be considered to be a very grave abuse when the liturgy in ecclesiastical functions is made to appear secondary to and in a manner at the service of the music, for the music is merely a part of the liturgy and its humble handmaid.

VIII. Principal Means

24. For the exact execution of what has been herein laid   68
down, the Bishops, if they have not already done so, are to
institute in their dioceses a special commission composed of
persons really competent in sacred music, and to this commission let them entrust in the manner they find most suitable the task of watching over the music executed in their
churches. Nor are they to see merely that the music is good
in itself, but also that it is adapted to the powers of the
singers and be always well executed.

25. In seminaries of clerics and in ecclesiastical institutions   69
let the above-mentioned traditional Gregorian Chant be
cultivated by all with diligence and love, according to the
Tridentine prescriptions, and let the superiors be liberal of
encouragement and praise towards their young subjects.
In like manner let "Scholae Cantorum" be established,
whenever possible, among the clerics for the execution of
sacred polyphony and of good liturgical music.

26. In the ordinary lessons of liturgy, morals, canon law   70
given to the students of theology, let care be taken to touch
on those points which regard more directly the principles
and laws of sacred music, and let an attempt be made to
complete the doctrine with some particular instruction in
the aesthetic side of the sacred art, so that the clerics may
not leave the seminary ignorant of all those notions, necessary as they are for complete ecclesiastical culture.

27. Let care be taken to restore, at least in the principal   71
churches, the ancient "Scholae Cantorum" as has been done
with excellent fruit in a great many places. It is not difficult
for a zealous clergy to institute such "Scholae" even in the
minor country churches--nay, in them they will find a very
easy means for gathering round them both the children and
the adults, to their own profit and the edification of the
people.

28. Let efforts be made to support and promote in the best   72
way possible the higher schools of sacred music where these

already exist, and to help in founding them where they do not. It is of the utmost importance that the Church itself provide for the instruction of its masters, organists and singers, according to the true principles of sacred art.

IX. Conclusion

73   29. Finally, it is recommended to choirmasters, singers, members of the clergy, superiors of seminaries, ecclesiastical institutions and religious communities, parish priests and rectors of churches, canons of collegiate churches and cathedrals, and above all, to the diocesan ordinaries to favor with all zeal these prudent reforms, long desired and demanded with united voice by all; so that the authority of the Church, which herself has repeatedly proposed them, and now inculcates them, may not fall into contempt.

74   Given from our Apostolic Palace at the Vatican, on the day of the Virgin and Martyr, St. Cecilia, November 22, 1903, in the first year of our Pontificate.

SACRA TRIDENTINA
Decree on Frequent and Daily Reception
of Holy Communion
December 20, 1905

The Holy Council of Trent, having in view the ineffable riches of grace which are offered to the faithful who receive the Most Holy Eucharist, makes the following declaration: "The Holy Council wishes indeed that at each Mass the faithful who are present should communicate, not only in spiritual desire, but sacramentally, by the actual reception of the Eucharist."[1] These words declare plainly enough the wish of the Church that all Christians should be daily nourished by this heavenly banquet and should derive therefrom more abundant fruit for their sanctification.

This wish of the Council fully conforms to that desire wherewith Christ our Lord was inflamed when He instituted this Divine Sacrament. For He Himself, more than once, and in clarity of word, pointed out the necessity of frequently eating His Flesh and drinking His Blood, especially in these words: This is the bread that has come down from heaven; not as your fathers ate the manna, and died. He who eats this bread shall live forever.[2] From this comparison of the Food of angels with bread and with manna, it was easily to be understood by His disciples that, as the body is daily nourished with bread, and as the Hebrews were daily fed with manna in the desert, so the Christian soul might daily partake of this heavenly bread and be refreshed thereby. Moreover, we are bidden in the Lord's Prayer to ask for "our daily bread" by which words, the holy Fathers of the Church all but unanimously teach, must be understood not so much that material bread which is the support of the body as the Eucharistic bread which ought to be our daily food.

77   Moreover, the desire of Jesus Christ and of the Church that all the faithful should daily approach the sacred banquet is directed chiefly to this end, that the faithful, being united to God by means of the Sacrament, may thence derive strength to resist their sensual passions, to cleanse themselves from the stains of daily faults, and to avoid these graver sins to which human frailty is liable; so that its primary purpose is not that the honor and reverence due to our Lord may be safe-guarded, or that it may serve as a reward or recompense of virtue bestowed on the recipients.[3] Hence the Holy Council calls the Eucharist "the antidote whereby we may be freed from daily faults and be preserved from mortal sin."[4]

78   The will of God in this respect was well understood by the first Christians; and they daily hastened to this Table of life and strength. They continued steadfastly in the teaching of the apostles and in the communion of the breaking of the bread.[5] The holy Fathers and writers of the Church testify that this practice was continued into later ages and not without great increase of holiness and perfection.

79   Piety, however, grew cold, and especially afterward because of the widespread plague of Jansenism, disputes began to arise concerning the dispositions with which one ought to receive frequent and daily Communion; and writers vied with one another in demanding more and more stringent conditions as necessary to be fulfilled. The result of such disputes was that very few were considered worthy to receive the Holy Eucharist daily, and to derive from this most health-giving Sacrament its more abundant fruits; the others were content to partake of it once a year, or once a month, or at most once a week. To such a degree, indeed, was rigorism carried that whole classes of persons were excluded from a frequent approach to the Holy Table, for instance, merchants or those who were married.

80   Some, however, went over to the opposite view. They held that daily Communion was prescribed by divine law and that no day should pass without communicating, and besides other

practices not in accord with the approved usage of the Church, they determined that the Eucharist must be received even on Good Friday and in fact so administered it.

Toward these conditions, the Holy See did not fail in its duty. A Decree of this Sacred Congregation which begins with the words *Cum ad aures*, issued on February 12, 1679, with the approbation of Pope Innocent XI, condemned these errors, and put a stop to such abuses; at the same time it declared that all the faithful of whatsoever class, merchants or married persons not at all excepted, could be admitted to frequent Communion according to the devotion of each one and the judgment of his confessor. Then on December 7, 1690, by the Decree of Pope Alexander VIII, *Sanctissimus Dominus noster*, the proposition of Baius was condemned, requiring a most pure love of God, without any admixture of defect, on the part of those who wished to approach the Holy Table.   81

The poison of Jansenism, however, which, under the pretext of showing due honor and reverence to the Eucharist, had infected the minds even of good men, was by no means a thing of the past. The question as to the dispositions for the proper and licit reception of Holy Communion survived the declarations of the Holy See, and it was a fact that certain theologians of good repute were of the opinion that daily Communion could be permitted to the faithful only rarely and subject to many conditions.   82

On the other hand, there were not wanting men endowed with learning and piety who offered an easier approach to this practice, so salutary and so pleasing to God. They taught, with the authority of the Fathers, that there is no precept of the Church which prescribes more perfect dispositions in the case of daily than of weekly or monthly Communion; while the fruits of daily Communion will be far more abundant than those of Communion received weekly or monthly.   83

In our own day the controversy has been continued with increased warmth, and not without bitterness, so that the minds of confessors and the consciences of the faithful have been disturbed, to the no small detriment of Christian piety and fervor. Certain distinguished men, themselves pastors of   84 souls, have as a result of this, urgently begged His Holiness, Pope Pius X, to deign to settle, by his supreme authority, the question concerning the dispositions required to receive the Eucharist daily; so that this practice, so salutary and so pleasing to God, not only might suffer no decrease among the faithful, but rather that it increase and everywhere be promoted, especially in these days when religion and the Catholic faith are attacked on all sides, and the true love of God and piety are so frequently lacking. His Holiness, being most earnestly desirous, out of his solicitude and zeal, that the faithful should be invited to the sacred banquet as often as possible, even daily, and should benefit by its most abundant fruits, committed the aforesaid question to this Sacred Congregation, to be studied and decided definitely (definiendam).

85   Accordingly, the Sacred Congregation of the Council, in a Plenary Session held on December 16, 1905, submitted this matter to a very careful study, and after sedulously examining the reasons adduced on either side, determined and declared as follows:

86   1. Frequent and daily Communion, as a practice most earnestly desired by Christ our Lord and by the Catholic Church, should be open to all the faithful, of whatever rank and condition of life; so that no one who is in the state of grace, and who approaches the Holy Table with a right and devout intention (*recta piaque mente*) can be prohibited therefrom.

87   2. A right intention consists in this: that he who approaches the Holy Table should do so, not out of routine, or vainglory, or human respect, but that he wish to please God, to be more closely united with Him by charity, and to have recourse to this divine remedy for his weakness and defects.

88   3. Although it is especially fitting that those who receive Communion frequently or daily should be free from venial sins, at least from such as are fully deliberate, and from any affection thereto, nevertheless, it is sufficient that they be free from mortal sin, with the purpose of never sinning in the future; and if they have this sincere purpose, it is impossible by that daily communicants should gradually free themselves even from venial sins, and from all affection thereto.

4. Since, however, the Sacraments of the New Law, though   89
they produce their effect *ex opere operato*, nevertheless,
produce a great effect in proportion as the dispositions of the
recipient are better, therefore, one should take care that Holy
Communion be preceded by careful preparation, and followed
by an appropriate thanksgiving, according to each one's
strength, circumstances and duties.

5. That the practice of frequent and daily Communion may   90
be carried out with greater prudence and more fruitful merit,
the confessor's advice should be asked. Confessors, however,
must take care not to dissuade anyone from frequent or daily
Communion, provided he is found to be in a state of grace
and approaches with a right intention.

6. But since it is plain that by the frequent or daily recep-   91
tion of the Holy Eucharist union with Christ is strengthened,
the spiritual life more abundantly sustained, the soul more
richly endowed with virtues, and the pledge of everlasting
happiness more securely bestowed on the recipient, therefore,
parish priests, confessors and preachers, according to the
approved teaching of the Roman Catechism[6] should exhort
the faithful frequently and with great zeal to this devout and
salutary practice.

7. Frequent and daily Communion is to be promoted es-   92
pecially in religious Institutes of all kinds; with regard to
which, however, the Decree *Quemadmodum* issued on December 17, 1890, by the Sacred Congregation of Bishops and
Regulars, is to remain in force. It is to be promoted especially
in ecclesiastical seminaries, where students are preparing for
the service of the altar; as also in all Christian establishments
which in any way provide for the care of the young (ephebeis).

8. In the case of religious Institutes, whether of solemn or   93
simple vows, in whose rules, or constitutions, or calendars,
Communion is assigned to certain fixed days, such regulations
are to be considered as directive and not preceptive. The prescribed number of Communions should be regarded as a
minimum but not a limit to the devotion of the religious.
Therefore, access to the Eucharistic Table, whether it be
rather frequently or daily, must always be freely open to
them according to the norms above laid down in this Decree.

Furthermore, in order that all religious of both sexes may clearly understand the prescriptions of this Decree, the Superior of each house will provide that it be read in community, in the vernacular, every year within the octave of the Feast of Corpus Christi.

94   9. Finally, after the publication of this Decree, all ecclesiastical writers are to cease from contentious controversy concerning the dispositions requisite for frequent and daily Communion.

95   All this having been reported to His Holiness, Pope Pius X, by the undersigned Secretary of the Sacred Congregation in an audience held on December 17, 1905, His Holiness ratified this Decree, confirmed it and ordered its publication, anything to the contrary notwithstanding. He further ordered that it should be sent to all local Ordinaries and regular prelates, to be communicated by them to their respective seminaries, parishes, religious institutes, and priests; and that in their report on the state of their dioceses or institutes they should inform the Holy See concerning the execution of the prescriptions therein enacted.

96   Given at Rome, the 20th day of December, 1905.

Vincent, Card. Bishop of Palestrina, *Prefect*

Cajetan DeLai, *Secretary*

QUAM SINGULARI
Decree of the Sacred Congregation of the Discipline
of the Sacraments
on First Communion
August 8, 1910

The pages of the Gospel show clearly how special was that love for children which Christ showed while He was on earth. It was His delight to be in their midst; He was wont to lay His hands on them; He embraced them; and He blessed them. At the same time He was not pleased when they would be driven away by the disciples, whom He rebuked gravely with these words: "Let the little children come to me, and do not hinder them, for of such is the kingdom of God."[1] It is clearly seen how highly He held their innocence and the open simplicity of their souls on that occasion when He called a little child to Him and said to the disciples: "Amen, I say to you, unless you turn and become like little children, you will not enter into the kingdom of heaven. . . .And whoever receives one such little child for my sake, receives me."[2]

The Catholic Church, bearing this in mind, took care 98 even from the beginning to bring the little ones to Christ through Eucharistic Communion, which was administered even to nursing infants. This, as was prescribed in almost all ancient Ritual books, was done at Baptism until the thirteenth century, and this custom prevailed in some places even later. It is still found in the Greek and Oriental Churches. But to remove the danger that infants might eject the Consecrated Host, the custom obtained from the beginning of administering the Eucharist to them under the species of wine only.

99   Infants, however, not only at the time of Baptism, but also frequently thereafter were admitted to the sacred repast. In some churches it was the custom to give the Eucharist to the children immediately after the clergy; in others, the small fragments which remained after the Communion of the adults were given to the children.

100   This practice later died out in the Latin Church, and children were not permitted to approach the Holy Table until they had come to the use of reason and had some knowledge of this august Sacrament. This new practice, already accepted by certain local councils, was solemnly confirmed by the Fourth Council of the Lateran, in 1215, which promulgated its celebrated Canon XXI, whereby sacramental Confession and Holy Communion were made obligatory on the faithful after they had attained the use of reason, in these words: "All the faithful of both sexes shall, after reaching the years of discretion, make private confession of all their sins to their own priest at least once a year, and shall, according to their capacity, perform the enjoined penance; they shall also devoutly receive the Sacrament of Holy Eucharist at least at Easter time unless on the advice of their own priest, for some reasonable cause, it be deemed well to abstain for a while."

101   The Council of Trent,[3] in no way condemning the ancient practice of administering the Eucharist to children before they had attained the use of reason, confirmed the Decree of the Lateran Council and declared anathema those who held otherwise: "If anyone denies that each and all Christians of both sexes are bound, when they have attained the years of discretion, to receive Communion every year at least at Easter, in accordance with the precept of Holy Mother Church, let him be anathema."[4]

102   In accord with this Decree of the Lateran Council, still in effect, the faithful are obliged, as soon as they arrive at the years of discretion, to receive the Sacraments of Penance and Holy Eucharist at least once a year.

However, in the precise determination of "the age of rea-   103
son or discretion" not a few errors and deplorable abuses
have crept in during the course of time. There were some
who maintained that one age of discretion must be assigned
to reception of the Sacrament of Penance and another to the
Holy Eucharist. They held that for Confession the age of
discretion is reached when one can distinguish right from
wrong, hence can commit sin; for Holy Eucharist, however,
a greater age is required in which a full knowledge of matters
of faith and a better preparation of the soul can be had. As a
consequence, owing to various local customs and opinions,
the age determined for the reception of First Communion
was placed at ten years or twelve, and in places fourteen
years or even more were required; and until that age children
and youth were prohibited from Eucharistic Communion.

This practice of preventing the faithful from receiving on   104
the plea of safeguarding the august Sacrament has been the
cause of many evils. It happened that children in their
innocence were forced away from the embrace of Christ
and deprived of the food of their interior life; and from this
it also happened that in their youth, destitute of this strong
help, surrounded by so many temptations, they lost their
innocence and fell into vicious habits even before tasting of
the Sacred Mysteries. And even if a thorough instruction and
a careful Sacramental Confession should precede Holy Communion, which does not everywhere occur, still the loss of
first innocence is always to be deplored and might have been
avoided by reception of the Eucharist in more tender years.

No less worthy of condemnation is that practice which   105
prevails in many places prohibiting from Sacramental Confession children who have not yet made their First Holy
Communion, or of not giving them absolution. Thus it
happens that they, perhaps having fallen into serious sin, remain in that very dangerous state for a long time.

But worse still is the practice in certain places which pro-   106
hibits children who have not yet made their First Communion
from being fortified by the Holy Viaticum, even when they
are in imminent danger of death; and thus, when they die

they are buried with the rites due to infants and are deprived of the prayers of the Church.

107   Such is the injury caused by those who insist on extraordinary preparations for First Communion, beyond what is reasonable; and they doubtless do not realize that such precautions proceed from the errors of the Jansenists who contended that the Most Holy Eucharist is a reward rather than a remedy for human frailty. The Council of Trent, indeed, teaches otherwise when it calls the Eucharist, "An antidote whereby we may be freed from daily faults and be preserved from mortal sins."[5] This doctrine was not long ago strongly emphasized by a Decree of the Sacred Congregation of the Council given on December 20, 1905. It declared that daily approach to Communion is open to all, old and young, and two conditions only are required: the state of grace and a right intention.

108   Moreover, the fact that in ancient times the remaining particles of the Sacred Species were even given to nursing infants seems to indicate that no extraordinary preparation should now be demanded of children who are in the happy state of innocence and purity of soul, and who, amidst so many dangers and seductions of the present time have a special need of this heavenly food.

109   The abuses which we are condemning are due to the fact that they who distinguished one age of discretion for Penance and another for the Eucharist did so in error. The Lateran Council required one and the same age for reception of either Sacrament when it imposed the one obligation of Confession and Communion.

110   Therefore, the age of discretion for Confession is the time when one can distinguish between right and wrong, that is, when one arrives at a certain use of reason, and so similarly, for Holy Communion is required the age when one can distinguish between the Bread of the Holy Eucharist and ordinary bread—again the age at which a child attains the use of reason.

111   The principal interpreters of the Lateran Council and contemporaries of that period had the same teaching concerning this Decree. The history of the Church reveals that a number

of synods and episcopal decrees beginning with the twelfth
century, shortly after the Lateran Council, admitted children
of seven years of age to First Communion. There is moreover
the word of St. Thomas Aquinas, who is an authority of the
highest order, which reads: "When children begin to have
some use of reason, so that they can conceive a devotion
toward this Sacrament (the Eucharist), then this Sacrament
can be given to them."[6] Ledesma thus explains these words:
"I say, in accord with common opinion, that the Eucharist
is to be given to all who have the use of reason, and just as
soon as they attain the use of reason, even though at the time
the child may have only a confused notion of what he is
doing."[7] Vasquez comments on the same words of St.
Thomas as follows: "When a child has once arrived at the
use of reason he is immediately bound by the divine law
from which not even the Church can dispense him."[8]

The same is the teachings of St. Antoninus, who wrote: 112
"But when a child is capable of doing wrong, that is of com-
mitting a mortal sin, then he is bound by the precept of Confession and consequently of Communion."[9] The Council of
Trent also forces us to the same conclusion when it declares:
"Children who have not attained the use of reason are not by
any necessity bound to Sacramental Communion of the Eucharist." It assigns as the only reason the fact that they cannot commit sin: "they cannot at that age lose the grace of
the sons of God already acquired."

From this it is the mind of the Council that children are   113
held to Communion by necessity and by precept when they
are capable of losing grace by sin. The words of the Roman
Synod, held under Benedict XIII, are in agreement with this
in teaching that the obligation to receive the Eucharist begins, "after boys and girls attain the age of discretion, that
is, at the age in which they can distinguish this Sacramental
food, which is none other than the true Body of Jesus Christ,
from common and ordinary bread; and that they know how
to receive it with proper religious spirit."[10]

The Roman Catechism adds this: "At what age children   114
are to receive the Holy Mysteries no one can better judge
than their father and the priest who is their confessor. For it

is their duty to ascertain by questioning the children whether they have any understanding of this admirable Sacrament and if they have any desire for it."[11]

115   From all this it is clear that the age of discretion for receiving Holy Communion is that at which the child knows the difference between the Eucharistic Bread and ordinary, material bread, and can therefore approach the altar with proper devotion. Perfect knowledge of the things of faith, therefore, is not required, for an elementary knowledge suffices—some knowledge (*aliqua cognitio*); similarly full use of reason is not required, for a certain beginning of the use of reason, that is, some use of reason (*aliqualis usus rationis*) suffices.

116   To postpone Communion, therefore, until later and to insist on a more mature age for its reception must be absolutely discouraged, and indeed such practice was condemned more than once by the Holy See. Thus Pope Pius IX, of happy memory, in a Letter of Cardinal Antonelli to the Bishops of France, March 12, 1866, severely condemned the growing custom existing in some dioceses of postponing the First Communion of children until more mature years, and at the same time sharply disapproved of the age limit which had been assigned. Again, the Sacred Congregation of the Council, on March 15, 1851, corrected a prescription of the Provincial Council of Rouen, which prohibited children under twelve years of age from receiving First Communion. Similarly, this Sacred Congregation of the Discipline of the Sacraments, on March 25, 1910, in a question proposed to it from Strasburg whether children of twelve or fourteen years could be admitted to Holy Communion, answered: "Boys and girls are to be admitted to the Holy Table when they arrive at the years of discretion or the use of reason."

117   After careful deliberation on all these points, this Sacred Congregation of the Discipline of the Sacraments, in a general meeting held on July 15, 1910, in order to remove the above-mentioned abuses and to bring about that children even from their tender years may be united to Jesus Christ, may live His life, and obtain protection from all danger of corruption, has deemed it needful to prescribe the following

rules which are to be observed everywhere for the First Communion of children.

1. The age of discretion, both for Confession and for Holy   118
Communion, is the time when a child begins to reason, that
is about the seventh year, more or less. From that time on
begins the obligation of fulfilling the precept of both Confession and Communion.

2. A full and perfect knowledge of Christian doctrine is   119
not necessary either for First Confession or for First Communion. Afterwards, however, the child will be obliged to
learn gradually the entire Catechism according to his ability.

3. The knowledge of religion which is required in a child   120
in order to be properly prepared to receive First Communion
is such that he will understand according to his capacity those
Mysteries of faith which are necessary as a means of salvation
(necessitate medii) and that he can distinguish between the
Bread of the Eucharist and ordinary, material bread, and thus
he may receive Holy Communion with a devotion becoming
his years.

4. The obligation of the precept of Confession and Com-   121
munion which binds the child particularly affects those who
have him in charge, namely, parents, confessor, teachers and
the pastor. It belongs to the father, or the person taking his
place, and to the confessor, according to the Roman Catechism, to admit a child to his First Communion.

5. The pastor should announce and hold a General Com-   122
munion of the children once a year or more often, and he
should on these occasions admit not only the First Communicants but also others who have already approached the
Holy Table with the above-mentioned consent of their parents or confessor. Some days of instruction and preparation
should be previously given to both classes of children.

6. Those who have charge of the children should zealously   123
see to it that after their First Communion these children frequently approach the Holy Table, even daily if possible, as
Jesus Christ and Mother Church desire, and let this be done
with a devotion becoming their age. They must also bear in
mind that very grave duty which obliged them to have the
children attend the public Catechism classes; if this is not

done, then they must supply religious instruction in some other way.

124   7. The custom of not admitting children to Confession or of not giving them absolution when they have already attained the use of reason must be entirely abandoned. The Ordinary shall see to it that this condition ceases absolutely, and he may, if necessary, use legal measures accordingly.

125   8. The practice of not administering the Viaticum and Extreme Unction to children who have attained the use of reason, and of burying them with the rite used for infants is a most intolerable abuse. The Ordinary should take very severe measures against those who do not give up the practice.

126   His Holiness, Pope Pius X, in an audience granted on the seventh day of this month, approved all the above decisions of this Sacred Congregation, and ordered this Decree to be published and promulgated.

127   He furthermore commanded that all the Ordinaries make this Decree known not only to the pastors and the clergy, but also to the people, and he wishes that it be read in the vernacular every year at the Easter time. The Ordinaries shall give an account of the observance of this Decree together with other diocesan matters every five years.

ABHINC DUOS ANNOS
Motu Proprio of Pope Pius X
October 23, 1913

Two years ago, in publishing Our Apostolic Constitution, *Divino Afflatu,* We had especially in sight the recitation, as far as possible in its entirety, of the Psalter on weekdays, and the restoration of the ancient Sunday offices. But Our mind was occupied with many other projects—some mere plans, others already on the way to realization—relating to the reform in the Roman Breviary.

However, because of the numerous difficulties preventing   129 Us from executing them, We had to postpone them for a more favorable moment. To change the composition of the Breviary to make it in accordance with Our desires, that is, to give it a finished perfection in every part, would involve:
—restoring the calendar of the Universal Church to its original arrangement and style, retaining meanwhile the splendid richness which the marvelous fruitfulness of the Church, the Mother of Saints, has brought to bear upon it.
—utilizing appropriate passages of Scripture, of the Fathers and Doctors, after having reestablished the authentic text;
—prudently correcting the lives of the Saints according to documentary evidence;
—perfecting the arrangment of numerous points of the liturgy, eliminating superfluous elements.

But in the judgment of wise and learned persons, all this   130 would require considerable work and time. For this reason, many years will have to pass before this type of liturgical edifice, composed with intelligent care for the Spouse of Christ to express her piety and faith, can appear purified of the imperfections brought by time, newly resplendent with dignity and fitting order.

131   In the meantime, through correspondence and conversations with a number of bishops, We have learned of their urgent deisre—shared by many priests—to find in the Breviary, together with the new arrangement of the Psalter and its rubrics, all the changes which already have come or which might come with this new Psalter.

132   They have repeatedly asked Us, indeed they have repeatedly manifested their earnest desire that the new psalter be used more often, that the Sundays be observed more conscientiously, that provision be made for the inconvience of transferred offices, and that certain other changes be effected which seem to be justified.

133   Because they are grounded in objectivity and completely conform to Our desire, We have agreed to these requests and We believe that the moment has come to grant them.

Minor modifications are then authorized, with the hope of a full reform later, but Pius X died less than ten months later.—Ed.

Code of Canon Law
Book III, Part 3
1917

Can. 1255.—1. The worship which is due to the Most Holy Trinity, to each of the Divine Persons, to our Lord Jesus Christ, even under the Sacramental Species, is *cultus latriae*; that which is due to the Blessed Virgin Mary is *cultus hyperdulia*; that which is due to others who reign with Christ in heaven is *cultus duliae*.

2. To sacred relics and images also there is due a veneration 135 and worship which is relative to the person to whom the relics and images refer.

Can. 1256.—If worship is offered in the name of the Church 136 by persons lawfully deputed for this function and through acts which, by institution of the Church are to be offered only to God, and the saints and blessed, the worship is *public*; otherwise, it is *private*.

Can. 1257.—It pertains exclusively to the Holy See to con- 137 trol the sacred liturgy and to approve liturgical books.

DIVINI CULTUS
Apostolic Constitution of Pope Pius XI
on Divine Worship
December 20, 1928

ince the Church has received from Christ her Founder the office of safeguarding the sanctity of divine worship, it is certainly incumbent upon her, while leaving intact the substance of the Sacrifice and the sacraments, to prescribe ceremonies, rites, formulæ, prayers and chant for the proper regulation of that august public ministry, whose special name is "Liturgy", as being the eminently sacred action.

139 For the liturgy is indeed a sacred thing, since by it we are raised to God and united to Him, thereby professing our faith and our deep obligation to Him for the benefits we have received and the help of which we stand in constant need. There is thus a close connection between dogma and the sacred liturgy, and between Christian worship and the sanctification of the faithful. Hence Pope Celestine I saw the standard of faith expressed in the sacred formulæ of the liturgy. "The rule of our faith," he says, "is indicated by the law of our worship. When those who are set over the Christian people fulfill the function committed to them, they plead the cause of the human race in the sight of God's clemency, and pray and supplicate in conjunction with the whole Church."

140 These public prayers, called at first "the work of God" and later "the divine office" or the daily "debt" which man owes to God, used to be offered both day and night in the presence of a great concourse of the faithful. From the earliest

times the simple chants which graced the sacred prayers and
the liturgy gave a wonderful impulse to the piety of the people. History tells us how in the ancient basilicas, where bishop, clergy and people alternately sang the divine praises, the
liturgical chant played no small part in converting many bar-
barians to Christianity and civilization. It was in the churches
that heretics came to understand more fully the meaning of
the communion of saints; thus the Emperor Valens, an Arian,
being present at Mass celebrated by St. Basil, was overcome
by an extraordinary seizure and fainted. At Milan, St. Ambrose was accused by heretics of attracting the crowds by
means of liturgical chants. It was due to these that St. Augustine made up his mind to become a Christian. It was in the
churches, finally, where practically the whole city formed
a great joint choir, that the workers, builders, artists, sculp-
tors and writers gained from the liturgy that deep knowledge of theology which is now so apparent in the monuments of the Middle Ages.

No wonder, then, that the Roman Pontiffs have been so   141
solicitous to safeguard and protect the liturgy. They have
used the same care in making laws for the regulation of the
liturgy, in preserving it from adulteration, as they have in
giving accurate expression to the dogmas of the faith. This is
the reason why the Fathers made both spoken and written
commentary upon the liturgy or "the law of worship"; for
this reason the Council of Trent ordained that the liturgy
should be expounded and explained to the faithful.

In our times too, the chief object of Pope Pius X, in the   142
Motu Proprio which he issued twenty-five years ago, making
certain prescriptions concerning Gregorian Chant and sacred
music, was to arouse and foster a Christian spirit in the faithful, by wisely excluding all that might ill befit the sacredness
and majesty of our churches. The faithful come to church in
order to derive piety from its chief source, by taking an
active part in the venerated mysteries and the public solemn
prayers of the Church. It is of the utmost importance, therefore, that anything that is used to adorn the liturgy should be
controlled by the Church, so that the arts may take their
proper place as most noble ministers in sacred worship. Far

from resulting in a loss to art, such an arrangement will certainly make for the greater splendor and dignity of the arts that are used in the Church. This has been especially true of sacred music. Wherever the regulations on this subject have been carefully observed, a new life has been given to this delightful art, and the spirit of religion has prospered; the faithful have gained a deeper understanding of the sacred liturgy, and have taken part with greater zest in the ceremonies of the Mass, in the singing of the psalms and the public prayers. Of this We Ourselves had happy experience when, in the first year of Our Pontificate, We celebrated solemn High Mass in the Vatican Basilica to the noble accompaniment of a choir of clerics of all nationalities, singing in Gregorian Chant.

143   It is, however, to be deplored that these most wise laws in some places have not been fully observed, and therefore their intended results not obtained. We know that some have declared that these laws, though so solemnly promulgated, were not binding upon their obedience. Others obeyed them at first, but have since come gradually to give countenance to a type of music which should be altogether banned from our churches. In some cases, especially when the memory of some famous musician was being celebrated, the opportunity has been taken of performing in church certain works which, however excellent, should never have been performed there, since they were entirely out of keeping with the sacredness of the place and of the liturgy.

144   In order to urge the clergy and faithful to a more scrupulous observance of these laws and directions which are to be carefully obeyed by the whole Church, We think it opportune to set down here something of the fruits of Our experience during the last twenty-five years. This We do the more willingly because in this year We celebrate not only the memory of the reform of sacred music to which We have referred, but also the centenary of the monk Guido of Arezzo. Nine hundred years ago Guido, at the bidding of the Pope, came to Rome and produced his wonderful invention, whereby the ancient and traditional liturgical chants might be more easily published, circulated and preserved intact for pos-

terity—to the great benefit and glory of the Church and of art.

It was in the Lateran Palace that Gregory the Great, having   145
made his famous collection of the traditional treasures of
plainsong, editing them with additions of his own, had wisely
founded his great *Schola* in order to perpetuate the true
interpretation of the liturgical chant. It was in the same
building that the monk Guido gave a demonstration of his
marvelous invention before the Roman clergy and the Roman
Pontiff himself. The Pope, by his full approbation and high
praise of it, was responsible for the gradual spread of the
new system throughout the whole world, and thus for the
great advantages that accrued therefrom to musical art in
general.

We wish, then, to make certain recommendations to the   146
Bishops and Ordinaries, whose duty it is, since they are the
custodians of the liturgy, to promote ecclesiastical art. We
are thus acceding to the requests which, as a result of many
musical congresses and especially that recently held at Rome,
have been made to Us by not a few Bishops and learned
masters in the musical art. To these We accord due meed of
praise; and We ordain that the following directions, as here-
under set forth, with the practical methods indicated, be put
into effect.

All those who aspire to the priesthood, whether in Sem-   147
inaries or in religious houses, from their earliest years are to
be taught Gregorian Chant and sacred music. At that age they
are able more easily to learn to sing, and to modify, if not
entirely to overcome, any defects in their voices, which in
later years would be quite incurable. Instruction in music and
singing must be begun in the elementary, and continued in
the higher classes. In this way, those who are about to receive
sacred orders, having become gradually experienced in chant,
will be able during their theological course quite easily to
undertake the higher and "aesthetic" study of plainsong and
sacred music, of polyphony and the organ, concerning which
the clergy certainly ought to have a thorough knowledge.

In seminaries, and in other houses of study for the for-   148
mation of the clergy both secular and regular there should be

a frequent and almost daily lecture or practice—however short— in Gregorian Chant and sacred music. If this is carried out in the spirit of the liturgy, the students will find it a relief rather than a burden to their minds, after the study of the more exacting subjects. Thus a more complete education of both branches of the clergy in liturgical music will result in the restoration to its former dignity and splendor of the choral Office, a most important part of divine worship; moreover, the *scholæ* and choirs will be invested again with their ancient glory.

149   Those who are responsible for, and engaged in divine worship in basilicas and cathedrals, in collegiate and conventual churches of religious, should use all their endeavors to see that the choral Office is carried out duly—i.e. in accordance with the prescriptions of the Church. And this, not only as regards the precept of reciting the divine Office "worthily, attentively and devoutly," but also as regards the chant. In singing the psalms attention should be paid to the right tone, with its appropriate mediation and termination, and a suitable pause at the asterisk; so that every verse of the psalms and every strophe of the hymns may be sung by all in perfect time together. If this were rightly observed, then all who worthily sing the psalms would signify their unity of intention in worshipping God and, as one side of the choir sings in answer to the other, would seem to emulate the everlasting praise of the Seraphim who cried one to the other "Holy, Holy, Holy."

150   Lest anyone in future should invent easy excuses for exempting himself from obedience to the laws of the Church, let every chapter and religious community deal with these matters at meetings held for the purpose; and just as formerly there used to be a "Cantor" or director of the choir, so in future let one be chosen from each chapter or choir of religious, whose duty it will be to see that the rules of the liturgy and of choral chant are observed and, both individually and generally, to correct the faults of the choir. In this connection it should be observed that, according to the ancient discipline of the Church and the constitutions of chapters still in force, all those at least who are bound to office in

choir, are obliged to be familiar with Gregorian Chant. And the Gregorian Chant which is to be used in every church of whatever order, is the text which, revised according to the ancient manuscripts, has been authentically published by the Church from the Vatican Press.

We wish here to recommend, to those whom it may concern, the formation of choirs. These in the course of time came to replace the ancient *scholæ* and were established in the basilicas and greater churches especially for the singing of polyphonic music. Sacred polyphony, We may here remark, is rightly held second only to Gregorian Chant. We are desirous, therefore, that such choirs, as they flourished from the fourteenth to the sixteenth century, should now also be created anew and prosper especially in churches where the scale on which the liturgy is carried out demands a greater number and a more careful selection of singers. **151**

Choir-schools for boys should be established not only for the greater churches and cathedrals, but also for smaller parish churches. The boys should be taught by the choirmaster to sing properly, so that, in accordance with the ancient custom of the Church, they may sing in the choir with the men, especially as in polyphonic music the highest part, the *cantus,* ought to be sung by boys. Choir-boys, especially in the sixteenth century, have given us masters of polyphony: first and foremost among them, the great Palestrina. **152**

As We have learned that in some places an attempt is being made to reintroduce a type of music which is not entirely in keeping with the performance of the sacred Office, particularly owing to the excessive use made of musical instruments, We hereby declare that singing with orchestra accompaniment is not regarded by the Church as a more perfect form of music or as more suitable for sacred purposes. Voices, rather than instruments, ought to be heard in the church: the voices of the clergy, the choir and the congregation. Nor should it be deemed that the Church, in preferring the human voice to any musical instrument, is obstructing the progress of music; for no instrument, however perfect, however excellent, can surpass the human voice in **153** expressing human thought, especially when it is used by the mind to offer up prayer and praise to Almighty God.

154   The traditionally appropriate musical instrument of the Church is the organ, which, by reason of its extraordinary grandeur and majesty, has been considered a worthy adjunct to the liturgy, whether for accompanying the chant or, when the choir is silent, for playing harmonious music at the prescribed times. But here too must be avoided that mixture of the profane with the sacred which, through the fault partly of organ-builders and partly of certain performers who are partial to the singularities of modern music, may result eventually in diverting this magnificent instrument from the purpose for which it is intended. We wish, within the limits prescribed by the liturgy, to encourage the development of all that concerns the organ; but We cannot but lament the fact that, as in the case of certain types of music which the Church has rightly forbidden in the past, so now attempts are being made to introduce a profane spirit into the Church by modern forms of music; which forms, if they began to enter in, the Church would likewise be bound to condemn. Let our churches resound with organ-music that gives expression to the majesty of the edifice and breathes the sacredness of the religious rites; in this way will the art both of those who build organs and of those who play them flourish afresh and render effective service to the sacred liturgy.

155   In order that the faithful may more actively participate in divine worship, let them be made once more to sing the Gregorian Chant, so far as it belongs to them to take part in it. It is most important that when the faithful assist at the sacred ceremonies, or when pious sodalities take part with the clergy in a procession, they should not be merely detached and silent spectators, but, filled with a deep sense of the beauty of the liturgy, they should sing alternately with the clergy or the choir, as it is prescribed. If this is done, then it will no longer happen that the people either make no answer at all to the public prayers—whether in the language of the liturgy or in the vernacular—or at best utter the responses in a low and subdued murmur.

Let the clergy, both secular and regular, under the lead of   156
their Bishops and Ordinaries devote their energies either
directly, or through other trained teachers, to instructing
the people in the liturgy and in music, as being matters
closely associated with Christian doctrine. This will be best
effected by teaching liturgical chant in schools, pious con-
fraternities and similar associations. Religious communities of
men or women should devote particular attention to the
achievement of this purpose in the various educational institutions committed to their care. Moreover, We are confident
that this object will be greatly furthered by those societies
which, under the control of ecclesiastical authority, are
striving to reform sacred music according to the laws of the
Church.

To achieve all that We hope for in this matter numerous   157
trained teachers will be required. And in this connection We
accord due praise to all the Schools and Institutes throughout
the Catholic world, which by giving careful instruction in
these subjects are forming good and suitable teachers. But We
have a special word of commendation for the "Pontifical
Higher School of Sacred Music," founded in Rome in the
year 1910. This School, which was greatly encouraged by
Pope Benedict XV and was by him endowed with new privileges, is most particularly favored by Us; for We regard it as
a precious heritage left to Us by two Sovereign Pontiffs, and
We therefore wish to recommend it in a special way to all the
Bishops.

We are well aware that the fulfillment of these injunctions   158
will entail great trouble and labor. But do we not all know
how many artistic works our forefathers, undaunted by difficulties, have handed down to posterity, imbued as they were
with pious zeal and with the spirit of the liturgy? Nor is this
to be wondered at; for anything that is the fruit of the interior life of the Church surpasses even the most perfect
works of this world. Let the difficulties of this sacred task,
far from deterring, rather stimulate and encourage the Bishops
of the Church, who, by their universal and unfailing obedience
to Our behests, will render to the Sovereign Bishop a service
most worthy of their episcopal office.

MYSTICI CORPORIS
Selection from Encyclical Letter of Pope Pius XII
on the Mystical Body of Christ
and Our Union in It with Christ
June 29, 1943

Introduction

The doctrine of the Mystical Body of Christ, which is the Church,[1] was first taught us by the Redeemer Himself. Illustrating as it does the great and inestimable privilege of our intimate union with so exalted a Head, this doctrine by its sublime dignity invites all those who are drawn by the Holy Spirit to study it, and gives them, in the truths of which it proposes to the mind, a strong incentive to the performance of such good works as are conformable to its teaching. For this reason, We deem it fitting to speak to you on this subject through this Encyclical Letter, developing and explaining above all, those points which concern the Church Militant. To this We are urged not only by the surpassing grandeur of the subject but also by the circumstances of the present time.

160   2. For We intend to speak of the riches stored up in this Church which Christ purchased with His own Blood,[2] and whose members glory in a thorn-crowned Head. The fact that they thus glory is a striking proof that the greatest joy and exaltation are born only of suffering, and hence that we should rejoice if we partake of the sufferings of Christ, that when His glory shall be revealed we may also be glad with exceeding joy.[3]

3. From the outset it should be noted that the society 161
established by the Redeemer of the human race resembles its
divine Founder who was persecuted, calumniated and tortured
by those very men whom He had undertaken to save. We do
not deny, rather from a heart filled with gratitude to God We
admit, that even in our turbulent times there are many who,
though outside the fold of Jesus Christ, look to the Church as
the only haven of salvation; but We are also aware that the
Church of God not only is despised and hated maliciously by
those who shut their eyes to the light of Christian wisdom
and miserably return to the teachings, customs and practices
of ancient paganism, but is ignored, neglected, and even at
times looked upon as irksome by many Christians who are
allured by specious error or caught in the meshes of the
world's corruption. In obedience, therefore, Venerable Brethren, to the voice of Our conscience and in compliance with
the wishes of many, We will set forth before the eyes of all
and extol the beauty, the praises, and the glory of Mother
Church to whom, after God, we owe everything.

4. And it is to be hoped that Our instructions and exhorta- 162
tions will bring forth abundant fruit in the souls of the faithful in the present circumstances. For We know that if all the
sorrows and calamities of these stormy times, by which countless multitudes are being sorely tried, are accepted from God's
hands with calm submission, they naturally lift souls above
the passing things of earth to those of heaven that abide forever, and arouse a certain secret thirst and intense desire for
spiritual things. Thus, urged by the Holy Spirit, men are
moved, and, as it were, impelled to seek the Kingdom of God
with greater diligence; for the more they are detached from
the vanities of this world and from inordinate love of temporal
things, the more apt they will be to perceive the light of
heavenly mysteries. But the vanity and emptiness of earthly
things are more manifest today than perhaps at any other
period, when Kingdoms and States are crumbling, when enormous quantities of goods and all kinds of wealth are being
sunk in the depths of the sea, and cities, towns and fertile
fields are strewn with massive ruins and defiled with the blood
of brothers.

163   5. Moreover, We trust that Our exposition of the doctrine of the Mystical Body of Christ will be acceptable and useful to those also who are without the fold of the Church, not only because their good will towards the Church seems to grow from day to day, but also because, while before their eyes nation rises up against nation, kingdom against kingdom and discord is sown everywhere together with the seeds of envy and hatred, if they turn their gaze to the Church, if they contemplate her divinely-given unity—by which all men of every race are united to Christ in the bond of brotherhood— they will be forced to admire this fellowship in charity, and with the guidance and assistance of divine grace will long to share in the same union and charity.

164   6. There is a special reason too, and one most dear to Us, which recalls this doctrine to Our mind and with it a deep sense of joy. During the year that has passed since the twenty-five anniversary of Our Episcopal consecration, We have had the great consolation of witnessing something that has made the image of the Mystical Body of Jesus Christ stand out most clearly before the whole world. Though a long and deadly war has pitilessly broken the bond of brotherly union between nations, We have seen Our children in Christ, in whatever part of the world they happened to be, one in will and affection, lift up their hearts to the common Father, who, carrying in his own heart the cares and anxieties of all, is guiding the barque of the Catholic Church in the teeth of a raging tempest. This is a testimony to the wonderful union existing among Christians; but it also proves that, as Our paternal love embraces all peoples, whatever their nationality and race, so Catholics the world over, though their countries may have drawn the sword against each other, look to the Vicar of Jesus Christ as to the loving Father of them all, who, with absolute impartiality and incorruptible judgment, rising above the conflicting gales of human passions, takes upon himself with all his strength the defence of truth, justice and charity.

165   7. We have been no less consoled to know that with spontaneous generosity a fund has been created for the erection of a church in Rome to be dedicated to Our saintly predecessor and patron Eugene I. As this temple, to be built by

the wish and through the liberality of all the faithful, will be a lasting memorial of this happy event, so We desire to offer this Encyclical Letter in testimony of Our gratitude. It tells of those living stones which rest upon the living corner-stone, which is Christ, and are built together into a holy temple, far surpassing any temple built by hands, into a habitation of God in the Spirit.[4]

8. But the chief reason for Our present exposition of this 166 sublime doctrine is Our solicitude for the souls entrusted to Us. Much indeed has been written on this subject; and We know that many today are turning with greater zest to a study which delights and nourishes Christian piety. This, it would seem, is chiefly because a revived interest in the sacred liturgy, the more widely spread custom of frequent Communion, and the more fervent devotion to the Sacred Heart of Jesus practised today, have brought many souls to a deeper consideration of the unsearchable riches of Christ which are preserved in the Church. Moreover recent pronouncements on Catholic Action, by drawing closer the bonds of union between Christians and between them and the ecclesiastical hierarchy and especially the Roman Pontiff, have undoubtedly helped not a little to place this truth in its proper light. Nevertheless, while We can derive legitimate joy from these considerations, We must confess that grave errors with regard to this doctrine are being spread among those outside the true Church, and that among the faithful, also inaccurate or thoroughly false ideas are being disseminated which turn minds aside from the straight path of truth.

(There follows the section on the Church as an organically constituted body.)—Ed.

18. Now we see that the human body is given the proper 167 means to provide for its own life, health and growth, and for that of all its members. Similarly the Saviour of mankind out of His infinite goodness has provided in a wonderful way for His Mystical Body, endowing it with the Sacraments, so that, as though by an uninterrupted series of graces, its members should be sustained from birth to death, and that generous

provision might be made for the social needs of the Church. Through the waters of Baptism those who are born into this world dead in sin are not only born again and made members of the Church, but being stamped with a spiritual seal they become able and fit to receive the other Sacraments. By the chrism of Confirmation, the faithful are given added strength to protect and defend the Church, their Mother, and the faith she has given them. In the Sacrament of Penance a saving medicine is offered for the members of the Church who have fallen into sin, not only to provide for their own health, but to remove from other members of the Mystical Body all danger of contagion, or rather to afford them an incentive to virtue, and the example of a virtuous act.

168   19. Nor is that all; for in the Holy Eucharist the faithful are nourished and strengthened at the same banquet and by a divine, ineffable bond are united with each other and with the Divine Head of the whole Body. Finally, like a devoted mother, the Church is at the bedside of those who are sick unto death; and if it be not always God's will that by the holy anointing she restore health to the mortal body, nevertheless she administers spiritual medicine to the wounded soul and sends new citizens to heaven—to be her new advocates—who will enjoy forever the happiness of God.

169   20. For the social needs of the Church Christ has provided in a particular way by the institution of two other Sacraments. Through Matrimony, in which the contracting parties are ministers of grace to each other, provision is made for the external and duly regulated increase of Christian society, and, what is of greater importance, for the correct religious education of the children, without which this Mystical Body would be in grave danger. Through Holy Orders men are set aside and consecrated to God, to offer the Sacrifice of the Eucharistic Victim, to nourish the flock of the faithful with the Bread of Angels and the food of doctrine, to guide them in the way of God's commandments and counsels and to strengthen them with all other supernatural helps.

170   21. In this connection it must be borne in mind that, as God at the beginning of time endowed man's body with most ample power to subject all creatures to himself, and to increase

and multiply and fill the earth, so at the beginning of the Christian era, He supplied the Church with the means necessary to overcome countless dangers and to fill not only the whole world but the realms of heaven as well.

(The role of the Liturgy is touched upon again.)—Ed.

51. Holiness begins from Christ; and Christ is its cause. For   171
no act conducive to salvation can be performed unless it proceeds from Him as from its supernatural source. "Without me" He says, "you can do nothing."[5] If we grieve and do penance for our sins, if with filial fear and hope, we turn again to God, it is because He is leading us. Grace and glory flow from His inexhaustible fulness. Our Saviour is continually pouring out His gifts of counsel, fortitude, fear and piety, especially on the leading members of His body, so that the whole Body may grow ever more and more in holiness and in integrity of life. When the Sacraments of the Church are administered by external rite, it is He who produces their effect in souls.[6] He nourishes the redeemed with His own flesh and blood and thus calms the turbulent passions of the soul; He gives increase of grace and prepares future glory for souls and bodies. All these treasures of His divine goodness He is said to bestow on the members of His Mystical Body, not merely because He, as the Eucharistic Victim on earth and the glorified Victim in heaven, through His wounds and His prayers pleads our cause before the Eternal Father, but because He selects, He determines, He distributes every single grace to every single person "according to the measure of the giving of Christ."[7] Hence it follows that from our Divine Redeemer as from a fountainhead "the whole body, being compacted and fitly joined together, by what ever joint supplieth according to the operation in the measure of every part, maketh increase of the body, unto the edifying of itself in charity."[8]

(Later the role of the Eucharist is again expounded.)—Ed.

81. It seems to Us that something would be lacking to what   172
We have thus far proposed concerning the close union of the

Mystical Body of Jesus Christ with its Head, were We not to add here a few words on the Holy Eucharist, by which this union during this mortal life reaches, as it were, a culmination.

173　　82. By means of the Eucharistic Sacrifice Christ our Lord willed to give to the faithful a striking manifestation of our union among oursleves and with our divine Head, wonderful as it is and beyond all praise. For in this Sacrifice the sacred minister acts as the vicegerent not only of our Saviour but of the whole Mystical Body and of each one of the faithful. In this act of Sacrifice through the hands of the priest, by whose word alone the Immaculate Lamb is present on the altar, the faithful themselves, united with him in prayer and desire, offer to the Eternal Father a most acceptable victim of praise and propitiation for the needs of the whole Church. And as the Divine Redeemer, when dying on the Cross, offered Himself to the Eternal Father as Head of the whole human race, so "in this clean oblation"[9] He offers to the heavenly Father not only Himself as Head of the Church, but in Himself His mystical members also, since He holds them all, even those who are weak and ailing, in His most loving Heart.

174　　83. The Sacrament of the Eucharist is itself a striking and wonderful figure of the unity of the Church, if we consider how in the bread to be consecrated many grains go to form one whole,[10] and that in it the very Author of supernatural grace is given to us, so that through Him we may receive the spirit of charity in which we are bidden to live now no longer our own life but the life of Christ, and to love the Redeemer Himself in all the members of His social Body.

175　　84. As then in the sad and anxious times through which we are passing there are many who cling so firmly to Christ the Lord hidden beneath the Eucharistic veils that neither tribulation, nor distress, nor famine, nor nakedness, nor danger, nor persecution, nor the sword can separate them from His love,[11] surely no doubt can remain that Holy Communion which once again in God's providence is much more frequented even from early childhood, may become a source of that fortitude which not infrequently makes Christians into heroes.

(Part 3 is a Pastoral Exhortation, calling for the avoidance of errors and for love of the Church. Then the conclusion runs as follows.)—Ed.

110. Venerable Brethren, may the Virgin Mother of God   176
hear the prayers of Our paternal heart—which are yours also—
and obtain for all a true love of the Church—she whose sinless
soul was filled with the divine Spirit of Jesus Christ above all
other created souls, and who "in the name of the whole human race" gave her consent "for a spiritual marriage between
the Son of God and human nature."[12] Within her virginal
womb Christ our Lord already bore the exalted title of Head
of the Church; in a marvellous birth she brought Him forth as
the source of all supernatural life and presented Him, newly
born, as Prophet, King, and Priest to those who, from among
Jews and Gentiles, were the first to come to adore Him. Furthermore, her only Son, condescending to His mother's prayer
in "Cana of Galilee," performed the miracle by which "his
disciples believed in him."[13] It was she, the second Eve, who,
free from all sin, original or personal, and always most intimately united with her Son, offered Him on Golgotha to the
Eternal Father for all the children of Adam, sin-stained by his
unhappy fall, and her mother's rights and mother's love were
included in the holocaust. Thus she who, according to the
flesh, was the mother of our Head, through the added title of
pain and glory became, according to the Spirit, the mother of
all His members. She it was who through her powerful prayers
obtained that the Spirit of our Divine Redeemer, already
given on the Cross, should be bestowed, accompanied by
miraculous gifts, on the newly founded Church at Pentecost;
and finally, bearing with courage and confidence the tremen-
dous burden of her sorrows and desolation, she, truly the
Queen of Martyrs, more than all the faithful "filled up those
things that are wanting of the sufferings of Christ . . . for His
Body, which is the Church";[14] and she continues to have for
the Mystical Body of Christ, born of the pierced Heart of the
Saviour,[15] the same motherly care and ardent love with which
she cherished and fed the Infant Jesus in the crib.

177   111. May she, then, the most holy Mother of all the members of Christ,[16] to whose Immaculate Heart We have trustfully consecrated all mankind, and who now reigns in heaven with her Son, her body and soul refulgent with heavenly glory—may she never cease to beg from Him that copious streams of grace may flow from its exalted Head into all the members of the Mystical Body. May she throw about the Church today, as in times gone by, the mantle of her protection and obtain from God that now at last the Church and all mankind may enjoy more peaceful days.

178   112. Confiding in this sublime hope, from an overflowing heart We impart to you, one and all, Venerable Brethren, and to the flocks entrusted to your care, as a pledge of heavenly graces and a token of Our special affection, the Apostolic Benediction.

179   113. Given at Rome, at St. Peter's, on the twenty-ninth day of June, the Feast of the Holy Apostles Peter and Paul, in the year 1943, the fifth of Our Pontificate.

MEDIATOR DEI
Encyclical Letter of Pope Pius XII
on the Sacred Liturgy
November 30, 1947

Introduction

Mediator between God and men[1] and High Priest who has gone before us into heaven, Jesus the Son of God[2] quite clearly had one aim in view when He undertook the mission of mercy which was to endow mankind with the rich blessings of supernatural grace. Sin had disturbed the right relationship between man and his Creator; the Son of God would restore it. The children of Adam were wretched heirs to the infection of original sin; He would bring them back to their heavenly Father, the primal source and final destiny of all things. For this reason He was not content, while He dwelt with us on earth, merely to give notice that redemption had begun, and to proclaim the long-awaited Kingdom of God, but gave Himself besides in prayer and sacrifice to the task of saving souls, even to the point of offering Himself, as He hung from the cross, a Victim unspotted unto God, to purify our conscience of dead works, to serve the living God.[3] Thus happily were all men summoned back from the byways leading them down to ruin and disaster, to be set squarely once again upon the path that leads to God. Thanks to the shedding of the blood of the Immaculate Lamb, now each might set about the personal task of achieving his own sanctification, so rendering to God the glory due to Him.

181   2. But what is more, the divine Redeemer has so willed it
that the priestly life begun with the supplication and sacrifice of His mortal body should continue without intermission down the ages in His Mystical Body which is the Church.
That is why He established a visible priesthood to offer
everywhere the clean oblation[4] which would enable men
from East to West, freed from the shackles of sin, to offer
God that unconstrained and voluntary homage which their
conscience dictates.

182   3. In obedience, therefore, to her Founder's behest, the
Church prolongs the priestly mission of Jesus Christ mainly
by means of the sacred liturgy. She does this in the first
place at the altar, where constantly the sacrifice of the cross
is re-presented[5] and, with a single difference in the manner
of its offering, renewed.[6] She does it next by means of the
sacraments, those special channels through which men are
made partakers in the supernatural life. She does it, finally,
by offering to God, all Good and Great, the daily tribute of
her prayer of praise. "What a spectacle for heaven and earth,"
observes Our predecessor of happy memory, Pius XI, "is not
the Church at prayer! For centuries without interruption,
from midnight to midnight, the divine psalmody of the inspired canticles is repeated on earth; there is no hour of the
day that is not hallowed by its special liturgy; there is no
stage of human life that has not its part in the thanksgiving,
praise, supplication and reparation of this common prayer
of the Mystical Body of Christ which is His Church!"[7]

183   4. You are of course familiar with the fact, Venerable
Brethren, that a remarkably widespread revival of scholarly
interest in the sacred liturgy took place towards the end of
the last century and has continued through the early years
of this one. The movement owed its rise to commendable
private initiative and more particularly to the zealous and
persistent labor of several monasteries within the distinguished
Order of Saint Benedict. Thus there developed in this field
among many European nations, and in lands beyond the seas
as well, a rivalry as welcome as it was productive of results.
Indeed, the salutary fruits of this rivalry among the scholars
were plain for all to see, both in the sphere of the sacred

sciences, where the liturgical rites of the Western and Eastern Church were made the object of extensive research and profound study, and in the spiritual life of considerable numbers of individual Christians.

5. The majestic ceremonies of the sacrifice of the altar became better known, understood and appreciated. With more widespread and more frequent reception of the sacraments, the worship of the Eucharist came to be regarded for what it really is: the fountain-head of genuine Christian devotion. Bolder relief was given likewise to the fact that all the faithful make up a single and very compact body with Christ for its Head, and that the Christian community is in duty bound to participate in the liturgical rites according to their station. 184

6. You are surely well aware that this Apostolic See has always made careful provision for the schooling of the people committed to its charge in the correct spirit and practice of the liturgy; and that it has been no less careful to insist that the sacred rites should be performed with due external dignity. In this connection We ourselves, in the course of our traditional address to the Lenten preachers of this gracious city of Rome in 1943, urged them warmly to exhort their respective hearers to more faithful participation in the Eucharistic sacrifice. Only a short while previously, with the design of rendering the prayers of the liturgy more correctly understood and their truth and unction more easy to perceive, We arranged to have the Book of Psalms, which forms such an important part of these prayers in the Catholic Church, translated once more into Latin from their original text.[8] 185

7. But while We derive no little satisfaction from the wholesome results of the movement just described, duty obliges Us to give serious attention to this "revival" as it is advocated in some quarters, and to take proper steps to preserve it at the outset from excess or outright perversion. 186

8. Indeed, though We are sorely grieved to note, on the one hand, that there are places where the spirit, understanding or practice of the sacred liturgy is defective, or all but inexistent, We observe with considerable anxiety and some misgiving, that elsewhere certain enthusiasts, over eager in their search for novelty, are straying beyond the path of sound doctrine 187

and prudence. Not seldom, in fact, they interlard their plans and hopes for a revival of the sacred liturgy with principles which compromise this holiest of causes in theory or practice, and sometimes even taint it with errors touching Catholic faith and ascetical doctrine.

188   9. Yet the integrity of faith and morals ought to be the special criterion of this sacred science, which must conform exactly to what the Church out of the abundance of her wisdom teaches and prescribes. It is, consequently, Our prerogative to commend and approve whatever is done properly, and to check or censure any aberration from the path of truth and rectitude.

189   10. Let not the apathetic or half-hearted imagine, however, that We agree with them when We reprove the erring and restrain the overbold. No more must the imprudent think that We are commending them when We correct the faults of those who are negligent and sluggish.

190   11. If in this encyclical letter We treat chiefly of the Latin liturgy, it is not because We esteem less highly the venerable liturgies of the Eastern Church, whose ancient and honorable ritual traditions are just as dear to Us. The reason lies rather in a special situation prevailing in the Western Church, of sufficient importance, it would seem, to require this exercise of Our authority.

191   12. With docile hearts, then, let all Christians hearken to the voice of their Common Father, who would have them, each and every one, intimately united with him as they approach the altar of God, professing the same faith, obedient to the same law, sharing in the same Sacrifice with a single intention and one sole desire. This is a duty imposed, of course, by the honor due to God. But the needs of our day and age demand it as well. After a long and cruel war which has rent whole peoples asunder with its rivalry and slaughter, men of good will are spending themselves in the effort to find the best possible way to restore peace to the world. It is, notwithstanding, Our belief that no plan or initiative can offer better prospect of success than that fervent religious spirit and zeal by which Christians must be formed and guided; in this way their common and whole-hearted acceptance of the

same truth, along with their united obedience and loyalty to their appointed pastors, while rendering to God the worship due to Him, makes of them one brotherhood: "for we, being many, are one body: all that partake of one bread."[9]

Part I: The Nature, Source and Development of the Liturgy

A. The Liturgy is Public Worship

13. It is unquestionably the fundamental duty of man to orientate his person and his life towards God. "For He it is to whom we must first be bound, as to an unfailing principle; to whom even our free choice must be directed as to an ultimate objective. It is He, too, whom we lose when carelessly we sin. It is He whom we must recover by our faith and trust."[10] But man turns properly to God when he acknowledges His supreme majesty and supreme authority; when he accepts divinely revealed truths with a submissive mind; when he scrupulously obeys divine law, centering in God his every act and aspiration; when he accords, in short, due worship to the One True God by practicing the virtue of religion.   192

14. This duty is incumbent, first of all, on men as individuals. But it also binds the whole community of human beings, grouped together by mutual social ties: mankind, too, depends on the sovereign authority of God.   193

15. It should be noted, moreover, that men are bound by this obligation in a special way in virtue of the fact that God has raised them to the supernatural order.   194

16. Thus we observe that when God institutes the Old Law, He makes provision besides for sacred rites, and determines in exact detail the rules to be observed by His people in rendering Him the worship He ordains. To this end He established various kinds of sacrifice and designated the ceremonies with which they were to be offered to Him. His enactments on all matters relating to the Ark of the Covenant, the Temple and the holy days are minute and clear. He established a sacerdotal tribe with its high priest, selected and described the vestments with which the sacred ministers were to be clothed, and every function in any way pertaining to divine worship.[11] Yet this   195

was nothing more than a faint foreshadowing[12] of the worship which the High Priest of the New Testament was to render to the Father in heaven.

196   17. No sooner, in fact, "is the Word made flesh"[18] than He shows Himself to the world vested with a priestly office, making to the Eternal Father an act of submission which will continue uninterruptedly as long as He lives: "When He cometh into the world He saith . . . 'behold I come . . . to do Thy will'."[14] This act He was to consummate admirably in the bloody Sacrifice of the Cross: "In the which will we are sanctified by the oblation of the Body of Jesus Christ once."[15] He plans His active life among men with no other purpose in view. As a child He is presented to the Lord in the Temple. To the Temple He returns as a grown boy, and often afterwards to instruct the people and to pray. He fasts for forty days before beginning His public ministry. His counsel and example summon all to prayer, daily and at night as well. As Teacher of the truth He "enlighteneth every man"[16] to the end that mortals may duly acknowledge the immortal God, "not withdrawing unto perdition, but faithful to the saving of the soul."[17] As Shepherd He watches over His flock, leads it to life-giving pasture, lays down a law that none shall wander from His side, off the straight path He has pointed out, and that all shall lead holy lives imbued with His spirit and moved by His active aid. At the Last Supper He celebrates a new Pasch with solemn rite and ceremonial, and provides for its continuance through the divine institution of the Eucharist. On the morrow, lifted up between heaven and earth, He offers the saving sacrifice of His life, and pours forth, as it were, from His pierced Heart the sacraments destined to impart the treasures of redemption to the souls of men. All this He does with but a single aim: the glory of His Father and man's ever greater sanctification.

197   18. But it is His will, besides, that the worship He instituted and practiced during His life on earth shall continue ever afterwards without any intermission. For he has not left mankind an orphan. He still offers us the support of His powerful, unfailing intercession, acting as our "advocate with the Fa-

ther."[18] He aids us likewise through His Church, where He
is present indefectibly as the ages run their course: through
the Church which He constituted "the pillar of truth"[19]
and dispenser of grace, and which by His sacrifice on the cross,
He founded, consecrated and confirmed forever.[20]

19. The Church has, therefore, in common with the Word   198
Incarnate the aim, the obligation and the function of teaching all men the truth, of governing and directing them aright,
of offering to God the pleasing and acceptable sacrifice; in
this way the Church re-establishes between the Creator and
His creatures that unity and harmony to which the Apostle
of the Gentiles alludes in these words: "Now, therefore, you
are no more strangers and foreigners; but you are fellow citizens with the saints and domestics of God, built upon the
foundation of the apostles and prophets, Jesus Christ Himself
being the chief corner-stone; in whom all the building, being
framed together, groweth up into a holy temple in the Lord,
in whom you also are built together into a habitation of God
in the Spirit."[21] Thus the society founded by the divine Redeemer, whether in her doctrine and government, or in the
sacrifice and sacraments instituted by Him, or finally, in the
ministry, which He has confided to her charge with the outpouring of His prayer and the shedding of His blood, has no
other goal or purpose than to increase ever in strength and
unity.

20. This result is, in fact, achieved when Christ lives and   199
thrives, as it were, in the hearts of men, and when men's
hearts in turn are fashioned and expanded as though by Christ.
This makes it possible for the sacred temple, where the Divine Majesty receives the acceptable worship which His law
prescribes, to increase and prosper day by day in this land of
exile on earth. Along with the Church, therefore, her Divine
Founder is present at every liturgical function: Christ is present at the august sacrifice of the altar both in the person of
His minister and above all under the eucharistic species. He is
present in the sacraments, infusing into them the power
which makes them ready instruments of sanctification. He
is present, finally, in the prayer of praise and petition we
direct to God, as it is written: "Where there are two or three

gathered together in My Name, there am I in the midst of them."[22] The sacred liturgy is, consequently, the public worship which our Redeemer as Head of the Church renders to the Father, as well as the worship which the community of the faithful renders to its Founder, and through Him to the heavenly Father. It is, in short, the worship rendered by the Mystical Body of Christ in the entirety of its Head and members.

200   21. Liturgical practice begins with the very founding of the Church. The first Christians, in fact, "were persevering in the doctrine of the apostles and in the communication of the breaking of bread and in prayers."[23] Whenever their pastors can summon a little group of the faithful together, they set up an altar on which they proceed to offer the sacrifice, and around which are ranged all the other rites appropriate for the saving of souls and for the honor due to God. Among these latter rites, the first place is reserved for the sacraments, namely, the seven principal founts of salvation. There follows the celebration of the divine praises in which the faithful also join, obeying the behest of the Apostle Paul, "In all wisdom, teaching and admonishing one another in psalms, hymns and spiritual canticles, singing in grace in your hearts to God."[24] Next comes the reading of the Law, the prophets, the gospel and the apostolic epistles; and last of all the homily or sermon in which the official head of the congregation recalls and explains the practical bearing of the commandments of the divine Master and the chief events of His life, combining instruction with appropriate exhortation and illustration for the benefit of all his listeners.

201   22. As circumstances and the needs of Christians warrant, public worship is organized, developed and enriched by new rites, ceremonies and regulations, always with the single end in view, "that we may use these external signs to keep us alert, learn from them what distance we have come along the road, and by them be heartened to go on further with more eager step; for the effect will be more precious the warmer the affection which precedes it."[25] Here then is a better and more suitable way to raise the heart to God. Thenceforth the priesthood of Jesus Christ is a living and continuous reality

through all the ages to the end of time, since the liturgy is nothing more nor less than the exercise of this priestly function. Like her divine Head, the Church is forever present in the midst of her children. She aids and exhorts them to holiness, so that they may one day return to the Father in heaven clothed in that beauteous raiment of the supernatural. To all who are born to life on earth she gives a second, supernatural kind of birth. She arms them with the Holy Spirit for the struggle against the implacable enemy. She gathers all Christians about her altars, inviting and urging them repeatedly to take part in the celebration of the Mass, feeding them with the Bread of Angels to make them ever stronger. She purifies and consoles the hearts that sin has wounded and soiled. Solemnly she consecrates those whom God has called to the priestly ministry. She fortifies with new gifts of grace the chaste nuptials of those who are destined to found and bring up a Christian family. When at last she has soothed and refreshed the closing hours of this earthly life by holy Viaticum and extreme unction, with the utmost affection she accompanies the mortal remains of her children to the grave, lays them reverently to rest, and confides them to the protection of the cross, against the day when they will triumph over death and rise again. She has a further solemn blessing and invocation for those of her children who dedicate themselves to the service of God in the life of religious perfection. Finally, she extends to the souls in purgatory, who implore her intercession and her prayers, the helping hand which may lead them happily at last to eternal blessedness in heaven.

B. The Liturgy is Exterior and Interior Worship

23. The worship rendered by the Church to God must be, in its entirety, interior as well as exterior. It is exterior because the nature of man as a composite of body and soul requires it to be so. Likewise, because divine Providence has disposed that "while we recognize God visibly, we may be drawn by Him to love of things unseen."[26] Every impulse of the human heart, besides, expresses itself naturally through

        202

the senses; and the worship of God, being the concern not merely of individuals but of the whole community of mankind, must therefore be social as well. This obviously it cannot be unless religious activity is also organized and manifested outwardly. Exterior worship, finally, reveals and emphasizes the unity of the Mystical Body, feeds new fuel to its holy zeal, fortifies its energy, intensifies its action day by day: "for although the ceremonies themselves can claim no perfection or sanctity in their own right, they are, nevertheless, the outward acts of religion, designed to rouse the heart, like signals of a sort, to veneration of the sacred realities, and to raise the mind to meditation on the supernatural. They serve to foster piety, to kindle the flame of charity, to increase our faith and deepen our devotion. They provide instruction for simple folk, decoration for divine worship, continuity of religious practice. They make it possible to tell genuine Christians from their false or heretical counterparts."[27]

203   24. But the chief element of divine worship must be interior. For we must always live in Christ and give ourselves to Him completely, so that in Him, with Him and through Him the heavenly Father may be duly glorified. The sacred liturgy requires, however, that both of these elements be intimately linked with each other. This recommendation the liturgy itself is careful to repeat, as often as it prescribes an exterior act of worship. Thus we are urged, when there is question of fasting, for example, "to give interior effect to our outward observance."[28] Otherwise religion clearly amounts to mere formalism, without meaning and without content. You recall, Venerable Brethren, how the divine Master expels from the sacred temple, as unworthy to worship there, people who pretend to honor God with nothing but neat and well-turned phrases, like actors in a theatre, and think themselves perfectly capable of working out their eternal salvation without plucking their inveterate vices from their hearts.[29] It is, therefore, the keen desire of the Church that all of the faithful kneel at the feet of the Redeemer to tell Him how much they venerate and love Him. She wants them present in crowds—like the children whose joyous cries accompanied

His entry into Jerusalem—to sing their hymns and chant their song of praise and thanksgiving to Him who is King of Kings and Source of every blessing. She would have them move their lips in prayer, sometimes in petition, sometimes in joy and gratitude, and in this way experience His merciful aid and power like the apostles at the lakeside of Tiberias, or abandon themselves totally, like Peter on Mount Tabor, to mystic union with the eternal God in contemplation.

25. It is an error, consequently, and a mistake to think of   204
the sacred liturgy as merely the outward or visible part of divine worship or as an ornamental ceremonial. No less erroneous is the notion that it consists solely in a list of laws and prescriptions according to which the ecclesiastical hierarchy orders the sacred rites to be performed.

26. It should be clear to all, then, that God cannot be   205
honored worthily unless the mind and heart turn to Him in quest of the perfect life, and that the worship rendered to God by the Church in union with her divine Head is the most efficacious means of achieving sanctity.

27. This efficacy, where there is question of the eucharistic   206
sacrifice and the sacraments, derives first of all and principally from the act itself *(ex opere operato)*. But if one considers the part which the Immaculate Spouse of Jesus Christ takes in the action, embellishing the sacrifice and sacraments with prayer and sacred ceremonies, or if one refers to the"sacramentals" and the other rites instituted by the hierarchy of the Church, then its effectiveness is due rather to the action of the Church *ex opere operantis Ecclesiae)*, inasmuch as she is holy and acts always in closest union with her Head.

28. In this connection, Venerable Brethren, We desire to   207
direct your attention to certain recent theories touching a so-called "objective" piety. While these theories attempt, it is true, to throw light on the mystery of the Mystical Body, on the effective reality of sanctifying grace, on the action of God in the sacraments and in the Mass, it is nonetheless apparent that they tend to belittle, or pass over in silence, what they call "subjective," or "personal" piety.

29. It is an unquestionable fact that the work of our re-   208
demption is continued, and that its fruits are imparted to us,

during the celebration of the liturgy, notably in the august sacrifice of the altar. Christ acts each day to save us, in the sacraments and in His holy sacrifice. By means of them He is constantly atoning for the sins of mankind, constantly consecrating it to God. Sacraments and sacrifice do, then, possess that "objective" power to make us really and personally sharers in the divine life of Jesus Christ. Not from any ability of our own, but by the power of God, are they endowed with the capacity to unite the piety of members with that of the Head, and to make this, in a sense, the action of the whole community. From these profound considerations some are led to conclude that all Christian piety must be centered in the mystery of the Mystical Body of Christ, with no regard for what is "personal" or "subjective," as they would have it. As a result they feel that all other religious exercises not directly connected with the sacred liturgy, and performed outside public worship, should be omitted.

209   30. But though the principles set forth above are excellent, it must be plain to everyone that the conclusions drawn from them respecting two sorts of piety are false, insidious and quite pernicious.

210   31. Very truly, the sacraments and the sacrifice of the altar, being Christ's own actions, must be held to be capable in themselves of conveying and dispensing grace from the divine Head to the members of the Mystical Body. But if they are to produce their proper effect, it is absolutely necessary that our hearts be properly disposed to receive them. Hence the warning of Paul the Apostle with reference to holy communion, "But let a man first prove himself; and then let him eat of this bread and drink of the chalice."[30] This explains why the Church in a brief and significant phrase calls the various acts of mortification, especially those practised during the season of Lent, "the Christian army's defenses."[31] They represent, in fact, the personal effort and activity of members who desire, as grace urges and aids them, to join forces with their Captain—"that we may discover . . . in our Captain," to borrow St. Augustine's words, "the fountain of grace itself."[32] But observe that these members are alive, endowed and equipped with an intelligence and will of their own. It

follows that they are strictly required to put their own lips to the fountain, imbibe and absorb for themselves the life-giving water, and rid themselves personally of anything that might hinder its nutritive effect in their souls. Emphatically, therefore, the work of redemption, which in itself is indepen-dent of our will, requires a serious interior effort on our part if we are to achieve eternal salvation.

32. If the private and interior devotion of individuals were   211
to neglect the august sacrifice of the altar and the sacraments, and to withdraw them from the stream of vital energy that flows from Head to members, it would indeed be sterile, and deserve to be condemned. But when devotional exer-cises, and pious practices in general, not strictly connected with the sacred liturgy, confine themselves to merely human acts, with the express purpose of directing these latter to the Father in heaven, of rousing people to repentance and holy fear of God, of weaning them from the seductions of the world and its vice, and leading them back to the difficult path of perfection, then certainly such practices are not only highly praiseworthy but absolutely indispensable, because they expose the dangers threatening the spiritual life; because they promote the acquisition of virtue; and because they in-crease the fervor and generosity with which we are bound to dedicate all that we are and all that we have to service of Jesus Christ. Genuine and real piety, which the Angelic Doctor calls "devotion," and which is the principal act of the virtue of religion—that act which correctly relates and fitly directs men to God; and by which they freely and spontaneously give themselves to the worship of God in its fullest sense[33]— piety of this authentic sort needs meditation on the super-natural realities and spiritual exercises, if it is to be nurtured, stimulated and sustained, and if it is to prompt us to lead a more perfect life. For the Christian religion, practiced as it should be, demands that the will especially be consecrated to God and exert its influence on all the other spiritual faculties. But every act of the will presupposes an act of the intelli-gence, and before one can express the desire and the intention of offering oneself in sacrifice to the eternal Godhead, a knowledge of the facts and truths which make religion a duty

of submission to our Creator; and, finally, the inexhaustible treasures of love with which God yearns to enrich us, as well as the necessity of supernatural grace for the achievement of our destiny, and that special path marked out for us by divine Providence in virtue of the fact that we have been united, one and all, like members of body, to Jesus Christ the Head. But further, since our hearts, disturbed as they are at times by the lower appetites, do not always respond to motives of love, it is also extremely helpful to let consideration and contemplation of the justice of God provoke us on occasion to salutary fear, and guide us thence to Christian humility, repentance and amendment.

212   33. But it will not do to possess these facts and truths after the fashion of an abstract memory lesson or lifeless commentary. They must lead to practical results. They must impel us to subject our senses and their faculties to reason, as illuminated by the Catholic faith. They must help to cleanse and purify the heart, uniting it to Christ more intimately every day, growing ever more to His likeness, and drawing from Him the divine inspiration and strength of which it stands in need. They must serve as increasingly effective incentives to action: urging men to produce good fruit, to perform their individual duties faithfully, to give themselves eagerly to the regular practice of their religion and the energetic exercise of virtue. "You are Christ's, and Christ is God's."[34] Let everything, therefore, have its proper place and arrangement; let everything be "theocentric," so to speak, if we really wish to direct everything to the glory of God through the life and power which flow from the divine Head into our hearts: "Having therefore, brethren, a confidence in the entering into the holies by the blood of Christ, a new and living way which He both dedicated for us through the veil, that is to say, His flesh, and a high priest over the house of God; let us draw near with a true heart, in fulness of faith, having our hearts sprinkled from an evil conscience and our bodies washed with clean water, let us hold fast the confession of our hope without wavering . . . and let us consider one another, to provoke unto charity and to good works."[35]

34. Here is the source of the harmony and equilibrium   213
which prevails among the members of the Mystical Body of
Jesus Christ. When the Church teaches us our Catholic faith
and exhorts us to obey the commandments of Christ, she is
paving a way for her priestly, sanctifying action in its highest
sense; she disposes us likewise for more serious meditation on
the life of the divine Redeemer and guides us to profounder
knowledge of the mysteries of faith where we may draw the
supernatural sustenance, strength and vitality that enable us
to progress safely, through Christ, towards a more perfect
life. Not only through her ministers but with the help of the
faithful individually, who have imbibed in this fashion the
spirit of Christ, the Church endeavors to permeate with this
same spirit the life and labors of men—their private and family life, their social, even economic and political life—that all
who are called God's children may reach more readily the end
He has proposed for them.

35. Such action on the part of individual Christians, then,   214
along with the ascetic effort prompting them to purify their
hearts, actually stimulates in the faithful those energies
which enable them to participate in the august sacrifice of
the altar with better dispositions. They now can receive the
sacraments with more abundant fruit, and come from the
celebration of the sacred rites more eager, more firmly resolved to pray and deny themselves like Christians, to answer
the inspirations and invitation of divine grace and to imitate
daily more closely the virtues of our Redeemer. And all of
this not simply for their own advantage, but for that of the
whole Church, where whatever good is accomplished proceeds from the power of her Head and redounds to the ad-
vancement of all her members.

36. In the spiritual life, consequently, there can be no op-   215
position between the action of God, who pours forth His
grace into men's hearts so that the work of the redemption
may always abide, and the tireless collaboration of man, who
must not render vain the gift of God.[36] No more can the efficacy of the external administration of the sacraments, which
comes from the rite itself *(ex opere operato),* be opposed to

the meritorious action of their ministers or recipients, which we call the agent's action *(opus operantis)*. Similarly, no conflict exists between public prayer and prayers in private, between morality and contemplation, between the ascetical life and devotion to the liturgy. Finally, there is no opposition between the jurisdiction and teaching office of the ecclesiastical hierarchy, and the specifically priestly power exercised in the sacred ministry.

216   37. Considering their special designation to perform the liturgical functions of the holy sacrifice and divine office, the Church has serious reason for prescribing that the ministers she assigns to the service of the sanctuary and members of religious institutes betake themselves at stated times to mental prayer, to examination of conscience, and to various other spiritual exercises.[37] Unquestionably, liturgical prayer, being the public supplication of the illustrious Spouse of Jesus Christ, is superior in excellence to private prayers. But this superior worth does not at all imply contrast or incompatibility between these two kinds of prayer. For both merge harmoniously in the single spirit which animates them, "Christ is all and in all."[38] Both tend to the same objective: until Christ be formed in us.[39]

C. The Liturgy Under the Hierarchy of the Church

217   38. For a better and more accurate understanding of the sacred liturgy another of its characteristic features, no less important, needs to be considered.

218   39. The Church is a society, and as such requires an authority and hierarchy of her own. Though it is true that all the members of the Mystical Body partake of the same blessings and pursue the same objective, they do not all enjoy the same powers, nor are they all qualified to perform the same acts. The divine Redeemer has willed, as a matter of fact, that His Kingdom should be built and solidly supported, as it were, on a holy order, which resembles in some sort the heavenly hierarchy.

219   40. Only to the apostles, and thenceforth to those on whom their successors have imposed hands, is granted the

power of the priesthood, in virtue of which they represent
the person of Jesus Christ before their people, acting at the
same time as representatives of their people before God. This
priesthood is not transmitted by heredity or human descent.
It does not emanate from the Christian community. It is not
a delegation from the people. Prior to acting as representative
of the community before the throne of God, the priest is the
ambassador of the divine Redeemer. He is God's vice-gerent
in the midst of his flock precisely because Jesus Christ is
Head of that body of which Christians are the members. The
power entrusted to him, therefore, bears no natural resemblance to anything human. It is entirely supernatural. It comes
from God. "As the Father hath sent me, I also send you[40]
. . . he that heareth you heareth me[41] . . . go ye into the
whole world and preach the gospel to every creature; he that
believeth and is baptized shall be saved."[42]

41. That is why the visible, external priesthood of Jesus   220
Christ is not handed down indiscriminately to all members
of the Church in general, but is conferred on designated men,
through what may be called the spiritual generation of holy
orders.

42. This latter, one of the seven sacraments, not only im-   221
parts the grace appropriate to the function and state of life,
but imparts an indelible "character" besides, indicating the
sacred ministers' conformity to Jesus Christ the Priest and
qualifying them to perform those official acts of religion by
which men are sanctified and God is duly glorified in keeping
with the divine laws and regulations.

43. In the same way, actually, that baptism is the distinctive   222
mark of all Christians, and serves to differentiate them from
those who have not been cleansed in this purifying stream
and consequently are not members of Christ, the sacrament
of holy orders sets the priest apart from the rest of the faithful who have not received this consecration. For they alone,
in answer to an inward supernatural call, have entered the
august ministry, where they are assigned to service in the
sanctuary and become, as it were, the instruments God uses
to communicate supernatural life from on high to the Mystical
Body of Jesus Christ. Add to this, as We have noted above,

the fact that they alone have been marked with the indelible sign "conforming" them to Christ the Priest, and that their hands alone have been consecrated "in order that whatever they bless may be blessed, whatever they consecrate may become sacred and holy, in the name of our Lord Jesus Christ."[43] Let all, then, who would live in Christ flock to their priests. By them they will be supplied with the comforts and food of the spiritual life. From them they will procure the medicine of salvation assuring their cure and happy recovery from the fatal sickness of their sins. The priest, finally, will bless their homes, consecrate their families and help them, as they breathe their last, across the threshold of eternal happiness.

223   44. Since, therefore, it is the priest chiefly who performs the sacred liturgy in the name of the Church, its organization, regulation and details cannot but be subject to Church authority. This conclusion, based on the nature of Christian worship itself, is further confirmed by the testimony of history.

224   45. Additional proof of this indefeasible right of the ecclesiastical hierarchy lies in the circumstances that the sacred liturgy is intimately bound up with doctrinal propositions which the Church proposes to be perfectly true and certain, and must as a consequence conform to the decrees respecting Catholic faith issued by the supreme teaching authority of the Church with a view to safeguarding the integrity of the religion revealed by God.

225   46. On this subject We judge it Our duty to rectify an attitude with which you are doubtless familiar, Venerable Brethren. We refer to the error and fallacious reasoning of those who have claimed that the sacred liturgy is a kind of proving ground for the truths to be held of faith, meaning by this that the Church is obliged to declare such a doctrine sound when it is found to have produced fruits of piety and sanctity through the sacred rites of the liturgy, and to reject it otherwise. Hence the epigram, *"Lex orandi, lex credendi"*—the law for prayer is the law for faith.

226   47. But this is not what the Church teaches and enjoins. The worship she offers to God, all good and great, is a con-

tinuous profession of Catholic faith and a continuous exercise of hope and charity, as Augustine puts it tersely. "God
is to be worshipped," he says, "by faith, hope and charity."[44]
In the sacred liturgy we profess the Catholic faith explicitly
and openly, not only by the celebration of the mysteries,
and by offering the holy sacrifice and administering the sacraments, but also by saying or singing the credo or Symbol of
the faith—it is indeed the sign and badge, as it were, of the
Christian—along with other texts, and likewise by the reading
of holy scripture, written under the inspiration of the Holy
Ghost. The entire liturgy, therefore, has the Catholic faith for
its content, inasmuch as it bears public witness to the faith
of the Church.

48. For this reason, whenever there was question of defin-   227
ing a truth revealed by God, the Sovereign Pontiff and the
Councils in their recourse to the "theological sources," as
they are called, have not seldom drawn many an argument
from this sacred science of the liturgy. For an example in
point, Our predecessor of immortal memory, Pius IX, so
argued when he proclaimed the Immaculate Conception of
the Virgin Mary. Similarly during the discussion of a doubtful or controversial truth, the Church and the Holy Fathers
have not failed to look to the age-old and age-honored
sacred rites for enlightenment. Hence the well-known and
venerable maxim, *"Legem credendi lex statuat supplicandi"*—
let the rule for prayer determine the rule of belief.[45] The
sacred liturgy, consequently, does not decide or determine
independently and of itself what is of Catholic faith. More
properly, since the liturgy is also a profession of eternal
truths, and subject, as such, to the supreme teaching authority
of the Church, it can supply proofs and testimony, quite
clearly of no little value, towards the determination of a
particular point of Christian doctrine. But if one desires to
differentiate and describe the relationship between faith and
the sacred liturgy in absolute and general terms, it is perfectly correct to say, *"Lex credendi legem statuat supplicandi"*—
let the rule of belief determine the rule of prayer. The same
holds true for the other theological virtues also, *"In . . . fide,*

spe, caritate continuato desiderio semper oramus"—we pray always, with constant yearning in faith, hope and charity.[46]

D. Progress and Development of the Liturgy

228   49. From time immemorial the ecclesiastical hierarchy has exercised this right in matters liturgical. It has organized and regulated divine worship, enriching it constantly with new splendor and beauty, to the glory of God and the spiritual profit of Christians. What is more, it has not been slow—keeping the substance of the Mass and sacraments carefully intact—to modify what it deemed not altogether fitting, and to add what appeared more likely to increase the honor paid to Jesus Christ and the august Trinity, and to instruct and stimulate the Christian people to greater advantage.[47]

229   50. The sacred liturgy does, in fact, include divine as well as human elements. The former, instituted as they have been by God, cannot be changed in any way by men. But the human components admit of various modifications, as the needs of the age, circumstance and the good of souls may require, and as the ecclesiastical hierarchy, under guidance of the Holy Spirit, may have authorized. This will explain the marvellous variety of Eastern and Western rites. Here is the reason for the gradual addition, through successive development, of particular religious customs and practices of piety only faintly discernible in earlier times. Hence likewise it happens from time to time that certain devotions long since forgotten are revived and practiced anew. All these developments attest the abiding life of the immaculate Spouse of Jesus Christ through these many centuries. They are the sacred language she uses, as the ages run their course, to profess to her divine Spouse her own faith along with that of the nations committed to her charge, and her own unfailing love. They furnish proof, besides, of the wisdom of the teaching method she employs to arouse and nourish constantly the "Christian instinct."

230   51. Several causes, really, have been instrumental in the progress and development of the sacred liturgy during the long and glorious life of the Church.

52. Thus, for example, as Catholic doctrine on the Incar-   231
nate Word of God, the eucharistic sacrament and sacrifice and
Mary the Virgin Mother of God came to be determined with
greater certitude and clarity, new ritual forms were introduced through which the acts of the liturgy proceeded to
reproduce this brighter light issuing from the decrees of the
teaching authority of the Church, and to reflect it, in a sense,
so that it might reach the minds and hearts of Christ's people
more readily.

53. The subsequent advances in ecclesiastical discipline for   232
the administering of the sacraments, that of penance for example; the institution and later suppression of the catechumenate; and again, the practice of eucharistic communion
under a single species, adopted in the Latin Church; these
developments were assuredly responsible in no little measure
for the modification of the ancient ritual in the course of
time, and for the gradual introduction of new rites considered
more in accord with prevailing discipline in these matters.

54. Just as notable a contribution to this progressive trans-   233
formation was made by devotional trends and practices not
directly related to the sacred liturgy, which began to appear,
by God's wonderful design, in later periods, and grew to be
so popular. We may instance the spread and ever mounting
ardor of devotion to the Blessed Eucharist, devotion to the
most bitter passion of our Redeemer, devotion to the most
Sacred Heart of Jesus, to the Virgin Mother of God and to
her most chaste spouse.

55. Other manifestations of piety have also played their   234
circumstantial part in this same liturgical development. Among
them may be cited the public pilgrimages to the tombs of the
martyrs prompted by motives of devotion, the special periods
of fasting instituted for the same reason, and lastly, in this
gracious city of Rome, the penitential recitation of the litanies
during the "station" processions, in which even the Sovereign
Pontiff frequently joined.

56. It is likewise easy to understand that the progress of   235
the fine arts, those of architecture, painting and music above
all, has exerted considerable influence on the choice and disposition of the various external features of the sacred liturgy.

236   57. The Church has further used her right of control over liturgical observance to protect the purity of divine worship against abuse from dangerous and imprudent innovations introduced by private individuals and particular churches. Thus it came about—during the 16th century, when usages and customs of this sort had become increasingly prevalent and exaggerated, and when private initiative in matters liturgical threatened to compromise the integrity of faith and devotion, to the great advantage of heretics and further spread of their errors—that in the year 1588, Our predecessor Sixtus V of immortal memory established the Sacred Congregation of Rites, charged with the defense of the legitimate rites of the Church and with the prohibition of any spurious innovattion.[48] This body fulfils even today the official function of supervision and legislation with regard to all matters touching the sacred liturgy.[49]

E. Its Development May Not be Left to Private Judgment

237   58. It follows from this that the Sovereign Pontiff alone enjoys the right to recognize and establish any practice touching the worship of God, to introduce and approve new rites, as also to modify those he judges to require modification.[50] Bishops, for their part, have the right and duty carefully to watch over the exact observance of the prescriptions of the sacred canons respecting divine worship.[51] Private individuals, therefore, even though they be clerics, may not be left to decide for themselves in these holy and venerable matters, involving as they do the religious life of Christian society along with the exercise of the priesthood of Jesus Christ and worship of God; concerned as they are with the honor due to the Blessed Trinity, the Word Incarnate and His august mother and the other saints, and with the salvation of souls as well. For the same reason no private person has any authority to regulate external practices of this kind, which are intimately bound up with Church discipline and with the order, unity and concord of the Mystical Body and frequently even with the integrity of Catholic faith itself.

59. The Church is without question a living organism, and   238
as an organism, in respect of the sacred liturgy also, she
grows, matures, develops, adapts and accommodates herself
to temporal needs and circumstances, provided only that the
integrity of her doctrine be safeguarded. This notwithstanding, the temerity and daring of those who introduce novel
liturgical practices, or call for the revival of obsolete rites out
of harmony with prevailing laws and rubrics, deserve severe
reproof. It has pained Us grievously to note, Venerable Brethren, that such innovations are actually being introduced, not
merely in minor details but in matters of major importance as
well. We instance, in point of fact, those who make use of the
vernacular in the celebration of the august eucharistic sacrifice; those who transfer certain feast-days—which have been
appointed and established after mature deliberation—to other
dates; those, finally, who delete from the prayer-books approved for public use the sacred texts of the Old Testament,
deeming them little suited and inopportune for modern times.

60. The use of the Latin language, customary in a consider-   239
able portion of the Church, is a manifest and beautiful sign of
unity, as well as an effective antidote for any corruption of
doctrinal truth. In spite of this, the use of the mother tongue
in connection with several of the rites may be of much advantage to the people. But the Apostolic See alone is empowered
to grant this permission. It is forbidden, therefore, to take
any action whatever of this nature without having requested
and obtained such consent, since the sacred liturgy, as We
have said, is entirely subject to the discretion and approval of
the Holy See.

61. The same reasoning holds in the case of some persons   240
who are bent on the restoration of all the ancient rites and
ceremonies indiscriminately. The liturgy of the early ages is
most certainly worthy of all veneration. But ancient usage
must not be esteemed more suitable and proper, either in its
own right or in its significance for later times and new situations, on the simple ground that it carries the savor and aroma
of antiquity. The more recent liturgical rites likewise deserve
reverence and respect. They, too, owe their inspiration to the
Holy Spirit, who assists the Church in every age even to the

consummation of the world.[52] They are equally the resources used by the majestic Spouse of Jesus Christ to promote and procure the sanctity of man.

241   62. Assuredly it is a wise and most laudable thing to return in spirit and affection to the sources of the sacred liturgy. For research in this field of study, by tracing it back to its origins, contributes valuable assistance towards a more thorough and careful investigation of the significance of feast-days, and of the meaning of the texts and sacred ceremonies employed on their occasion. But it is neither wise nor laudable to reduce everything to antiquity by every possible device. Thus, to cite some instances, one would be straying from the straight path were he to wish the altar restored to its primitive table-form; were he to want black excluded as a color for the liturgical vestments; were he to forbid the use of sacred images and statues in Churches; were he to order the cricifix so designed that the divine Redeemer's body shows no trace of His cruel sufferings; and lastly were he to disdain and reject polyphonic music or singing in parts, even where it conforms to regulations issued by the Holy See.

242   63. Clearly no sincere Catholic can refuse to accept the formulation of Christian doctrine more recently elaborated and proclaimed as dogmas by the Church, under the inspiration and guidance of the Holy Spirit with abundant fruit for souls, because it pleases him to hark back to the old formulas. No more can any Catholic in his right senses repudiate existing legislation of the Church to revert to prescriptions based on the earliest sources of canon law. Just as obviously unwise and mistaken is the zeal of one who in matters liturgical would go back to the rites and usage of antiquity, discarding the new patterns introduced by disposition of divine Providence to meet the changes of circumstances and situation.

243   64. This way of acting bids fair to revive the exaggerated and senseless antiquarianism to which the illegal Council of Pistoia gave rise. It likewise attempts to reinstate a series of errors which were responsible for the calling of that meeting as well as for those resulting from it, with grievous harm to souls, and which the Church, the ever watchful guardian of the "deposit of faith" committed to her charge by her divine

Founder, had every right and reason to condemn.[53] For perverse designs and ventures of this sort tend to paralyze and weaken that process of sanctification by which the sacred liturgy directs the sons of adoption to their Heavenly Father for their souls' salvation.

65. In every measure taken, then, let proper contact with   244
the ecclesiastical hierarchy be maintained. Let no one arrogate to himself the right to make regulations and impose them on others at will. Only the Sovereign Pontiff, as the successor of Saint Peter, charged by the divine Redeemer with the feeding of His entire flock,[54] and with him, in obedience to the Apostolic See, the bishops "whom the Holy Ghost has placed . . . to rule the Church of God,"[55] have the right and the duty to govern the Christian people. Consequently, Venerable Brethren, whenever you assert your authority—even on occasion with wholesome severity—you are not merely acquitting yourselves of your duty; you are defending the very will of the Founder of the Church.

Part II: Eucharistic Worship

A. The Nature of the Eucharistic Sacrifice

66. The mystery of the most Holy Eucharist which Christ,   245
the High Priest instituted, and which He commands to be continually renewed in the Church by His ministers, is the culmination and center, as it were, of the Christian religion. We consider it opportune in speaking about the crowning act of the sacred liturgy, to delay for a little while and call your attention, Venerable Brethren, to this most important subject.

67. Christ the Lord, "Eternal Priest according to the order   246
of Melchisedech,"[56] "loving His own who were in the world,"[57] "at the last supper, on the night He was betrayed, wishing to leave His beloved Spouse, the Church, a visible sacrifice such as the nature of men requires, that would represent the bloody sacrifice offered once on the cross, and perpetuate its memory to the end of time, and whose salutary virtue might be applied in remitting those sins which we daily commit, . . . offered His body and blood under the species of bread and wine to God the Father, and under the same species

allowed the apostles, whom He at that time constituted the priests of the New Testament, to partake thereof; commanding them and their successors in the priesthood to make the same offering."[5 8]

247   68. The august sacrifice of the altar, then, is no mere empty commemoration of the passion and death of Jesus Christ, but a true and proper act of sacrifice, whereby the High Priest by an unbloody immolation offers Himself a most acceptable victim to the Eternal Father, as He did upon the cross. "It is one and the same victim; the same person now offers it by the ministry of His priests, who then offered Himself on the cross, the manner of offering alone being different."[5 9]

248   69. The priest is the same, Jesus Christ, whose sacred Person His minister represents. Now the minister, by reason of the sacerdotal consecration which he has received, is made like to the High Priest and possesses the power of performing actions in virtue of Christ's very person.[6 0] Wherefore in his priestly activity he in a certain manner "lends his tongue, and gives his hand" to Christ.[6 1]

249   70. Likewise the victim is the same, namely, our divine Redeemer in His human nature with His true body and blood. The manner, however, in which Christ is offered is different. On the cross He completely offered Himself and all His sufferings to God, and the immolation of the victim was brought about by the bloody death, which He underwent of His free will. But on the altar, by reason of the glorified state of His human nature, "death shall have no more dominion over Him,"[6 2] and so the shedding of His blood is impossible; still, according to the plan of divine wisdom, the sacrifice of our Redeemer is shown forth in an admirable manner, by external signs which are the symbols of His death. For by the "transubstantiation" of bread into the body of Christ and of wine into His blood, His body and blood are both really present: now the eucharistic species under which He is present symbolize the actual separation of His body and blood. Thus the commemorative representation of His death, which actually took place on Calvary, is repeated in every sacrifice of the altar, seeing that Jesus Christ is symbolically shown by separate symbols to be in a state of victimhood.

71. Moreover, the appointed ends are the same. The first of   250
these is to give glory to the Heavenly Father. From His birth
to His death Jesus Christ burned with zeal for the divine glory;
and the offering of His blood upon the cross rose to heaven in
an odor of sweetness. To perpetuate this praise, the members
of the Mystical Body are united with their divine Head in the
eucharistic sacrifice, and with Him, together with the Angels
and Archangels, they sing immortal praise to God[63] and give
all honor and glory to the Father Almighty.[64]

72. The second end is duly to give thanks to God. Only   251
the divine Redeemer, as the eternal Father's most beloved
Son whose immense love He knew, could offer Him a worthy
return of gratitude. This was His intention and desire at the
Last Supper when He "gave thanks."[65] He did not cease to
do so when hanging upon the cross, nor does He fail to do so
in the august sacrifice of the altar, which is an act of thanksgiving or a "eucharistic" act; since this "is truly meet and
just, right and availing unto salvation."[66]

73. The third end proposed is that of expiation, propitia-   252
tion and reconciliation. Certainly, no one was better fitted to
make satisfaction to almighty God for all the sins of men than
was Christ. Therefore, He desired to be immolated upon the
cross "as a propitiation for our sins, not for ours only but also
for those of the whole world."[67] And likewise He daily offers Himself upon our altars for our redemption, that we may
be rescued from eternal damnation and admitted into the
company of the elect. This He does, not for us only who are
in this mortal life, but also "for all who rest in Christ, who
have gone before us with the sign of faith and repose in the
sleep of peace;"[68] for whether we live, or whether we die
"still we are not separated from the one and only Christ."[69]

74. The fourth end, finally, is that of impetration. Man,   253
being the prodigal son, has made bad use of and dissipated
the goods which he received from his heavenly Father. Accordingly, he has been reduced to the utmost poverty and to
extreme degradation. However, Christ on the cross "offering
prayers and supplications with a loud cry and tears, has been
heard for His reverence."[70] Likewise upon the altar He is our

mediator with God in the same efficacious manner, so that we may be filled with every blessing and grace.

254   75. It is easy, therefore, to understand why the holy Council of Trent lays down that by means of the eucharistic sacrifice the saving virtue of the cross is imparted to us for the remission of the sins we daily commit.[71]

255   76. Now the Apostle of the Gentiles proclaims the copious plenitude and the perfection of the sacrifice of the cross, when he says that Christ by one oblation has perfected for ever them that are sanctified.[72] For the merits of this sacrifice, since they are altogether boundless and immeasurable, know no limits; for they are meant for all men of every time and place. This follows from the fact that in this sacrifice the God-Man is the priest and victim; that His immolation was entirely perfect, as was His obedience to the will of His eternal Father; and also that He suffered death as the Head of the human race: "See how we were bought: Christ hangs upon the cross, see at what a price He makes His purchase. . . . He sheds His blood, He buys with His blood, He buys with the blood of the Spotless Lamb, He buys with the blood of God's only Son. He who buys is Christ; the price is His blood; the possession bought is the world."[73]

256   77. This purchase, however, does not immediately have its full effect; since Christ, after redeeming the world at the lavish cost of His own blood, still must come into complete possession of the souls of men. Wherefore, that the redemption and salvation of each person and of future generations unto the end of time may be effectively accomplished, and be acceptable to God, it is necessary that men should individually come into vital contact with the sacrifice of the cross, so that the merits, which flow from it, should be imparted to them. In a certain sense it can be said that on Calvary Christ built a font of purification and salvation which He filled with the blood He shed; but if men do not bathe in it and there wash away the stains of their iniquities, they can never be purified and saved.

257   78. The cooperation of the faithful is required so that sinners may be individually purified in the blood of the Lamb. For though, speaking generally, Christ reconciled by His painful death the whole human race with the Father, He wished

that all should approach and be drawn to His cross, especially by means of the sacraments and the eucharistic sacrifice, to obtain the salutary fruits produced by Him upon it. Through this active and individual participation, the members of the Mystical Body not only become daily more like to their divine Head, but the life flowing from the Head is imparted to the members, so that we can each repeat the words of St. Paul, "With Christ I am nailed to the cross: I live, now not I, but Christ liveth in me."[74] We have already explained sufficiently and of set purpose on another occasion, that Jesus Christ "when dying on the cross, bestowed upon His Church, as a completely gratuitous gift, the immense treasure of the redemption. But when it is a question of distributing this treasure, He not only commits the work of sanctification to His Immaculate Spouse, but also wishes that, to a certain extent, sanctity should derive from her activity."[75]

79. The august sacrifice of the altar is, as it were, the supreme instrument whereby the merits won by the divine Redeemer upon the cross are distributed to the faithful: "as often as this commemorative sacrifice is offered, there is wrought the work of our Redemption."[76] This, however, so far from lessening the dignity of the actual sacrifice on Calvary, rather proclaims and renders more manifest its greatness and its necessity, as the Council of Trent declares.[77] Its daily immolation reminds us that there is no salvation except in the cross of our Lord Jesus Christ[78] and that God Himself wishes that there should be a continuation of this sacrifice "from the rising of the sun till the going down thereof,"[79] so that there may be no cessation of the hymn of praise and thanksgiving which man owes to God, seeing that he requires His help continually and has need of the blood of the Redeemer to remit sin which challenges God's justice. **258**

B. Participation of the Faithful in the Eucharistic Sacrifice

80. It is, therefore, desirable, Venerable Brethren, that all the faithful should be aware that to participate in the eucharistic sacrifice is their chief duty and supreme dignity, and that not in an inert and negligent fashion, giving way to distractions and day-dreaming, but with such earnestness and **259**

concentration that they may be united as closely as possible with the High Priest, according to the Apostle, "Let this mind be in you which was also in Christ Jesus."[80] And together with Him and through Him let them make their oblation, and in union with Him let them offer up themselves.

260   81. It is quite true that Christ is a priest; but He is a priest not for Himself but for us, when in the name of the whole human race He offers our prayers and religious homage to the eternal Father; He is also a victim and for us since He substitutes Himself for sinful man. Now the exhortation of the Apostle, "Let this mind be in you which was also in Christ Jesus," requires that all Christians should possess, as far as is humanly possible, the same dispositions as those which the divine Redeemer had when He offered Himself in sacrifice: that is to say, they should in a humble attitude of mind, pay adoration, honor, praise and thanksgiving to the supreme majesty of God. Moreover, it means that they must assume to some extent the character of a victim, that they deny themselves as the Gospel commands, that freely and of their own accord they do penance and that each detests and satisfies for his sins. It means, in a word, that we must all undergo with Christ a mystical death on the cross so that we can apply to ourselves the words of St. Paul, "With Christ I am nailed to the Cross."[81]

261   82. The fact, however, that the faithful participate in the eucharistic sacrifice does not mean that they also are endowed with priestly power. It is very necessary that you make this quite clear to your flocks.

262   83. For there are today, Venerable Brethren, those who, approximating to errors long since condemned,[82] teach that in the New Testament by the word "priesthood" is meant only that priesthood which applies to all who have been baptised; and hold that the command by which Christ gave power to His apostles at the Last Supper to do what He Himself had done, applies directly to the entire Christian Church, and that thence, and thence only, arises the hierarchical priesthood. Hence they assert that the people are possessed of a true priestly power, while the priest only acts in virtue of an office committed to him by the community. Wherefore, they look

on the eucharistic sacrifice as a "concelebration," in the literal meaning of that term, and consider it more fitting that priests should "concelebrate" with the people present than that they should offer the sacrifice privately when the people are absent.

84. It is superfluous to explain how captious errors of this   263
sort completely contradict the truths which we have just stated above, when treating of the place of the priest in the Mystical Body of Jesus Christ. But we deem it necessary to recall that the priest acts for the people only because he represents Jesus Christ, who is Head of all His members and offers Himself in their stead. Hence, he goes to the altar as the minister of Christ, inferior to Christ but superior to the people.[83] The people, on the other hand, since they in no sense represent the divine Redeemer and are not mediator between themselves and God, can in no way possess the sacerdotal power.

85. All this has the certitude of faith. However, it must   264
also be said that the faithful do offer the divine Victim, though in a different sense.

86. This has already been stated in the clearest terms by   265
some of Our predecessors and some Doctors of the Church. "Not only," says Innocent III of immortal memory, "do the priests offer the sacrifice, but also all the faithful: for what the priest does personally by virtue of his ministry, the faithful do collectively by virtue of their intention."[84] We are happy to recall one of St. Robert Bellarmine's many statements on this subject. "The sacrifice," he says "is principally offered in the person of Christ. Thus the oblation that follows the consecration is a sort of attestation that the whole Church consents in the oblation made by Christ, and offers it along with Him."[85]

87. Moreover, the rites and prayers of the eucharistic sacri-   266
fice signify and show no less clearly that the oblation of the Victim is made by the priests in company with the people. For not only does the sacred minister, after the oblation of the bread and wine when he turns to the people, say the significant prayer: "Pray brethren, that my sacrifice and yours may be acceptable to God the Father almighty;"[86] but also the prayers by which the divine Victim is offered to God are

generally expressed in the plural number: and in these it is indicated more than once that the people also participate in this august sacrifice inasmuch as they offer the same. The following words, for example, are used: "For whom we offer, or who offer up to Thee. . . . We therefore beseech thee, O Lord, to be appeased and to receive this offering of our bounden duty, as also of thy whole household. . . . We thy servants, as also thy whole people . . . do offer unto thy most excellent majesty, of thine own gifts bestowed upon us, a pure victim, a holy victim, a spotless victim."[8 7]

267   88. Nor is it to be wondered at, that the faithful should be raised to this dignity. By the waters of baptism, as by common right, Christians are made members of the Mystical Body of Christ the Priest, and by the "character" which is imprinted on their souls, they are appointed to give worship to God. Thus they participate, according to their condition, in the priesthood of Christ.

268   89. In every age of the Church's history, the mind of man, enlightened by faith, has aimed at the greatest possible knowledge of things divine. It is fitting, then, that the Christian people should also desire to know in what sense they are said in the canon of the Mass to offer up the sacrifice. To satisfy such a pious desire, then, We shall here explain the matter briefly and concisely.

269   90. First of all the more extrinsic explanations are these: it frequently happens that the faithful assisting at Mass join their prayers alternately with those of the priest, and sometimes— a more frequent occurrence in ancient times—they offer to the ministers at the altar bread and wine to be changed into the body and blood of Christ, and, finally, by their alms they get the priest to offer the divine victim for their intentions.

270   91. But there is also a more profound reason why all Christians, especially those who are present at Mass, are said to offer the sacrifice.

271   92. In this most important subject it is necessary, in order to avoid giving rise to a dangerous error, that we define the exact meaning of the word "offer." The unbloody immolation at the words of consecration, when Christ is made present upon the altar in the state of a victim, is performed by the

priest and by him alone, as the representative of Christ and not as the representative of the faithful. It is because the priest places the divine victim upon the altar that he offers it to God the Father as an oblation for the glory of the Blessed Trinity and for the good of the whole Church. Now the faithful participate in the oblation, understood in this limited sense, after their own fashion and in a twofold manner, namely, because they not only offer the sacrifice by the hands of the priest, but also, to a certain extent, in union with him. It is by reason of this participation that the offering made by the people is also included in liturgical worship.

93. Now it is clear that the faithful offer the sacrifice by the hands of the priest from the fact that the minister at the altar, in offering a sacrifice in the name of all His members, represents Christ, the Head of the Mystical Body. Hence the whole church can rightly be said to offer up the victim through Christ. But the conclusion that the people offer the sacrifice with the priest himself is not based on the fact that, being members of the Church no less than the priest himself, they perform a visible liturgical rite; for this is the privilege only of the minister who has been divinely appointed to this office: rather it is based on the fact that the people unite their hearts in praise, impetration, expiation and thanksgiving with the prayers or intention of the priest, even of the High Priest himself, so that in the one and same offering of the victim and according to a visible sacerdotal rite, they may be presented to God the Father. It is obviously necessary that the external sacrificial rite should, of its very nature, signify the internal worship of the heart. Now the sacrifice of the New Law signifies that supreme worship by which the principal Offerer himself, who is Christ, and, in union with Him and through Him all the members of the Mystical Body pay God the honor and reverence that are due to Him.

94. We are very pleased to learn that this teaching, thanks to a more intense study of the liturgy on the part of many, especially in recent years, has been given full recognition. We must, however, deeply deplore certain exaggerations and overstatements which are not in agreement with the true teaching of the Church.

272

273

274   95. Some in fact disapprove altogether of those Masses which are offered privately and without any congregation, on the ground that they are a departure from the ancient way of offering the sacrifice; moreover, there are some who assert that priests cannot offer Mass at different altars at the same time, because, by doing so, they separate the community of the faithful and imperil its unity; while some go so far as to hold that the people must confirm and ratify the sacrifice if it is to have its proper force and value.

275   96. They are mistaken in appealing in this matter to the social character of the eucharistic sacrifice, for as often as a priest repeats what the divine Redeemer did at the Last Supper, the sacrifice is really completed. Moreover, this sacrifice, necessarily and of its very nature, has always and everywhere the character of a public and social act, inasmuch as he who offers it acts in the name of Christ and of the faithful, whose Head is the divine Redeemer, and he offers it to God for the holy Catholic Church, and for the living and the dead.[88] This is undoubtedly so, whether the faithful are present—as we desire and commend them to be in great numbers and with devotion—or are not present, since it is in no wise required that the people ratify what the sacred minister has done.

276   97. Still, though it is clear from what We have said that the Mass is offered in the name of Christ and of the Church and that it is not robbed of its social effects though it be celebrated by a priest without a server, nonetheless, on account of the dignity of such an august mystery, it is our earnest desire—as Mother Church has always commanded—that no priest should say Mass unless a server is at hand to answer the prayers, as canon 813 prescribes.

277   98. In order that the oblation by which the faithful offer the divine Victim in this sacrifice to the heavenly Father may have its full effect, it is necessary that the people add something else, namely, the offering of themselves as a victim.

278   99. This offering in fact is not confined merely to the liturgical sacrifice. For the Prince of the Apostles wishes us, as living stones built upon Christ, the cornerstone, to be able as "a holy priesthood, to offer up spiritual sacrifices, acceptable to God by Jesus Christ."[89] St. Paul the Apostle addresses the

following words of exhortation to Christians, without distinction of time, "I beseech you therefore, . . . that you present your bodies, a living sacrifice, holy, pleasing unto God, your reasonable service."[90] But at that time especially when the faithful take part in the liturgical service with such piety and recollection that it can truly be said of them: "whose faith and devotion is known to Thee,"[91] it is then, with the High Priest and through Him they offer themselves as a spiritual sacrifice, that each one's faith ought to become more ready to work through charity, his piety more real and fervent, and each one should consecrate himself to the furthering of the divine glory, desiring to become as like as possible to Christ in His most grievous sufferings.

100. This we are also taught by those exhortations which the Bishop, in the Church's name, addresses to priests on the day of their ordination, "Understand what you do, imitate what you handle, and since you celebrate the mystery of the Lord's death, take good care to mortify your members with their vices and concupiscences."[92] In almost the same manner the sacred books of the liturgy advise Christians who come to Mass to participate in the sacrifice: "At this . . . altar let innocence be in honor, let pride be sacrificed, anger slain, impurity and every evil desire laid low, let the sacrifice of chastity be offered in place of doves and instead of the young pigeons the sacrifice of innocence.[93] While we stand before the altar, then, it is our duty so to transform our hearts, that every trace of sin may be completely blotted out, while whatever promotes supernatural life through Christ may be zealously fostered and strengthened even to the extent that, in union with the immaculate Victim, we become a victim acceptable to the eternal Father.

279

101. The prescriptions in fact of the sacred liturgy aim, by every means at their disposal, at helping the Church to bring about this most holy purpose in the most suitable manner possible. This is the object not only of readings, homilies and other sermons given by priests, as also the whole cycle of mysteries which are proposed for our commemoration in the course of the year, but it is also the purpose of vestments, of sacred rites and their external splendor. All these things aim

280

at "enhancing the majesty of this great Sacrifice, and raising the minds of the faithful by means of these visible signs of religion and piety, to the contemplation of the sublime truths contained in this sacrifice."[94]

281   102. All the elements of the liturgy, then, would have us reproduce in our hearts the likeness of the divine Redeemer through the mystery of the cross, according to the words of the Apostle of the Gentiles, "With Christ I am nailed to the cross. I live, now not I, but Christ liveth in me."[95] Thus we become a victim, as it were, along with Christ to increase the glory of the eternal Father.

282   103. Let this, then, be the intention and aspiration of the faithful, when they offer up the divine Victim in the Mass. For if, as St. Augustine writes, our mystery is enacted on the Lord's table, that is Christ our Lord Himself,[96] who is the Head and symbol of that union through which we are the body of Christ[97] and members of His Body;[98] if St. Robert Bellarmine teaches, according to the mind of the Doctor of Hippo, that in the sacrifice of the altar there is signified the general sacrifice by which the whole Mystical Body of Christ, that is, all the city of the redeemed, is offered up to God through Christ, the High Priest:[99] nothing can be conceived more just or fitting than that all of us in union with our Head, who suffered for our sake, should also sacrifice ourselves to the eternal Father. For in the sacrament of the altar, as the same St. Augustine has it, the Church is made to see that in what she offers she herself is offered.[100]

283   104. Let the faithful, therefore, consider to what a high dignity they are raised by the sacrament of baptism. They should not think it enough to participate in the eucharistic sacrifice with that general intention which befits members of Christ and children of the Church, but let them further, in keeping with the spirit of the sacred liturgy, be most closely united with the High Priest and His earthly minister, at the time the consecration of the divine Victim is enacted, and at that time especially when those solemn words are pronounced, "By Him and with Him and in Him, is to Thee, God the Father almighty, in the unity of the Holy Ghost, all honor and glory for ever and ever";[101] to these words in fact the

people answer, "Amen." Nor should Christians forget to offer themselves, their cares, their sorrows, their distress and their necessities in union with their divine Saviour upon the cross.

105. Therefore, they are to be praised who, with the idea   284
of getting the Christian people to take part more easily and more fruitfully in the Mass, strive to make them familiar with the "Roman Missal," so that the faithful, united with the priest, may pray together in the very words and sentiments of the Church. They also are to be commended who strive to make the liturgy even in an external way a sacred act in which all who are present may share. This can be done in more than one way, when, for instance, the whole congregation, in accordance with the rules of the liturgy, either answer the priest in an orderly and fitting manner, or sing hymns suitable to the different parts of the Mass, or do both, or finally in high Masses when they answer the prayers of the minister of Jesus Christ and also sing the liturgical chant.

106. These methods of participation in the Mass are to be   285
approved and commended when they are in complete agreement with the precepts of the Church and the rubrics of the liturgy. Their chief aim is to foster and promote the people's piety and intimate union with Christ and His visible minister and to arouse those internal sentiments and dispositions which should make our hearts become like to that of the High Priest of the New Testament. However, though they show also in an outward manner that the very nature of the sacrifice, as offered by the Mediator between God and men,[102] must be regarded as the act of the whole Mystical Body of Christ, still they are by no means necessary to constitute it a public act or to give it a social character. And besides, a "dialogue" Mass of this kind cannot replace the high Mass, which, as a matter of fact, though it should be offered with only the sacred ministers present, possesses its own special dignity due to the impressive character of its ritual and the magnificence of its ceremonies. The splendor and grandeur of a high Mass, however, are very much increased if, as the Church desires, the people are present in great numbers and with devotion.

286   107. It is to be observed, also, that they have strayed from the path of truth and right reason who, led away by false opinions, make so much of these accidentals as to presume to assert that without them the Mass cannot fulfill its appointed end.

287   108. Many of the faithful are unable to use the Roman missal even though it is written in the vernacular; nor are all capable of understanding correctly the liturgical rites and formulas. So varied and diverse are men's talents and characters that it is impossible for all to be moved and attracted to the same extent by community prayers, hymns and liturgical services. Moreover, the needs and inclinations of all are not the same, nor are they always constant in the same individual. Who, then, would say, on account of such a prejudice, that all these Christians cannot participate in the Mass nor share its fruits? On the contrary, they can adopt some other method which proves easier for certain people; for instance, they can lovingly meditate on the mysteries of Jesus Christ or perform other exercises of piety or recite prayers which, though they differ from the sacred rites, are still essentially in harmony with them.

288   109. Wherefore We exhort you, Venerable Brethren, that each in his diocese or ecclesiastical jurisdiction supervise and regulate the manner and method in which the people take part in the liturgy, according to the rubrics of the missal and in keeping with the injunctions which the Sacred Congregation of Rites and the Code of canon law have published. Let everything be done with due order and dignity, and let no one, not even a priest, make use of the sacred edifices according to his whim to try out experiments. It is also Our wish that in each diocese an advisory committee to promote the liturgical apostolate should be established, similar to that which cares for sacred music and art, so that with your watchful guidance everything may be carefully carried out in accordance with the prescriptions of the Apostolic See.

289   110. In religious communities let all those regulations be accurately observed which are laid down in their respective constitutions, nor let any innovations be made which the superiors of these communities have not previously approved.

111. But however much variety and disparity there may   290
be in the exterior manner and circumstances in which the
Christian laity participate in the Mass and other liturgical
functions, constant and earnest effort must be made to
unite the congregation in spirit as much as possible with the
divine Redeemer, so that their lives may be daily enriched
with more abundant sanctity, and greater glory be given
to the heavenly Father.

C. Holy Communion

112. The august sacrifice of the altar is concluded with   291
communion or the partaking of the divine feast. But, as all
know, the integrity of the sacrifice only requires that the
priest partake of the heavenly food. Although it is most
desirable that the people should also approach the holy
table, this is not required for the integrity of the sacrifice.

113. We wish in this matter to repeat the remarks which   292
Our predecessor Benedict XIV makes with regard to the
definitions of the Council of Trent: "First We must state
that none of the faithful can hold that private Masses, in
which the priest alone receives holy communion, are therefore unlawful and do not fulfill the idea of the true, perfect
and complete unbloody sacrifice instituted by Christ our
Lord. For the faithful know quite well, or at least can easily
be taught, that the Council of Trent, supported by the
doctrine which the uninterrupted tradition of the Church
has preserved, condemned the new and false opinion of
Luther as opposed to this tradition"[103] "If anyone shall
say that Masses in which the priest only receives communion,
are unlawful, and therefore should be abolished, let him be
anathema."[104]

114. They, therefore, err from the path of truth who do   293
not want to have Masses celebrated unless the faithful communicate; and those are still more in error who, in holding
that it is altogether necessary for the faithful to receive holy
communion as well as the priest, put forward the captious
argument that here there is question not of a sacrifice merely,
but of a sacrifice and a supper of brotherly union, and con-

sider the general communion of all present as the culminating point of the whole celebration.

294   115. Now it cannot be over-emphasized that the eucharistic sacrifice of its very nature is the unbloody immolation of the divine Victim, which is made manifest in a mystical manner by the separation of the sacred species and by their oblation to the eternal Father. Holy communion pertains to the integrity of the Mass and to the partaking of the august sacrament; but while it is obligatory for the priest who says the Mass, it is only something earnestly recommended to the faithful.

295   116. The Church, as the teacher of truth, strives by every means in her power to safeguard the integrity of the Catholic faith, and like a mother solicitous for the welfare of her children, she exhorts them most earnestly to partake fervently and frequently of the richest treasure of our religion.

296   117. She wishes in the first place that Christians—especially when they cannot easily receive holy communion—should do so at least by desire, so that with renewed faith, reverence, humility and complete trust in the goodness of the divine Redeemer, they may be united to Him in the spirit of the most ardent charity.

297   118. But the desire of Mother Church does not stop here. For since by feasting upon the bread of angels we can by a "sacramental" communion, as we have already said, also become partakers of the sacrifice, she repeats the invitation to all her children individually, "Take and eat. . . .Do this in memory of Me"[105] so that "we may continually experience within us the fruit of our redemption"[106] in a more efficacious manner. For this reason the Council of Trent, reechoing, as it were, the invitation of Christ and His immaculate Spouse, has earnestly exhorted "the faithful when they attend Mass to communicate not only by a spiritual communion but also by a sacramental one, so that they may obtain more abundant fruit from this most holy sacrifice."[107] Moreover, our predecessor of immortal memory, Benedict XIV, wishing to emphasize and throw fuller light upon the truth that the faithful by receiving the Holy Eucharist become partakers of the divine sacrifice itself, praises the de-

votion of those who, when attending Mass, not only elicit a desire to receive holy communion but also want to be nourished by hosts consecrated during the Mass, even though, as he himself states, they really and truly take part in the sacrifice should they receive a host which has been duly consecrated at a previous Mass. He writes as follows: "And although in addition to those to whom the celebrant gives a portion of the Victim he himself has offered in the Mass, they also participate in the same sacrifice to whom a priest distributes the Blessed Sacrament that has been reserved; however, the Church has not for this reason ever forbidden, nor does she now forbid, a celebrant to satisfy the piety and just request of those who, when present at Mass, want to become partakers of the same sacrifice, because they likewise offer it after their own manner, nay more, she approves of it and desires that it should not be omitted and would reprehend those priests through whose fault and negligence this participation would be denied to the faithful."[108]

119. May God grant that all accept these invitations of the Church freely and with spontaneity. May He grant that they participate even every day, if possible, in the divine sacrifice, not only in a spiritual manner, but also by reception of the august sacrament, receiving the body of Jesus Christ which has been offered for all to the eternal Father. Arouse, Venerable Brethren, in the hearts of those committed to your care, a great and insatiable hunger for Jesus Christ. Under your guidance let the children and youth crowd to the altar rails to offer themselves, their innocence and their works of zeal to the divine Redeemer. Let husbands and wives approach the holy table so that nourished on this food they may learn to make the children entrusted to them conformed to the mind and heart of Jesus Christ.   298

120. Let the workers be invited to partake of this sustaining and never failing nourishment that it may renew their strength and obtain for their labors an everlasting recompense in heaven; in a word, invite all men of whatever class and compel them to come in;[109] since this is the bread of life   299

which all require. The Church of Jesus Christ needs no other bread than this to satisfy fully our souls' wants and desires, and to unite us in the most intimate union with Jesus Christ, to make us "one body,"[110] to get us to live together as brothers who, breaking the same bread, sit down to the same heavenly table, to partake of the elixir of immortality.[111]

300   121. Now it is very fitting, as the liturgy otherwise lays down, that the people receive holy communion after the priest has partaken of the divine repast upon the altar; and, as we have written above, they should be commended who, when present at Mass, receive hosts consecrated at the same Mass, so that it is actually verified, "that as many of us as, at this altar, shall partake of and receive the most holy body and blood of thy Son, may be filled with every heavenly blessing and grace."[112]

301   122. Still sometimes there may be a reason, and that not unfrequently, why holy communion should be distributed before or after Mass and even immediately after the priest receives the sacred species—and even though hosts consecrated at a previous Mass should be used. In these circumstances—as we have stated above—the people duly take part in the eucharistic sacrifice and not seldom they can in this way more conveniently receive holy communion. Still, though the Church with the kind heart of a mother, strives to meet the spiritual needs of her children, they, for their part, should not readily neglect the directions of the liturgy and, as often as there is no reasonable difficulty, should aim that all their actions at the altar manifest more clearly the living unity of the Mystical Body.

302   123. When the Mass, which is subject to special rules of the liturgy, is over, the person who has received holy communion is not thereby freed from his duty of thanksgiving; rather, it is most becoming that, when the Mass is finished, the person who has received the Eucharist should recollect himself, and in intimate union with the divine Master hold loving and fruitful converse with Him. Hence they have departed from the straight way of truth, who, adhering to the letter rather than the sense, assert and teach that, when Mass has ended, no such thanksgiving should be added, not only

because the Mass is itself a thanksgiving, but also because this pertains to a private and personal act of piety and not to the good of this community.

124. But, on the contrary, the very nature of the sacrament   303
demands that its reception should produce rich fruits of Christian sanctity. Admittedly the congregation has been officially dismissed, but each individual, since he is united with Christ, should not interrupt the hymn of praise in his own soul, "always returning thanks for all in the name of our Lord Jesus Christ to God the Father."[113] The sacred liturgy of the Mass also exhorts us to do this when it bids us pray in these words, "Grant, we beseech thee, that we may always continue to offer thanks[114]. . .and may never cease from praising thee."[115] Wherefore, if there is no time when we must not offer God thanks, and if we must never cease from praising Him, who would dare to reprehend or find fault with the Church, because she advises her priests[116] and faithful to converse with the divine Redeemer for at least a short while after holy communion, and inserts in her liturgical books, fitting prayers, enriched with indulgences, by which the sacred ministers may make suitable preparation before Mass and holy communion or may return thanks afterwards? So far is the sacred liturgy from restricting the interior devotion of individual Christians, that it actually fosters and promotes it so that they may be rendered like to Jesus Christ and through Him be brought to the heavenly Father; wherefore this same discipline of the liturgy demands that whoever has partaken of the sacrifice of the altar should return fitting thanks to God. For it is the good pleasure of the divine Redeemer to hearken to us when we pray, to converse with us intimately and to offer us a refuge in His loving Heart.

125. Moreover, such personal colloquies are very necessary   304
that we may all enjoy more fully the supernatural treasures that are contained in the Eucharist and, according to our means, share them with others, so that Christ our Lord may exert the greatest possible influence on the souls of all.

126. Why then, Venerable Brethren, should we not ap-   305
prove of those who, when they receive holy communion, remain on in closest familiarity with their divine Redeemer

even after the congregation has been officially dismissed, and that not only for the consolation of conversing with Him, but also to render Him due thanks and praise and especially to ask help to defend their souls against anything that may lessen the efficacy of the sacrament and to do everything in their power to cooperate with the action of Christ who is so intimately present. We exhort them to do so in a special manner by carrying out their resolutions, by exercising the Christian virtues, as also by applying to their own necessities the riches they have received with royal liberality. The author of that golden book *The Imitation of Christ* certainly speaks in accordance with the letter and the spirit of the liturgy, when he gives the following advice to the person who approaches the altar, "Remain on in secret and take delight in your God; for He is yours whom the whole world cannot take away from you."[117]

306   127. Therefore, let us all enter into closest union with Christ and strive to lose ourselves, as it were, in His most holy soul and so be united to Him that we may have a share in those acts with which He adores the Blessed Trinity with a homage that is most acceptable, and by which He offers to the eternal Father supreme praise and thanks which find an harmonious echo throughout the heavens and the earth, according to the words of the prophet, "All ye works of the Lord, bless the Lord."[118] Finally, in union with tnese sentiments of Christ, let us ask for heavenly aid at that moment in which it is supremely fitting to pray for and obtain help in His name.[119] For it is especially in virtue of these sentiments that we offer and immolate ourselves as a victim, saying, "make of us thy eternal offering."[120]

307   128. The divine Redeemer is ever repeating His pressing invitation, "Abide in Me."[121] Now by the sacrament of the Eucharist, Christ remains in us and we in Him, and just as Christ, remaining in us, lives and works, so should we remain in Christ and live and work through Him.

D. Adoration of the Eucharist

129. The Eucharistic Food contains, as all are aware,   308
"truly, really and substantially the Body and Blood together
with the soul and divinity of our Lord Jesus Christ."[122] It
is no wonder, then, that the Church, even from the beginning,
adored the body of Christ under the appearance of bread;
this is evident from the very rites of the august sacrifice,
which prescribe that the sacred ministers should adore the
most holy sacrament by genuflecting or by profoundly
bowing their heads.

130. The Sacred Councils teach that it is the Church's   309
tradition right from the beginning, to worship "with the same
adoration the Word Incarnate as well as His own flesh,"[123]
and St. Augustine asserts that, "No one eats that flesh, without first adoring it," while he adds that "not only do we not
commit a sin by adoring it, but that we do sin by not adoring
it."[124]

131. It is on this doctrinal basis that the cult of adoring   310
the Eucharist was founded and gradually developed as something distinct from the sacrifice of the Mass. The reservation
of the sacred species for the sick and those in danger of death
introduced the praiseworthy custom of adoring the Blessed
Sacrament which is reserved in our churches. This practice of
adoration, in fact, is based on strong and solid reasons. For
the Eucharist is at once a sacrifice and a sacrament; but it
differs from the other sacraments in this that it not only produces graces, but contains in a permanent manner the Author
of grace Himself. When, therefore, the Church bids us adore
Christ hidden behind the eucharistic veils and pray to Him
for spiritual and temporal favors, of which we ever stand in
need, she manifests living faith in her divine Spouse who is
present beneath these veils, she professes her gratitude to
Him and she enjoys the intimacy of His friendship.

132. Now, the Church in the course of centuries has intro-   311
duced various forms of this worship which are ever increasing
in beauty and helpfulness: as, for example, visits of devotion
to the tabernacles, even every day; benediction of the Blessed

Sacrament; solemn processions, especially at the time of Eucharistic Congress, which pass through cities and villages; and adoration of the Blessed Sacrament publicly exposed. Sometimes these public acts of adoration are of short duration. Sometimes they last for one, several and even for forty hours. In certain places they continue in turn in different churches throughout the year, while elsewhere adoration is perpetual day and night, under the care of religious communities, and the faithful quite often take part in them.

312   133. These exercises of piety have brought a wonderful increase in faith and supernatural life to the Church militant upon earth and they are re-echoed to a certain extent by the Church triumphant in heaven which sings continually a hymn of praise to God and to the Lamb "who was slain."[125] Wherefore, the Church not merely approves these pious practices, which in the course of centuries have spread everywhere throughout the world, but makes them her own, as it were, and by her authority commends them.[126] They spring from the inspiration of the liturgy and if they are performed with due propriety and with faith and piety, as the liturgical rules of the Church require, they are undoubtedly of the very greatest assistance in living the life of the liturgy.

313   134. Nor is it to be admitted that by this Eucharistic cult men falsely confound the historical Christ, as they say, who once lived on earth, with the Christ who is present in the august Sacrament of the altar, and who reigns glorious and triumphant in heaven and bestows supernatural favors. On the contrary, it can be claimed that by this devotion the faithful bear witness to and solemnly avow the faith of the Church that the Word of God is identical with the Son of the Virgin Mary, who suffered on the cross, who is present in a hidden manner in the Eucharist and who reigns upon His heavenly throne. Thus St. John Chrysostom states: "When you see It [the Body of Christ] exposed, say to yourself: Thanks to this body, I am no longer dust and ashes, I am no more a captive but a freeman: hence I hope to obtain heaven and the good things that are there in store for me, eternal life, the heritage of the angels, companionship with Christ; death has not destroyed this body which was pierced by nails

and scourged, . . .this is that body which was once covered
with blood, pierced by a lance, from which issued saving
fountains upon the world, one of blood and the other of
water. . . .This body He gave to us to keep and eat, as a mark
of His intense love."[127]

135. That practice in a special manner is to be highly   314
praised according to which many exercises of piety, customary among the faithful, end with benediction of the
blessed sacrament. For excellent and of great benefit is that
custom which makes the priest raise aloft the Bread of Angels
before congregations with heads bowed down in adoration,
and forming with It the sign of the cross implores the heavenly
Father to deign to look upon His Son who for love of us was
nailed to the cross, and for His sake and through Him who
willed to be our Redeemer and our brother, be pleased to
shower down heavenly favors upon those whom the immaculate blood of the Lamb has redeemed.[128]

136. Strive then, Venerable Brethren, with your customary   315
devoted care so that the churches, which the faith and piety
of Christian peoples have built in the course of centuries for
the purpose of singing a perpetual hymn of glory to God almighty and of providing a worthy abode for our Redeemer
concealed beneath the eucharistic species, may be entirely at
the disposal of greater numbers of the faithful who, called to
the feet of their Savior, hearken to His most consoling invitation, "Come to Me all you who labor and are heavily burdened, and I will refresh you."[129] Let your churches be the
house of God where all who enter to implore blessings rejoice in obtaining whatever they ask[130] and find there heavenly consolation.

137. Only thus can it be brought about that the whole   316
human family settling their differences may find peace, and
united in mind and heart may sing this song of hope and
charity, "Good Pastor, truly bread—Jesus have mercy on us—
feed us, protect us—bestow on us the vision of all good
things—in the land of the living."[131]

Part III: The Divine Office and the Liturgical Year

A. The Divine Office

317   138. The ideal of Christian life is that each one be united
to God in the closest and most intimate manner. For this reason, the worship that the Church renders to God, and which
is based especially on the eucharistic sacrifice and the use of
the sacraments, is directed and arranged in such a way that
it embraces, by means of the divine office, the hours of the
day, the weeks and the whole cycle of the year, and reaches
all the aspects and phases of human life.

318   139. Since the divine Master commanded "that we ought
always to pray and not to faint,"[132] the Church faithfully
fulfills this injunction and never ceases to pray: She urges us
in the words of the Apostle of the Gentiles, "by him [Jesus]
let us offer the sacrifice of praise always to God."[133]

319   140. Public and common prayer offered to God by all at
the same time was customary in antiquity only on certain
days and at certain times. Indeed, people prayed to God not
only in groups but in private houses and occasionally with
neighbors and friends. But soon in different parts of the
Christian world the practice arose of setting aside special
times for praying, as for example, the last hour of the day
when evening set in and the lamps were lighted; or the first,
heralded, when the night was coming to an end, by the crow-
ing of the cock and the rising of the morning star. Other
times of the day, as being more suitable for prayer are indicated in Sacred Scripture, in Hebrew customs or in keeping
with the practice of every-day life. According to the Acts of
the Apostles, the disciples of Jesus Christ all came together
to pray at the third hour, when they were all filled with the
Holy Ghost;[134] and before eating, the Prince of the Apostles
went up to the higher parts of the house to pray, about the
sixth hour;[135] Peter and John "went up into the Temple at
the ninth hour of prayer"[136] and "at midnight Paul and Silas
praying...praised God."[137]

141. Thanks to the work of the monks and to those who   320
practise asceticism, these various prayers in the course of time
become ever more perfected and by the authority of the
Church are gradually incorporated into the sacred liturgy.

142. The divine office is the prayer of the Mystical Body   321
of Jesus Christ, offered to God in the name and on behalf of
all Christians, when recited by priests and other ministers
of the Church and by religious who are deputed by the
Church for this.

143. The character and value of the divine office may be   322
gathered from the words recommended by the Church to be
said before starting the prayers of the office, namely, that
they be said "worthily, with attention and devotion."

144. By assuming human nature, the Divine Word intro-   323
duced into this earthly exile a hymn which is sung in heaven
for all eternity. He unites to Himself the whole human race
and with it sings this hymn to the praise of God. As we must
humbly recognize that "we know not what we should pray
for, as we ought, the Spirit Himself asketh for us with unspeakable groanings."[138] Moreover, through His Spirit in
us, Christ entreats the Father, "God could not give a greater
gift to men ... [Jesus] prays for us, as our Priest; He prays in
us as our Head; we pray to Him as our God ... we recognize
in Him our voice and His voice in us ... He is prayed to as
God, He prays under the appearance of a servant; in heaven
He is Creator; here, created though not changed, He assumes
a created nature which is to be changed and makes us with
Him one complete man, head and body."[139]

145. To this lofty dignity of the Church's prayer, there   324
should correspond earnest devotion in our souls. For when in
prayer the voice repeats those hymns written under the inspiration of the Holy Ghost and extolls God's infinite per-
fections, it is necessary that the interior sentiment of our
soul should accompany the voice so as to make those sentiments our own in which we are elevated to heaven, adoring
and giving due praise and thanks to the Blessed Trinity; "so let
us chant in choir that mind and voice may accord together."[140] It is not merely a question of recitation or of singing

which, however perfect according to norms of music and the sacred rites, only reaches the ear, but it is especially a question of the ascent of the mind and heart to God so that, united with Christ, we may completely dedicate ourselves and all our actions to Him.

325   146. On this depends in no small way the efficacy of our prayers. These prayers, in fact, when they are not addressed directly to the Word made man, conclude with the phrase "through Jesus Christ our Lord." As our Mediator with God, He shows to the heavenly Father His glorified wounds, "always living to make intercession for us."[141]

326   147. The Psalms, as all know, form the chief part of the divine office. They encompass the full round of the day and sanctify it. Cassiodorus speaks beautifully about the Psalms as distributed in his day throughout the divine office: "With the celebration of matins they bring a blessing on the coming day, they set aside for us the first hour and consecrate the third hour of the day, they gladden the sixth hour with the breaking of bread, at the ninth they terminate our fast, they bring the evening to a close and at nightfall they shield our minds from darkness."[142]

327   148. The Psalms recall to mind the truths revealed by God to the chosen people, which were at one time frightening and at another filled with wonderful tenderness; they keep repeating and fostering the hope of the promised Liberator which in ancient times was kept alive with song, either around the hearth or in the stately temple; they show forth in splendid light the prophesied glory of Jesus Christ: first, His supreme and eternal power, then His lowly coming to this terrestial exile, His kingly dignity and priestly power and, finally, His beneficent labors, and the shedding of His blood for our redemption. In a similar way they express the joy, the bitterness, the hope and fear of our hearts and our desire of loving God and hoping in Him alone, and our mystic ascent to divine tabernacles.

328   149. "The psalm is . . . a blessing for the people, it is the praise of God, the tribute of the nation, the common language and acclamation of all, it is the voice of the Church, the harmonious confession of faith, signifying deep attachment to

authority; it is the joy of freedom, the expression of happiness, an echo of bliss."[143]

150. In an earlier age, these canonical prayers were attended by many of the faithful. But this gradually ceased, and, as We have already said, their recitation at present is the duty only of the clergy and of religious. The laity have no obligation in this matter. Still, it is greatly to be desired that they participate in reciting or chanting vespers sung in their own parish on feast days. We earnestly exhort you, Venerable Brethren, to see that this pious practice is kept up, and that wherever it has ceased you restore it if possible. This, without doubt, will produce salutary results when vespers are conducted in a worthy and fitting manner and with such helps as foster the piety of the faithful. Let the public and private observance of the feasts of the Church, which are in a special way dedicated and consecrated to God, be kept inviolable; and especially the Lord's day which the Apostles, under the guidance of the Holy Ghost, substituted for the sabbath. Now, if the order was given to the Jews: "Six days shall you do work; in the seventh day is the sabbath, the rest holy to the Lord. Every one that shall do any work on this day, shall die;"[144] how will these Christians not fear spiritual death who perform servile work on feast-days, and whose rest on these days is not devoted to religion and piety but given over to the allurements of the world? Sundays and holy-days, then, must be made holy by divine worship, which gives homage to God and heavenly food to the soul. Although the Church only commands the faithful to abstain from servile work and attend Mass and does not make it obligatory to attend evening devotions, still she desires this and recommends it repeatedly. Moreover, the needs of each one demand it, seeing that all are bound to win the favor of God if they are to obtain His benefits. Our soul is filled with the greatest grief when We see how the Christian people of today profane the afternoon of feast days; public places of amusement and public games are frequented in great numbers while the churches are not as full as they should be. All should come to our churches and there be taught the truth of the Catholic faith, sing the praises of God, be enriched

with benediction of the blessed sacrament given by the
priest and be strengthened with help from heaven against
the adversities of this life. Let all try to learn those prayers
which are recited at vespers and fill their souls with their
meaning. When deeply penetrated by these prayers, they will
experience what St. Augustine said about himself: "How
much did I weep during hymns and verses, greatly moved at
the sweet singing of thy Church. Their sound would penetrate
my ears and their truth melt my heart, sentiments of piety
would well up, tears would flow and that was good for
me."[145]

B. The Cycle of the Mysteries in the Liturgical Year

330   151. Throughout the entire year, the Mass and the divine
office center especially around the person of Jesus Christ.
This arrangement is so suitably disposed that our Saviour
dominates the scene in the mysteries of His humiliation, of
His redemption and triumph.

331   152. While the sacred liturgy calls to mind the mysteries
of Jesus Christ, it strives to make all believers take their part
in them so that the divine Head of the Mystical Body may
live in all the members with the fulness of His holiness.
Let the souls of Christians be like altars on each one of which
a different phase of the sacrifice, offered by the High Priest,
comes to life again, as it were: pains and tears which wipe
away and expiate sin; supplication to God which pierces
heaven; dedication and even immolation of oneself made
promptly, generously and earnestly; and, finally, that intimate union by which we commit ourselves and all we have
to God, in whom we find our rest. "The perfection of religion
is to imitate whom you adore."[146]

332   153. By these suitable ways and methods in which the
liturgy at stated times proposes the life of Jesus Christ for
our meditation, the Church gives us examples to imitate,
points out treasures of sanctity for us to make our own,
since it is fitting that the mind believes what the lips sing,
and that what the mind believes should be practiced in public
and private life.

154. In the period of Advent, for instance, the Church 333
arouses in us the consciousness of the sins we have had the
misfortune to commit, and urges us, by restraining our desires and practicing voluntary mortification of the body, to
recollect ourselves in meditation, and experience a longing
desire to return to God who alone can free us by His grace
from the stain of sin and from its evil consequences.

155. With the coming of the birthday of the Redeemer, 334
she would bring us to the cave of Bethlehem and there teach
that we must be born again and undergo a complete reformation; that will only happen when we are intimately
and vitally united to the Word of God made man and participate in His divine nature, to which we have been elevated.

156. At the solemnity of the Epiphany, in putting before 335
us the call of the Gentiles to the Christian faith, she wishes us
daily to give thanks to the Lord for such a blessing; she wishes
us to seek with lively faith the living and true God, to penetrate deeply and religiously the things of heaven, to love
silence and meditation in order to perceive and grasp more
easily heavenly gifts.

157. During the days of Septuagesima and Lent, our Holy 336
Mother the Church over and over again strives to make each
of us seriously consider our misery, so that we may be urged
to a practical emendation of our lives, detest our sins heart-
ily and expiate them by prayer and penance. For constant
prayer and penance done for past sins obtain for us divine
help, without which every work of ours is useless and un-
availing.

158. In Holy Week, when the most bitter sufferings of 337
Jesus Christ are put before us by the liturgy, the Church
invites us to come to Calvary and follow in the blood-stained
footsteps of the divine Redeemer, to carry the cross willingly
with Him, to reproduce in our own hearts His spirit of expiation and atonement, and to die together with Him.

159. At the Paschal season, which commemorates the 338
triumph of Christ, our souls are filled with deep interior joy:
we, accordingly, should also consider that we must rise, in
union with the Redeemer, from our cold and slothful life to
one of greater fervour and holiness by giving ourselves com-

pletely and generously to God, and by forgetting this wretched world in order to aspire only to the things of heaven: "If you be risen with Christ, seek the things that are above . . . mind the things that are above."[147]

339   160. Finally, during the time of Pentecost, the Church by her precept and practice urges us to be more docile to the action of the Holy Spirit who wishes us to be on fire with divine love so that we may daily strive to advance more in virtue and thus become holy as Christ our Lord and His Father are holy.

340   161. Thus, the liturgical year should be considered as a splendid hymn of praise offered to the heavenly Father by the Christian family through Jesus, their perpetual Mediator. Nevertheless, it requires a diligent and well ordered study on our part to be able to know and praise our Redeemer ever more and more. It requires a serious effort and constant practice to imitate His mysteries, to enter willingly upon His path of sorrow and thus finally share His glory and eternal happiness.

341   162. From what We have already explained, Venerable Brethren, it is perfectly clear how much modern writers are wanting in the genuine and true liturgical spirit who, deceived by the illusion of a higher mysticism, dare to assert that attention should be paid not to the historic Christ but to a "pneumatic" or glorified Christ. They do not hesitate to assert that a change has taken place in the piety of the faithful by dethroning, as it were, Christ from His position; since they say that the glorified Christ, who liveth and reigneth forever and sitteth at the right hand of the Father, has been overshadowed and in His place has been substituted that Christ who lived on earth. For this reason, some have gone so far as to want to remove from the churches images of the divine Redeemer suffering on the cross.

342   163. But these false statements are completely opposed to the solid doctrine handed down by tradition. "You believe in Christ born in the flesh," says St. Augustine, "and you will come to Christ begotten of God."[148] In the sacred liturgy, the whole Christ is proposed to us in all the circumstances of His life, as the Word of the eternal Father, as born of the Vir-

gin Mother of God, as He who teaches us truth, heals the sick, consoles the afflicted, who endures suffering and who dies; finally, as He who rose triumphantly from the dead and who, reigning in the glory of heaven, sends us the Holy Paraclete and who abides in His Church forever; "Jesus Christ, yesterday and today, and the same forever."[149] Besides, the liturgy shows us Christ not only as a model to be imitated but as a Master to whom we should listen readily, a Shepherd whom we should follow, Author of our salvation, the Source of our holiness and the Head of the Mystical Body whose members we are, living by His very life.

164. Since His bitter sufferings constitute the principal   343
mystery of our redemption, it is only fitting that the Catholic faith should give it the greatest prominence. This mystery is the very center of divine worship since the Mass re-presents and renews it every day and since all the sacraments are most closely united with the cross.[150]

165. Hence, the liturgical year, devotedly fostered and   344
accompanied by the Church, is not a cold and lifeless representation of the events of the past, or a simple and bare record of a former age. It is rather Christ Himself who is ever living in His Church. Here He continues that journey of immense mercy which He lovingly began in His mortal life, going about doing good,[151] with the design of bringing men to know His mysteries and in a way live by them. These mysteries are ever present and active not in a vague and uncertain way as some modern writers hold, but in the way that Catholic doctrine teaches us. According to the Doctors of the Church, they are shining examples of Christian perfection, as well as sources of divine grace, due to the merit and prayers of Christ; they still influence us because each mystery brings its own special grace for our salvation. Moreover, our holy Mother the Church, while proposing for our contemplation the mysteries of our Redeemer, asks in her prayers for those gifts which would give her children the greatest possible share in the spirit of these mysteries through the merits of Christ. By means of His inspiration and help and through the cooperation of our wills we can receive from Him living vitality as branches do from the tree and members from the head; thus slowly and

laboriously we can transform ourselves "unto the measure of the age of the fulness of Christ."[152]

C. Feasts of the Saints

345   166. In the course of the liturgical year, besides the mysteries of Jesus Christ, the feasts of the saints are celebrated. Even though these feasts are of a lower and subordinate order, the Church always strives to put before the faithful examples of sanctity in order to move them to cultivate in themselves the virtues of the divine Redeemer.

346   167. We should imitate the virtues of the saints just as they imitated Christ, for in their virtues there shines forth under different aspects the splendor of Jesus Christ. Among some of these saints the zeal of the apostolate stood out, in others courage prevailed even to the shedding of blood, constant vigilance marked others out as they kept watch for the divine Redeemer, while in others the virginal purity of soul was resplendent and their modesty revealed the beauty of Christian humility; there burned in all of them the fire of charity towards God and their neighbor. The sacred liturgy puts all these gems of sanctity before us so that we may consider them for our salvation, and "rejoicing at their merits, we may be inflamed by their example."[153] It is necessary, then, to practice "in simplicity innocence, in charity concord, in humility modesty, diligence in government, readiness in helping those who labor, mercy in serving the poor, in defending truth, constancy, in the strict maintenance of discipline, justice, so that nothing may be wanting in us of the virtues which have been proposed for our imitation. These are the footprints left by the saints in their journey homeward, that guided by them we might follow them into glory."[154] In order that we may be helped by our senses, also, the Church wishes that images of the saints be displayed in our churches, always, however, with the same intention "that we imitate the virtues of those whose images we venerate."[155]

347   168. But there is another reason why the Christian people should honor the saints in heaven, namely, to implore their help and "that we be aided by the pleadings of those whose

praise is our delight."[156] Hence, it is easy to understand why the sacred liturgy provides us with many different prayers to invoke the intercession of the saints.

169. Among the saints in heaven the Virgin Mary Mother   348
of God is venerated in a special way. Because of the mission she received from God, her life is most closely linked with the mysteries of Jesus Christ, and there is no one who has followed in the footsteps of the Incarnate Word more closely and with more merit than she: and no one has more grace and power over the most Sacred Heart of the Son of God and through Him with the Heavenly Father. Holier than the Cherubim and Seraphim, she enjoys unquestionably greater glory than all the other saints, for she is "full of grace,"[157] she is the Mother of God, who happily gave birth to the Redeemer for us. Since she is, therefore, "Mother of mercy, our life, our sweetness and our hope," let us all cry to her "mourning and weeping in this vale of tears,"[158] and confidently place ourselves and all we have under her patronage. She became our Mother also when the divine Redeemer offered the sacrifice of Himself; and hence by this title also, we are her children. She teaches us all the virtues; she gives us her Son and with Him all the help we need, for God "wished us to have everything through Mary."[159]

170. Throughout this liturgical journey which begins anew   349
for us each year under the sanctifying action of the Church, and strengthened by the help and example of the saints, especially of the Immaculate Virgin Mary, "let us draw near with a true heart, in fulness of faith having our hearts sprinkled from an evil conscience, and our bodies washed with clean water,"[160] let us draw near to the "High Priest"[161] that with Him we may share His life and sentiments and by Him penetrate "even within the veil,"[162] and there honor the heavenly Father for ever and ever.

171. Such is the nature and the object of the sacred liturgy: 350
it treats of the Mass, the sacraments, the divine office; it aims at uniting our souls with Christ and sanctifying them through the divine Redeemer in order that Christ be honored and, through Him and in Him, the most Holy Trinity. *Glory be to the Father and to the Son and to the Holy Ghost.*

Part IV: Pastoral Directives

A. Other Devotions Not Strictly Liturgical Warmly Recommended

351   172. In order that the errors and inaccuracies, mentioned above, may be more easily removed from the Church, and that the faithful following safer norms may be able to use more fruitfully the liturgical apostolate, We have deemed it opportune, Venerable Brethren, to add some practical applications of the doctrine which We have explained.

352   173. When dealing with genuine and solid piety We stated that there could be no real opposition between the sacred liturgy and other religious practices, provided they be kept within legitimate bounds and performed for a legitimate purpose. In fact, there are certain exercises of piety which the Church recommends very much to clergy and religious.

353   174. It is Our wish also that the faithful, as well, should take part in these practices. The chief of these are: meditation on spiritual things, diligent examination of conscience, enclosed retreats, visits to the blessed sacrament, and those special prayers in honor of the Blessed Virgin Mary among which the rosary, as all know, has pride of place.[163]

354   175. From these multiple forms of piety, the inspiration and action of the Holy Spirit cannot be absent. Their purpose is, in various ways, to attract and direct our souls to God, purifying them from their sins, encouraging them to practice virtue and, finally, stimulating them to advance along the path of sincere piety by accustoming them to meditate on the eternal truths and disposing them better to contemplate the mysteries of the human and divine natures of Christ. Besides, since they develop a deeper spiritual life of the faithful, they prepare them to take part in sacred public functions with greater fruit, and they lessen the danger of liturgical prayers becoming an empty ritualism.

355   176. In keeping with your past oral solicitude, Venerable Brethren, do not cease to recommend and encourage these exercises of piety from which the faithful, entrusted to your

care, cannot but derive salutary fruit. Above all, do not allow—
as some do, who are deceived under the pretext of restoring
the liturgy or who idly claim that only liturgical rites are of
any real value and dignity—that churches be closed during the
hours not appointed for public functions, as has already happened in some places: where the adoration of the august sacrament and visits to our Lord in the tabernacles are neglected;
where confession of devotion is discouraged; and devotion to
the Virgin Mother of God, a sign of "predestination" according to the opinion of holy men, is so neglected, especially
among the young, as to fade away and gradually vanish. Such
conduct most harmful to Christian piety is like posionous
fruit, growing on the infected branches of a healthy tree,
which must be cut off so that the life-giving sap of the tree
may bring forth only the best fruit.

177. Since the opinions expressed by some about frequent   356
confession are completely foreign to the spirit of Christ and
His Immaculate Spouse and are also most dangerous to the
spiritual life, let Us call to mind what with sorrow We wrote
about this point in the encyclical on the Mystical Body. We
urgently insist once more that what We expounded in very
serious words be proposed by you for the serious consideration and dutiful obedience of your flock, especially to students for the priesthood and young clergy.

178. Take special care that as many as possible, not only   357
of the clergy but of the laity and especially those in religious
organizations and in the ranks of Catholic Action, take part in
monthly days of recollection and in retreats of longer duration
made with a view to growing in virtue. As We have previously
stated, such spiritual exercises are most useful and even necessary to instill into souls solid virtue, and to strengthen them
in sanctity so as to be able to derive from the sacred liturgy
more efficacious and abundant benefits.

179. As regards the different methods employed in these   358
exercises, it is perfectly clear to all that in the Church on earth,
no less in the Church in heaven, there are many mansions,[164]
and that asceticism cannot be the monopoly of anyone. It is
the same Spirit who breatheth where He will,[165] and who
with differing gifts and in different ways enlightens and guides

souls to sanctity. Let their freedom and the supernatural action of the Holy Spirit be so sacrosanct that no one presume to disturb or stifle them for any reason whatsoever.

359   180. However, it is well known that the spiritual exercises according to the method and norms of St. Ignatius have been fully approved and earnestly recommended by Our predecessor on account of their admirable efficacy. We, too, for the same reason have approved and commended them and willingly do We repeat this now.

360   181. Any inspiration to follow and practise extraordinary exercises of piety must most certainly come from the Father of Lights, from whom every good and perfect gift descends;[166] and, of course, the criterion of this will be the effectiveness of these exercises in making the divine cult loved and spread daily ever more widely, and in making the faithful approach the sacraments with more longing desire, and in obtaining for all things holy due respect and honor. If, on the contrary, they are an obstacle to the principles and norms of divine worship, or if they oppose or hinder them, one must surely conclude that they are not in keeping with prudence and enlightened zeal.

361   182. There are, besides, other exercises of piety which, although not strictly belonging to the sacred liturgy, are, nevertheless, of special import and dignity, and may be considered in a certain way to be an addition to the liturgical cult; they have been approved and praised over and over again by the Apostolic See and by the bishops. Among these are the prayers usually said during the month of May in honor of the Blessed Virgin Mother of God, or during the month of June to the most Sacred Heart of Jesus: also novenas and triduums, stations of the cross and other similar practices.

362   183. These devotions make us partakers in a salutary manner of the liturgical cult, because they urge the faithful to go frequently to the sacrament of penance, to attend Mass and receive communion with devotion, and, as well, encourage them to meditate on the mysteries of our redemption and imitate the example of the saints.

363   184. Hence, he would do something very wrong and dangerous who would dare to take on himself to reform all these

exercises of piety and reduce them completely to the methods and norms of liturgical rites. However, it is necessary that the spirit of the sacred liturgy and its directives should exercise such a salutary influence on them that nothing improper be introduced nor anything unworthy of the dignity of the house of God or detrimental to the sacred functions or opposed to solid piety.

185. Take care then, Venerable Brethren, that this true and solid piety increases daily and more under your guidance and bears more abundant fruit. Above all, do not cease to inculcate into the minds of all that progress in the Christian life does not consist in the multiplicity and variety of prayers and exercises of piety, but rather in their helpfulness towards spiritual progress of the faithful and constant growth of the Church universal. For the eternal Father "chose us in Him [Christ] before the foundation of the world that we should be holy and unspotted in His sight."[167] All our prayers, then, and all our religious practices should aim at directing our spiritual energies towards attaining this most noble and lofty end.

B. Liturgical Spirit and Liturgical Apostolate

186. We earnestly exhort you, Venerable Brethren, that after errors and falsehood have been removed, and anything that is contrary to truth or moderation has been condemned, you promote a deeper knowledge among the people of the sacred liturgy so that they more readily and easily follow the sacred rites and take part in them with true Christian dispositions.

187. First of all, you must strive that with due reverence and faith all obey the decrees of the Council of Trent, of the Roman Pontiffs, and the Sacred Congregation of Rites, and what the liturgical books ordain concerning external public worship.

188. Three characteristics of which Our predecessor Pius X spoke should adorn all liturgical services: sacredness, which abhors any profane influence; nobility, which true and genuine arts should serve and foster; and universality, which,

364

365

366

367

while safeguarding local and legitimate custom, reveals the catholic unity of the Church.[168]

368   189. We desire to commend and urge the adornment of churches and altars. Let each one feel moved by the inspired word, "the zeal of thy house hath eaten me up";[169] and strive as much as in him lies that everything in the church, including vestments and liturgical furnishing, even though not rich nor lavish, be perfectly clean and appropriate, since all is consecrated to the Divine Majesty. If we have previously disapproved of the error of those who would wish to outlaw images from churches on the plea of reviving an ancient tradition, We now deem it Our duty to censure the inconsiderate zeal of those who propose for veneration in the Churches and on the altars, without any just reason, a multitude of sacred images and statues, and also those who display unauthorized relics, those who emphasize special and insignificant practices, neglecting essential and necessary things. They thus bring religion into derision and lessen the dignity of worship.

369   190. Let us recall, as well, the decree about "not introducing new forms of worship and devotion."[170] We commend the exact observance of this decree to your vigilance.

370   191. As regards music, let the clear and guiding norms of the Apostolic See be scrupulously observed. Gregorian chant, which the Roman Church considers her own as handed down from antiquity and kept under her close tutelage, is proposed to the faithful as belonging to them also. In certain parts of the liturgy the Church definitely prescribes it;[171] it makes the celebration of the sacred mysteries not only more dignified and solemn but helps very much to increase the faith and devotion of the congregation. For this reason, Our predecessors of immortal memory, Pius X and Pius XI, decreed—and We are happy to confirm with Our authority the norms laid down by them—that in seminaries and religious institutes, Gregorian chant be diligently and zealously promoted, and moreover that the old *Scholæ Cantorum* be restored, at least in the principal churches. This has already been done with happy results in not a few places.[172]

371   192. Besides, "so that the faithful take a more active part in divine worship, let Gregorian chant be restored to popular use

in the parts proper to the people. Indeed it is very necessary that the faithful attend the sacred ceremonies not as if they were outsiders or mute onlookers, but let them fully appreciate the beauty of the liturgy and take part in the sacred ceremonies, alternating their voices with the priest and the choir, according to the prescribed norms. If, please God, this is done, it will not happen that the congregation hardly ever or only in a low murmur answer the prayers in Latin or in the vernacular."[172] A congregation that is devoutly present at the sacrifice, in which our Saviour together with His children redeemed with His sacred blood sings the nuptial hymn of His immense love, cannot keep silent, for "song befits the lover"[174] and, as the ancient saying has it, "he who sings well prays twice." Thus the Church militant, faithful as well as clergy, joins in the hymns of the Church triumphant and with the choirs of angels, and, all together, sing a wondrous and eternal hymn of praise to the most Holy Trinity in keeping with words of the preface, "with whom our voices, too, thou wouldst bid to be admitted."[175]

193. It cannot be said that modern music and singing should be entirely excluded from Catholic worship. For, if they are not profane nor unbecoming to the sacredness of the place and function, and do not spring from a desire of achieving extraordinary and unusual effects, then our churches must admit them since they can contribute in no small way to the splendor of the sacred ceremonies, can lift the mind to higher things and foster true devotion of soul.   372

194. We also exhort you, Venerable Brethren, to promote with care congregational singing, and to see to its accurate execution with all due dignity, since it easily stirs up and arouses the faith and piety of large gatherings of the faithful. Let the full harmonious singing of our people rise to heaven like the bursting of a thunderous sea[176] and let them testify by the melody of their song to the unity of their hearts and minds[177], as becomes brothers and the children of the same Father.   373

195. What We have said about music, applies to the other fine arts, especially to architecture, sculpture and painting. Recent works of art which lend themselves to the materials   374

of modern composition, should not be universally despised and rejected through prejudice. Modern art should be given free scope in the due and reverent service of the church and the sacred rites, provided that they preserve a correct balance between styles tending neither to extreme realism nor to excessive "symbolism," and that the needs of the Christian community are taken into consideration rather than the particular taste or talent of the individual artist. Thus modern art will be able to join its voice to that wonderful choir of praise to which have contributed, in honor of the Catholic faith, the greatest artists throughout the centuries. Nevertheless, in keeping with the duty of Our office, We cannot help deploring and condemning those works of art, recently introduced by some, which seem to be a distortion and perversion of true art and which at times openly shock Christian taste, modesty and devotion, and shamefully offend the true religious sense. These must be entirely excluded and banished from our churches, like "anything else that is not in keeping with the sanctity of the place."[178]

375   196. Keeping in mind, Venerable Brethren, pontifical norms and decrees, take great care to enlighten and direct the minds and hearts of the artists to whom is given the task today of restoring or rebuilding the many churches which have been ruined or completely destroyed by war. Let them be capable and willing to draw their inspiration from religion to express what is suitable and more in keeping with the requirements of worship. Thus the human arts will shine forth with a wondrous heavenly splendor, and contribute greatly to human civilization, to the salvation of souls and the glory of God. The fine arts are really in conformity with religion when "as noblest handmaids they are at the service of divine worship."[179]

376   197. But there is something else of even greater importance, Venerable Brethren, which We commend to your apostolic zeal, in a very special manner. Whatever pertains to the external worship has assuredly its importance; however, the most pressing duty of Christians is to live the liturgical life, and increase and cherish its supernatural spirit.

377   198. Readily provide the young clerical student with facilities to understand the sacred ceremonies, to appreciate their

majesty and beauty and to learn the rubrics with care, just as you do when he is trained in ascetics, in dogma and in canon law and pastoral theology. This should not be done merely for cultural reasons and to fit the student to perform religious rites in the future, correctly and with due dignity, but especially to lead him into closest union with Christ, the Priest, so that he may become a holy minister of sanctity.

199. Try in every way, with the means and helps that your prudence deems best, that the clergy and people become one in mind and heart, and that the Christian people take such an active part in the liturgy that it becomes a truly sacred action of due worship to the eternal Lord in which the priest, chiefly responsible for the souls of his parish, and the ordinary faithful are united together. 378

200. To attain this purpose, it will greatly help to select carefully good and upright young boys from all classes of citizens who will come generously and spontaneously to serve at the altar with careful zeal and exactness. Parents of higher social standing and culture should greatly esteem this office for their children. If these youths, under the watchful guidance of the priests, are properly trained and encouraged to fulfill the task committed to them punctually, reverently and constantly, then from their number will readily come fresh candidates for the priesthood. The clergy will not then complain— as, alas, sometimes happens even in Catholic places—that in the celebration of the august sacrifice they find no one to answer or serve them. 379

201. Above all, try with your constant zeal to have all the faithful attend the eucharistic sacrifice from which they may obtain abundant and salutary fruit; and carefully instruct them in all the legitimate ways We have described above so that they may devoutly participate in it. The Mass is the chief act of divine worship; it should also be the source and center of Christian piety. Never think that you have satisfied your apostolic zeal until you see your faithful approach in great numbers the celestial banquet which is a sacrament of devotion, a sign of unity and a bond of love.[180] 380

202. By means of suitable sermons and particularly by periodic conferences and lectures, by special study weeks and the 381

like, teach the Christian people carefully about the treasures of piety contained in the sacred liturgy so that they may be able to profit more abundantly by these supernatural gifts. In this matter, those who are active in the ranks of Catholic Action will certainly be a help to you, since they are ever at the service of the hierarchy in the work of promoting the Kingdom of Jesus Christ.

382   203. But in all these matters, it is essential that you watch vigilantly lest the enemy come into the field of the Lord and sow cockle among the wheat;[181] in other words, do not let your flocks be deceived by the subtle and dangerous errors of false mysticism or quietism—as you know We have already condemned these errors;[182] also do not let a certain dangerous "humanism" lead them astray, nor let there be introduced a false doctrine destroying the notion of Catholic faith, nor finally an exaggerated zeal for antiquity in matters liturgical. Watch with like diligence lest the false teaching of those be propagated who wrongly think and teach that the glorified human nature of Christ really and continually dwells in the "just" by His presence and that one and numerically the same grace, as they say, united Christ with the members of His Mystical Body.

383   204. Never be discouraged by the difficulties that arise, and never let your pastoral zeal grow cold. "Blow the trumpet in Sion . . . call an assembly, gather together the people, sanctify the Church, assemble the ancients, gather together the little ones, and them that suck at the breasts,"[183] and use every help to get the faithful everywhere to fill the churches and crowd around the altars so that they may be restored by the graces of the sacraments and joined as living members to their divine Head, and with Him and through Him celebrate together the august sacrifice that gives due tribute of praise to the Eternal Father.

Epilogue

384   205. These, Venerable Brethren, are the subjects We desired to write to you about. We are moved to write that your children, who are also Ours, may more fully understand and

appreciate the most precious treasures which are contained in the sacred liturgy: namely, the eucharistic sacrifice, representing and renewing the sacrifice of the cross, the sacraments which are the streams of divine grace and of divine life, and the hymn of praise, which heaven and earth daily offer to God.

206. We cherish the hope that these Our exhortations will not only arouse the sluggish and recalcitrant to a deeper and more correct study of the liturgy, but also instill into their daily lives its supernatural spirit according to the words of the Apostle, "extinguish not the spirit."[184]   385

207. To those whom an excessive zeal occasionally led to say and do certain things which saddened Us and which We could not approve, We repeat the warning of St. Paul, "But prove all things, hold fast that which is good."[185] Let Us paternally warn them to imitate in their thoughts and actions the Christian doctrine which is in harmony with the precepts of the immaculate Spouse of Jesus Christ, the mother of saints.   386

208. Let Us remind all that they must generously and faithfully obey their holy pastors who possess the right and duty of regulating the whole life, especially the spiritual life, of the Church. "Obey your prelates and be subject to them. For they keep watch as having to render an account of your souls; that they may do this with joy and not with grief."[186]   387

209. May God, whom we worship, and who is "not the God of dissension but of peace,"[187] graciously grant to us all that during our earthly exile we may with one mind and one heart participate in the sacred liturgy which is, as it were, a preparation and a token of that heavenly liturgy in which we hope one day to sing together with the most glorious Mother of God and our most loving Mother, "To Him that sitteth on the throne, and to the Lamb, benediction and honor, and glory and power for ever and ever."[188]   388

210. In this joyous hope, We most lovingly impart to each and every one of you, Venerable Brethren, and to the flocks confided to your care, as a pledge of divine gifts and as a witness of Our special love, the apostolic benediction.   389

211. Given at Castel Gandolfo, near Rome, on the 20th day of November in the year 1947, the 9th of Our Pontificate.   390

Sacred Congregation of Rites
Decree Restoring Easter Vigil
February 9, 1951

Since early times the Church solemnly celebrates the Easter Vigil, which St. Augustine calls "the mother of all the holy vigils." This vigil was celebrated during the early hours of the morning preceding the Resurrection of Our Lord. But in the course of centuries and for various reasons, the celebration was put ahead, first to the early evening, then to the afternoon, and finally to the morning of Holy Saturday; at the same time some modifications were introduced to the detriment of the primitive symbolism.

392 However in our times, which are distinguished for development in researches on ancient liturgy, has witnessed the fulfillment of the ardent desire of bringing back the Easter Vigil to its primitive splendor and of assigning to it the time observed in the beginning, that is, the early hours of the night preceding Resurrection Sunday. In favor of such a return there is added a special motive of pastoral order: that of facilitating the presence of numerous faithful. In fact, as Holy Saturday is no longer a holyday, as it once was, the greater part of the faithful cannot assist at the sacred rite, if it takes place in the morning.

CHRISTUS DOMINUS
Apostolic Constitution of Pope Pius XII
on Eucharistic Fast
January 6, 1953

C hrist the Lord, "on the night in which he was betrayed,"[1] when for the last time he celebrated the Pasch of the old law, after supper was finished,[2] took bread and, giving thanks, broke and gave to his disciples, saying: "This is my body, which shall be given up for you";[3] and in like manner he handed them the chalice, saying: "This is my blood of the new covenant, which is being shed for many";[4] do this in remembrance of me."[5] From these passages of holy Scripture it is clearly evident that the divine Redeemer wished to substitute for this final paschal celebration, in which a lamb was eaten according to the Hebrew rites, a new Pasch to endure to the end of the world, that is, the eating of the immaculate Lamb, who was to be immolated for the life of the world, so that new Pasch of the new law should bring the ancient Passover to an end, and the shadow be dispelled by the reality.[6]

However, since this conjunction of the two suppers was designed to signify the transition from the old Pasch to the new, it is easy to see why the Church, in renewing the eucharistic sacrifice by command of the divine Redeemer in remembrance of him, could depart from the practice of the ancient love feast and introduce that of the eucharistic fast.   394

For from ancient times the custom developed of administering the Eucharist to the faithful fasting.[7] Toward the end of the fourth century, fasting was already prescribed by several   395 councils for those who were going to celebrate the eucharistic sacrifice. Thus in the year 393 the Council of Hippo decreed: "Let the sacrament of the altar be celebrated only by those who are fasting";[8] a little later, that is, in the year 397, this precept was set forth in the same words by the Third Council of Carthage;[9] and by the beginning of the fifth century this custom was quite common and could be called immemorial. Hence St. Augustine states that the most holy Eucharist is always received fasting, and that this usage is observed throughout the world.[10]

396   Undoubtedly this practice was based on very serious reasons, among which may be mentioned first of all the circumstance which the apostle of the Gentiles deplores in speaking of the fraternal love feast of the Christians.[11] Abstinence from food and drink is in keeping with the profound reverence which we owe to the supreme majesty of Jesus Christ when we are about to receive him hidden under the eucharistic veils. Moreover, when we receive his most precious body and blood before taking any other food, we clearly show that it is the first and greatest nourishment by which our soul is supported and its holiness increased. Hence, the same St. Augustine reminds us: "It has pleased the Holy Spirit that in honor of so great a sacrament the body of the Lord should enter the mouth of a Christian before any other foods."[12]

397   Not only does this fast discharge the obligation of honor to the divine Redeemer, but it also fosters devotion; and so it can help to augument those most salutary fruits of holiness which Christ, the fountainhead and Author of all good, demands that we who are enriched by his grace bring forth.

398   Besides, everyone knows from experience that by the very laws of human nature, when the body is not burdened with food the mind is rendered more alert and is more strongly moved to meditate on that hidden and sublime mystery which is enacted in the soul as in a temple, to the increase of divine charity.

399   The solicitude of the Church for the observance of the eucharistic fast can be gathered also from the fact that she imposed severe penalties for the violation of this precept. Thus the Seventh Council of Toledo in the year 646 threatened

with excommunication anyone who should celebrate Mass without fasting;[13] and in the year 572 the Third Council of Braga,[14] as well as in the year 585 the Second Council of Macon,[15] had already decreed that anyone who should be proved guilty of this act should be deposed from his office and dignity.

Nevertheless, as the centuries rolled by, diligent consideration was also given to the fact that at times it was expedient in view of special circumstances to relax somewhat this law of fasting as it affected the faithful. Accordingly, the Council of Constance in the year 1415, while reaffirming the sacrosanct law of fasting, also added a certain modification:" ... the authority of the sacred canons and approved custom of the Church have prescribed and now prescribe that this sacrament must not be celebrated after supper, nor be received by the faithful not fasting, except in the case of illness or other necessity recognized or permitted by the law or by the Church."[16]

It has seemed good to recall these things to mind so that all may understand that, although we have been induced by new conditions of time and circumstances to grant not a few faculties and permissions in this matter, nevertheless we intend by this apostolic letter to confirm the full force of the law and custom concerning the eucharistic fast; and that we also wish to remind those who are able to comply with that law, that they diligently continue to do so, so that only those who need these concessions may make use of them, according to their need.

We are filled with the sweetest consolation—and we are happy to mention it here, though briefly—when we behold devotion to the august Sacrament of the altar daily increasing not only in the souls of the faithful but also in the splendor of divine worship, a thing which has been very frequently shown in the public manifestations of the people. To this effect undoubtedly the solicitous attentions of the sovereign pontiffs have contributed not a little, especially in the case of Blessed Pius X who, calling upon all to renew the ancient custom of the Church, exhorted them to approach the table of the angels as frequently as possible and even daily if possi-

400

401

402

ble;[17] and, inviting also the little ones to this heavenly food, wisely decreed that the precept of confession and holy communion applied to each and every person who had attained the use of reason;[18] and this is also prescribed by the code of canon law.[19] Spontaneously and willingly responding to these wishes of the sovereign pontiffs, the faithful have come to holy communion in ever increasing numbers. And would that this hunger for the bread of heaven and thirst for the precious blood were enkindled in all men of every age and of every social rank!

403   It should be observed, however, that the times in which we live and their special conditions have introduced into common currency and the ordinary course of life many circumstances which occasion grave difficulties, apt to deter people from participating in the divine mysteries, if all most absolutely observe the law of the eucharistic fast as it has been observed up to the present time.

404   In the first place, obviously priests today are numerically unequal to the task of ministering to the growing necessities of the faithful. On feast days especially they must often put up with excessive labors, as they have to celebrate the eucharistic sacrifice at a late hour and not infrequently two or three times on the same day; and at times they must travel long distances in order that considerable sections of their flock may not be without Mass. Exhausting apostolic labors of this sort unquestionably undermine the health of priests, as they must not only celebrate Mass, explain the Gospel, hear confessions, teach catechism and attend to the other duties of their office, which demand of them more and more application and work, but must also carefully plan and provide the ways and means of combating the relentless assault which in these days has been launched on such a wide front and with such shrewdness and bitterness against God and his Church.

405   But our mind and heart go out above all to those who are working in distant countries far from their native land, and who have generously responded to that invitation and command of the divine Master: "Go, therefore, and make disciples of all nations."[20] We are speaking of the heralds of the Gospel who, enduring exhausting labors and conquering all the

difficulties of communication, are striving with all their power to bring the light of the Christian religion to all according to their capacity, and to nourish their people, who often are but recent converts to the Catholic faith, with the bread of angels which fosters virtue and rekindles devotion.

In almost the same situation are those faithful who live in 406 the many areas cared for by Catholic missionaries or in other places where they do not have their own resident priest, but must await until a late hour the arrival of another priest before they can participate in the eucharistic sacrifice and be nourished with the divine food.

Moreover, now that machines of every sort have been 407 brought into general use, it very often happens that not a few workmen employed in factories, or in transportation, shipping or other public utilities, are occupied day and night on swing shifts, so that their weakened conditions sometimes compel them to take some nourishment, and thus they are prevented from approaching the eucharistic table fasting.

Mothers of families also are often unable to come to the 408 holy table until they have attended to their household duties, . which often demand many hours of work.

It also happens that in schools and academies for boys and 409 girls there are very many who desire to answer that divine invitation: "Let the little children come to me,"[21] perfectly trusting that he who "feedeth among the lilies,"[22] will guard the innocence of their souls and the purity of their lives against the enticements of youth and the snares of the world. And yet at times it is very difficult for them, before going to school, to go to church and there nourish themselves with the bread of angels and afterward return home to their necessary nourishment.

Moreover, we must remember that today large numbers of 410 people cross from place to place in the afternoon or early evening to take part in religious services or to attend meetings on social questions. If, then, it were permitted to celebrate on such occasions the eucharistic mystery, which is the living font of divine grace and incites the will to glow with the desire of virtue, there is no doubt that all could draw from this source the strength to adopt a thoroughly Christian way of thought and action and to obey just laws.

411   These special considerations may well be supplemented by others which are of universal application. Although in these our times medical science and the study of hygiene have made such progress and have contributed so much to diminishing the death rate, especially among the young, yet the conditions of modern life and the hardships resulting from the frightful wars of this century are such that they have to a great extent undermined constitutions and weakened physical health.

412   For these reasons and especially in order the better to promote the reawakened devotion toward the Eucharist, not a few bishops of various countries have respectfully petitioned by letter that this law of fasting be somewhat mitigated; and this Apostolic See has already graciously granted special faculties and permissions in this matter to the sacred ministers and to the faithful. In this connection we may recall the decree entitled *Post editum*, which was issued by the Sacred Congregation of the Council, December 7, 1906, for the sick;[2 3] and the letter of March 22, 1923 given to local ordinaries for priests, by the Supreme Sacred Congregation of the Holy Office.[2 4]

413   In these latter times the petitions of the bishops in this matter have been more frequent and more insistent and the faculties granted have been correspondingly greater, especially those bestowed at the time of the war. Without doubt, that is an excellent indication that there exist new, serious continuing and sufficiently general causes which make it exceedingly difficult in many circumstances both for priests to celebrate the eucharistic sacrifice and for the faithful to receive the bread of angels fasting.

414   Wherefore, in order to meet these grave inconveniences and difficulties and in order that diversity of indults may not lead to differences in practice, we think it necessary to decree a mitigation of the eucharistic fast in such a way that, as far as possible, even in the special conditions of time and place and persons, all may more easily be able to observe that law. In issuing this decree we are confident that we will be able to contribute much to the increase of devotion to the Eucharist,

and thus better persuade and induce all to partake at the table of the angels, with an undoubted increase of glory to God and of holiness to the mystical body of Jesus Christ.

Accordingly, by our apostolic authority we decree and pro- 415 vide as follows:

1. The law of the eucharistic fast from midnight continues 416 in force for all those who are not in the special conditions which we are about to explain in this apostolic letter. However, for the future, it is to be a general and common principle for all, whether priests or faithful, that natural water does not break the eucharistic fast.

2. The sick, even though not confined to bed, may with 417 the prudent advice of a confessor take something by way of drink or of true medicine, exclusive of alcoholics. The same faculty is granted to priests who are ill yet intend to celebrate Mass.

3. Priests who are going to celebrate either at a rather late 418 hour, or after fatiguing work in the sacred ministry or after a long journey, may take something by way of drink, exclusive of alcoholic beverages; however, they must abstain from such drink for at least the space of one hour before saying Mass.

4. Those who are to celebrate Mass twice or three times 419 may take the ablutions, but in the case the ablutions are to consist of water only, without wine.

5. In the manner the faithful, even though not ill, who be- 420 cause of serious inconvenience—that is, fatiguing work, the lateness of the hour at which alone they can receive holy communion, or a long journey which they must make—cannot approach the eucharistic table completely fasting, may, with the prudent advice of a confessor, for as long as the need lasts, take something by way of drink, exclusive of alcoholic beverages; however, they must abstain from such drink for at least the space of one hour before receiving communion.

6. We grant to local ordinaries, if the circumstances demand 421 it, the faculty to permit the celebration of Mass in the evening, as we have said, but with the understanding that the Mass shall not begin before four o'clock in the afternoon, on the following days: on holy days of obligation which are still in effect, or on those which were formerly observed; on the first

Friday of each month; on the occasion of solemnities which are celebrated with a large concourse of people; and also in addition to these days, once each week. The priest must observe the fast for three hours as to solid food and alcoholic drink, and for one hour as to nonalcoholic drink. During these Masses, moreover, the faithful may receive holy communion, observing the same rule as regards the eucharistic fast, and without prejudice to the prescription of canon 857.

422   In mission territories, considering the very special conditions which prevail there and because of which, generally speaking, it is rare for priests to be able to visit distant stations, local ordinaries can grant to missionaries the same faculty also for other days of the week.

423   Local ordinaries, however, should carefully see to it that every interpretation be avoided which would enlarge the faculties granted, and that all abuse and irreverence in this matter be precluded. For in bestowing these faculties which are demanded today by circumstances of persons, times and places, we wish most emphatically to confirm the importance, force and efficacy of the eucharistic fast for those who are about to receive the divine Redeemer hidden under the eucharistic veils. And moreover, as bodily inconvenience is diminished, the soul ought as far as possible to make up for it, either by interior penance or in other ways, according to the traditional practice of the Church which usually prescribes other works when it mitigates the obligation to fast. Therefore, those who make use of the faculties here granted should direct more fervent prayers to heaven, adore God, thank him and especially expiate their faults and implore new graces from above. Since all should clearly realize that the Eucharist was instituted by Jesus Christ "as an everlasting memorial of his passion,"[25] they should stir up in hearts those sentiments of Christian humility and Christian penance which meditation on the sufferings and death of the divine Redeemer ought to arouse. Likewise, let all offer to the same divine Redeemer, ever immolating himself on the altar and thus renewing the greatest proof of his love, increased fruits of charity toward their neighbor. In this way certainly all will contribute to the daily better fulfillment of that saying of the apostle of the

Gentiles: "The bread is one, we though many are one body, all of us who partake of the one bread."[26]

It is our will that all the decrees contained in this letter be established, ratified and valid, notwithstanding anything to the contrary, even though worthy of most special mention; and all other privileges and faculties which have been granted in any way whatsoever by the Holy See are hereby abolished, so that everywhere all persons may uniformly and duly observe this discipline.   424

All the provisions herein set forth shall be operative from the day of promulgation in the *Acta Apostolicae Sedis.*[27]   425

Given at Rome at St. Peter's, in the year of the Lord 1953, on the sixth day of January, the Epiphany of the Lord, in the fourteenth year of our pontificate.   426

Sacred Congregation of Rites
Decree on the Restoration of the Holy Week Order
November 16, 1955

General Decree

From apostolic times holy Mother Church has taken care each year to celebrate the principal mysteries of our redemption, namely the passion, death and resurrection of our Lord Jesus Christ, with an absolutely singular commemoration.

At first the supreme moments of these mysteries, those of "the crucified, buried and risen" Christ (St. Augustine, *Ep.* 55, 14), were recalled in a special three-day period. Soon a solemn commemoration of the institution of the most holy Eucharist was added. Finally, on the Sunday immediately preceding the passion, a liturgical celebration of the triumphant messianic entry of our Lord and King into the Holy City was added. Thus there arose a special liturgical week which, by reason of the greatness of the mysteries celebrated, was designated as "Holy" and was enriched with exceptionally complete and sacred ceremonies.

In the beginning these rites were performed on the same days of the week and at the same hours of the day that the sacred mysteries occurred. Thus, the institution of the holy Eucharist was recalled on Thursday evening by the solemn Mass of the Lord's Supper. On Friday there was a special liturgical function in the hours after noon, recalling the Lord's passion and death. Finally, on Holy Saturday night there began solemn vigil which ended the following morning with the joy of the resurrection.

During the middle ages they began, for various pertinent reasons to set an earlier time for the performance of liturgical services on those days, so that toward the end of that period all of these liturgical services had been transferred to the morning. This did not take place without detriment to the ligurgical meaning, nor without causing some confusion between the Gospel narratives and the liturgical ceremonies attached to them. The solemn liturgy of the Easter vigil in particular lost its original clarity and the meaning of its words and symbols when it was torn from its proper nocturnal setting. Moreover, Holy Saturday, with too early a recollection of the Easter gladness intruding into it, lost its original character as a day of mourning for the burial of the Lord.   430

In more recent times another change, very serious from the pastoral point of view, took place. For many centuries, Thursday, Friday and Saturday of Holy Week were holy days of obligation, so that the Christian people, freed from servile works, could be present at the ceremonies taking place on those days. But in the course of the seventeenth century the Roman pontiffs themselves were compelled, because of the complete change in the conditions of social life, to reduce the number of the holy days of obligation. And so Urban VIII was compelled in his apostolic constitution *Universa per orbem* of September 24, 1642, to declare that the last three days of Holy Week were no longer holy days of obligation, and to classify them as working days.   431

Hence the attendance of the faithful at these ceremonies necessarily decreased, especially because the services had long been moved back to the morning hours, when schools, factories and public business of every kind are usually open and functioning on working days throughout the world. As a matter of fact, common and almost universal experience shows that these solemn and important liturgical services of the last three days of Holy Week are often conducted by the clergy in church buildings that are almost deserted.   432

This is certainly to be regretted, since these liturgical services of Holy Week are endowed not only with a singular dignity,   433 but also with a special sacramental force and efficacy for nourishing Christian life.

434   Nor can there be proper compensation for the loss of these liturgical functions through those pious devotional exercises which are usually called extra-liturgical and which are performed in the afternoon hours of these three days.

435   For these reasons during recent years experts on the liturgy, priests having the care of souls, and especially the bishops have sent earnest petitions to the Holy See begging that the liturgical functions of the last three days of Holy Week be restored to the hours after noon, as formerly, so that all the faithful might more easily be present at these services.

436   After carefully considering the matter, Pope Pius XII restored the liturgy of the sacred vigil of Easter in 1951. The celebration was to be held at the discretion of the ordinary and as an experiment.

437   This experiment was highly successful everywhere, as many ordinaries reported to the Holy See. These same ordinaries also renewed their petitions for a liturgical restoration for the other days of Holy Week, asking that the sacred functions be moved back to the evening hours as had been done in the case of the Easter vigil. Moreover, evening Masses, provided for in the apostolic constitution *Christus Dominus* of January 6, 1953, were being said everywhere and were attended by many. With all these things in mind Pope Pius XII commanded the Commission for the Restoration of the Liturgy established by him to examine the question of restoring the order of Holy Week and to propose a solution. After obtaining that answer, His Holiness decreed, as the seriousness of the affair demanded, that the entire question be subjected to a special examination by the Cardinals of the Sacred Congregation of Rites.

438   The cardinals gathered in an extraordinary session at the Vatican on July 19 of this year. They considered the matter thoroughly and voted unanimously that the restored ordo of Holy Week be approved and prescribed, subject to the approval of the Holy Father.

439   After all this had been reported in detail to the Holy Father by the undersigned Cardinal Prefect, His Holiness deigned to approved what the cardinals had decided.

(Details of the restoration followed:)—Ed.

MUSICAE SACRAE DISCIPLINA
Encyclical Letter of Pope Pius XII
on Sacred Music
December 25, 1955

To Our Venerable Brethren, the Patriarchs, Primates, Archbishops, Bishops and other Local Ordinaries in peace and communion with the Apostolic See: Health and Apostolic Benediction.

The subject of sacred music has always been very close to Our heart. Hence it has seemed appropriate to Us in this encyclical letter to give an orderly explanation of the topic and also to answer somewhat more completely several questions which have been raised and discussed during the past decades. We are doing so in order that this noble and distinguished art may contribute more every day to greater splendor in the celebration of divine worship and to the more effective nourishment of spiritual life among the faithful. 441

At the same time We have desired to grant what many of you, venerable brethren, have requested in your wisdom and also what has been asked by outstanding masters of this liberal art and distinguished students of sacred music at meet ings devoted to the subject. The experience of pastoral life and the advances being made in the study of this art have persuaded Us that this step is timely. 442

We hope, therefore, that what St. Pius X rightly decreed in the document which he accurately called the "legal code of sacred music"[1] may be confirmed and inculcated anew, shown in a new light and strengthened by new proofs. We hope that the noble art of sacred music—adapted to contem- 443 porary conditions and in some way enriched—may ever more perfectly accomplish its mission.

I

444   Music is among the many and great gifts of nature with which God, in Whom is the harmony of the most perfect concord and the most perfect order, has enriched men, whom He has created in His image and likeness.[2] Together with the other liberal arts, music contributes to spiritual joy and the delight of the soul.

445   On this subject St. Augustine has accurately written: "Music, that is the science or the sense of proper modulation, is likewise givien by God's generosity to mortals having rational souls in order to lead them to higher things."[3]

446   No one, therefore, will be astonished that always and everywhere, even among pagan peoples, sacred song and the art of music have been used to ornament and decorate religious ceremonies. This is proved by many documents, both ancient and new. No one will be astonished that these arts have been used especially for the worship of the true and sovereign God from the earliest times. Miraculously preserved unharmed from the Red Sea by God's power, the people of God sang a song of victory to the Lord, and Miriam, the sister of Moses, their leader, endowed with prophetic inspiration, sang with the people while playing a tambourine.[4]

447   Later, when the ark of God was taken from the house of Abinadab to the city of David, the king himself and "all Israel played before the Lord on all manner of instruments made of wood, on harps and lutes and timbrels and cornets and cymbals."[5] King David himself established the order of the music and singing used for sacred worship.[6] This order was restored after the people's return from exile and was observed faithfully until the Divine Redeemer's coming.

448   St. Paul showed us clearly that sacred chant was used and held in honor from the very beginning in the Church founded by the divine Redeemer when he wrote to the Ephesians: "Be filled with the Spirit, speaking to one another in psalms and hymns and spiritual songs."[7] He indicates that this custom of

singing hymns was in force in the assemblies of Christians when he says: "When you come together each of you has a hymn."[8]

Pliny testifies that the same thing held true after apostolic times. He writes that apostates from the Faith said that "this was their greatest fault or error, that they were accustomed to gather before dawn on a certain day and sing a hymn to Christ as if He were God."[9] These words of the Roman proconsul in Bithynia show very clearly that the sound of church singing was not completely silenced even in times of persecution. 449

Tertullian confirms this when he says that in the assemblies of the Christians "the Scriptures are read, the psalms are sung, sermons are preached."[10] 450

There are many statements of the Fathers and ecclesiastical writers testifying that after freedom and peace had been restored to the Church the psalms and hymns of liturgical worship were in almost daily use. Moreover, new forms of sacred chant were gradually created and new types of songs were invented. These were developed more and more by the choir schools attached to cathedrals and other important churches, especially by the School of Singers in Rome. 451

According to tradition, Our predecessor of happy memory, St. Gregory the Great, carefully collected and wisely arranged all that had been handed down by the elders and protected the purity and integrity of sacred chant with fitting laws and regulations. 452

From Rome, the Roman mode of singing gradually spread to other parts of the West. Not only was it enriched by new forms and modes, but a new kind of sacred singing, the religious song, frequently sung in the vernacular, was also brought into use. 453

The choral chant began to be called "Gregorian" after St. Gregory, the man who revived it. It attained new beauty in almost all parts of Christian Europe after the 8th or 9th century because of its accompaniment by a new musical instrument called the "organ." Little by little, beginning in the 9th century, polyphonic singing was added to this choral chant. The study and use of polyphonic singing were developed 454 more and more during the centuries that followed and were raised to a marvelous perfection under the guidance of magnificent composers during the 15th and 16th centuries.

455   Since the Church always held this polyphonic chant in the highest esteem, it willingly admitted this type of music even in the Roman basilicas and in pontifical ceremonies in order to increase the glory of the sacred rites. Its power and splendor were increased when the sounds of the organ and other musical instruments were joined with the voices of the singers.

456   Thus, with the favor and under the auspices of the Church the study of sacred music has gone a long way over the course of the centuries. In this journey, although sometimes slowly and laboriously, it has gradually progressed from the simple and ingenuous Gregorian modes to great and magnificent works of art. To these works not only the human voice, but also the organ and other musical instruments, add dignity, majesty and a prodigious richness.

457   The progress of this musical art clearly shows how sincerely the Church has desired to render divine worship ever more splendid and more pleasing to the Christian people. It likewise shows why the Church must insist that this art remain within its proper limits and must prevent anything profane and foreign to divine worship from entering into sacred music along with genuine progress, and perverting it.

458   The Sovereign Pontiffs have always diligently fulfilled their obligation to be vigilant in this matter. The Council of Trent also forbids "those musical works in which something lascivious or impure is mixed with organ music or singing."[11] In addition, not to mention numerous other Sovereign Pontiffs, Our predecessor Benedict XIV of happy memory in an encyclical letter dated February 19, 1749, which prepared for a Holy Year and was outstanding for its great learning and abundance of proofs, particularly urged Bishops to firmly forbid the illicit and immoderate elements which had arrogantly been inserted into sacred music.[12]

459   Our predecessors Leo XII, Pius VIII[13] followed the same line.

460   Nevertheless it can rightly be said that Our predecessor of immortal memory, St. Pius X, made as it were the highest

contribution to the reform and renewal of sacred music when he restated the principles and standards handed down from the elders and wisely brought them together as the conditions of modern times demanded.[14] Finally, like Our immediate predecessor of happy memory, Pius XI, in his Apostolic Constitution *Divini cultus sanctitatem (The Holiness of Divine Worship)*, issued December 20, 1929,[15] We ourself in the encyclical *Mediator Dei (On the Sacred Liturgy)*, issued November 20, 1947,[16] have enriched and confirmed the orders of the older Pontiffs.

Certainly no one will be astonished that the Church is so vigilant and careful about sacred music. It is not a case of drawing up laws of aesthetics or technical rules that apply to the subject of music. It is the intention of the Church, however, to protect sacred music against anything that might lessen its dignity, since it is called upon to take part in something as important as divine worship. 461

On this score sacred music obeys laws and rules which are no different from those prescribed for all religious art and, indeed, for art in general. Now we are aware of the fact that during recent years some artists, gravely offending against Christian piety, have dared to bring into churches works devoid of any religious inspiration and completely at variance with the right rules of art. They try to justify this deplorable conduct by plausible-looking arguments which they claim are based on the nature and character of art itself. They go on to say that artistic inspiration is free and that it is wrong to impose upon it laws and standards extraneous to art, whether they are religous or moral, since such rules seriously hurt the dignity of art and place bonds and shackles on the activity of an inspired artist. 462

Arguments of this kind raise a question which is certainly difficult and serious, and which affects all art and every artist. It is a question which is not to be answered by an appeal to the principles of art or of aesthetics, but which must be decided in terms of the supreme principle of the final end, which is the inviolate and sacred rule for every man and every human act. 463

The ordination and direction of man to his ultimate end—which is God—by absolute and necessary law based on the nature and the infinite perfection of God Himself is so solid that not even God could exempt anyone from it. This eternal and unchangeable law commands that man himself and all his actions should manifest and imitate, so far as possible, God's infinite perfection for the praise and glory of the Creator. Since man is born to attain this supreme end, he ought to conform himself and through his actions direct all the powers of his body and his soul, rightly ordered among themselves and duly subjected to the end they are meant to attain, to the divine Model. Therefore even art and works of art must be judged in the light of their conformity and concord with man's last end.

Art certainly must be listed among the noblest manifestations of human genius. Its purpose is to express in human works the infinite divine beauty of which it is, as it were, the reflection. Hence that outworn dictum "art for art's sake" ·entirely neglects the end for which every creature is made. Some people wrongly assert that art should be exempted entirely from every rule which does not spring from art itself. Thus this dictum either has no worth at all or is gravely offensive to God Himself, the Creator and Ultimate End.

Since the freedom of the artist is not a blind instinct to act in accordance with his own whim or some desire for novelty, it is in no way restricted or destroyed, but actually ennobled and perfected, when it is made subject to the divine law.

Since this is true of works of art in general, it obviously applies also to religious and sacred art. Actually religious art is even more closely bound to God and the promotion of His praise and glory, because its only purpose is to give the faithful the greatest aid in turning their minds piously to God through the works it directs to their senses of sign and hearing. Consequently the artist who does not profess the truths of the faith or who strays far from God in his attitude or conduct should never turn his hand to religious art. He lacks, as it were, that inward eye with which he might see what God's majesty and His worship demand. Nor can he hope that his works, devoid of religion as they are, will ever really breathe the piety and faith that befit God's temple and His holiness, even though they may show him to be an expert artist who is endowed with visible talent. Thus he cannot hope that his works will be worthy of admission into the sacred buildings of the Church, the guardian and arbiter of religious life.

But the artist who is firm in his faith and leads a life worthy   468
of a Christian, who is motivated by the love of God and reverently uses the powers the Creator has given him, expresses and manifests the truths he holds and the piety he possesses so skillfully, beautifully and pleasingly in colors and lines or sounds and harmonies that this sacred labor of art is an act of worship and religion for him. It also effectively arouses and inspires people to profess the faith and cultivate piety.

The Church has always honored and always will honor this   469
kind of artist. It opens wide the doors of its temples to them because what these people contribute through their art and industry is a welcome and important help to the Church in carrying out its apostolic ministry more effectively.

These laws and standards for religious art apply in a   470
stricter and holier way to sacred music because sacred music enters more intimately into divine worship than many other liberal arts, such as architecture, painting and sculpture. These last serve to prepare a worthy setting for the sacred ceremonies. Sacred music, however, has an important place in the actual performance of the sacred ceremonies and rites themselves. Hence the Church must take the greatest care to prevent whatever might be unbecoming to sacred worship or anything that might distract the faithful in attendance from lifting their minds up to God from entering into sacred music, which is the servant, as it were, of the sacred liturgy.

The dignity and lofty purpose of sacred music consist in the   471
fact that its lovely melodies and splendor beautify and embellish the voices of the priest who offers Mass and of the Christian people who praise the Sovereign God. Its special power and excellence should lift up to God the minds of the faithful who are present. It should make the liturgical prayers of the Christian community more alive and fervent so that

everyone can praise and beseech the Triune God more powerfully, more intently and more effectively.

472   The power of sacred music increases the honor given to God
by the Church in union with Christ, its Head. Sacred music
likewise helps to increase the fruits which the faithful, moved
by the sacred harmonies, derive from the holy liturgy. These
fruits, as daily experience and many ancient and modern
literary sources show, manifest themselves in a life and conduct worthy of a Christian.

473   St. Augustine, speaking of chants characterized by "beautiful voice and most apt melody," says: "I feel that our souls
are moved to the ardor of piety by the sacred words more
piously and powerfully when these words are sung than when
they are not sung, and that all the affections of our soul in
their variety have modes of their own in song and chant by
which they are stirred up by an indescribable and secret
sympathy."[17]

474   It is easy to infer from what has just been said that the
dignity and force of sacred music are greater the closer sacred
music itself approaches to the supreme act of Christian worship, the Eucharistic sacrifice of the altar. There can be nothing more exalted or sublime than its function of accompanying with beautiful sound the voice of the priest offering up
the Divine Victim, answering him joyfully with the people
who are present and enhancing the whole liturgical ceremony
with its noble art.

475   To this highest function of sacred music We must add
another which closely resembles it, that is its function of
accompanying and beautifying other liturgical ceremonies,
particularly the recitation of the Divine Office in choir.
Thus the highest honor and praise must be given to liturgical
music.

476   We must also hold in honor that music which is not primarily a part of the sacred liturgy, but which by its power
and purpose greatly aids religion. This music is therefore
rightly called religious music. The Church has possessed such
music from the beginning and it has developed happily under
the Church's auspices. As experience shows, it can exercise
great and salutary force and power on the souls of the faith-

ful, both when it is used in churches during nonliturgical services and ceremonies, or when it is used outside churches at various solemnities and celebrations.

The tunes of these hymns, which are often sung in the   477
language of the people, are memorized with almost no effort or labor. The mind grasps the words and the music. They are frequently repeated and completely understood. Hence even boys and girls, learning these sacred hymns at a tender age, are greatly helped by them to know, appreciate and memorize the truths of the faith. Therefore they also serve as a sort of catechism. These religious hymns bring pure and chaste joy to young people and adults during times of recreation. They give a kind of religious grandeur to their more solemn assemblies and gatherings. They bring pious joy, sweet consolation and spiritual progress to Christian families themselves. Hence these popular religious hymns are of great help to the Catholic apostolate and should be carefully cultivated and promoted.

Therefore when We praised the manifold power and the   478
apostolic effectiveness of sacred music, We spoke of something that can be a source of great joy and solace to all who have in any way dedicated themselves to its study and practice. All who use the art they possess to compose such musical compositions, to teach them or to perform them by singing or using musical instruments, undoubtedly exercise in many and various ways a true and genuine apostolate. They will receive from Christ the Lord the generous rewards and honors of apostles for the work they have done so faithfully.

Consequently they should hold their work in high esteem,   479
not only as artists and teachers of art, but also as ministers of Christ the Lord and as His helpers in the work of the apostolate. They should likewise show in their conduct and their lives the dignity of their calling.

III

Since, as We have just shown, the dignity and effectiveness   480
of sacred music and religious chant are so great, it is very necessary that all of their parts should be diligently and care-

fully arranged to produce their salutary results in a fitting manner.

481   First of all the chants and sacred music which are immediately joined with the Church's liturgical worship should be conducive to the lofty end for which they are intended. This music—as our predecessor St. Pius X has already wisely warned us—"must possess proper liturgical qualities, primarily holiness and goodness of form; from which its other note, universality, is derived."[18]

482   It must be *holy*. It must not allow within itself anything that savors of the profane nor allow any such thing to slip into the melodies in which it is expressed. The Gregorian chant which has been used in the Church over the course of so many centuries, and which may be called, as it were, its patrimony, is gloriously outstanding for this holiness.

483   This chant, because of the close adaptation of the melody to the sacred text, is not only most intimately conformed to the words, but also in a way interprets their force and efficacy and brings delight to the minds of the hearers. It does this by the use of musical modes that are simple and plain, but which are still composed with such sublime and holy art that they move everyone to sincere admiration and constitute an almost inexhaustible source from which musicians and composers draw new melodies.

484   It is the duty of all those to whom Christ the Lord has entrusted the task of guarding and dispensing the Church's riches to preserve this precious treasure of Gregorian chant diligently and to impart it generously to the Christian people. Hence what Our predecessors, St. Pius X, who is rightly called the renewer of Gregorian chant,[19] and Pius XI[20] have wisely ordained and taught, We also, in view of the outstanding qualities which genuine Gregorian chant possesses, will and prescribe that this be done. In the performance of the sacred liturgical rites this same Gregorian chant should be most widely used and great care should be taken that it should be performed properly, worthily and reverently. And if, because of recently instituted feast days, new Gregorian melodies must be composed, this should be done by true masters of the art. It should be done in such a way that these

new compositions obey the laws proper to genuine Gregorian chant and are in worthy harmony with the older melodies in their virtue and purity.

If these prescriptions are really observed in their entirety, **485** the requirements of the other property of sacred music—that property by virtue of which it should be an *example of true art*—will be duly satisfied. And if in Catholic churches throughout the entire world Gregorian chant sounds forth without corruption or diminution, the chant itself, like the sacred Roman liturgy, will have a characteristic of *universality,* so that the faithful, wherever they may be, will hear music that is familiar to them and a part of their own home. In this way they may experience, with much spiritual consolation, the wonderful unity of the Church. This is one of the most important reasons why the Church so greatly desires that the Gregorian chant traditionally associated with the Latin words of the sacred liturgy be used.

We are not unaware that, for serious reasons, some quite **486** definite exceptions have been conceded by the Apostolic See. We do not want these exceptions extended or propagated more widely, nor do We wish to have them transferred to other places without due permission of the Holy See. Furthermore, even where it is licit to use these exemptions, local Ordinaries and the other pastors should take great care that the faithful from their earliest years should learn at least the easier and more frequently used Gregorian melodies, and should know how to employ them in the sacred liturgical rites, so that in this way also the unity and the universality of the Church may shine forth more powerfully every day.

Where, according to old or immemorial custom, some pop- **487** ular hymns are sung in the language of the people after the sacred words of the liturgy have been sung in Latin during the solemn Eucharistic sacrifice, local Ordinaries can allow this to be done "if, in the light of the circumstances of the locality and the people, they believe that (custom) cannot prudently be removed."[21] The Law by which it is forbidden to sing the liturgical words themselves in the language of the people remains in force, according to what has been said.

488 In order that singers and the Christian people may rightly understand the meaning of the liturgical words joined to the musical melodies, it has pleased Us to make Our own the exhortation made by the Fathers of the Council of Trent. "Pastors and all those who have care of souls," were especially urged that "often, during the celebration of Mass, they or others whom they delegate explain something about what is read in the Mass and, among other things, tell something about the mystery of this most holy sacrifice. This is to be done particularly on Sundays and holy days."[22]

489 This should be done especially at the time when catechetical instruction is being given to the Christian people. This may be done more easily and readily in this age of ours than was possible in times past, because translations of the liturgical texts into the vernacular tongues and explanations of these texts in books and pamphlets are available. These works, produced in almost every country by learned writers, can effectively help and enlighten the faithful to understand and share in what is said by the sacred ministers in the Latin language.

490 It is quite obvious that what We have said briefly here about Gregorian chant applies mainly to the Latin Roman Rite of the Church. It can also, however, be applied to a certain extent to the liturgical chants of other rites—either to those of the West, such as the Ambrosian, Gallican or Mozarabic, or to the various eastern rites.

491 For as all of these display in their liturgical ceremonies and formulas of prayer the marvelous abundance of the Church, they also, in their various liturgical chants, preserve treasures which must be guarded and defended to prevent not only their complete disappearance, but also any partial loss or distortion.

492 Among the oldest and most outstanding monuments of sacred music the liturgical chants of the different eastern rites hold a highly important place. Some of the melodies of these chants, modified in accordance with the character of the Latin liturgy, had a great influence on the composition of the musical works of the Western Church itself. It is Our hope that the selection of sacred eastern rite hymns—which the Pontifical Institute of Oriental Studies, with the help of the Pontifical

Institute of Sacred Music, is busily working to complete—will achieve good doctrinal and practical results. Thus eastern rite seminarians, well trained in sacred chant, can make a significant contribution to enhancing the beauty of God's house after they have been ordained priests.

It is not Our intention in what We have just said in praise 493 and commendation of the Gregorian chant to exclude sacred polyphonic music from the rites of the Church. If this polyphonic music is endowed with the proper qualities, it can be of great help in increasing the magnificent of divine worship and of moving the faithful to religious dispositions. Everyone certainly knows that many polyphonic compositions, especially those that date from the 16th century, have an artistic purity and richness of melody which render them completely worthy of accompanying and beautifying the Church's sacred rites.

Although over the course of the centuries genuine poly- 494 phonic art gradually declined and profane melodies often crept into it, during recent decades the indefatigable labors of experts have brought about a restoration. The works of the old composers have been carefully studied and proposed as models to be imitated and rivalled by modern composers.

So it is that in the basilicas, cathedrals and churches of 495 religious communities these magnificent works of the old masters and the polyphonic compositions of more recent musicians can be performed, contributing greatly to the beauty of the sacred rite. Likewise We know that simpler but genuinely artistic polyphonic compositions are often sung even in smaller churches.

The Church favors all these enterprises. As Our predecessor 496 of immortal memory, St. Pius X, says, the Church "unceasingly encourages and favors the progress of the arts, admitting for religious use all the good and the beautiful that the mind of man has discovered over the course of the centuries, but always respecting the liturgical laws."[2 3]

These laws warn that great prudence and care should be 497 used in this serious matter in order to keep out of churches polyphonic music which, because of its heavy and bombastic style, might obscure the sacred words of the liturgy by a kind of exaggeration, interfere with the conduct of the liturgical service or, finally, lower the skill and competence of the singers to the disadvantage of sacred worship.

498   These norms must be applied to the use of the organ or other musical instruments. Among the musical instruments that have a place in church the organ rightly holds the principal position, since it is especially fitted for the sacred chants and sacred rites. It adds a wonderful splendor and a special magnificence to the ceremonies of the Church. It moves the souls of the faithful by the grandeur and minds an almost heavenly joy and it lifts them up powerfully to God and to higher things.

499   Besides the organ, other instruments can be called upon to give great help in attaining the lofty purpose of sacred music, so long as they play nothing profane, nothing clamorous or strident and nothing at variance with the sacred services or the dignity of the place. Among these the violin and other musical instruments that use the bow are outstanding because, when they are played by themselves or with other stringed instruments or with the organ, they express the joyous and sad sentiments of the soul with an indescribable power. Moreover, in the encyclical *Mediator Dei*, We Ourselves gave detailed and clear regulations concerning the musical modes that are to be admitted into the worship of the Catholic religion.

500   "For, if they are not profane or unbecoming to the sacredness of the place and function and do not spring from a desire to achieve extraordinary and unusual effects, then our churches must admit them, since they can contribute in no small way to the splendor of the sacred ceremonies, can lift the mind to higher things, and can foster true devotion of the soul."[24]

501   It should hardly be necessary to add the warning that, when the means and talent available are unequal to the task, it is better to forego such attempts than to do something which would be unworthy of divine worship and sacred gatherings.

502   As We have said before, besides those things that are intimately associated with the Church's sacred liturgy, are also popular religious hymns which derive their origin from the

liturgical chant itself. Most of these are written in the language of the people. Since these are closely related to the mentality and temperament of individual national groups, they differ considerably among themselves according to the character of different races and localities.

If hymns of this sort are to bring spiritual fruit and advan- 503 tage to the Christian people, they must be in full conformity with the doctrine of the Catholic faith. They must also express and explain that doctrine accurately. Likewise they must use plain language and simple melody and must be free from violent and vain excess of words. Despite the fact that they are short and easy, they should manifest a religious dignity and seriousness. When they are fashioned in this way these sacred canticles, born as they are from the most profound depths of the people's soul, deeply move the emotions and spirit and stir up pious sentiments. When they are sung at religious rites by a great crowd of people singing as with one voice, they are powerful in raising the minds of the faithful to higher things.

As we have written above, such hymns cannot be used in 504 Solemn High Masses without the express permission of the Holy See. Nevertheless at Masses that are not sung solemnly these hymns can be a powerful aid in keeping the faithful from attending the Holy Sacrifice like dumb and idle spectators. They can help to make the faithful accompany the sacred services both mentally and vocally and to join their own piety to the prayers of the priest. This happens when these hymns are properly adapted to the individual parts of the Mass, as We rejoice to know is being done in many parts of the Catholic world.

In rites that are not completely liturgical religious hymns 505 of this kind—when, as We have said, they are endowed with the right qualities—can be of great help in the salutary work of attracting the Christian people and enlightening them, in imbuing them with sincere piety and filling them with holy joy. They can produce these effects not only within churches, but outside of them also, especially on the occasion of pious processions and pilgrimages to shrines and at the time of national or international congresses. They can be especially useful, as experience has shown, in the work of instructing boys and girls in Catholic truth, in societies for youth and in meetings of pious associations.

506   Hence We can do no less than urge you, venerable brethren, to foster and promote diligently popular religious singing of this kind in the dioceses entrusted to you. There is among you no lack of experts in this field to gather hymns of this sort into one collection, where this has not already been done, so that all of the faithful can learn them more easily, memorize them and sing them correctly.

507   Those in charge of the religious instruction of boys and girls should not neglect the proper use of these effective aids. Those in charge of Catholic youth should make prudent use of them in the highly important work entrusted to them. Thus there will be hope of happily attaining what everyone desires, namely the disappearance of worldly songs which because of the quality of their melodies or the frequently voluptuous and lascivious words that go with them are a danger to Christians especially the young, and their replacement by songs that give chaste and pure pleasure, that foster and increase faith and piety.

508   May it thus come about that the Christian people begin even on this earth to sing that song of praise it will sing forever in heaven: "To Him who sits upon the throne, and to the Lamb, blessing and honor and glory and dominion forever and ever."[2][5]

509   What we have written thus far applies primarily to those nations where the Catholic religion is already firmly established. In mission lands it will not be possible to accomplish all these things until the number of Christians has grown sufficiently, larger church buildings have been erected, the children of Christians properly attend schools established by the Church and, finally, until there is an adequate number of sacred ministers. Still We urgently exhort apostolic workers who are laboring strenuously in these extensive parts of the Lord's vineyard to pay careful attention to this matter as one of the serious problems of their ministry.

510   Many of the peoples entrusted to the ministry of the missionaries take great delight in music and beautify the cere-

monies dedicated to the worship of idols with religious singing. It is not prudent, then, for the heralds of Christ, the true God, to minimize or neglect entirely this effective help in their apostolate. Hence the preachers of the Gospel in pagan lands should sedulously and willingly promote in the course of their apostolic ministry the love for religious song which is cherished by the men entrusted to their care. In this way these people can have, in contrast to their own religious music which is frequently admired even in cultivated countries, sacred Christian hymns in which the truths of the faith, the life of Christ the Lord and the praises of the Blessed Virgin Mary and the Saints can be sung in a language and in melodies familiar to them.

Missionaries should likewise be mindful of the fact that,   511
from the beginning, when the Catholic Church sent preachers of the Gospel into lands not yet illumined by the light of faith, it took care to bring into those countries, along with the sacred liturgical rites, musical compositions, among which were the Gregorian melodies. It did this so that the people who were to be converted might be more easily led to accept the truths of the Christian religion by the attractiveness of these melodies.

IV

So that the desired effect may be produced by what We   512
have recommended and ordered in this encyclical, following in the footsteps of Our predecessors, you, venerable brethren, must carefully use all the aids offered by the lofty function entrusted to you by Christ the Lord and committed to you by the Church. As experience teaches, these aids are employed to great advantage in many churches throughout the Christian world.

First of all see to it that there is a good school of singers   513
in the cathedral itself and, as far as possible, in other major churches of your dioceses. This school should serve as an example to others and influence them to carefully develop and perfect sacred chant.

514   Where it is impossible to have schools of singers or where there are not enough choir boys, it is allowed that "a group of men and women or girls, located in a place outside the sanctuary set apart for the exclusive use of this group, can sing the liturgical texts at Solemn Mass, as long as the men are completely separated from the women and girls and everything unbecoming is avoided. The Ordinary is bound in conscience in this matter."[26]

515   Great care must be taken that those who are preparing for the reception of sacred orders in your seminaries and in missionary or religious houses of study are properly instructed in the doctrine and use of sacred music and Gregorian chant according to the mind of the Church by teachers who are experts in this field, who esteem the traditional customs and teachings and who are entirely obedient to the precepts and norms of the Holy See.

516   If, among the students in the seminary or religious house of study, anyone shows remarkable facility in or liking for this art, the authorities of the seminary or house of study should not neglect to inform you about it. Then you may avail yourself of the opportunity to cultivate these gifts further and send him either to the Pontifical Institute of Sacred Music in Rome or to some other institution of learning in which this subject is taught, provided that the student manifests the qualities and virtues upon which one can base a hope that he will become an excellent priest.

517   In this matter care must also be taken that local Ordinaries and heads of religious communities have someone whose help they can use in this important area which, weighed down as they are by so many occupations, they cannot easily take care of themselves.

518   It would certainly be best if in diocesan Councils of Christian Art there were someone especially expert in the fields of religious music and chant who could carefully watch over what is being done in the diocese, inform the Ordinary about what has been done and what is going to be done, receive the Ordinary's commands and see that they are obeyed. If in any diocese there is one of these associations, which have been wisely instituted to foster sacred music and have been

greatly praised and commended by the Sovereign Pontiffs, the Ordinary in his prudence may employ this association in the task of fulfilling responsibility.

Pious associations of this kind, which have been founded to instruct the people in sacred music or for advanced study in this subject, can contribute greatly by words and example to the advance of sacred music.   519

Help and promote such associations, venerable brethren, so that they may lead an active life, may employ the best and the most effective teachers, and so that, throughout the entire diocese, they may diligently promote the knowledge, love and use of sacred music and religious harmonies, with due observance of the Church's laws and due obedience to Ourselves.   520

Moved by paternal solicitude, We have dealt with this matter at some length. We are entirely confident that you, venerable brethren, will diligently apply all of your pastoral solicitude to this sacred subject which contributes so much to the more worthy and magnificent conduct of divine worship.   521

It is Our hope that whoever in the Church supervises and directs the work of sacred music under your leadership may be influenced by Our encyclical letter to carry on this glorious apostolate with new ardor and new effort, generously, enthusiastically and strenuously.   522

Hence, We hope that this most noble art, which has been so greatly esteemed throughout the Church's history and which today has been brought to real heights of holiness and beauty, will be developed and continually perfected and that on its own account it will happily work to bring the children of the Church to give due praise, expressed in worthy melodies and sweet harmonies, to the Triune God with stronger faith, more flourishing hope and more ardent charity.   523

May it produce even outside the walls of churches—in Christian families and gatherings of Christians—what St. Cyprian beautifully spoke of to Donatus, "Let the sober banquet resound with Psalms. And if your memory be good and your voice pleasant, approach this work according to custom. You give more nourishment to those dearest to you   524 if we hear spiritual things and if religious sweetness delights the ears."[27]

525 In the meantime, buoyed up by the hope of richer and more joyous fruits which We are confident will come from this exhortation of Ours, as a testimony of Our good will and as an omen of heavenly gifts to each one of you, venerable brethren, to the flock entrusted to your care and to those who observe Our wishes and work to promote sacred music, with abundant charity, We impart the Apostolic Benediction.

526 Given at St. Peter's in Rome, December 25, on the feast of the Nativity of Our Lord Jesus Christ, in the year 1955, the 17th of Our Pontificate.

Address of Pope Pius XII
to the International Congress on Pastoral Liturgy
on the Liturgical Movement
September 22, 1956

You have asked Us to deliver an address upon the closing of the International Congress on Pastoral Liturgy which has just been held in Assisi. We readily accede to your request and bid you welcome.

If the position of the liturgical movement today is compared to that of thirty years ago, undeniable progress in its extent and in its depth becomes evident. Interest in the liturgy, practical accomplishments, and the active participation of the faithful have undergone a development which would then have been difficult to anticipate.

The chief driving force, both in doctrinal matters and in practical applications, came from the Hierarchy and, in particular, from Our saintly Predecessor, Pius X, who gave the liturgical movement a decisive impulse by his *Motu Proprio* of October 23, 1913, *"Abhinc duos annos."*[1]

The faithful received these directives gratefully and showed themselves ready to comply with them. Liturgists applied themselves to their task with zeal and, as a result, many interesting and rewarding projects were soon under way, although, at times, certain deviations had to be corrected by the Church's authority.

Of the many documents published on this subject in recent times, it will suffice for Us to mention three: the Encyclical *"Mediator Dei," "On the Liturgy,"* of November 20, 1947[2]; the new decree on Holy Week, dated November 16, 1955,[3] which has helped the faithful to achieve a better understanding and fuller participation in the love, sufferings and triumph of our Savior; and finally, the Encyclical *"De musica sacra"* of December 25, 1955.[4]

532   Thus the liturgical movement has appeared as a sign of God's providential dispositions for the present day, as a movement of the Holy Spirit in His Church, intended to bring men closer to those mysteries of the faith and treasures of grace which derive from the active participation of the faithful in liturgical life.

533   The Congress which is just concluding has had for its particular end a demonstration of the inestimable value of the liturgy in the sanctification of souls, and, consequently, in the Church's pastoral activity.

534   You have studied this aspect of the liturgy as it is revealed in history and has continued to be revealed. You have also seen how this aspect of the liturgy is founded in the nature of things, that is, how it is derived from essential elements of the liturgy.

535   Your Congress, then, included a study of historical developments, some reflections on existing conditions, and an examination both of objectives to be sought in the future and of means suitable for their attainment. After careful consideration of your program, We express Our hope that this new sowing of seed, added to those of the past, will produce rich harvests for the benefit of individuals and the whole Church.

536   In this address, instead of presenting to you in greater detail norms on which the Holy See has already spoken sufficiently, We have decided it would be more useful to touch on a few important points which are actually under discussion in the field of liturgy and dogma, and which hold Our special interest. We shall group these considerations under two headings. These will be simple pointers rather than the express themes We propose to develop: the Liturgy and the Church, the Liturgy and the Lord.

I. The Liturgy and the Church

As We have said in the Encyclical *"Mediator Dei,"* the   537
liturgy is a vital function of the whole Church, and not
simply of a group or of a limited movement. "The Sacred
Liturgy is the whole public worship of the Mystical Body of
Jesus Christ, Head and members."[5]

The Mystical Body of our Lord lives on the truth of Christ   538
and on the graces which flow through its members, giving them
life and uniting them to one another and their Head. This is
what St. Paul means when he says in the first Epistle to the
Corinthians: *"All are yours, and you are Christ's, and Christ
is God's."*[6] All then is directed toward God, His service, and
His glory.

The Church, filled with the gifts and the life of God,   539
devotes herself with a deep and spontaneous movement to
the adoration and praise of the infinite God. Through the
liturgy she renders to Him, as a corporate body, that worship
which is His due.

To this unique liturgy, all the members, those clothed with   540
episcopal power and those belonging to the body of the faithful, bring all that they have received from God, all the
powers of their minds and hearts and all of their achievements. This is true, above all, of the Hierarchy, since it holds
the *"depositum fidei"* and the *"depositum gratiae."*

From the *"depositum fidei,"* from the truth of Christ con-   541
tained in Scripture and Tradition, the Hierarchy draws the
great mysteries of the faith, in particular, those of the Trinity,
the Incarnation and the Redemption, and causes them to pass
into the liturgy. But it would be difficult to find a truth of
the Christian faith which is not expressed in some manner in
the liturgy, whether in readings from the Old and the New
Testament during Holy Mass and the Divine Office, or in the
riches which the mind and heart discover in the Psalms.

Moreover, the solemn ceremonies of the liturgy are a pro-   542
fession of faith in action. They give concrete expression to
the great truths of the faith which concern the inscrutable

designs of God's generosity and His inexhaustible benefits to men, the love and mercy of the heavenly Father for the world, the salvation for which He sent His Son and delivered Him to death.

543   It is thus that the Church communicates in abundance in the liturgy the treasures of the *"depositum fidei,"* of the truth of Christ.

544   Through the liturgy also are diffused the riches of the *"depositum gratiae"* which the Savior has transmitted to His Apostles: sanctifying grace, the virtues and gifts, the power to baptize, to confer the Holy Spirit, to forgive sins through the sacraments of Penance, and to ordain priests.

545   At the heart of the liturgy is the celebration of the Eucharist, the sacrifice and the repast. In the liturgy also are all the sacraments gathered up, and the Church, by means of the sacramentals, generously multiplies gifts of grace in the most varied circumstances.

546   The Hierarchy also extends its care to all that helps increase the beauty and dignity of liturgical ceremonies: the places of worship, their furnishing, the liturgical vestments, sacred music, and sacred art.

547   If the Hierarchy communicates the truth and the grace of Christ by means of the liturgy, the faithful, on their side, have a duty to receive them, to give them their whole-hearted consent, to transform them into values for life. They accept all that is offered to them—the graces of the sacrifice of the altar, of the sacraments and sacramentals—not as mere passive recipients of the graces flowing over them, but cooperating in these graces with all their will and strength, and, above all, participating in the liturgical offices, or at least following their performance with fervor.

548   The laity have contributed in large measure, and by a constant effort continue to contribute, to increase the external solemnity of worship, to build churches and chapels, to adorn them, to enhance the beauty of the liturgical ceremonies with all the splendors of sacred art.

549   The contributions which are brought to the liturgy by the Hierarchy and by the faithful are not to be reckoned as two separate quantities, but represent the joint work of members

of the same organism, which acts as a single living entity. The shepherds and the flock, the teaching Church and the Church taught, form a single and unique body of Christ. So there is no reason for entertaining suspicion, rivalries, open or hidden opposition, either in one's thought or in one's manner of speaking and acting. Among members of the same body there ought to reign, before all else, harmony, union and cooperation. It is within this unity that the Church prays, makes its offering, grows in holiness. One can declare therefore with justice that the liturgy is the work of the *Church whole and entire.*

But We have to add: public worship is not on that account   550
the *whole Church.* It does not exhaust the field of her activities.

Alongside public worship, which is that of the community,   551
there is still place for private worship, which the individual pays to God in the secret of his heart or expresses by exterior acts. This private worship has as many variations as there are Christians, though it proceeds from the same faith and the same grace of Christ. The Church not only tolerates this kind of worship, but gives it full recognition and approval, without however raising it in any way to the primary position of liturgical worship.

But when We say that public worship does not exhaust the   552
field of the Church's activities, We are thinking in particular of the tasks of teaching and pastoral care, of the *"Tend the flock of God, which is among you."*[7]

We have recalled the role which the Magisterium the depos   553
itory of the truth of Christ, exercises through the liturgy. The influence of the governing power upon it is also evident. For it belongs to the Popes to give recognition to rites which are in force, to introduce any new practices, to establish rules for the manner of worship. It pertains to the Bishops to watch carefully that the prescriptions of canon law with regard to divine worship are observed.[8]

But the functions of teaching and control extend even be   554
yond that. To ascertain this it is sufficient to glance at canon law and its statements concerning the Pope, the Roman Congregations, the Bishops, Councils, the Magisterium, and ecclesiastical discipline. The same conclusion may be reached by

observing the life of the Church, and in Our two Allocutions of May 31 and November 2, 1954, on the threefold function of the Bishop, We expressly insisted on the extent of his obligations. They are not limited to teaching and government, but embrace also all other human activities in the measure in which religious and moral interests are involved.[9]

555   If then the duties and the interests of the Church on this point are universal, the priests and the faithful will be cautious in their manner of thinking and acting, lest they fall into narrowness of view or lack of understanding.

556   Our Encyclical *"Mediator Dei"* has already corrected certain erroneous statements which were tending either to orientate religious and pastoral teaching into a form exclusively liturgical, or to raise obstacles to the liturgical movement because it was not understood.

557   In reality, there exists no objective difference between the end pursued by the liturgy and that of the other functions of the Church. As for differences of opinion, though they are genuine, they do not present insuperable obstacles.

558   These considerations will suffice to show, We hope, that the liturgy is the work of the whole Church, and that all the faithful, as members of the Mystical Body, ought to love and value it, and take part in it, while understanding that the tasks of the Church extend well beyond it.

II. The Liturgy and the Lord

559   We wish to consider now in a special manner the liturgy of the Mass and the Lord Who in it is both Priest and Oblation. As some inaccuracies nd some misunderstandings are coming to light here and there with regard to certain points, We shall say a word about the *"actio Christi,"* about the *"praesentia Christi,"* and about the *"infinita et divina maiestas Christi."*

1. "Actio Christi"

560   The liturgy of the Mass has for its end the expression through the senses of the grandeur of the mystery which is accomplished in it, and efforts are being made today which

tend to make the faithful participate in as active and intelligent a manner as possible. Though this aim is justified, there is risk of lessening reverence if attention is distracted from the main action to direct it to the splendor of other ceremonies.

What is this main action of the Eucharist sacrifice?   561

We have spoken explicitly of it in the Allocution of November 2, 1954.[10] We there cited first the teaching of the Council of Trent: *"In this divine sacrifice which takes place at Mass, the same Christ is present and is immolated in an unbloody manner, Who once on the altar of the Cross offered Himself in a bloody manner . . . For the victim is one and the same, now offering Himself through the ministry of priests, Who then offered Himself on the Cross; only the manner of offering is different."*[11]   562

And We continued in these words: *"Thus the priest-celebrant, putting on the person of Christ, alone offers sacrifice, and not the people, nor the clerics, nor even the priests who reverently assist. All, however, can and should take an active part in the sacrifice."*[12]   563

We then emphasized that, from a failure to distinguish between the participation of the celebrant in the fruits of the sacrifice of the Mass and the nature of the action which he performs, the conclusion was reached that *"the offering of one Mass, at which a hundred priests assist with religious devotion, is the same as a hundred Masses celebrated by a hundred priests."* Concerning this statement We said: *"It must be rejected as an erroneous opinion."*   564

And We added by way of explanation: *"With regard to the offering of the Eucharistic Sacrifice, the actions of Christ, the High Priest, are as many as are the priests celebrating, not as many as are the priests reverently hearing the Mass of a Bishop or a priest; for those present at the Mass in no sense sustain, or act in, the person of Christ sacrificing, but are to be compared to the faithful layfolk who are present at the Mass."*[13]   565

On the subject of liturgical congresses, We remarked on the same occasion: *"These meetings sometimes follow a definite program, so that only one offers the Mass, and others (all or the majority) assist at this one Mass, and receive the Holy Eucharist during it from the hands of the celebrant. If this be*   566 *done for a good and sound reason, . . . the practice is not to be opposed, so long as the error We have mentioned above is not underlying it,"* that is to say, the error of equating the offering of a hundred Masses by a hundred priests to the offering of one Mass at which a hundred priests are devoutly present.

567   According to this, the central element of the Eucharisti Sacrifice is that in which Christ intervenes as *"se ipsum offerens"* —to adopt the words of the Council of Trent. (Sess. XXII, cap. 2) That happens at the consecration when, in the very act of transubstantiation worked by the Lord,[14] the priest-celebrant is *"personam Christi gerens."*

568   Even if the consecration takes place without pomp and in all simplicity, it is the central point of the whole liturgy of the sacrifice, the central point of the *"actio Christi cuius personam gerit sacerdos celebrans,"* or *"sacerdotes concelebrantes"* in the case of a true concelebration.

569   Some recent events give Us the occasion to speak with precision on certain points regarding this matter. When the consecration of the bread and wine is validly brought about, the whole action of Christ is actually accomplished. Even if all that remains could not be completed, still, nothing essential is wanting to the Lord's oblation.

570   After the consecration is performed, the *"oblatio hostiae super altare positae"* can be accomplished and is accomplished by the priest-celebrant, by the Church, by the other priests, by each of the faithful. But this action is not *"actio ipsus Christi per sacerdotem ipsius personam sustinentem et gerentem."* In reality the action of the consecrating priest is the very action of Christ Who acts through His minister. In the case of a concelebration in the proper sense of the word, Christ, instead of acting through one minister, acts through several. On the other hand, in a merely ceremonial concelebration, which could also be the act of a lay person, there is no question of simultaneous consecration, and this fact raises the important point: "What intention and what exterior action are required to have a true concelebration and simultaneous consecration?"

On this subject let Us recall what We said in Our Apostolic   571
Constitution *"Episcopalis Consecrationis"* of November 30,
1944.[15] We there laid down that in an episcopal consecration
the two Bishops who accompany the consecrator must have
the intention of consecrating the Bishop-Elect, and that, consequently, they must perform the exterior actions and pronounce the words by which the power and the grace to trans-
mit are signified and transmitted. It is, then, not sufficient
for them to unite their wills with that of the chief consecrator, and to declare that they make his words and actions
their own. They must themselves perform the actions and
pronounce the essential words.

The same thing likewise happens in concelebration in the   572
true sense. It is not sufficient to have and to indicate the will
to make one's own the words and the actions of the celebrant.
The concelebrants must themselves say over the bread and the
wine, "This is my Body," "This is my Blood." Otherwise,
their concelebration is purely ceremonial.

And so it may not be affirmed that, "in the last analysis the   573
only decisive question is to know in what measure personal
participation, supported by the grace which one receives in
the offering of worship, increases the participation in the
cross and in the grace of Christ, Who unites us to Himself and
with each other." This inaccurate manner of putting the question We have already rejected in the Allocution of November
2, 1954; but certain theologians still cannot reconcile themselves to it. We therefore repeat it: the decisive question (for
concelebration as for the Mass of a single priest) is not to know
the fruit of the soul draws from it, but the nature of the act
which is performed: does or does not the priest, as minister
of Christ, perform *"actio Christi se ipsum sacrificantis et
offerentis?"*

Likewise for the sacraments, it is not a question of knowing   574
the fruit produced by them, but whether the essential elements of the sacramental sign (the performing of the sign by
the minister himself who performs the gestures and pronounces the words with intention *saltem faciendi quod facit
ecclesia*) have been validly performed.

575   Likewise, in celebration and concelebration, one must see whether, along with the necessary interior intention, the celebrant completes the external action, and, above all, pronounces the words which constitute the *"actio Christi se ipsum sacrificantis et offerentis."* This is not verified when the priest does not pronounce over the bread and the wine our Lord's words: "This is my Body," "This is my Blood."

2. "Praesentia Christi"

576   Just as altar and sacrifice dominate liturgical worship, the life of Christ must be said to be completely dominated by the sacrifice of the Cross.

577   The Angel's words to His foster father: *"He shall save his people from their sins,"*[16] those of John the Baptist: *"Behold the lamb of God, who takes away the sin of the world,"*[17] those of Christ Himself to Nicodemus: *"Even so must the Son of Man be lifted up, that those who believe in him . . . may have life everlasting,"*[18] to His disciples: *"But I have a baptism to be baptized with; and how distressed I am until it is accomplished,"*[19] and the words especially which He spoke at the Last Supper and on Calvary, all show that the core of our divine Lord's life and thought was the Cross and the offering of Himself to the Father in order to reconcile men to God and to save them.

578   But is not He who offers sacrifice somehow greater than the sacrifice itself? So now we would like to speak to you about the Lord Himself, and first of all to call your attention to the fact that in the Eucharist the Church possesses the Lord, flesh and blood, body and soul and divinity. This is solemnly defined by the Council of Trent, in its thirteenth Session, canon 1. It suffices, moreover, to take the words pronounced by Jesus in their clear, literal, unambiguous meaning to arrive at the same conclusion: "Take and eat. This is my Body, which shall be given for you. Take and drink, this is my Blood, which shall be shed for you." And St. Paul uses the same clear and simple words in his first letter to Corinthians.[20]

579   On this subject there is neither doubt nor divergence of opinion among Catholics. But as soon as speculative theology

begins to discuss the manner in which Christ is present in the Eucharist, serious differences of opinion rise on a number of points. We do not wish to go into these speculative con- troversies. We would like, however, to point out certain limits and insist on a fundamental principle of interpretation whose neglect causes Us some anxiety.

Speculation must take as its norm that the literal meaning   580 of scriptural texts, the faith and teaching of the Church, take precedence over a scientific system and theoretical consider- ations. Science must conform to revelation, not revelation to science. When a philosophical concept distorts the genuine meaning of a revealed truth, it is either inaccurate or is being applied incorrectly.

This principle finds application in the doctrine of the real   581 presence. Certain theologians, though they accept the Coun- cil's teaching on the real presence and on transubstantiation, interpret the words of Christ and those of the Council in such a way that nothing more remains of the presence of Christ than a sort of envelope empty of its natural content.

In their opinion, what the species of bread and wine sub-   582 stantially and actually contain is "the Lord in heaven," with Whom the species have a so-called real and substantial relation of content and presence. Such a speculative interpretation raises serious objections when presented as one fully ade- quate, since the Christian sense of the faithful, the constant catechetical teaching of the Church, the terms of the Coun- cil, and above all the words of our Lord require that the Eucharist contain the Lord Himself.

The sacramental species are not the Lord, even if they   583 have a so-called essential relation of container and presence contained with the substance of the heavenly Christ. The Lord said: "This is my Body! This is my Blood!" He did not say, "This is something apparent to the senses which signifies the presence of My Body and Blood."

No doubt He could effect that those perceptible signs of a   584 true relation of presence should also be perceptible and efficacious signs of sacramental grace; but there is question here of the essential content of the "eucharistic species," not of their sacramental efficacy. Therefore it cannot be admitted that the theory We have just described gives full satisfaction to the words of Christ; that the presence of Christ in the Eucharist means nothing more; or that this theory is adequate to enable us to say in all truth of the Eucharist: "It is the Lord."[21]

585   Undoubtedly, the majority of the faithful is unable to grasp the difficult speculative problems and the attempts to explain the nature of Christ's presence. The Roman Catechism, moreover, advises against discussing such questions before the faithful,[22] but it neither mentions nor proposes the theory outlined above. Still less does it affirm that such a theory exhausts the meaning of Christ's words and gives them a full explanation. One can still search for scientific explanations and interpretations, but they must not, so to speak, drive Christ from the Eucharist and leave in the tabernacle only a Eucharistic species retaining a so-called real and essential relation with the true Lord Who is in heaven.

586   It is surprising that those who are not satisfied with the theory We have just described should be listed as adversaries, among the non-scientific "physicists," or that there is no hesitation in saying, with regard to the so-called scientific conception of Christ's presence: "This truth is not for the masses."

587   To these consideraions We must add some remarks concerning the tabernacle. Just as We said above: "The Lord is somehow greater than the altar and the sacrifice," so now We might say: "Is the tabernacle, where dwells the Lord Who has come down amongst His people, greater than altar and sacrifice?" The altar is more important than the tabernacle, because on it is offered the Lord's sacrifice. No doubt the tabernacle holds the *"Sacramentum permanens"*; but it is not an *"altare permanens,"* for the Lord offers Himself in sacrifice only on the altar during the celebration of Holy Mass, not after or outside the Mass.

588   In the tabernacle, on the other hand, He is present as long as the consecrated species last, yet is not making a permanent sacrificial offering.

589   One has a perfect right to distinguish between the offering of the sacrifice of the Mass and the *"cultus latreuticus"* offered

to the God-Man hidden in the Eucharist. A decision of the Sacred Congregation of Rites, dated July 7, 1927, severely limits exposition of the Blessed Sacrament during Mass.[23] But this is easily explained by a concern to keep habitually separate the act of sacrifice and the worship of simple adoration, in order that the faithful may clearly understand the characteristics proper to each.

Still, an awareness of their unity is more important than a   590
realization of their differences. It is one and the same Lord Who is immolated on the altar and honored in the tabernacle, and Who pours out His blessings from the tabernacle.

A person who was thoroughly convinced of this would   591
avoid many difficulties. He would be wary of exaggerating the significance of one to the detriment of the other, and of opposing decisions of the Holy See.

The Council of Trent has explained the disposition of soul   592
required concerning the Blessed Sacrament: *"If anyone says that Christ, the only-begotten Son of God, is not to be adored in the holy sacrament of the Eucharist with the worship of latria, including the external worship, and that the sacrament, therefore, is not to be honored with extraordinary festive celebrations nor solemnly carried from place to place in processions according to the praiseworthy universal rite and custom of the holy Church; or that the sacrament is not to be publicly exposed for the people's adoration, and that those who adore it are idolators: let him be anathema."*[24]

*"If anyone says that it is not permissible to keep the sacred   593
Eucharist in a holy place, but that it must necessarily be distributed immediately after the consecration to those who are present; or that it is not permissible to carry the Eucharist respectfully to the sick: let him be anathema."*[25]

He who clings wholeheartedly to this teaching has no   594
thought of formulating objections against the presence of the tabernacle on the altar.

In the instruction of the Holy Office, *"De arte sacra,"* of   595
June 20, 1952,[26] the Holy See insists, among other things, on this point: *"This Supreme Sacred Congregation strictly commands that the prescriptions of Canons 1268, #2, and 1269, #1, be faithfully observed: 'The Most Blessed Eucharist*

should be kept in the most distinguished and honorable place in the church, and hence as a rule at the main altar unless some other be considered more convenient and suitable for the veneration and worship due to so great a Sacrament. . . . The Most Blessed Sacrament must be kept in an immovable tabernacle set in the middle of the altar.' "²⁷

596   There is question, not so much of the material presence of the tabernacle on the altar, as of a tendency to which We should like to call your attention, that of a lessening of esteem for the presence and action of Christ in the tabernacle. The sacrifice of the altar is held sufficient, and the importance of Him who accomplishes it is reduced.

597   Yet the person of our Lord must hold the central place in worship, for it is His person that unifies the relations of the altar and the tabernacle and gives them their meaning.

598   It is through the sacrifice of the altar, first of all, that the Lord becomes present in the Eucharist, and He is in the tabernacle only as a *"memoria sacrificii et passionis suae."*

599   To separate tabernacle from altar is to separate two things which by their origin and their nature should remain united.

600   Specialists will offer various opinions for solving the problem of so placing the tabernacle on the altar as not to impede the celebration of Mass when the priest is facing the congregation. The essential point is to understand that it is the same Lord present on the altar and in the tabernacle.

601   One might also stress the attitude of the Church regarding certain pious practices: visits to the Blessed Sacrament, which she earnestly recommends, the Forty Hours devotion or "perpetual adoration," the holy hour, the solemn carrying of Holy Communion to the sick, processions of the Blessed Sacrament. The most enthusiastic and convinced liturgist must be able to understand and appreciate what our Lord in the tabernacle means to the solidly pious faithful, be they unlearned or educated. He is their counsellor, their consoler, their strength and refuge, their hope in life and in death.

602   Not satisfied simply with letting the faithful come to their Lord in the tabernacle, the liturgical movement, then, will strive to draw them there even more.

3. "Infinita Et Divina Maiestas Christi"

The third and final point We would like to treat is that of   603
the *"infinita et divina Maiestas"* of Christ, which the words
"Christus Deus" express.

Certainly the Incarnate Word is Lord and Savior of men;   604
but He is and remains the Word, the infinite God. In the
Athanasian creed it is said: *"Our Lord Jesus Christ, Son of
God, is God and Man."*

The humanity of Christ has a right also to the worship of   605
"latria" because of its hypostatic union with the Word, but
His divinity is the reason and source of this worship. And so,
the divinity of Christ cannot remain on the outer edge of
liturgical thought.

It is normal to go *"ad Patrem per Christum,"* since Christ   606
is Mediator between God and men. But He is not only Mediator; He is also within the Trinity, equal to the Father and
the Holy Spirit. Let it suffice to recall the magnificent pro-
logue of St. John's Gospel: "The Word was God. . . . All
things were made through him, and without him nothing was
made that has been made."[28] Christ is First and Last, Alpha
and Omega.

At the end of the world, when all enemies shall have been   607
overcome, and last of all, death itself, Christ, the Word sub-
sisting in human nature, will give over the Kingdom to God
His Father, and the Son will subject Himself to Him Who has
subjected all to the Son, so that "God may be all in all."[29]

Meditation on the *"infinita, summa, divina Maiestas"* of   608
Christ can surely contribute to a deeper appreciation of the
litrugy. That is why We wished to call your attention to this
point.

In closing We would like to add two remarks on the   609
"liturgy and the past" and the "liturgy and the present."

The Liturgy and the Past. In liturgical matters, as in many   610
other fields, one must avoid two exaggerated viewpoints concerning the past: blind attachment and utter contempt. The
liturgy contains immutable elements, a sacred content which

transcends time; but changeable, transitory, occasionally even defective, elements are also to be found there.

611 It seems to Us that the present day attitude of liturgical circles toward the past is quite balanced. They seek and study seriously, hold on to what is really worthwhile without, however, falling into excess. Yet here and there erroneous tendencies appear, resistances, enthusiasms or condemnations, whose concrete manifestations you know well, and which We briefly mentioned above.

612 *The Liturgy and the Present.* The liturgy stamps a characteristic mark on the life of the Church, even on the whole religious attitude of the day. Especially noteworthy is the active and conscientious participation of the faithful at liturgical functions.

613 From the Church's side, today's liturgy involves a concern for progress, but also for conservation and defense. It returns to the past, but does not slavishly imitate. It creates new elements in the ceremonies themselves, in using the vernacular, in popular chant and in the building of churches.

614 Yet it would be superfluous to call once more to mind that the Church has grave motives for firmly insisting that in the Latin rite the priest celebrating Mass has an absolute obligation to use Latin, and also, when Gregorian chant accompanies the Holy Sacrifice, that this be done in the Church's tongue.

615 For their part the faithful are careful to respond to the measures taken by the Church, but adopt divergent attitudes: some manifest promptness and enthusiasm, even at times a too lively fervor which provokes the intervention of authority. Others show indifference and even opposition. Thus are laid bare differences of temperament, and preferences for individual piety or for community worship.

616 Present day liturgy interests itself likewise in many special problems. Among these are the relation of liturgy to the religious ideas of the world of today, contemporary culture, social questions, depth psychology.

617 This mere enumeration is enough to show you that the various aspects of today's liturgy not only arouse Our interest, but keep Our vigilance on the alert. We sincerely desire the progress of the liturgical movement, and wish to help it, but

it is also Our duty to forestall whatever might be a source of error or danger.

It is, however, a consolation and joy for Us to know that in these matters We can rely on your help and understanding. 618

May these considerations, along with the labors which occupied your attention these past days, produce abundant fruit and contribute to the attainment of the goal towards which the sacred liturgy is striving. In token of divine blessings, which We beg for you and the souls confided to you, We impart to you from Our heart Our Apostolic Benediction. 619

SACRAM COMMUNIONEM
Motu Proprio of Pope Pius XII
on Further Modifications of the Eucharistic Fast
March 19, 1957

Early in 1953 We promulgated the Apostolic Constitution *Christus Dominus* in order that the faithful could receive Holy Communion frequently and satisfy more easily for precept for hearing Mass on holydays. By this Constitution We mitigated the severity of the Eucharistic fast and gave local ordinaries power to permit, under fixed conditions, the celebration of Mass and reception of Holy Communion in the afternoon.

621   We also defined the period during which one must fast before celebrating Mass or receiving Holy Communion after noon, as three hours preceding celebration or reception, for solid foods, and one hour for non-alcoholic beverages.

622   Inspired by the abundant benefits which resulted from this concession, the Bishops have extended their deepest thanks to Us, and many of them, for the greater good of their flocks, have asked Us in repeated and insistent requests to permit the daily celebration of Mass during the hours after noon. They also ask that We prescribe this same period of time for the fast when Mass is celebrated, or Holy Communion received, before noon.

623   Out of consideration for the notable changes which have occurred in working and office hours, and in social life generally, We have decided to fulfill the earnest requests of the Hierarchy, and therefore decree:

1. Local Ordinaries, except for Vicars General without special mandate, are empowered to permit the daily celebration of Mass after noon if the spiritual good of a considerable number of the faithful demands it.   624

2. The period for observing the Eucharistic fast by priests before Mass and by the faithful before Holy Communion—whether before or after noon—is reduced to three hours from solid food and alcoholic beverages, but to one hour from non-alcoholic beverages. The fast is not broken by drinking water.   625

3. Those who celebrate Mass or receive Holy Communion at midnight or in the very early hours of the morning are bound to observe the Eucharistic fast according to the rules laid down above.   626

4. The sick, even though they are not confined to bed, can consume non-alcoholic beverages and real and appropriate medicines, whether liquids or solids, before celebrating Mass or receiving Holy Communion, without any restriction of time.   627

But We earnestly exhort priests and faithful who are able to do so, to preserve the venerable and ancient form of Eucharistic fast before Mass or Holy Communion.   628

Finally, all who enjoy these concessions are to endeavor seriously to compensate for the benefits received by becoming illustrious examples of the Christian life, especially by works of penance and charity.   629

The instructions contained in this Apostolic Letter, issued *motu proprio,* shall take effect from the twenty-fifth day of March, the feast of the Annunciation of the Blessed Virgin Mary.   630

Anything to the contrary notwithstanding, even though worthy of special mention.   631

Given at Rome, in St. Peter's, on the 19th day of March, on the feast of St. Joseph, Patron of the universal Church, in the year 1957, the 19th of Our Pontificate.   632

Sacred Congregation of Rites
Instruction on Sacred Music and Sacred Liturgy
September 3, 1958

Three important documents on sacred music have been published in recent times by the Supreme Pontiffs. They are: the Motu Proprio, *Tra le sollecitudini,* of St. Pius X, November 22, 1903; the Apostolic Constitution of Pope Pius XI of happy memory, *Divini cultus,* December 20, 1928; and finally the Encyclical, *Musicae sacrae disciplina,* December 25, 1955, of the Supreme Pontiff Pius XII, happily reigning. There have also been other briefer papal documents and various decrees of this Sacred Congregation of Rites pertaining to sacred music.

634   Everyone is aware that sacred music and the sacred liturgy are by their nature so closely linked that laws and norms cannot be given for one without regard for the other. As a matter of fact, there is material common to both sacred music and the sacred liturgy in the papal documents and decrees of the Sacred Congregation which were mentioned above.

635   Since the Supreme Pontiff Pius XII issued, before his Encyclical on sacred music, an important Encyclical on the sacred music, an important Encyclical on the sacred liturgy— *Mediator Dei* of November 20, 1947—in which liturgical doctrine and pastoral needs are admirably explained in their relation to one another, it seems opportune that the principal points on sacred liturgy and sacred music and their pastoral efficacy be taken from these aforementioned documents and set down concisely in one special Instruction, so that their

content may be more easily and surely put into practice.

For this purpose, experts on sacred music and members   636
of the Pontifical Commission for the General Renovation of
the Liturgy have undertaken to draw up the present Instruction.

The contents of this Instruction are organized in the fol-   637
lowing manner:

Chapter I—*General Concepts*
Chapter II—*General Norms*
Chapter III—*Special Norms:*

1. Regarding the principal liturgical services in which sacred   638
   music is used:
   A. On the Mass.
      a. Some general principles concerning the participation
         of the faithful (numbers 22-23).
      b. Participation of the faithful in the sung Mass (num-
         bers 24-27).
      c. Participation of the faithful in the low Mass (numbers
         28-34).
      d. The conventual Mass, which is also called Mass in
         choir (numbers 35-37).
      e. Assistance of priests in the Holy Sacrifice of the Mass,
         and what are called "synchoronized" Masses (num-
         bers 38-39).
   B. The Divine Office (numbers 40-46).
   C. Benediction of the Blessed Sacrament (number 47).

2. On the various kinds of sacred music: 639
   A. Sacred polyphony (numbers 48-49).
   B. Modern sacred music (number 50).
   C. Popular religious song (numbers 51-53).
   D. Religious music (numbers 54-55).

3. On books on liturgical chant (numbers 56-59).   640

4. On musical instruments and bells: 641
   A. Some general principles (number 60).
   B. The classic organ and similar instruments (numbers 61-
      67).
   C. Instrumental sacred music (numbers 68-69).

    D. Musical instruments and mechanical devices (numbers 70-73).

    E. The transmission of sacred functions over radio and television (numbers 74-79).

    F. The times when the playing of musical instruments is forbidden (numbers 80-85).

    G. Bells (numbers 86-92).

642   5. On the persons who have the principal roles in sacred music and the sacred liturgy (numbers 93-103).

643   6. On the necessity of fostering sacred music and the sacred liturgy:

    A. On training the clergy and the people in sacred music and the sacred liturgy (numbers 104-112).

    B. On public and private schools for the advancement of sacred music (numbers 113-118).

644   After explaining a few general concepts (Chapter I), there is a statement of general norms on the use of sacred music in the liturgy (Chapter II). With this foundation laid, the entire subject is explained in Chapter III. The separate paragraphs of this chapter establish some of the more important principles from which special norms are then drawn.

Chapter I
General Concepts

645   1. "The sacred Liturgy comprises the whole public worship of the Mystical Body of Jesus Christ, that is, of the Head and of His members" (*Mediator Dei,* November 20, 1947: *Acta Apostolicae Sedis* 39 [1947] 528-529).

646   "Liturgical services" [*actiones liturgicae*] are therefore those sacred actions which have been instituted by Jesus Christ or the Church and are performed in their name by legitimately appointed persons according to liturgical books approved by the Holy See, in order to give due worship to God, the Saints, and the Blessed (cf. can. 1256). Other sacred acts performed inside or outside the church, even if performed by a priest or in his presence, are called "pious exercises" [*pia exercitia*].

2. The Holy Sacrifice of the Mass is an act of public wor- 647
ship offered to God in the name of Christ and the Church,
wherever or in whatever manner it is celebrated. The expression "private Mass" should, then, be avoided.

3. There are two kinds of Masses: the "sung" Mass [*Missa* 648
in cantu] and the "read" Mass [*Missa lecta*].

The Mass is called a "sung Mass" if the priest celebrant 649
actually sings those parts which are to be sung according to
the rubrics. Otherwise it is a "read" Mass.

Furthermore, if a "sung" Mass is celebrated with the as- 650
sistance of sacred ministers, it is called a "solemn" Mass. If
it is celebrated without the sacred ministers it is called a
"Missa cantata."

4. By "sacred music" is meant: *a.* Gregorian chant; *b.* 651
sacred polyphony; *c.* modern sacred music; *d.* sacred organ
music; *e.* popular religious singing; *f* religious music.

5. The "Gregorian chant" used in liturgical functions is 652
the sacred song of the Roman Church and is to be found
for liturgical use in various books approved by the Holy See,
piously and faithfully copied from ancient and venerable tradition or composed in recent times on the pattern of ancient
tradition. Of its nature Gregorian chant does not require the
accompaniment of an organ or other musical instrument.

6. By "sacred polyphony" is meant that measured song 653
which is derived from the motifs of Gregorian chant and performed in several voices without instrumental accompaniment. It began to flourish in the Latin Church in the Middle
Ages. Giovanni Pierluigi da Palestrine (1525-1594), was its
principal exponent in the second half of the 16th century and
today it is promoted by illustrious masters of that art.

7. "Modern sacred music" is music which has many parts, 654
does not exclude instrumental accompaniment, and is composed in accord with the progress of musical art. When this
is intended specifically for liturgical use, it must be pious
and preserve a religious character. On this condition it is accepted in liturgical service.

8. "Sacred organ music" is music composed solely for the 655
organ. Ever since the pipe organ was perfected as a concert
instrument, it has been cultivated by illustrious masters. If

the laws of sacred music are scrupulously observed, organ music can greatly contribute to the beauty of the sacred liturgy.

656   9. "Popular religious song" is that which springs spontaneously from that religious sentiment with which human beings have been endowed by the Creator Himself. For this reason, such song is universal and flourishes among all peoples.

657   Since this song is very suitable for imbuing the private and social life of the faithful with a Christian spirit, it has been cultivated in the Church from very earliest times (Cf. *Eph.* 5:18-20; *Col.* 3:16), and, is recommended today for arousing the piety of the faithful and for giving beauty to pious exercises. Sometimes it can even be permitted in liturgical functions themselves.

658   10. By "religious music" is meant any music which, either because of the intention of the composer or because of the subject and purpose of the composition, is likely to express and arouse pious and religious sentiments and therefore "most helpful to religion" *(Musicae sacrae disciplina: AAS* 48 [1956] 13-14). But, since it is not meant for sacred worship and is expressed in a rather free form, it is not permitted in liturgical services.

Chapter II
General Norms

659   11. This Instruction applies to all the rites of the Latin Church. Therefore, what is said concerning *Gregorian* chant also applies to the liturgical chant, if any, proper to the other Latin rites.

660   The term "sacred music" in this Instruction sometimes refers to "chant *and* the playing of musical instruments" and sometimes only to "the playing of musical instruments," as can be easily understood from the context.

661   Finally, the term "church" ordinarily, applies to any "sacred place," that is to say: a church in the strict sense, or a public, semipublic, or private oratory (Cf. can. 1154, 1161, 1188), unless it is apparent from the context that the expression refers only to a church in the strict sense of the word.

12. Liturgical services must be performed according to the   662
liturgical books approved by the Apostolic See, whether for
the entire Church or for some specific church or religious
family (Cf. can. 1257); pious exercises, however, are performed according to those usages and traditions of places
or communities, which have been approved by competent
ecclesiastical authority (Cf. can. 1259).

It is unlawful to mix liturgical services and pious exer-   663
cises; but if circumstances require, pious exercises may precede or follow liturgical functions.

13. a. Latin is the language of liturgical services, unless   664
the above mentioned liturgical books (either general or
specific ones) explicitly permit another language. Other exceptions will be mentioned further on in this instruction.

b. In sung liturgical services no liturgical text translated   665
verbatim into the vernacular may be sung except by special
permission (Motu Proprio *Tra le sollecitudini,* November 22,
1903: *AAS* 36 [1903-1904] 334; *Decr. auth. S.R.C.* 4121).

c. Special exceptions granted by the Holy See from this   666
law on the exclusive use of Latin in liturgical functions remain in force, but one may not give them a broader interpretation or transfer them to other regions without authorization from the Holy See.

d. In pious exercises, any language may be used which is   667
convenient to the faithful.

14. a. In *sung* Masses, Latin must be used not only by the   668
priest celebrant and the ministers, but also by the choir and
the faithful.

"Yet wherever ancient or immemorial custom permits the   669
singing of popular hymns in the vernacular after the sacred
liturgical words have been sung in Latin at the Eucharistic
Sacrifice (that is, during sung Mass), local Ordinaries may allow the practice to continue, 'if they judge that because of
circumstances of place and persons, such customs cannot
prudently be eliminated.' (can. 5). But the rule forbidding
the chanting of liturgical texts in the vernacular has no exceptions." *(Musicae sacra disciplina: AAS* 48 [1956] 16-17).

b. In a *read* Mass, the priest celebrant, his ministers, and   670
the faithful who participate directly in the liturgical services

with the celebrant must pronounce in a clear voice those parts of the Mass which apply to them and may use only the Latin language.

671   Then, if the faithful wish to add some popular prayers or hymns to this *direct* liturgical participation, according to local custom, this may be done in the vernacular.

672   c. It is strictly forbidden to say aloud the parts of the *Proper, Ordinary and Canon of the Mass* together with the priest celebrant, in Latin or in translation, and this applies both to the faithful and to a commentator, with the exceptions laid down in number 31.

673   It is desirable, however, that in read Masses on Sundays and feastdays, the Gospel and Epistle be read by a lector in the vernacular for the convenience of the faithful. From the Consecration up to the *Pater noster* a sacred silence is proper.

674   15. In sacred processions, described by liturgical books, the language prescribed and accepted by these books should be the one used. In other processions held as pious exercises, however, the language most suited to the faithful may be used.

675   16. *Gregorian chant* is the Roman Church's very own sacred song, and preeminently so. Therefore, not only can it be used in all liturgical actions, but unless there are mitigating circumstances, it is preferable to use it instead of other kinds of sacred music.

676   Accordingly:

677   a. The language of Gregorian chant, insofar as it is a liturgical chant, is solely Latin.

678   b. Those parts of a liturgical service which according to the rubrics must be sung by the priest celebrant and by his ministers, must be sung exclusively in Gregorian chant, as given in the "typical" editions. Accompaniment by any instrument is forbidden.

679   The choir and the people, when they respond according to the rubrics to the chant of the priest and ministers, must also use only Gregorian melodies.

680   c. Finally, at sung Masses in places where particular indults permit the priest celebrant, deacon or subdeacon or lector, after having sung the texts of the Epistle or Lesson and Gospel in Gregorian, to repeat them in the vernacular, this must

be done by reading in a loud and clear voice, without any kind of Gregorian chant, authentic or improvised (cf. n. 96-e).

17. *Sacred polyphony* may be used in all liturgical services, on condition, however, that there is a choir which knows how to perform it artistically. This kind of sacred music is more suitable to the liturgical functions celebrated in greater splendor.   **681**

18. In the same way, *modern sacred music* is permitted in all liturgical services, if it is really in accord with the dignity, seriousness, and sacredness of the liturgy, and if there is a choir capable of performing it artistically.   **682**

19. *Popular religious song* may be freely used in pious exercises; but in liturgical services what has been established in numbers 13-15 must be strictly observed.   **683**

20. *Religious music,* however, must be excluded from all liturgical services. It may, however, be admitted in pious exercises. As regards its performance in sacred places, the rues which will be given in numbers 54 and 55 must be observed.   **684**

21. Everything which the liturgical books require to be sung by the priest and his ministers, or by the choir and people, is an integral part of the sacred liturgy. Hence: **685**

a. It is strictly forbidden to change in any manner the arrangement of the text to be chanted, to alter or omit or improperly repeat words. In sacred polyphony and sacred modern music, the individual words of the text must be clearly and distinctly audible.   **686**

b. For the same reason, unless otherwise established by the rubrics, it is strictly forbidden to omit, wholly or in part, any liturgical text which, should be sung.   **687**

c. However, if there is a reasonable cause (for example, because of an insufficient number of singers, or because of their inexperience in singing, or even because of the length of the function or some piece of music) such that one cannot chant one or another liturgical text as given in the notations of the liturgical books for performance by the choir, only the following is allowed: that these texts be chanted in their entirety on a single note *(recto tono)* or in the manner of the psalms. If desired, organ accompaniment may be used.   **688**

Chapter III

*(Special Norms then follow, giving details as outlined above.)—
Ed.*

689   Given at Rome, from the office of the Sacred Congregation
of Rites, on the feastday of St. Pius X, Sept. 3, 1958.

Gaetano Cardinal Cicognani, *Prefect*
Archbishop Alfonso Carinci, *Secretary*

Motu Proprio of Pope John XXIII
on the New Rubrical Code
July 25, 1960

It has been the constant aim of the Apostolic See, especially since the Council of Trent, to define more accurately and arrange more suitable the body of rubrics by which the Church's public worship is ordered and governed. Thus many things have been emended, changed and added in the course of time. The consequent growth of the system of rubrics has sometimes been unsystematic and detrimental to the original clarity and simplicity of the whole system.

Hence, it is not surprising that our predecessor Pope Pius XII, of happy memory, acceding to the wishes of many of the bishops, should have judged it expedient to reduce the rubrics of the Roman breviary and missal to a simpler form in certain respects. This simplification was enacted by a decree of the Sacred Congregation of Rites dated March 23, 1955.   691

Then, in the following year, 1956, when preparatory studies were being conducted for a general liturgical reform, our predecessor decided to survey the opinions of the bishops on the liturgical improvement of the Roman breviary. After duly weighing the answers of the bishops he judged that it was time to attack the problem of a general and systematic revision of the rubrics of the breviary and missal. This question he referred to the special committee of experts who have been appointed to study the general liturgical reform.   692

693   Then the problem became ours. After we had decided, under the inspiration of God, to convene an ecumenical council, we turned over in our mind what was to be done about this project begun by our predecessor. After mature reflection, we came to the conclusion that the more important principles governing a general liturgical reform should be laid before the members of the hierarchy at the forthcoming ecumenical council, but that the above-mentioned improvement of the rubrics of the breviary and missal should no longer be put off.

694   We ourselves, therefore, *of our own accord [motu proprio]* and with full knowledge, have seen fit to approve by our apostolic authority the body of these rubrics of the Roman breviary and missal prepared by the experts of the Sacred Congregation of Rites and carefully revised by the aforesaid pontifical commission for general liturgical reform. And we decree as follows:

695   1. We command that, beginning on the first day of January of next year, 1961, all those who follow the Roman rite shall observe the new code of rubrics of the Roman breviary and missal arranged under three headings—"General Rubrics," "General Rubrics of the Roman Breviary," and "General Rubrics of the Roman Missal"—to be published shortly by our Sacred Congregation of Rites. As for those who observe some other Latin rite, they are bound to conform as soon as possible both to the new code of rubrics and to the calendar, in all those things which are not strictly proper to their own rite.

696   2. On the same day, January 1, 1961, the "General Rubrics" of the Roman breviary and missal, as well as the "Additions and Variations" to the rubrics of the Roman breviary and missal according to the bull *Divino afflatu* of our predecessor St. Pius X, which have hitherto been prefixed to these books, shall become inoperative. As the provisions of the decree, *The Reduction of the Rubrics to a Simpler Form,* dated March 23, 1955, have been incorporated into this new edition of the rubrics, this general decree of the Sacred Congregation of Rites shall likewise become inoperative. Finally, any decrees and replies on doubtful points issued by the same

Congregation which do not agree with this new form of the rubrics shall be abrogated.

3. Likewise, statutes, priveleges, indults and customs of   697
any kind whatsoever, including those that are centenary and immemorial, even if they are worthy of special and individual mention, shall be revoked if they are opposed to these rubrics.

4. The publishers of liturgical books who are duly approved   698
by the Holy See may prepare new editions of the Roman breviary and missal arranged according to the new code of rubrics. In order to insure the necessary uniformity of the new editions, however, the Sacred Congregation of Rites shall issue special instructions.

5. In the new editions of the Roman breviary or missal, the   699
texts of the rubrics mentioned in no. 2 above shall be omitted, and the texts of the new rubrics put in their place. That is, the "General Rubrics" and the "General Rubrics of the Roman Breviary" shall be prefixed to the breviary; and similarly, the "General Rubrics" and the "General Rubrics of the Roman Missal" shall be prefixed to the missal.

6. Finally, all those whose responsibility it is, shall see to it   700
as soon as possible that the special calendars and propers, whether diocesan or religious, conform to the principles and ideals of the new edition of the rubrics and of the calendar. These calendars and propers are subject to the approval of the Sacred Congregation of Rites.

Having firmly established these points, we consider it   701
fitting to our apostolic office to add some advice.

The fact is that this new arrangement of the rubrics has   702
two effects. On the one hand, the whole structure of the rubrics of the Roman breviary and missal is reduced to a better form, distributed in a clearer order and brought together into a single text. On the other hand, some special modifications have also been introduced, by which the divine office is somewhat shortened. This shortening was petitioned by very many of the bishops, in view especially of the constantly increasing burden of pastoral cares laid upon many priests. In a fatherly spirit we urge these and all who are bound to the recitation of the divine office to make up for any shortening of that office by greater attentiveness and

devotion. Moreover, since the reading of the fathers of the Church is sometimes cut down to a certain extent, we earnestly exhort all the clergy to be sure to have at hand for reading and meditation the works of the fathers, which are so full of wisdom and piety.

703   Now let those things which we have decreed and established by this letter, given of our own accord, be considered as ratified and confirmed, anything to the contrary notwithstanding, including that which is worthy of special and individual mention.

704   Given at Rome, at St. Peter's, on the twenty-fifth day of July, in the year 1960, the second of our pontificate.

Address of Pope John XXIII
to a Gathering of Young Choristers
January 1, 1961

Dear children! Welcome today to the Vatican Basilica! See how your lively, cheerful presence today has transformed and brought to life these vast precincts, which were made primarily to gather together crowds and to allow united prayer and acclaim of the glory of God to spring from the hearts of a whole people. Four thousand children from many different countries! An incomparable sight! It stirs us to the very bottom of our heart and we are sure that the priests and the faithful around you share our feelings.

The first thing that we experience at the sight of you is the purest spiritual joy. This joy has its source in the holy liturgy that is unfolding before the eyes of everyone here and that goes deep into the innermost fibers of the being of each of us, the priest who is its minister and the believers who share in it. 706

Your wonderful role as "little singers" gives you a very close connection with the splendors of this liturgy, dear children. And so you ought to be even more familiar with it than other Christians. It is first of all, as you know, a prayer: the official prayer of the Church, the liturgy. As soon as you mention prayer, you are talking about communication with God, homage paid to his infinite majesty, the trust of a child who runs to his Father in heaven to praise him, to beg his pardon, to bless him, to thank him, to plead for what he needs. There are different levels and degrees in this elevation 707 of the soul. The soul starts out by answering an inner urge inviting it to pray; then, little by little, it goes deeper and deeper into the mysterious and sacred meaning that underlies our obligation to offer up prayer in all its forms, from individual and private prayer on up to public, collective prayer and its supreme expression: the holy Mass.

708   Dear children, you have the great joy of assisting at holy Mass very often and of adding to its external beauty by your singing, so please allow us to tell you that this participation of the Christian people in the most solemn act of the whole liturgy is one of our constant preoccupations. It is true that private devotions deserve respect and have their value; but nothing should hold a higher place in the esteem of a Christian than the holy sacrifice of the Mass.

709   How we would like to see priests and the faithful always be careful about preparing for this divine action and carrying it out perfectly! An altar with nothing missing, where everything is just as it should be; servers who are well-trained, devout and attentive; a few words from the priest that are short but to the point, well-adapted to the audience, listened to with the attention and respect that the word of God deserves; active participation, through dialogue and chant, yet with that discretion which leaves room for personal, silent prayer; finally and above all, holy communion, as frequently as possible, to make participation in the sacrifice really complete.

710   These are the things that bring the soul its truest and purest joy during its stay here on earth. And the foundation on which the dignity of a Christian rests, the point from which his activity radiates out upon his brothers is divine worship, with its most sublime expression in turn being the holy Mass.

711   Well, dear children, there you have the main thing that we wanted to say to you, to you and to all those who have come with you this morning to assist at the Pope's Mass.

712   But your presence here today, on January 1, stirs up still another feeling in our soul: one of hope, of a well-founded hope.

713   Of course, it is true that the year that is beginning is the civil year, not the liturgical one. But it is a day that strikes a

Christian note as well; it brings us all together around the crib of the divine Infant who has just been born. Beneath his gaze, we exchange wishes and look forward to all the good that the year just opening may contain: fresh beginnings always fill the heart with hope.

And you too—you are a beginning, you are a dawn that   714
promises life. Those pure and innocent eyes that are turned toward the altar bear in them the reflection of God's plan for each of you: you are the future heads of families, some of you the future priests of the Lord, all of you future witnesses to Jesus in the world of tomorrow, the guardians and defenders of our great and unique treasure, the faith! The heart of your Father is deeply touched at this thought and we would like to sweep all of you in our arms and offer you to the Lord. Truly a moving and encouraging sight is the one that you offer us this morning: the joyous dawn of generations to come, a harbinger of life and consolation for holy Church!

Finally, as a pledge of this great hope that you represent,   715
as the fruit and the spiritual culmination of this meeting with the Vicar of Jesus Christ, permits us to offer you this resolution: to dare all and to do all for God and for the Church. Really, what can you possibly have to fear if faith is inspiring you and hope dwells in your souls? So here on the occasion of this very solemn meeting, have the courage to promise always to grow in virtue and in grace. Promise it with all the enthusiasm of your youth, following in the footsteps of the children of the Hebrews—*Pueri Hebraeorum*—who acclaimed Jesus with their hosannas on the day he entered Jerusalem. He will hear your child's voices and will bless the generous resolutions you have made in the presence of his Vicar.

And the place to find the strength to live up to your reso-   716
lution will always be the holy altar, where the "memorial of his passion" unfolds, for the greater good of our souls: *the mind is filled with grace and a pledge of future glory is given to us*, as the Church reminds us and as you yourselves sang so well just a while ago. With a gift like this, what more could we ask of the Lord Jesus? The *Pueri Cantores* of today stand close to him in his Eucharist and they will, on the morrow and for all their lives, know how to uncover the secret of

making divine joy sing in their souls, of keeping alive there a source of holy joy and a spiritual vigor that will never flag.

717   Dear children and young people here in St. Peter's today! God bless you. And may your lives always reflect what is expressed so eloquently in the innocence of your eyes, the sweetness of your voice, the dignity of your posture and deportment!

718   Lord Jesus, who became a child for love of us and whom we contemplate these days in the cave of Bethlehem! Permit us to place all these children, the jewels of our Christian families who have come here from all over the world, close to you and alongside of Mary, your Mother and ours, alongside of Joseph, the "just man," and of the good and simple shepherds. We offer you their melodious song, their pure hearts, their warm and stirring resolution to do honor to holy Church and to the wonderful traditions of the peoples whom they represent here. Bless them, Lord, as we ourself bless them in your name. Go with them along the road so filled with promise that is opening before them. May they carry joy and beauty everywhere. May they follow your example and grow in age and grace and wisdom before God and men!

719   We have to end by letting you share in some sad news that has just come and that has caused us deep pain: the sudden death of Joseph Cardinal Wendel, Archbishop of Munich, which occurred last night just after he had presided over a ceremony marking the close of the year in his cathedral.

720   We can recall the wonderful contribution that the Little Singer's made to the success of the great international congress at Munich this past summer. And that is why we invite you to raise one last hymn to God as a tribute and a prayer for the repose of the soul of this great servant of the Church.

Vatican II
SACROSANCTUM CONCILIUM
Constitution on the Sacred Liturgy
December 4, 1963

This sacred council has several aims in view: it desires to impart an ever increasing vigor to the Christian life of the faithful; to adapt more suitably to the needs of our own times those institutions which are subject to change; to foster whatever can promote union among all who believe in Christ; to strengthen whatever can help to call the whole of mankind into the household of the Church. The Council therefore sees particularly cogent reasons for undertaking the reform and promotion of the liturgy.

2. For the liturgy, through which "the work of our redemption is accomplished,"[1] most of all in the divine Sacrifice of the Eucharist, is the supreme means whereby the faithful may express in their lives, and manifest to others, the mystery of Christ and the real nature of the true Church. It is of the essence of the Church that she be both human and divine, visible and yet equipped with invisible elements, eager to act and yet intent on contemplation, present in this world and yet not at home in it; and she is all these things in such wise that in her the human is directed and subordinated to the divine, the visible likewise to the invisible, action to contemplation, and this present world to that city yet to come, which we seek.[2] Hence, while the liturgy daily builds up those who are within into a holy temple in the Lord, into a dwelling place of God in the Spirit,[3] to the mature measure of the fullness of Christ,[4] at the same

time it marvelously strengthens their power to preach Christ, and thus shows forth the Church to those who are outside as a sign lifted up among the nations[5] under which the scattered children of God may be gathered together,[6] until there is one sheepfold and one shepherd.[7]

723   3. Wherefore the sacred Council judges that the following principles concerning the promotion and reform of the liturgy should be called to mind, and that norms for practice should be established.

724   Among these principles and norms there are some which can and should be applied both to the Roman rite and also to all the other rites. The practical norms which follow, however, should be taken as applying only to the Roman rite, except for those which, in the very nature of things, affect other rites as well.

725   4. Lastly, in faithful obedience to tradition, the sacred Council declares that holy Mother Church holds all lawfully acknowledged rites to be of equal right and dignity; that she wishes to preserve them in the future and to foster them in every way. The Council also desires that, where necessary, the rites be revised carefully in the light of sound tradition, and that they be given new vigor to meet the circumstances and needs of modern times.

CHAPTER I

General Principles for the Restoration and Promotion of the Sacred Liturgy

I. The Nature of the Sacred Liturgy and Its Importance in the Church's Life

726   5. God who "wishes all men to be saved and to come to the knowledge of the truth,"[8] "who at sundry times and in divers manners spoke in times past to the fathers by the prophets,"[9] when the fullness of time had come sent His Son, the Word made flesh, anointed by the Holy Spirit, to preach the Gospel to the poor, to heal the contrite of heart,[10] to be a "bodily and spiritual medicine,"[11] the

Mediator between God and man.[12] For His humanity, united with the person of the Word, was the instrument of our salvation. Therefore in Christ "the perfect achievement of our reconciliation came forth, and the fullness of divine worship was given to us."[13]

The wonderful works of God among the people of the Old Testament were but a prelude to the work of Christ the Lord in redeeming mankind and giving perfect glory to God. He achieved His task principally by the paschal mystery of His blessed Passion, Resurrection from the dead, and glorious Ascension, whereby "dying, he destroyed our death and, rising, he restored our life."[14] For it was from the side of Christ as He slept the sleep of death upon the cross that there came forth "the wondrous sacrament of the whole Church."[15]   727

6. Therefore, just as Christ was sent by the Father, so also He sent the apostles, filled with the Holy Spirit. This He did that, by preaching the Gospel to every creature,[16] they might proclaim that the Son of God, by His death and resurrection, had freed us from the power of Satan[17] and from death, and brought us into the kingdom of His Father. His purpose also was that they might accomplish the work of salvation which they were proclaiming, by means of sacrifice and sacraments, around which the entire liturgical life revolves. Thus by baptism men are plunged into the paschal mystery of Christ: they die with Him, are buried with Him, are raised up with Him;[18] they receive the spirit of adoption as sons, " by virtue of which we cry: Abba, Father,"[19] and thus become the true adorers whom the Father seeks.[20] In like manner, as often as they eat the supper of the Lord they proclaim the death of the Lord until He comes.[21] For that reason, on the very day of Pentecost, when the Church appeared before the world, "those who received the word" of Peter "were baptized." And "they continued steadfastly in the teaching of the apostles and in the communion of the breaking of the bread and in the prayers. . . . praising God and being in favor with all the people."[22] From that time onwards the Church has never failed to come together to celebrate the paschal mystery: reading those things "which   728

were in all the scriptures concerning him,"[23] celebrating the Eucharist in which "the victory and triumph of his death are again made present,"[24] and at the same time giving thanks "to God for his unspeakable gift"[25] in Christ Jesus, "to the praise of his glory,"[26] through the power of the Holy Spirit.

729   7. To accomplish so great a work, Christ is always present in His Church, especially in her liturgical celebrations. He is present in the Sacrifice of the Mass, not only in the person of His minister, "the same person now offering, through the ministry of priests, who formerly offered himself on the cross,"[27] but especially under the eucharistic species. By His power He is present in the sacraments, so that when a man baptizes it is really Christ Himself who baptizes.[28] He is present in His word, since it is He Himself who speaks when the holy Scriptures are read in the Church. He is present, lastly, when the Church prays and sings, for He promised: "For where two or three are gathered together for my sake, there am I in the midst of them."[29]

730   Christ indeed always associates the Church with Himself in this great work wherein God is perfectly glorified and men are sanctified. The Church is His beloved Bride who calls upon her Lord, and through Him offers worship to the Eternal Father.

731   Rightly, then, the liturgy is considered as an exercise of the priestly office of Jesus Christ. In the liturgy the sanctification of man is signified by signs perceptible to the senses, and is effected in a way which corresponds with each of these signs; in the liturgy the whole public worship is performed by the Mystical Body of Jesus Christ, that is, by the Head and His members.

732   From this it follows that every liturgical celebration, because it is an action of Christ the Priest and of His Body, which is the Church, is a sacred action surpassing all others; no other action of the Church is equal to it in effectiveness either from the point of view of its basis or in degree.

733   8. In the earthly liturgy we take part in a foretaste of that heavenly liturgy which is celebrated in the holy city of Jerusalem toward which we journey as pilgrims, where Christ is sitting at the right hand of God, as minister of all that is holy

and of the true tabernacle;[30] we sing a hymn to the Lord's glory with all the warriors of the heavenly army; venerating the memory of the saints, we hope for some part and fellowship with them; we eagerly await the Saviour, our Lord Jesus Christ, until He, our life, shall appear and we too will appear with Him in glory.[31]

9. The sacred liturgy does not exhaust the entire activity   734
of the Church. Before men can come to the liturgy they must be called to faith and to conversion: "How then are they to call upon him in whom they have not believed? But how are they to believe him whom they have not heard? And how are they to hear, if no one preaches? And how are men to preach unless they be sent?"[32]

Therefore the Church announces the good tidings of salva-   735
tion to those who do not believe, so that all men may know the true God and Jesus Christ whom He has sent, and may be converted from their ways, doing penance.[33] To believers also the Church must ever preach faith and penance; she must prepare them for the sacraments, teach them to observe all that Christ has commanded,[34] and invite them to all the works of charity, piety, and the apostolate. For all these works make it clear that Christ's faithful, though not of this world, are to be the light of the world and to glorify the Father before men.

10. Nevertheless the liturgy is the high point toward which   736
the activity of the Church is directed; at the same time it is the fount from which all her power flows. For the aim and object of apostolic works is that all who are made sons of God by faith and baptism should come together to praise God in the midst of His Church, to take part in the Sacrifice, and to eat the Lord's supper.

The liturgy in its turn moves the faithful, filled with "the   737
paschal sacraments," to be "one in holiness";[35] it prays that "they may hold fast in their lives to what they have grasped by their faith";[36] the renewal in the Eucharist of the covenant between the Lord and man draws the faithful into the compelling love of Christ and sets them on fire. From the liturgy, therefore, and especially from the Eucharist, as from a fount, grace is poured forth upon us; and the sanctification

of men in Christ and the glorification of God, to which all other activities of the Church are directed as toward their end, is achieved in the most efficacious way possible.

738   11. But in order that the liturgy may be able to produce its full effects, it is necessary that the faithful come to it with proper dispositions, that their minds should be attuned to their voices, and that they should co-operate with divine grace lest they receive it in vain.[37] Pastors of souls must therefore see to it that, when the liturgy is celebrated, something more is achieved than the mere observation of the laws governing valid and licit celebration; it is their duty also to ensure that the faithful take part fully aware of what they are doing, actively engaged in the rite, and enriched by its effects.

739   12. The spiritual life, however, is not limited solely to participation in the liturgy. The Christian is indeed called to pray with his brethren, but he must also enter into his chamber to pray to the Father in secret;[38] yet more, according to the teaching of the Apostle, he should pray without ceasing.[39] We learn from the same Apostle that we must always bear about in our body the mortification of Jesus, so that the life also of Jesus may be made manifest in our bodily frame.[40] This is why we ask the Lord in the Sacrifice of the Mass that, "receiving the offering of the spiritual victim," He may fashion us for Himself "as an eternal gift."[41]

740   13. Popular devotions of the Christian people are to be highly commended, provided they accord with the laws and norms of the Church, above all when they are ordered by the Apostolic See.

741   Devotions proper to individual Churches also have a special dignity when they are undertaken by mandate of the bishops, according to customs or books lawfully approved.

742   But these devotions should be so drawn up that they harmonize with the liturgical seasons, accord with the sacred liturgy, are in some fashion derived from it, and lead the people to it, since, in fact, the liturgy by its very nature far surpasses any of them.

II. The Promotion of Liturgical Instruction
and Active Participation

14. Mother Church earnestly desires that all the faithful 743
should be led to that full, conscious, and active participation
in liturgical celebrations which is demanded by the very
nature of the liturgy. Such participation by the Christian
people as "a chosen race, a royal priesthood, a holy nation,
a purchased people,"[42] is their right and duty by reason of
their baptism.

In the restoration and promotion of the sacred liturgy, this 744
full and active participation by all the people is the aim to be
considered before all else; for it is the primary and indispensable source from which the faithful are to derive the true
Christian spirit; and therefore pastors of souls must zealously
strive to achieve it, by means of the necessary instruction, in
all their pastoral work.

Yet it would be futile to entertain any hopes of realizing 745
this unless the pastors themselves, in the first place, become
thoroughly imbued with the spirit and power of the liturgy,
and undertake to give instruction about it. A prime need,
therefore, is that attention be directed, first of all, to the
liturgical instruction of the clergy. Wherefore the sacred
Council has decided to enact as follows.

15. Professors who are appointed to teach liturgy in 746
seminaries, religious houses of study, and theological faculties
are to be properly trained for their work in institutes which
specialize in this subject.

16. The study of sacred liturgy is to be ranked among the 747
compulsory and major courses in seminaries and religious
houses of studies; in theological faculties it is to rank among
the principal courses. It is to be taught under its theological,
historical, spiritual, pastoral, and juridical aspects. Moreover,
other professors, while striving to expound the mystery of
Christ and the history of salvation from the angle proper to
each of their own subjects, must nevertheless do so in a way
which will clearly bring out the connection between their

subjects and the liturgy, as also the unity which underlies all priestly training. This consideration is especially important for professors of dogmatic, spiritual, and pastoral theology and for those of Holy Scripture.

748   17. In seminaries and houses of religious, clerics shall be given a liturgical formation in their spiritual life. This should be accomplished through leading them in suitable fashion to understand the sacred rites and to take part in them wholeheartedly through the actual celebration of the mysteries and through other devotions which are imbued with the spirit of the liturgy. In addition they must learn how to observe the liturgical laws, so that life seminaries and houses of religious may be thoroughly influenced by the spirit of the liturgy.

749   18. Priests, both secular and religious, who are already working in the Lord's vineyard are to be helped by every suitable means to understand ever more fully what it is that they are doing when they perform sacred rites; they are to be aided to live the liturgical life and to share it with the faithful entrusted to their care.

750   19. With zeal and patience, pastors of souls must promote the liturgical instruction of the faithful, and also their active participation in the liturgy both internally and externally, taking into account their age and condition, their way of life, and level of religious training. By so doing, pastors will be fulfilling one of the chief duties of a faithful dispenser of the mysteries of God; and in this matter they should lead their flock not only in word but also by example.

751   20. Transmissions of the sacred rites by radio and television shall be done with discretion and dignity, under the leadership and direction of a suitable person appointed for this office by the bishops. This is especially important when the service to be broadcast is the Mass.

III. The Reform of the Sacred Liturgy

752   21. In order that the Christian people may more certainly derive an abundance of graces from the sacred liturgy, Holy Mother Church desires to undertake with great care a general

restoration of the liturgy itself. For the liturgy is made up of immutable elements divinely instituted, and of elements subject to change. These not only may but ought to be changed with the passage of time if they have suffered from the intrusion of anything out of harmony with the inner nature of the liturgy or have become unsuited to it.

In this restoration, both texts and rites should be drawn   753
up so that they express more clearly the holy things which they signify; the Christian people, so far as possible, should be enabled to understand them with ease and to take part in them fully, actively, and as befits a community.

Wherefore the sacred Council establishes the following   754
general norms.

A) General Norms

22. § 1. Regulation of the sacred liturgy depends solely on   755
the authority of the Church, that is, on the Apostolic See and, as laws may determine, on the bishop.

§ 2. In virtue of power conceded by the law, the regulation   756
of the liturgy within certain defined limits belongs also to various kinds of competent territorial bodies of bishops legitimately established.

§ 3. Therefore no other person, even if he be a priest, may   757
add, remove, or change anything in the liturgy on his own authority.

23. That sound tradition may be retained, and yet the way   758
remain open to legitimate progress, a careful investigation is always to be made into each part of the liturgy which is to be revised. This investigation should be theological, historical, and pastoral. Also the general laws governing the structure and meaning of the liturgy must be studied in conjunction with the experience derived from recent liturgical reforms and from the indults conceded to various places. Finally, there must be no innovations unless the good of the Church genuinely and certainly requires them; and care must be taken that any new forms adopted should in some way grow organically from forms already existing.

As far as possible, notable differences between the rites   759
used in adjacent regions must be carefully avoided.

760   24. Sacred Scripture is of the greatest importance in the celebration of the liturgy. For it is from Scripture that lessons are read and explained in the homily, and psalms are sung; the prayers, collects, and liturgical songs are scriptural in their inspiration, and it is from the Scriptures that actions and signs derive their meaning. Thus to achieve the restoration, progress, and adaptation of the sacred liturgy, it is essential to promote that warm and living love for Scripture to which the venerable tradition of both Eastern and Western rites gives testimony.

761   25. The liturgical books are to be revised as soon as possible; experts are to be employed in the task, and bishops are to be consulted from various parts of the world.

B) Norms Drawn from the Hierarchic and Communal Nature of the Liturgy

762   26. Liturgical services are not private functions, but are celebrations of the Church, which is the "sacrament of unity," namely, the holy people united and ordered under the bishops.[43]

763   Therefore liturgical services pertain to the whole Body of the Church; they manifest it and have effects upon it; but they concern the individual members of the Church in different ways, according to their differing rank, office, and actual participation.

764   27. It is to be stressed that whenever rites, according to their specific nature, make provision for communal celebration involving the presence and active participation of the faithful, this way of celebrating them is to be preferred, so far as possible, to a celebration that is individual and quasi-private.

765   This principle applies with special force to the celebration of Mass and the administration of the sacraments, while granting that every Mass has of itself a public and social nature.

766   28. In liturgical celebrations each person, minister or layman, who has an office to perform, should do all of, but only, those parts which pertain to his office by the nature of the rite and the norms of liturgy.

29. Servers, lectors, commentators, and members of the   767
choir also exercise a genuine liturgical function. They ought,
therefore, to discharge their office with the sincere piety and
decorum demanded by so exalted a ministry and rightly
expected of them by God's people.

Consequently they must all be deeply imbued with the   768
spirit of the liturgy, each in his own measure, and they must
be trained to perform their functions in a correct and orderly
manner.

30. To promote active participation, the people should be   769
encouraged to take part by means of verbal expression of
praise, responses, the singing of psalms, antiphons, and songs,
as well as by actions, gestures, and bodily attitudes. And at
the proper times all should observe a reverent silence.

31. The revision of the liturgical books must carefully   770
attend to the provision of rubrics also for the people's
parts.

32. The liturgy makes distinctions between persons accord-   771
ing to their liturgical function and sacred Orders, and there
are liturgical laws providing for due honors to be given to
civil authorities. Apart from these instances, no special
honors are to be paid in the liturgy to any private persons or
classes of persons, either in the ceremonies or by external
display.

C) Norms Based Upon the Didactic and Pastoral Nature of the Liturgy

33. Although the sacred liturgy is above all things the wor- 772
ship of the divine Majesty, it likewise contains much instruction for the faithful.[44] For in the liturgy God speaks to
His people and Christ is still proclaiming His Gospel. And the
people reply to God both by song and prayer.

Moreover, the prayers addressed to God by the priest who   773
presides over the assembly in the place of Christ are said in
the name of the entire holy people and of all present. And
the visible signs used by the liturgy to signify invisible divine
things have been chosen by Christ or the Church. Thus not
only when things are read which "have been written for our

instruction,"[45] but also when the Church prays or sings or acts, the faith of those taking part is nourished and their minds are raised to God, so that they may offer Him their reasonable homage and more abundantly receive His grace.

774   Wherefore, in the revision of the liturgy, the following general norms should be observed.

775   34. The rites should be distinguished by a noble simplicity; they should be short, clear, and unencumbered by useless repetitions; they should be accommodated to the minds of the people, and normally should not require much explanation.

776   35. That the intimate connection between words and rites may be apparent in the liturgy:

777   1) In sacred celebrations there is to be more reading from Holy Scripture, and it is to be more varied and suitable.

778   2) Because the sermon is part of the liturgical service, a suitable place is to be assigned to it as far as the nature of the rite will allow, and this is to be indicated in the rubrics; the ministry of preaching is to be carried out with exactitude and fidelity. The sermon, moreover, should draw its content mainly from scriptural and liturgical sources, and its character should be that of a proclamation of God's wonderful works in the history of salvation, the mystery of Christ, ever made present and active within us, especially in the celebration of the liturgy.

779   3) Instruction which is more explicitly liturgical should also be given in a variety of ways; if necessary, provision should be made for short directives to be spoken by the priest or proper minister within the rites themselves. But they should occur only at the more suitable moments, and be in prescribed or similar words.

780   4) Bible services should be encouraged, especially on the vigils of the more solemn feasts, in some weekdays in Advent and Lent, and on Sundays and feast days. They are particularly to be commended in places where no priest is available; when this is so, a deacon or some other person authorized by the bishop should preside over the celebration.

781   36. §1. Particular law remaining in force, the use of the Latin language is to be preserved in the Latin rites.

§2. But since the use of the mother tongue, whether in   782
the Mass, the administration of the sacraments, or other
parts of the liturgy, frequently may be of great advantage to
the people, the limits of its employment may be extended.
This will apply in the first place to the readings and directives, and to some of the prayers and chants, according to the
regulations on this matter to be laid down separately in subsequent chapters.

§3. These norms being observed, it is for the competent   783
territorial ecclesiastical authority mentioned in Art. 22,
§2, to decide whether, and to what extent, the vernacular
language is to be used; their decrees are to be approved, that
is, confirmed, by the Apostolic See. And, whenever it seems
to be called for, this authority is to consult with bishops of
neighboring regions which have the same language.

§4. Translations from the Latin Text into the mother   784
tongue intended for use in the liturgy must be approved by
the competent territorial ecclesiastical authority mentioned
above.

D) Norms for Adapting the Liturgy to the Culture and Traditions of Peoples

37. Not even in the liturgy does the Church wish to impose   785
a rigid uniformity in matters which do not involve the faith
or the good of the whole community; rather does she respect
and foster the genius and talents of the various races and
peoples. Anything in these peoples' way of life which is not
indissolubly bound up with superstition and error she studies
with sympathy and, if possible, preserves intact. Sometimes
in fact she admits such things into the liturgy itself, so long
as they harmonize with its true and authentic spirit.

38. Provisions shall also be made, when revising the liturgi- 786
cal books, for legitimate variations and adaptations to different groups, regions, and peoples, especially in mission
lands, provided that the substantial unity of the Roman rite
is preserved; and this should be borne in mind when drawing
up the rites and devising rubrics.

39. Within the limits set by the typical editions of the   787
liturgical books, it shall be for the competent territorial

ecclesiastical authority mentioned in Art. 22, § 2, to specify adaptations, especially in the case of the administration of the sacraments, the sacramentals, processions, liturgical language, sacred music, and the arts, but according to the fundamental norms laid down in this Constitution.

788   40. In some places and circumstances, however, an even more radical adaptation of the liturgy is needed, and this entails greater difficulties. Wherefore:

789   1) The competent territorial ecclesiastical authority mentioned in Art. 22, § 2, must, in this matter, carefully and prudently consider which elements from the traditions and culture of individual peoples might appropriately be admitted into divine worship. Adaptations which are judged to be useful or necessary should then be submitted to the Apostolic See, by whose consent they may be introduced.

790   2) To ensure that adaptations may be made with all the circumspection which they demand, the Apostolic See will grant power to this same territorial ecclesiastical authority to permit and to direct, as the case requires, the necessary preliminary experiments over a determined period of time among certain groups suited for the purpose.

791   3) Because liturgical laws often involve special difficulties with respect to adaptation, particularly in mission lands, men who are experts in these matters must be employed to formulate them.

IV. Promotion of Liturgical Life in Diocese and Parish

792   41. The bishop is to be considered as the high priest of his flock, from whom the life in Christ of his faithful is in some way derived and dependent.

793   Therefore all should hold in great esteem the liturgical life of the diocese centered around the bishop, especially in his cathedral church; they must be convinced that the pre-eminent manifestation of the Church consists in the full active participation of all God's holy people in these liturgical celebrations, especially in one and the same Eucharist, in one

single prayer, at one alter at which the bishop presides, surrounded by his priests and by his ministers.[46]

42. But because it is impossible for the bishop always and   794
everywhere to preside over the whole flock in his Church, he cannot do other than establish lesser groupings of the faithful. Among these, the parishes, set up locally under a pastor who takes the place of the bishop, are the most important: for in some manner they represent the visible Church constituted throughout the world.

And therefore the liturgical life of the parish and its re-   795
lationship to the bishop must be fostered theoretically and practically among the faithful and clergy; efforts also must be made to encourage a sense of community within the parish, above all in the celebration in common of the Sunday Mass.

V. The Promotion of Pastoral Liturgical Action

43. Zeal for the promotion and restoration of the liturgy   796
is rightly held to be a sign of the providential dispositions of God in our time, as a movement of the Holy Spirit in His Church. It is today a distinguishing mark of the Church's life, indeed of the whole tenor of contemporary religious thought and action.

So that this pastoral liturgical action may become even   797
more vigorous in the Church, the sacred Council decrees the following.

44. It is desirable that the competent territorial ecclesi-   798
astical authority mentioned in Art. 22, §2, set up a liturgical commission, to be assisted by experts in liturgical science, sacred music, art, and pastoral practice. So far as possible, the commission should be aided by some kind of Institute for Pastoral Liturgy, consisting of persons who are eminent in these matters, and including laymen as circumstances suggest. Under the direction of the above-mentioned territorial ecclesiastical authority, the commission is to regulate pastoral liturgical action throughout the territory, and to promote studies and necessary experiments whenever there is question of adaptations to be proposed to the Apostolic See.

799   45. For the same reason every diocese is to have a commission on the sacred liturgy under the direction of the bishop, for promoting liturgical activity.

800   Sometimes it may be expedient that several dioceses should form between them one single commission which will be able to promote the liturgy by common consultation.

801   46. Besides the commission on the sacred liturgy, every diocese, as far as possible, should have commissions for sacred music and sacred art.

802   These three commissions must work in closest collaboration; indeed it will often be best to fuse the three of them into one single commission.

CHAPTER II

The Most Sacred Mystery of the Eucharist

803   47. At the Last Supper, on the night when He was betrayed, our Saviour instituted the Eucharistic Sacrifice of His Body and Blood. He did this in order to perpetuate the Sacrifice of the Cross throughout the centuries until He should come again, and so to entrust to His beloved Spouse, the Church, a memorial of His Death and Resurrection: a sacrament of love, a sign of unity, a bond of charity,[47] a paschal banquet in which Christ is eaten, the mind is filled with grace, and a pledge of future glory is given to us.[48]

804   48. The Church, therefore, earnestly desires that Christ's faithful, when present at this mystery of faith, should not be there as strangers or silent spectators; on the contrary, through a good understanding of the rites and prayers they should take part in the sacred action, conscious of what they are doing, with devotion, and actively. They should be instructed by God's word and be nourished at the table of the Lord's Body; they should give thanks to God; by offering the Immaculate Victim, not only through the hands of the priest, but also with him, they should learn also to offer themselves; through Christ the Mediator,[49] they should be

drawn day by day into ever more perfect union with God and with each other, so that finally God may be all in all.

49. For this reason the sacred Council, having in mind those Masses which are celebrated with a large attendance of the faithful, especially on Sundays and holy days of obligation, has made the following decrees in order that the Sacrifice of the Mass, even in the ritual forms of its celebration, may become pastorally efficacious to the fullest degree.   805

50. The rite of the Mass is to be revised in such a way that the intrinsic nature and purpose of its several parts, as well as the connection between them, may be more clearly manifested, and that devout and active participation by the faithful may be more easily achieved.   806

For this purpose the rites are to be simplified, due care being taken to preserve their substance; elements which, with the passage of time, came to be duplicated, or were added with but little advantage, are now to be discarded; other elements which have suffered injury through accidents of history are now to be restored according to the pristine norm of the holy Fathers, to the extent that they may seem useful or necessary.   807

51. The treasures of the Bible are to be opened up more lavishly, so that richer fare may be provided for the faithful at the table of God's word. In this way a more notable portion of the Holy Scriptures will be read to the people in the course of a prescribed number of years.   808

52. By means of the homily the mysteries of the faith and the guiding principles of the Christian life are expounded from the sacred text, during the course of the liturgical year; the homily, therefore, is to be highly esteemed as part of the liturgy itself; in fact, at those Masses which are celebrated with a large attendance of the people on Sundays and holydays of obligation, it should not be omitted except for a serious reason.   809

53. Especially on Sundays and holydays of obligation there is to be restored, after the Gospel and the homily, "the common prayer" or "the prayer of the faithful." By   810

this prayer, in which the people are to take part, intercession will be made for Holy Church, for the civil authorities, for those oppressed by various needs, for all mankind, and for the salvation of the entire world.[50]

811   54. In Masses which are celebrated with the people, a suitable place may be allotted to their mother tongue. This is to apply in the first place to the readings and "the common prayer," but also, as local conditions may warrant, to those parts which pertain to the people, subject to the norms laid down in Art. 36 of this Constitution.

812   Nevertheless steps should be taken so that the faithful may also be able to say or to sing together in Latin those parts of the Ordinary of the Mass which pertain to them.

813   And wherever a more extended use of the mother tongue within the Mass appears desirable, the regulation laid down in Art. 40 of this Constitution is to be observed.

814   55. That more perfect form of participation in the Mass whereby the faithful, after the priest's Communion, receive the Lord's Body from the same Sacrifice, is strongly commended.

815   The dogmatic principles which were laid down by the Council of Trent remaining intact,[51] Communion under both species may be granted when the bishops think fit, not only to clerics and religious, but also to the laity, in cases to be determined by the Apostolic See, as, for instance, to the newly ordained in the Mass of their sacred ordination, to the newly professed in the Mass of their religious profession, and to the newly baptized in the Mass which follows their Baptism.

816   56. The two parts which, in a certain sense, go to make up the Mass, namely, the liturgy of the word and the eucharistic liturgy, are so closely connected with each other that they form but one single act of worship. Accordingly this sacred Synod strongly urges pastors of souls that, when instructing the faithful, they insistently teach them to take their part in the entire Mass, especially on Sundays and holydays of obligation.

817   57. §1. Concelebration, whereby the unity of the priesthood is appropriately manifested, has remained in use to this

day in the Church both in the East and in the West. For this reason it has seemed good to the Council to extend permission for concelebration to the following cases:

1. *a*) on the Thursday of the Lord's Supper, not only at   818
the Mass of the Chrism, but also at the evening Mass;

b) at Masses during councils, bishops' conferences, and   819
synods;

c) at the Mass for the blessing of an abbot.   820

2. Also, with permission of the ordinary, to whom it be-   821
longs to decide whether concelebration is opportune:

a) at conventual Mass, and at the principal Mass in   822
churches when the needs of the faithful do not require that
all the priests available should celebrate individually;

b) at Masses celebrated at any kind of priests' meetings, 823
whether the priests be secular clergy or religious.

§2. 1. The regulation, however, of the discipline of con-   824
celebration in the diocese pertains to the bishop.

2. Nevertheless, each priest shall always retain his right 825
to celebrate Mass individually, though not at the same time
in the same church as a concelebrated Mass, nor on Thursday
of the Lord's Supper.

58. A new rite for concelebration is to be drawn up and   826
inserted into the Pontifical and into the Roman Missal.

CHAPTER III

The Other Sacraments and the Sacramentals

59. The purpose of the sacraments is to sanctify men, to   827
build up the Body of Christ, and finally, to give worship to
God; because they are signs they also instruct. They not only
presuppose faith, but by words and objects they also nourish,
strengthen, and express it; that is why they are called "sacraments of faith." They do indeed impart grace, but, in addition, the very act of celebrating them most effectively disposes the faithful to receive this grace in a fruitful manner,
to worship God duly, and to practice charity.

It is therefore of the highest importance that the faithful 828
should easily understand the sacramental signs, and should

frequent with great eagerness those sacraments which were instituted to nourish the Christian life.

829   60. Holy Mother Church has, moreover, instituted sacramentals. These are sacred signs which bear a resemblance to the sacraments: they signify effects, particularly of a spiritual kind, which are obtained through the Church's intercession. By them men are disposed to receive the chief effect of the sacraments, and various circumstances of life are rendered holy.

830   61. Thus, for well-disposed members of the faithful, the liturgy of the sacraments and sacramentals sanctifies almost every event in their lives; they are given access to the stream of divine grace which flows from the paschal mystery of the Passion, Death, and Resurrection of Christ, the fount from which all sacraments and sacramentals draw their power. There is hardly any proper use of material things which cannot thus be directed toward the sanctification of man and the praise of God.

831   62. With the passage of time, however, there have crept into the rites of the sacraments and sacramentals certain features which have rendered their nature and purpose far from clear to the people of today; hence some changes have become necessary to adapt them to the needs of our own times. For this reason the sacred Council decrees as follows concerning their revision.

832   63. Because the use of the mother tongue in the administration of the sacraments and sacramentals can often be of considerable help to the people, this use is to be extended according to the following norms:

833   *a*) The vernacular language may be used in administering the sacraments and sacramentals, according to the norm of Art. 36.

834   *b*) In harmony with the new edition of the Roman Ritual, particular rituals shall be prepared without delay by the competent territorial ecclesiastical authority mentioned in Art. 22, §2, of this Constitution. These rituals, which are to be adapted, also as regards the language employed, to the needs of the different regions, are to be reviewed by the Apostolic See and then used in the regions for which they

have been prepared. But in drawing up these rituals or particular collections of rites, the instructions prefixed to the individual rites in the Roman Ritual, whether they be pastoral and rubrical or whether they have special social import, shall not be omitted.

64. The catechumenate for adults, comprising several distinct steps, is to be restored and to be taken into use at the discretion of the local ordinary. By this means the time of the catechumenate, which is intended as a period of suitable instruction, may be sanctified by sacred rites to be celebrated at successive intervals of time.   835

65. In mission lands it is found that some of the peoples already make use of initiation rites, aside from those already found in Christian tradition. Elements from these that are capable of being adapted to Christian ritual may be admitted, in accordance with the norms laid down in Art. 37-40 of this Constitution.   836

66. Both of the rites for the baptism of adults are to be revised: not only the simpler rite, but also the more solemn one, which must take into account the restored catechumenate. A special Mass "for the conferring of Baptism" is to be inserted into the Roman Missal.   837

67. The rite for the baptism of infants is to be revised, and it should be adapted to the circumstance that those to be baptized are, in fact, infants. The roles of parents and godparents, and also their duties, should be brought out more clearly in the rite itself.   838

68. The Baptismal rite should contain variants, to be used at the discretion of the local ordinary, for occasions when a very large number are to be baptized together. Moreover, a shorter rite is to be drawn up, especially for mission lands, to be used by catechists, but also by the faithful in general when there is danger of death, and neither priest nor deacon is available.   839

69. In place of the rite called the "order of supplying what was omitted in the baptism of an infant, " a new rite is to be drawn up. This should manifest more fittingly and clearly that the infant, baptized by the short rite, has already been received into the Church.   840

841 And a new rite is to be drawn up for converts who have already been validly baptized; it should indicate that they are now admitted to communion with the Church.

842 70. Except during Eastertide, baptismal water may be blessed within the rite of Baptism itself by an approved shorter formula.

843 71. The rite of Confirmation is to be revised and the intimate connection which this sacrament has with the whole of Christian initiation is to be more clearly set forth; for this reason it is fitting for candidates to renew their baptismal promises just before they are confirmed.

844 Confirmation may be given within the Mass when convenient; when it is given outside the Mass, the rite that is used should be introduce by a formula to be drawn up for this purpose.

845 72. The rite and formulas for the sacraments of Penance are to be revised so that they more clearly express both the nature and effect of the sacrament.

846 73. "Extreme Unction," which may also and more fittingly be called "anointing of the sick," is not a sacrament for those only who are at the point of death. Hence, as soon as any one of the faithful begins to be in danger of death from sickness or old age, the fitting time for him to receive this sacrament has certainly already arrived.

847 74. In addition to the separate rites for the anointing of the sick and for Viaticum, a continuous rite shall be prepared according to which the sick man is anointed after he has made his confession and before he receives Viaticum.

848 75. The number of the anointings is to be adapted to the occasion, and the prayers which belong to the rite of anointing are to be revised so as to correspond with the varying conditions of the sick who receive the sacrament.

849 76. Both the ceremonies and texts of the ordination rites are to be revised. The address given by the bishop at the beginning of each ordination or consecration may be in the mother tongue.

850 When a bishop is consecrated, the laying on of hands may be done by all the bishops present.

77. The marriage rite now found in the Roman Ritual is to   851
be revised and enriched in such a way that the grace of the
sacrament is more clearly signified and the duties of the
spouses are taught.

"If any regions are wont to use other praiseworthy cus-   852
toms and ceremonies when celebrating the sacrament of Matrimony, the sacred Synod earnestly desires that these by all
means be retained."[5][2]

Moreover the competent territorial ecclesiastical authority   853
mentioned in Art.22, § 2, of this Constitution is free to draw
up its own rite suited to the usages of place and people, subject to the provision of Art. 63. But the rite must always conform to the law that the priest assisting at the marriage must
ask for and obtain the consent of the contracting parties.

78. Matrimony is normally to be celebrated within the   854
Mass, after the reading of the Gospel and the homily, and before "the prayer of the faithful." The prayer for the bride,
duly amended to remind both spouses of their equal obligation to remain faithful to each other, may be said in the
mother tongue.

But if the sacrament of Matrimony is celebrated apart   855
from Mass, the Epistle and Gospel from the nuptial Mass are
to be read at the beginning of the rite, and the blessing
should always be given to the spouses.

79. The sacramentals are to undergo a revision which takes   856
into account the primary principle of enabling the faithful
to participate intelligently, actively, and easily; the needs of
our own days must also be considered. When rituals are revised, laid down in Art. 63, new sacramentals may also be
added as the need for these becomes apparent.

Reserved blessings shall be very few; reservations shall be   857
in favor only of bishops or ordinaries.

Let provision be made that some sacramentals, at least in   858
special circumstances and at the discretion of the ordinary,
may be administered by qualified lay persons.

80. The rite for the Consecration of Virgins at present   859
found in the Roman Pontifical is to be revised.

Moreover, a rite of religious profession and renewal of   860
vows shall be drawn up in order to achieve greater unity,

solemnity, and dignity. Apart from exceptions in particular law, this rite should be adopted by those who make their profession or renewal of vows within the Mass.

861   It is a good idea for religious profession to be made within the Mass.

862   81. The rite for the burial of the dead should express more clearly the paschal character of Christian death, and should correspond more closely to the circumstances and traditions found in various regions. The latter holds good also for the liturgical color to be used.

863   82. The rite for the burial of infants is to be revised, and a special Mass for the occasion should be provided.

CHAPTER IV

The Divine Office

864   83. Christ Jesus, High Priest of the New and eternal Covenant, taking human nature, introduced into this earthly exile that hymn which is sung throughout all ages in the halls of heaven. He joins the entire community of mankind to Himself, associating it with Him in singing this canticle of divine praise.

865   For He continues His priestly work through the agency of His Church, which is ceaselessly engaged in praising the Lord and interceding for the salvation of the whole world. She does this, not only by celebrating the Eucharist, but also in other ways, especially by praying the Divine Office.

866   84. By tradition going back to early Christian times, the Divine Office is devised so that the whole course of the day and night is made holy by the praises of God. Therefore, when this wonderful song of praise is rightly performed by priests and others who are deputed for this purpose by the Church's ordinance, or by the faithful praying together with the priest in the approved form, then it is truly the voice of the Bride addressed to her Bridegroom; it is the very prayer which Christ Himself, together with His Body, addresses to the Father.

85. Hence all who render this service are not only ful-   867
filling an office and duty of the Church, but also are sharing
in the greatest honor of Christ's Spouse, for by offering these
praises to God they are Standing before God's throne in the
name of the Church their Mother.

86. Priests who are engaged in the sacred pastoral ministry   868
will offer the praises of the hours with greater fervor the
more vividly they realize that they must heed St. Paul's
exhortation: "Pray without ceasing."[53] For the work in
which they labor will effect nothing and bring forth no fruit
except by the power of the Lord, who said: "Without me
you can do nothing."[54] That is why the apostles, instituting
deacons, said: "But we will devote ourselves to prayer and to
the ministry of the word."[55]

87. In order that the Divine Office may be better and more   869
perfectly prayed in existing circumstances, whether by priests
or by other members of the Church, the sacred Council,
carrying further the restoration already so happily begun by
the Apostolic See, has seen fit to decree as follows concerning the Office of the Roman rite.

88. Because the purpose of the Office is to sanctify the   870
day, the traditional sequence of the hours is to be restored so
that once again they may be genuinely related to the time of
the day when they are prayed, as far as this may be possible.
At the same time, it will be necessary to take into account
the modern conditions in which daily life has to be lived,
especially by those who are engaged in apostolic works.

89. Therefore, when the Office is revised, these norms are   871
to be observed:

a) By the venerable tradition of the universal Church,   872
Lauds as morning prayer and Vespers as evening prayer are
the two hinges on which the daily Office turns; hence they
are to be considered as the chief hours and are to be celebrated as such.

b) Compline is to be drawn up so that it will be a suitable   873
prayer for the end of the day.

c) The hour known as Matins, although it should retain the   874
character of nocturnal praise when celebrated in choir, shall

be adapted so that it may be recited at any hour of the day; it shall be made up of fewer psalms and longer readings.

875   *d*) The hour of Prime is to be suppressed.

876   *e*) In choir the minor hours of Terce, Sext, and None are to be observed. But outside choir it will be lawful to select any one of these three, according to the respective time of the day.

877   90. The Divine Office, because it is the public prayer of the Church, is a source of piety and nourishment for personal prayer. And therefore priests and all others who take part in the Divine Office are earnestly exhorted in the Lord to attune their minds to their voices when praying it. The better to achieve this, let them take steps to improve their understanding of the liturgy and of the Bible, especially of the psalms.

878   In revising the Roman Office, its ancient and venerable treasures are to be so adapted that all those to whom they are handed on may more extensively and easily draw profit from them.

879   91. So that it may really be possible in practice to observe the course of the hours proposed in Art. 89, the psalms are no longer to be distributed throughout one week, but through some longer period of time.

880   The work of revising the Psalter, already happily begun, is to be finished as soon as possible, and is to take into account the style of Christian Latin, the liturgical use of psalms also when sung, and the entire tradition of the Latin Church.

881   92. As regards the readings, the following shall be observed:

882   *a*) Readings from Sacred Scripture shall be arranged so that the riches of God's word may be easily accessible in more abundant measure.

883   *b*) Readings excerpted from the works of the Fathers, doctors, and ecclesiastical writers shall be better selected.

884   *c*) The accounts of martyrdom or the lives of the saints are to accord with the facts of history.

885   93. To whatever extent may seem desirable, the hymns are to be restored to their original form, and whatever smacks of mythology or ill accords with Christian piety is to be removed

or changed. Also, as occasion may arise, let other selections from the treasury of hymns be incorporated.

94. That the day may be truly sanctified, and that the   886
hours themselves may be recited with spiritual advantage, it is best that each of them be prayed at a time which most closely corresponds with its true canonical time.

95. Communities obliged to choral Office are bound to   887
celebrate the Office in choir every day in addition to the conventual Mass. In particular:

a) Orders of canons, of monks and of nuns, and of other   888
religious bound by law or constitutions to choral Office must celebrate the entire Office.

b) Cathedral or collegiate chapters are bound to recite   889
those parts of the Office imposed on them by general or particular law.

c) All members of the above communities who are in major   890
orders or who are solemnly professed, except for lay brothers, are bound to recite individually those canonical hours which they do not pray in choir.

96. Clerics not bound to Office in choir, if they are in major   891
orders, are bound to pray the entire Office every day, either in common or individually, as laid down in Art. 89.

97. Appropriate instances are to be defined by the rubrics   892
in which a liturgical service may be substituted for the Divine Office.

In particular cases, and for a just reason, ordinaries can dispense   893
their subjects wholly or in part from the obligation of reciting the Divine Office, or may commute the obligation.

98. Members of any institute dedicated to acquiring perfection   894
who, according to their constitutions, are to recite any parts of the Divine Office are thereby performing the public prayer of the Church.

They too perform the public prayer of the Church who, in   895
virtue of their constitutions, recite any little Office, provided this is drawn up after the pattern of the Divine Office and is duly approved.

99. Since the Divine Office is the voice of the Church, that   896
is, of the whole Mystical Body publicly praising God, those

clerics who are not obliged to Office in choir, especially priests who live together or who assemble for any purpose, are urged to pray at least some part of the Divine Office in common.

897   All who pray the Divine Office, whether in choir or in common, should fulfill the task entrusted to them as perfectly as possible: this refers not only to the internal devotion of their external manner of celebration.

898   It is, moreover, fitting that the Office, both in choir and in common, be sung when convenient.

899   100. Pastors of souls should see to it that the chief hours, especially Vespers, are celebrated in common in church on Sundays and the more solemn feasts. And the laity, too, are encouraged to recite the Divine Office, either with the priests, or among themselves, or even individually.

900   101. § 1. In accordance with the centuries-old tradition of the Latin rite, the Latin language is to be retained by clerics in the Divine Office. But in individual cases the ordinary has the power of granting the use of a vernacular translation to those clerics for whom the use of Latin constitutes a grace obstacle to their praying the Office properly. The vernacular version, however, must be one that is drawn up according to the provision of Art. 36.

901   § 2. The competent superior has the power to grant the use of the vernacular in the celebration of the Divine Office, even in choir, to nuns and to members of institutes dedicated to acquiring perfection, both men who are not clerics and women. The version, however, must be one that is approved.

902   § 3. Any cleric bound to the Divine Office fulfills his obligation if he prays the Office in the vernacular together with a group of the faithful or with those mentioned in § 2 above, provided that the text of the translation is approved.

CHAPTER V

The Liturgical Year

903   102. Holy Mother Church is conscious that she must celebrate the saving work of her divine Spouse by devoutly recall-

ing it on certain days throughout the course of the year. Every week, on the day which she has called the Lord's day, she keeps the memory of the Lord's Resurrection, which she also celebrates once in the year, together with His blessed Passion, in the most solemn festival of Easter.

Within the cycle of a year, moreover, she unfolds the whole mystery of Christ, from His incarnation and birth through His ascension, the day of Pentecost, and the expectation of blessed hope and of the coming of the Lord. 904

Recalling thus the mysteries of Redemption, the Church opens to the faithful the riches of her Lord's powers and merits, so that these are in some way made present in every age, and the faithful are enabled to lay hold upon them and become filled with saving grace. 905

103. In celebrating this annual cycle of Christ's mysteries, Holy Church honors with special love the Blessed Mary, Mother of God, who is joined by an inseparable bond to the saving work of her Son. In her the Church extols and admires the most excellent fruit of the Redemption, and joyfully contemplates, as in a faultless image, that which she herself desires and hopes wholly to be. 906

104. The Church has also included in the annual cycle days devoted to the memory of the martyrs and the other saints. Raised up to perfection by the manifold grace of God, and already in possession of eternal salvation, they sing God's perfect praise in heaven and offer prayers for us. By celebrating the passage of these saints from earth to heaven the Church proclaims the paschal mystery achieved in the saints who have suffered and been glorified with Christ; she proposes them to the faithful as examples drawing all to the Father through Christ, and through their merits she pleads for God's favors. 907

105. Finally, in the various seasons of the year and according to her traditional discipline, the Church completes the formation of the faithful by means of pious practices for soul and body, by instruction, prayer, and works of penance and of mercy. 908

Accordingly the sacred Council has seen fit to decree as follows. 909

910   106. By a tradition handed down from the apostles which took its origin from the very day of Christ's Resurrection, the Church celebrates the paschal mystery every eighth day; with good reason this, then, bears the name of the Lord's day or Sunday. For on this day Christ's faithful should come together into one place so that, by hearing the word of God and taking part in the Eucharist, they may call to mind the Passion, the Resurrection, and the glorification of the Lord Jesus, and may thank God who "has begotten them again, through the resurrection of Jesus Christ from the dead, unto a living hope."[56] Hence the Lord's day is the original feast day, and it should be proposed to the piety of the faithful ,and taught to them so that it may become in fact a day of joy and of freedom from work. Other celebrations, unless they be truly of greatest importance, shall not have precedence over it since it is the foundation and kernel of the whole liturgical year.

911   107. The liturgical year is to be revised so that the traditional customs and discipline of the sacred seasons shall be preserved or restored in keeping with the conditions of modern times; their specific character is to be retained, so that they duly nourish the piety of the faithful who celebrate the mysteries of Christian redemption, and above all the paschal mystery. If certain adaptations are considered necessary on account of local conditions, they are to be made in accordance with the provisions of Art 39 and 40.

912   108. The minds of the faithful must be directed primarily toward the feasts of the Lord whereby the mysteries of salvation are celebrated in the course of the year. Therefore, the proper of the time shall be given the preference which is its due over the feasts of the saints, so that the entire cycle of the mysteries of salvation may be suitably recalled.

913   109. The season of Lent has a two-fold character: particularly by recalling or preparing for baptism and by penance, it disposes the faithful, who devote themselves more diligently to listening to the word of God and to prayer, to celebrate the paschal mystery. This twofold character is to be brought into greater prominence both in the liturgy and in liturgical catechesis. Hence:

a) More use is to be made of the baptismal features proper   914
to the Lenten liturgy; some of them, which used to flourish
in bygone days, are to be restored as may seem desirable.

b) The same is to apply to the penitential elements. As   915
regards instruction, it is important to impress on the minds
of the faithful not only the social consequences of sin but
also that essence of the virtue of penance which leads to the
detestation of sin as an offence against God; the role of the
Church in penitential practices is not to be passed over, and
the people are to be exhorted to pray for sinners.

110. During Lent penance should not be only internal and   916
individual, but also external and social. The practice of penance should be fostered in ways that are possible in our own
times and in different regions, and according to the circumstances of the faithful; it should be encouraged by the
authorities mentioned in Art. 22.

Nevertheless, let the paschal fast be kept sacred. Let it be   917
celebrated everywhere on Good Friday and, where feasible,
prolonged throughout Holy Saturday, so that the joys of the
Sunday of the Resurrection may be attained with uplifted
and clear mind.

111. The saints have been traditionally honored in the   918
Church and their authentic relics and images held in veneration. For the feasts of the saints proclaim the wonderful
works of Christ in His servants, and display to the faithful
fitting examples for their imitation.

Lest the feasts of the saints should take precedence over   919
the feasts which commemorate the very mysteries of salvation, many of them should be left to be celebrated by a
particular Church or nation or family of religious; only those
should be extended to the universal Church which commemorate saints who are truly of universal importance.

CHAPTER VI

Sacred Music

112. The musical tradition of the universal Church is a   920
treasure of inestimable value that stands out among other

expression of art, especially since, as sacred song united to the words, it forms a necessary or integral part of the solemn liturgy.

921   Holy Scripture, indeed, has bestowed praise upon sacred song,[57] and the same may be said of the Fathers of the Church and of the Roman pontiffs who in recent times, led by St. Pius X, have explained more precisely the ministerial function of sacred music in the service of the Lord.

922   Therefore sacred music is to be considered the more holy in proportion as it is the more closely connected with the liturgical action, whether it adds delight to prayer, fosters unity of minds, or confers greater solemnity upon the sacred rites. But the Church approves all forms of true art having the needed qualities, and admits them into divine worship.

923   Accordingly, the sacred Council, keeping to the norms and precepts of ecclesiastical tradition and discipline, and having regard to the purpose of sacred music, which is the glory of God and the sanctification of the faithful, decrees as follows.

924   113. Liturgical worship is given a more noble form when the divine offices are celebrated solemnly in song, with the assistance of sacred ministers and the active participation of the people.

925   As regards the language to be used, the provisions of Art. 36 are to be observed; the language for the Mass, Art. 54; for the sacraments, Art. 63; for the Divine Office, Art. 101.

926   114. The treasure of sacred music is to be preserved and fostered with great care. Choirs must be diligently promoted, especially in cathedral churches; bishops and other pastors of souls must be at pains to ensure that whenever the sacred action is to be celebrated with song, the whole body of the faithful may be able to contribute that active participation which is rightly theirs, in accordance with Art. 28 and 30.

927   115. Great importance is to be attached to the teaching and practice of music in seminaries, in the novitiates and houses of study of religious of both sexes, and also in other Catholic institutions and schools. To impart this instruction, the teachers who are to be put in charge of the teaching of sacred music are to be carefully trained.

It is desirable also to found higher institutes of sacred   928
music whenever this can be done.

Composers and singers, especially bodys, must also be given   929
a genuine liturgical training.

116. The Church acknowledges Gregorian chant as proper   930
to the Roman liturgy: therefore, other things being equal,
it should be given pride of place in liturgical services.

But other kinds of sacred music, especially polyphony,   931
are by no means excluded from liturgical celebrations, so
long as they accord with the spirit of the liturgical action, as
laid down in Art. 30.

117. The typical edition of the books of Gregorian chant   932
is to be completed; and a more critical edition is to be prepared of those books published since the restoration by St.
Pius X.

It is desirable also than an edition be prepared containing   933
simpler melodies, for use in small churches.

118. Religious singing by the people is to be carefully   934
fostered, so that in devotions and sacred exercises, as also
during liturgical services, the voices of the faithful may ring
out according to the norms and requirements of the rubrics.

119. In certain parts of the world, especially mission lands,   935
there are peoples who have their own musical traditions, and
these play a great part in their religious and social life. For
this reason due importance is to be attached to their music,
and a suitable place is to be given to it, not only in forming
their attitude toward religion, but also in adapting worship
to their native genius, as indicated in Art. 39 and 40.

Therefore, when missionaries are being given training in   936
music, every effort should be made to see that they become
competent in promoting the traditional music of these peoples, both in schools and in sacred services, as far as may be
practicable.

120. In the Latin Church the pipe organ is to be held in   937
high esteem, for it is the traditional musical instrument
which adds a wonderful splendor to the Church's ceremonies
and powerfully lifts up man's mind to God and to higher
things.

938   But other instruments also may be admitted for use in divine worship, with the knowledge and consent of the competent territorial authority, as laid down in Art. 22, § 2, 37, and 40. This may be done, however, only on condition that the instruments are suitable, or can be made suitable, for sacred use, accord with the dignity of the temple, and truly · contribute to the edification of the faithful.

939   121. Composers, imbued with the Christian spirit, should feel that they have a vocation to cultivate sacred music and increase its store of treasures.

940   Let them produce compositions which have the qualities proper to genuine sacred music, not confining themselves to works which can be sung only by large choirs, but providing also works that will meet the needs of small choirs and foster the active participation of the entire assembly of the faithful.

941   The texts intended to be sung must always be in conformity with Catholic doctrine; indeed they should be drawn chiefly from Holy Scripture and from liturgical sources.

CHAPTER VII

Sacred Art and Sacred Furnishings

942   122. Very rightly the fine arts are considered to rank among the noblest activities of man's genius, and this applies especially to religious art and to its highest achievement, which is sacred art. These arts, by their very nature, are oriented toward the infinite beauty of God, which they attempt in some way to portray by the work of human hands; they achieve their purpose of redounding to God's praise and glory in proportion as they are directed the more exclusively to the single aim of turning men's minds devoutly toward God.

943   Holy Mother Church has therefore always been the friend of the fine arts and has ever sought their noble help, with the special aim that all things set apart for use in divine worship should be truly worthy, becoming, and beautiful, signs

and symbols of heavenly things; and for this purpose she has instructed artists. In fact, the Church has, with good reason, always reserved to herself the right to pass judgment upon the arts, deciding which of the works of artists are in accordance with faith, piety, and cherished traditional laws, and thereby fitted for sacred use.

The Church has been particularly careful to see that sacred 944 furnishings should worthily and beautifully serve the dignity of worship, and has admitted changes in materials, style, or ornamentation prompted by the progress of the technical arts with the passage of time.

Wherefore it has pleased the Fathers to issue the following 945 decrees on these matters.

123. The Church has not adopted any particular style of 946 art as her very own; she has admitted styles from every period according to the natural characteristics and circumstances of peoples, and the needs of the various rites. Thus, in the course of the centuries, she has brought into being a treasury of art which must be very carefully preserved. The art of our own days, coming from every race and region, shall also be given free scope in the Church, provided that it serves the sacred buildings and holy rites with due reverence and honor; thereby it is enabled to contribute its own voice to that wonderful chorus of praise in honor of the Catholic faith sung by great men in times gone by.

124. Ordinaries, by the encouragement and favor they 947 show to art which is truly sacred, should strive after noble beauty rather than sumptuous display. This principle is to apply also in the matter of sacred vestments and ornaments.

Let bishops carefully keep out of the house of God and 948 other sacred places those works of artists which are repugnant to faith, morals, and Christian piety, and which offend genuine religious feeling either by depraved forms or by lack of artistic worth, mediocrity, and pretense.

And when churches are to be built, let great care be taken 949 that they be suitable for the celebration of liturgical services and for the active participation of the faithful.

125. The practice of placing sacred images in churches so 950 that they may be venerated by the faithful is to be main-

tained. Nevertheless their number should be moderate and their relative positions should reflect right order. For otherwise they may create surprise among the Christian people and foster devotion that is less correct.

951   126. When passing judgment on works of art, local ordinaries shall give a hearing to the diocesan commission on sacred art and, if needed, also to others who are especially expert, and to the commissions referred to in Art. 44, 45, and 46.

952   Ordinaries must be very careful to see that sacred furnishings and works of value are not disposed of or dispersed; for they are the ornaments of the house of God.

953   127. Bishops should have a special concern for artists, so as to imbue them with the spirit of sacred art and of the sacred liturgy. This they may do in person or through suitable priests who are gifted with a knowledge and love of art.

954   It is also desirable that schools or academies of sacred art should be founded in those areas where it would be useful, so that artists may be trained.

955   All artists who, prompted by their talents, desire to serve God's glory in Holy Church, should ever bear in mind that they are engaged in a kind of sacred imitation of God the Creator, and are concerned with works destined to be used in Catholic worship, to edify the faithful, and to foster their piety and their religious formation.

956   128. Along with the revision of the liturgical books, as laid down in Art. 25, there is to be a revision as soon as possible of the canons and ecclesiastical statutes which govern the provision of material things involved in sacred worship. These laws refer especially to the worthy and well planned construction of sacred buildings, the shape and construction of altars, the nobility, placing, and safety of the eucharistic tabernacle, the dignity and suitability of the baptistery, the proper ordering of sacred images, embellishments, and vestments. Laws which seem less suited to the reformed liturgy are to be brought into harmony with it, or else abolished; and any which are helpful are to be retained if already in use, or introduced where they are lacking.

According to the norm of Art. 22 of this Constitution,   957
the territorial bodies of bishops are empowered to adapt
such things to the needs and customs of their different
regions; this applies especially to the materials and form of
sacred furnishings and vestments.

129. During their philosophical and theological studies,   958
clerics are to be instructed in the history and development of
sacred art, and the sound principles governing the production
of its works. In consequence they will be able to appreciate
and preserve the Church's venerable monuments, and be in
a position to aid, by good advice, artists who are engaged in
producing works of art.

130. It is fitting that the use of pontificals be reserved to   959
those ecclesiastical persons who have episcopal rank or some
particular jurisdiction.

APPENDIX

A Declaration of the Second Ecumenical Council of the Vatican on Revision of the Calendar

The Second Ecumenical Sacred Council of the Vatican, re-   960
cognizing the importance of the wishes expressed by many
concerning the assignment of the feast of Easter to a fixed
Sunday and concerning an unchanging calendar, having carefully considered the effects which could result from the introduction of a new calendar, declares as follows:

1. The sacred Council would not object if the feast of   961
Easter were assigned to a particular Sunday of the Gregorian
Calendar, provided that those whom it may concern, especially
the brethren who are not in communion with the Apostolic
See, give their assent.

2. The sacred Council likewise declares that it does not   962
oppose efforts designed to introduce a perpetual calendar into civil society.

But, among the various systems which are being suggested   963
to stabilize a perpetual calendar and to introduce it into
civil life, the Church has no objection only in the case of
those systems which retain and safeguard a seven-day week

with Sunday, without the introduction of any days outside the week, so that the succession of weeks may be left intact, unless there is question of the most serious reasons. Concerning these the Apostolic See shall judge.

964   In the Name of the Most Holy and Individual Trinity Father and Son and Holy Spirit. The matters which have just been read in this Sacrosanct and Universal Second Council of the Vatican which has legitimately met have met with the approval of the Fathers.

965   And We, by the Apostolic power handed on to Us by Christ, approve them, decree them and establish them, and We command that the things that have thus been decreed by the Council be promulgated for the glory of God.

Motu Proprio of Pope Paul VI
on Certain Prescriptions of
the Constitution *Sacram Liturgiam*
January 25, 1964

I t has always been the great concern of the papacy, of us, and of the bishops of the Church, to preserve, foster and, at need, reform the sacred liturgy. This is evident from numerous acts of public record, but especially from the constitution on this matter which the Second Ecumenical Council of the Vatican approved in solemn session on December 4, 1963, and we ordered promulgated.

This interest derives immediately from the fact that "in the earthly liturgy we take part in a foretaste of that heavenly liturgy which is celebrated in the holy city of Jerusalem toward which we journey as pilgrims, where Christ is sitting at the right hand of God, a minister of the holies and of the true tabernacle; we sing a hymn to the Lord's glory with all the warriors of the heavenly army; venerating the memory of the saints, we hope for some part and fellowship with them; we eagerly await the Savior, our Lord Jesus Christ, until he, our life, shall appear and we too will appear with Him in glory" *(The Constitution on the Sacred Liturgy,* no. 8).

Thus it is that Christians who worship God, the source and exemplar of all holiness, are drawn and even impelled to achieve that holiness by becoming on this earthly journey "seekers of holy Sion" (hymn at lauds, feast of the Dedication of a Church).

It should be immediately evident that for us nothing takes precedence over the necessity of all Christians and especially priests studying the above-mentioned constitution with care, with a view to observing its requirements with complete fidelity once they have come into force. Since in the nature of the case a knowledge and diffusion of the constitution's liturgical prescriptions should be effected immediately, we earnestly exhort the bishops of the several dioceses with the aid of their priests, "dispensers of the divine mysteries" (see *I Cor.* 4:1), to act swiftly in promoting both the liturgical instruction of the faithful and their active participation in the liturgy internally and externally, taking into account their age and condition, their way of life, and standard of religious culture.

970   It is clear that many prescriptions of the constitution cannot be effected within a short space, since the various rites must be revised thoroughly and the liturgical books carefully worked on. So that this task may go forward with the wisdom and courageous balance required, we initiate a special commission the chief obligation of which will be to bring to completion the matters prescribed in the constitution on liturgy.

971   There are certain norms of the constitution, however, which surely can be fulfilled now; therefore we wish them to take effect immediately, lest Christians be deprived any longer of the benefits they may expect in the order of grace.

972   By our apostolic authority and on our own initiative, we decree that from the First Sunday of Lent, February 16, 1964, at the end of the interim prescribed, the following norms should begin to take effect.

973   1. We would have the requirements indicated in nos. 15, 16 and 17, concerning the teaching of liturgy in seminaries, in houses of religious formation, and in theological faculties, studied in the light of curriculum changes now, so that they can be put into effect at the beginning of the next school year.

974   2. It is likewise our decision that, in accordance with nos. 45 and 46, in every diocese there shall be set up a commission, under the direction of the bishop, for promoting the liturgical apostolate.

At times it may be advisable for several dioceses to have   975
one commission in common.

In every diocese two other commissions should be set up;   976
one on sacred music and the other on sacred art.

These three diocesan commissions may be merged into one   977
if necessary.

3. From the date above [February 16, 1964], we would   978
have a homily preached every Sunday and feast day of obligation, in accord with no. 52.

4. We prescribe that that part of no. 71 which allows con-   979
firmation within the eucharistic sacrifice when convenient
shall take immediate effect.

5. As regards no. 78, we point out strongly to all con-   980
cerned that the sacrament of marriage must ordinarily take
place during Mass, after the gospel and homily. When marriage is celebrated apart from the eucharistic sacrifice, we prescribe the following order until a new rite is devised for the
occasion: at the beginning of the ceremony, after a brief exhortation, the epistle and gospel of the nuptial Mass are to
be read in the vernacular; subsequently the nuptial blessing
of the Roman ritual, tit. 8, ch. 3, is to be given.

6. Although the divine office has not yet been revised and   981
restored in accord with the norms of no. 89, we allow from
now onward that those who are not bound by the obligation
of choir may, once this law becomes effective, omit prime
and may choose from among the other little hours, one
that best suits the time of day.

We grant this in complete confidence that the sacred   982
ministers will forfeit none of their piety, but will go about
their priestly tasks full of love for God and united with him
in thought through every hour of the day.

7. Again as regards the office, we prescribe that hence-   983
forward bishops may for just cause and in particular cases dispense their subjects wholly or in part from reciting it, or may
substitute something else for it.

8. Further with respect to the office, we state that mem-   984
bers of any institute dedicated to acquiring perfection who,
according to their constitutions, are to recite any parts of

the divine office or any short office—provided this is drawn up after the pattern of the divine office and is duly approved—are to be considered performing the public prayer of the Church.

985   9. Since according to no. 101 of the constitution those who are obliged to recite the divine office may in various ways be granted the faculty to use translation in their mother tongue instead of Latin, we deem it opportune to specify that the various versions be prepared and approved by the competent territorial ecclesiastical authorities according to the norm of no. 36c and d; and the acts of this authority must be approved or confirmed by the Apostolic See according to the norm of the same article 36c. We prescribe the observance of this practice whenever a liturgical Latin text is translated into the vernacular by the aforesaid legitimate authority.

986   10. Whenever, in the constitution the regulation of the liturgy within the prescribed limits falls under the competence of various legitimately constituted territorial episcopal conferences, we establish that, for now, this term be taken to be understood as national.

987   In addition to the residential bishops, all who are mentioned in canon 292 of the code of canon law may participate in these national conferences with the right to vote; coadjutor and auxiliary bishops; may also be added.

988   In these conferences, two-thirds of the votes taken by secret ballot are required for legitimate passage of the decrees.

989   11. Finally, we wish it to be noted that, beyond what we in this apostolic letter on liturgical matters, have either changed or ordered to be carried out before the established time, the regulation of the sacred liturgy carried out before the established time, the regulation of the sacred liturgy comes solely within the competence of the Church: that is, this Apostolic See and, in accord with the law, the bishop; therefore, no other person, not even if he be a priest, may add or omit or change anything in the liturgy.

We ordain that all we have established by this *motu*   990
proprio letter shall remain firmly in possession, anything to
the contrary notwithstanding.

Given at Rome, at St. Peter's January 25, 1964, the feast   991
of the Conversion of St. Paul the Apostle, in the first year of
our pontificate.

INTER OECUMENICI
Instruction of the Sacred Congregation of Rites
on Putting into Effect the Constitution
on the Sacred Liturgy
September 26, 1964

FORWARD

I. *The nature of this Instruction*

The Constitution on the Sacred Liturgy justly ranks among the first fruits of the Second Ecumenical Vatican Council. Its legislation governs what is noblest in the Church's activity. The amount of good that will come from it will depend on how deeply the clergy and the faithful learn to appreciate its genuine spirit and on their wholeheartedness in putting the Constitution into effect.

993   2. The Commission for implementing the Constitution on the Sacred Liturgy, set up by the reigning Sovereign Pontiff, Paul VI, through his Apostolic Letter, *Sacram Liturgiam*, has already begun its work, which is to put into effect the directives of the Constitution and of the said Apostolic Letter and to make full provision for the correct understanding and fulfillment of these documents.

994   3. It is supremely important, however, that from the outset what these documents lay down shall be applied everywhere correctly, and that any doubts about their interpretation shall be resolved. Hence, by order of the Sovereign Pontiff, this Commission has prepared the present Instruction, defining more clearly the duties of bishops' conferences regarding the Liturgy, explaining more precisely some of the principles stated in general terms in the above-mentioned documents,

and allowing, or in some cases decreeing, that certain matters may be brought into effect even now before the liturgical books are revised.

II. *Some principles to be noted*

4. In deciding what is to be brought into effect even at this stage the intention has been to make the Liturgy reflect ever more perfectly the mind of the Council concerning the active participation of the faithful.   995

Moreover, the general renewal of the sacred Liturgy is much more likely to be welcomed by the faithful if it proceeds gradually, step by step, and if it is presented to them and explained to them by their pastors by means of planned instructions.   996

5. But first it must be clearly understood that the aim of the Second Vatican Council's Constitution on the Sacred Liturgy is not simply to bring about changes in the liturgical forms and texts but rather to give inspiration and encouragement to that instruction of the faithful and that pastoral activity which has the Liturgy for its source and finds in the Liturgy the height of its expression (cf. Const. art. 10). Changes which have so far been introduced as well as those which are to be introduced later into the sacred Liturgy have this as their end and object.   997

6. The value of organizing pastoral activity around the Liturgy lies in this, that it expresses the paschal mystery by actually living it. The paschal mystery is the mystery in which the Son of God became man, accepted an obedience which brought him even to death on the cross, and now, when he is risen from the dead and ascended into heaven, makes it possible for the world to share in his divine life. So it is that men now die to a life of sin, fashion themselves anew according to the model which is Christ, and now no longer live with their own life but with the life of him who died for them and who rose again (*2 Cor.* 5:15).   998

This comes about through faith and through the sacraments of faith, principally baptism (cf. Const. art. 6), and that cycle of feasts which in the course of the year unfold   999

Christ's paschal mystery in the Church (cf. Const. art. 102-107).

1000   7. And so, although the Liturgy does not exhaust the entire activity of the Church (cf. Const. art. 9), it is only right to give some attention to the problem of linking up pastoral work with the sacred Liturgy, and of making pastoral liturgical activity not a thing separate and distinct from other pastoral works, but something intimately united with them.

1001   It is particularly necessary that there should be an intimate connection between the Liturgy and such things as catechizing, religious instruction, and preaching.

III. *The awaited harvest*

1002   8. Bishops, therefore, and all who labour with them in the priesthood should organize the whole of their pastoral mission more and more around the Liturgy. In this way the faithful, sharing fully in the sacred rites, drinking deeply from the source of divine life, will become Christ's leaven and the salt of the earth. They will bear witness to that divine life and be instrumental in transmitting it to others.

Chapter I

Some General Rules

I. *The application of these rules*

1003   9. The practical rules found in the Constitution or in this Instruction, and everything which this Instruction permits or decrees to take effect even before the revision of the liturgical books, apply only to the Roman rite, but, with the proper reservations, they may be applied to other Latin rites also.

1004   10. Everything which this Instruction commits to the competent regional ecclesiastical authority can and must be put into effect only by the lawful decrees of that authority.

1005   In each and every case a clear indication should be given of the date and under what circumstances these decrees are to take effect. A reasonable interval of time should always be allowed for the instruction of the faithful and their training in carrying out the decrees.

II. *The liturgical education of clerics* (Const. art. 15-16, and 18)

11. As regards the liturgical education of clerics: 1006

(*a*) Wherever theological degrees are given there should be 1007 a chair of liturgy so that all students may acquire a proper liturgical training. In seminaries and in religious houses of studies local Ordinaries and major superiors must see to it that a special, well-trained teacher of liturgy is provided soon.

(*b*) In accordance with art. 15 of the Constitution, the 1008 training of teachers to take charge of liturgical studies ought to be begun with as little delay as possible.

(*c*) Institutes of pastoral liturgy for the further liturgical 1009 education of the clergy, those especially already working in the Lord's vineyard, are to be set up as soon as arrangements can be made.

12. In accordance with art. 16 of the Constitution, liturgy 1010 must be taught for a suitable regular period to be indicated by the competent authority in the timetable of studies and according to a teaching-method likely to be effective.

13. Liturgical ceremonies must be performed as perfectly 1011 as possible, i.e.:

(*a*) Rubrics must be carefully observed and the ceremonies 1012 performed with decorum under the careful eye of those in charge and after the necessary practice.

(*b*) Those clerics who are deacons, sub-deacons, acolytes, 1013 or lectors should frequently perform the liturgical duties of their respective orders. Clerics should also learn how to be commentators and cantors.

(*c*) Churches and oratories, sacred furnishings generally, 1014 and sacred vestments must conform to a decent standard of Christian art—and this applies also to modern art forms.

III. *The liturgical formation of the spiritual life of the clergy* (Const. art. 17)

14. In order that clerical students may be trained to take a 1015 full part in liturgical ceremonies, to draw their spiritual life from them and thereafter impart it to others, the Constitu-

tion on the Sacred Liturgy is to be fully implemented in seminaries and religious houses of studies in accordance with the ruling given in the documents of the Holy See. This must be given the full support and cooperation of superiors and teachers. The early stages of a cleric's training in the sacred Liturgy should be through books on the Liturgy, those particularly which deal with its theological and spiritual aspect (and such books should be in plentiful supply in the library), through sermons and meditations which draw their main inspiration from the sacred Scripture and the Liturgy (cf. Const. art. 35, 2), and through the carrying out of those ceremonies which are customary and are part of Christian formation according to the various seasons of the liturgical year.

1016   15. The Holy Eucharist, the centre of the whole spiritual life, is to be celebrated daily, adopting different forms of celebration according to the clerical status of those who take part (cf. Const. art. 19).

1017   On Sundays, however, and on the major feasts, Mass should be sung, and everyone in the house should be present. There should be a homily and, as far as possible, all those who are not priests should receive holy Communion. When need of the faithful does not require priests to say a separate Mass, these will be able to concelebrate, especially on the more solemn feasts, once the new rite has been promulgated.

1018   It is greatly to be desired that, at least on major feastdays, church students should take part in the Eucharist with the bishops in the cathedral church (cf. Const. art. 41).

1019   16. It is especially fitting that clerics, even those not yet bound by obligation to say the divine Office, should recite or sing Lauds in common each morning as a morning prayer, and in the evening, Vespers as an evening prayer, or Compline at the end of the day. The staff too, as far as possible, should take part in this common recitation. Furthermore, the daily time-table must allow clerics in sacred orders sufficient time for the fulfillment of their obligations to say the divine Office.

1020   It is fitting that, at least on major feastdays, church students sing Vespers in the cathedral church, wherever this can be arranged.

17. Devotional practices organized in accordance with the laws or customs of the locality or of the particular institute are to be held in due regard. Care must be taken, however, to ensure that they are in harmony with the sacred Liturgy (see Const. art. 13) and that they take account of the seasons of the liturgical year. **1021**

IV. *The liturgical formation of religious*

18. What is stated in the preceding paragraphs about the liturgical formation of the spiritual life of clerics is also to be applied, with the necessary reservations, to religious, both men and women. **1022**

V. *The liturgical instruction of the faithful*

19. Pastors of souls should strive to carry out, sedulously and patiently, the Constitution's ruling concerning the instruction of the faithful in the Liturgy and their internal and external active participation in it, 'having regard to their age and social standing, their way of life and their standard of religious culture' (Const. art. 19). They must take particular care to secure the liturgical instruction and active participation of those who belong to religious sodalities for the laity. Such people have a duty to share more intimately in the Church's life and to co-operate with their priests in promoting the liturgical life of the parish (cf. Const. art. 42). **1023**

VI. *The competent liturgical authority* (Const. art. 22)

20. The regulation of the sacred Liturgy is a matter for the authority of the Church. No one may proceed on his own initiative. (This reacts only too often to the detriments of the Liturgy and of its development by competent authority.) **1024**

21. It is for the Holy See to revise and approve the general liturgical books, to regulate the sacred Liturgy in matters affecting the universal Church, to give its approval or confirmation to the decrees and decisions of the regional authority, and to receive from the regional authority their proposals and requests. **1025**

1026   22. It is for the bishop to make regulations concerning the Liturgy in his own diocese, in accordance with the letter and the spirit of the Constitution on the Sacred Liturgy, and of the decrees of the Holy See and of the competent regional authority.

1027   23. The various kinds of regional bishops' conferences which, in virtue of art. 22, 2 of the Constitution, having power to make regulations concerning the Liturgy, are to be understood, *for the time being*, to be as follows:

1028   Either (*a*) a conference of all the bishops of a particular nation, in accordance with the Apostolic Letter, *Sacram Liturgiam*, n. X;

or (*b*) a lawfully constituted group of bishops—or of bishops and other local Ordinaries—of several nations;

or (*c*) a conference to be set up with leave from the Holy See of bishops and other local Ordinaries of several countries, especially in the case of those countries where the bishops are so few that it is better for them to form a conference of several different countries having the same language and cultural outlook.

1029   Where special local conditions call for still other arrangements, the matter should be referred to the Holy See.

1030   24. The following are to be summoned to the above-mentioned conferences:

(*a*) residential bishops;

(*b*) abbots and prelates *nullius;*

(*c*) vicars and prefects apostolic;

(*d*) those who have a permanent appointment as administrators apostolic of dioceses;

(*e*) all other local Ordinaries, excepting vicars general.

1031   Co-adjutor and auxiliary bishops may be invited by the president on the simple majority vote of those who have a deliberative voice in the conference.

1032   25. The summoning of the conference, unless other provision is lawfully made in certain localities and in view of special circumstances, is the responsibility of:

(*a*) the respective president, in the case of conferences already lawfully established;

(*b*) in other cases, the archbishop or bishop who lawfully has the right of precedence.

26. The president, with the consensus of the Fathers, decides on the order to be observed in the matters for discussion, and he it is who opens, adjourns, defers, and closes the actual conference.   1033

27. All the persons mentioned in paragraph 24 are entitled to a deliberative vote, not excepting co-adjutor and auxiliary bishops, unless expressly stated otherwise in the deed of convocation.   1034

28. For the lawful passing of decrees, a two-thirds majority is required on a secret ballot.   1035

29. An account of the proceedings of a competent regional authority is to be forwarded to the Holy See for approval or confirmation, and should include the following items: 1036

(*a*) the names of those present at the conference;

(*b*) a report on the matters dealt with;

(*c*) the result of the ballot on each of the decrees.

These 'Acta', prepared in duplicate, should bear the signature of the president and secretary of the conference, together with the appropriate seals, and should be sent to the Commission for implementing the Constitution on the Sacred Liturgy.   1037

30. 'Acta' which include decrees concerning the use and the degree of the vernacular to be admitted in the Liturgy should, in accordance with art. 36, 3 of the Constitution and the Apostolic Letter, *Sacram Liturgiam*, n. IX, contain the following items in addition to those set out in the preceding paragraph: 1038

(*a*) an indication of the individual parts of the Liturgy which it is decided to have said in the vernacular;

(*b*) two copies of the vernacular liturgical texts, one of which will be returned to the bishops of the conference;

(*c*) a short account of the criteria on which the work of translation has been based.

31. The decrees of a regional authority which need the Holy See's approval or confirmation, may not be promulgated and put into effect until the Holy See has given its approval or confirmation.   1039

VII. *The office of individuals in the Liturgy* (Const. art. 28)

1040   32. Those parts which concern the choir and the people, if they are in fact said or sung by them, are not said privately by the celebrant.

1041   33. Neither are the lessons which are read or sung by the competent minister or by a server, recited privately by the celebrant.

VIII. *Special honours not to be paid to private persons* (Const. art. 32)

1042   34. Individual bishops or, if considered desirable, regional and national conferences of bishops must see to it that the ruling of the Council which forbids the giving of special honours to private persons or social classes, whether in the ceremonies or by external display, shall be put into practice in their respective territories.

1043   35. For the rest, let priests in charge of souls in all prudence and charity spare no pains to demonstrate even externally the equality of the faithful particularly in the celebration of Mass and the administration of the sacraments and sacramentals. Moreover, they should avoid anything that would give the impression that their thought is of monetary reward.

IX. *The simplification of certain rites* (Const. art. 34)

1044   36. In order that liturgical actions may evince that noble simplicity which accords better with the present-day mentality:

(*a*) bowing to the choir by the celebrant and ministers is to be restricted to the beginning and the end of the sacred function;

(*b*) the incensation of the clergy (other than those who are bishops) is to be one triple swing of the censer towards each side of the choir;

(*c*) the incensation of the altar is to take place only at the altar at which the liturgical function is being celebrated;

(*d*) kissing of the hands and of things given or received is to be omitted.

X. *Services of the Word of God* (Const. art. 35, 4)

37. In places where there is ro priest and no possibility of   1045
celebrating Mass on Sundays or Holydays of Obligation an
effort should be made, if the bishop thinks fit, to hold a service of the 'Word of God', led by a deacon, or even by a layman deputed to do so.

The service should take much the same shape as the Liturgy   1046
of the Word celebrated at Mass. As a rule, the epistle and
gospel from the day's Mass should be read in the vernacular,
preceded by and interspersed with some singing, especially of
the psalms. If the one who presides is a deacon, he should
give a homily. If he is not a deacon, he should read a homily
indicated by the bishop or parish priest. The rite as a whole
should conclude with 'community prayer'—that is, 'the prayer
of the faithful'—and the Sunday collect.

38. It is fitting that services also of the sacred Word of   1047
God, which are to be encouraged on the vigils of more solemn
feasts, on some of the weekdays of Advent and Lent and on
Sundays and Holydays, should be planned on the model of
the Liturgy of the Word at Mass, although there need only be
one reading from sacred Scripture.

But if there are several lessons a reading from the Old   1048
Testament should generally precede one from the New Testament, and the reading of the holy gospel should be the climax.
In this way the history of salvation will be put into clear perspective.

39. To ensure that these services are dignified and devo-   1049
tional, the liturgical commissions in the various dioceses
should make it part of their business to offer help and advice.

XI. *Translations of liturgical texts into the language of the peo-*
    ple (Const. art. 36, 3)

40. In translating liturgical texts into the language of the   1050
people, it is fitting that the following rules be observed:

(*a*) Translations of liturgical texts are to be made from the
liturgical Latin. Translations of passages from Scripture must
also conform to the liturgical Latin text, although it is always

allowed, in order to make the meaning clearer, to have regard to the original or to another translation.

(*b*) The work of preparing a translation of liturgical texts is to be entrusted especially to the liturgical commission referred to in art. 44 of the Constitution and paragraph 44 of this Instruction, aided where possible by the Institute of Pastoral Liturgy. If there is no such commission, responsibility for the work of translation should be given to two or three bishops who should select a team, laymen not excluded, of those well versed in scripture, in liturgy, in the biblical and Latin languages, in the vernacular language and also in music. If liturgical texts are to be properly translated into the language of the people attention must be paid at one and the same time to a number of factors.

(*c*) Where the occasion demands it, a joint plan concerning translations should be formed with the bishops of neighboring territories.

(*d*) In the case of multi-lingual nations, translations should be made into each of the various languages and submitted to the special examination of the bishops concerned.

(*e*) Attention must be paid to the dignified appearance of the book from which the vernacular liturgical text is read. The very appearance of the book should arouse in the faithful a greater reverence for the word of God and for sacred things generally.

1051   41. In those liturgical functions which happen in some places, with a congregation that speaks a different language from that spoken locally—a gathering of people for example who have come from abroad or of people who are cared for not by a local parish priest but by a priest appointed to care for a language group—the local Ordinary may allow the use of a version in their own language if this translation has been properly approved by the competent authority of a country where their language is spoken.

1052   42. New melodies for the singing of the vernacular parts by the celebrant and ministers are to be approved by the competent regional ecclesiastical authority.

1053   43. Particular liturgical books duly authorized before the promulgation of the Constitution on the Sacred Liturgy and

indults granted up to that time shall retain their validity unless they are contrary to the Constitution, until the partial or
total revision of the Liturgy determines otherwise.

XII. *The liturgical commission within the bishops' conference*
    (Const. art. 44)

44. The liturgical commission to be set up by the regional   1054
authority should be chosen as far as possible from among the
bishops themselves; it should at least consist of one or two
bishops with the addition of a number of priests, well versed
in liturgical and pastoral matters and especially nominated
for this work.

It is desirable for the members of the commission together   1055
with the consultors to meet several times a year and discuss
things.

45. To this commission the regional authority may very   1056
well entrust the following business:

(*a*) the promoting of studies and experiments in accordance
with art. 40, 1 and 40, 2 of the Constitution;

(*b*) the furthering throughout the entire region of projects
designed to foster the Liturgy and the application of the Constitution;

(*c*) the preparation of study-schemes and practical aids
made necessary by the decrees of the full conference of bishops;

(*d*) the task of regulating liturgical-pastoral action in the
entire nation, of supervising the fulfillment of decrees of the
plenary conference, and of reporting on all these matters to
the conference;

(*e*) the organization of frequent meetings and the promotion of joint projects among the societies or groups in the
same region whose interest is in scripture, catechetics, pastoral
problems, music, and sacred art, and indeed with every type
of religious association for the laity.

46. Members of the Institute of Pastoral Liturgy, and any   1057
who by reason of their knowledge and experience may have
been invited to assist the liturgical commission, should be
ready and willing to offer their services also to individual

bishops for the more effective promotion of pastoral-liturgical action in their diocese.

1058   47. The following are the duties of the diocesan liturgical commission, under the direction of the bishop:

(*a*) to be conversant with the state of pastoral-liturgical activity in the diocese;

(*b*) to put into effect the proposals of the competent authority in liturgical matters, and also to keep themselves informed of all that is being said and done in this matter in other countries;

(*c*) to suggest and to promote practical schemes likely to further the liturgical movement especially such as will help priests already working among the people;

(*d*) to help individuals, or even the whole diocese, to draw up a pastoral-liturgical programme, to be completed in stages and with due regard to all the circumstances; where need arises to be able to give the names, and even secure the services of those qualified to help the priests concerned, and also to give advice about the best means of putting the programme into effect;

(*e*) to ensure in a way similar to that indicated for the commission set up within the bishops' conference (para. 45*e*) that the diocesan schemes for the promotion of the Liturgy have the good will and co-operation of other associations.

1059   *Interim directives then follow in this order:*

Chapter II, Eucharist
Chapter III, Other Sacraments and Sacramentals
Chapter IV, The Divine Office.—Ed.

Chapter V

The Proper Construction of Churches and Altars in Order to Facilitate the Active Participation of the Faithful

I. *The lay-out of churches*

1060   90. In building new churches and in repairing or adapting old ones great care must be taken to ensure that they lend themselves to the celebration of divine services as these are meant to be celebrated, and to achieve the active participation of the faithful (cf. Const. art. 124).

II. *The high altar*

91. It is better for the high altar to be constructed away   1061
from the wall so that one can move round it without difficulty, and so that it can be used for a celebration facing the
people. It ought to occupy a central position in the sacred
edifice, thus becoming naturally the focal point of attention
for the whole congregation.

In choosing the material for the construction and decora-   1062
tion of the altar, existing laws are to be observed.

The sanctuary must be large enough to allow plenty of   1063
room for the ceremonies.

III. *Seating for the celebrant and ministers*

92. Taking into account the general shape of each individ-   1064
ual church the seats for the celebrant and for the ministers
are to be so placed as to be easily seen by the congregation.

The celebrant when seated should appear as truly presiding   1065
over the whole gathering.

At the same time, if the seat for the celebrant is behind the   1066
altar all appearance of a throne must be avoided, since that
belongs only to the bishop.

IV. *Side altars*

93. Side altars are to be few in number. As far as the gen-   1067
eral shape of the building allows, they should be placed in
chapels in some way cut off from the main body of the
church.

V. *The ornamentation of altars*

94. The cross and candlesticks normally required to be   1068
placed on the altar for the various liturgical services, may, at
the discretion of the local Ordinary, be placed instead in
close proximity to it.

VI. *The reservation of the Blessed Sacrament*

1069   95. the Blessed Sacrament is to be reserved in a solid, bur-
glar-proof tabernacle in the centre of the high altar or of another altar if this is really outstanding and distinguished.
Where there is a lawful custom, and in particular cases to be
approved by the local Ordinary, the Blessed Sacrament may
be reserved in some other place in the church; but it must be
a very special place, having nobility about it, and it must be
suitably decorated.

1070   It is lawful to celebrate Mass facing the people even if on
the altar there is a small but adequate tabernacle.

VII. *The ambo*

1071   96. There should be, if possible, a pulpit (ambo) or pulpits
for the public reading of the sacred texts. They should be so
arranged that the minister can be clearly seen and heard by
the congregation.

VIII. *The position of the choir and organ*

1072   97. The choir and organ shall be so arranged that it is clear
to all that the singers and the organist form part of the congregation and can indeed fulfill their liturgical function.

IX. *The places of the faithful*

1073   98. The congregation must be accommodated in such a
way as to ensure that they can pay full attention both outwardly and inwardly to all that is happening in the sanctuary.
It is a good thing, as usually is the case, for benches or seats
to be provided for their use; but the custom of reserving seats
for private individuals is to be discontinued forthwith in accordance with art. 32 of the Constitution.

1074   Care too must be taken that the faithful can not only see
the celebrant and ministers, but also hear them. Modern technical aids should be used.

X. *The baptistry*

99. In the construction and furnishing of the baptistry,   1075
careful attention must be paid to making the dignity of the
sacrament of baptism clearly evident. It must be a place
which lends itself on occasion to the more public administration of the sacrament (cf. Const. art. 27).

* * *

The present Instruction, prepared by order of His Holiness   1076
Pope Paul VI by the Commission for implementing the Constitution on the Sacred Liturgy, was presented to His Holiness
by James Cardinal Lercaro, President of the Commission.

The Holy Father, after he had given due consideration to   1077
this Instruction with the assistance of the above-mentioned
Commission and of this Sacred Congregation of Rites, in an
Audience granted to Arcadio Maria Cardinal Larraona, Prefect of the Sacred Congregation of Rites, gave it both in its
entirety and in detail his special approval, confirmed it by his
authority and ordered it to be published and carefully observed by all concerned, as from 7 March 1965, the First
Sunday of Lent.

All things to the contrary notwithstanding.   1078
Rome, 26 September 1964.   1079

U.S. Bishops' Commission
on the Liturgical Apostolate
October 29, 1964

I. *Understanding Liturgical Texts in the Vernacular*

T*he Constitution on the Liturgy,* issued by the Second
Vatican Council, states that it is of the highest importance that the faithful understand the rites because the
sacraments "not only presuppose faith but by words and objects they also nourish, strengthen, and express it;" moreover,
"they do indeed impart grace, but in addition, the very act
of celebrating them most effectively disposes the faithful to
receive this grace in a fruitful manner, to worship God duly,
and to practice charity" (59). Another basic principle taught
by the Constitution is that "Christ is always present in His
Church, especially in her liturgical celebrations." Among the
ways He is present is "in His word, since it is He Himself who
speaks when the Holy Scriptures are read in the Church."
He is present also "when the Church prays and sings, for He
promised: 'Where two or three are gathered together in my
name, there am I in the midst of them'" (7).

1081   The widespread interest in the Council and particularly in
the discussions on vernacular in the liturgy have prepared
the people for changes. Many are filled with hope for a great
advance in meaningful participation by all the people in the
sacred rites. At the same time it is evident or will soon be evident that beyond use of the language which the people understand there must be developed an understanding of the "lan-

guage" of the liturgy in a deeper sense. No one can find the meaning in the allusions to Abraham's bosom or to Jerusalem in the funeral rites unless he knows Abraham as our father and Jerusalem as the place of God's presence with His people, the prefiguring of the Church on earth and in heaven. We all know how necessary is a grasp of Scriptural idiom to understand the Epistles. This is also necessary to appreciate the use of water, oil, bread, and wine, and to know the significance of such phrases as "now and eternal covenant" and "Lamb of God." The simple phrase, "through Christ our Lord," or "through Him and with Him and in Him," expresses a direction in devotion, a union with Christ's worship of the Father that is not yet the spontaneous manner of praying among our people. The same is true of praying the psalms as Christian prayers.

Understanding the liturgy is not merely a matter of vocab-   1082
ulary or of remembering Biblical events. Christ's earthly life followed in large part its Old Testament prefigurings and He established the basic rites of His Church on the basis of meanings already indicated in the Scriptures. He made the inspired psalms and canticles His own prayers. His great act of worship and sacrifice for mankind, "the paschal mystery" (5, 6, 47, 61, 102, 106), was intended as a new Exodus, a passing from this world to the Father, and it took place at the time of the Passover celebration.

Because of the Scriptural basis of liturgical language and   1083
actions, the Constitution on the Liturgy provides for more extensive reading of Scripture in the liturgy and also for the integration of preaching with Scripture. It states that the sermon is part of the liturgical service and that it "should draw its content mainly from scriptural and liturgical sources, and its character should be that of a proclamation of God's wonderful works in the history of salvation, the mystery of Christ, ever made present and active within us, especially in the celebration of the liturgy"(35).

The Constitution also states that Bible services should be   1084
encouraged (35) which include of their nature a sermon on the texts read to the people and said or sung by them. And it states that it is essential to "promote that warm and living

love for Scripture to which the venerable tradition of both eastern and western rites give testimony"(24)—a love which may be possessed by the simplest as well as the most learned members of the Church, as history shows us.

1085   Since, as the Constitution states, it is now a primary pastoral duty to enable the people to take their full internal and external part of the liturgy (14, 19), it is clearly our duty to equip ourselves at once to carry out this task and to begin to carry it out among our people. Providentially, the Scriptural, catechetical, and liturgical renewals of recent decades have already produced an abundance of reading matter, at many levels, which can serve to enrich our basic structure of its rites and prayers and, at the same time, help us to inform our people. A brief bibliography of some basic books which serve both these purposes it included herewith.

1086   But what is most necessary of all is that we begin, if we have not begun already, to meet with Christ as He speaks to us through the liturgical rites and the inspired word of Scripture. This should best start with the use of the primal form of Christian "mental prayer" or "meditation," traditionally known as "lectio divina"—(or, as we might call it in English, "praying the Bible."). This means, very simply, prayerfully "hearing," by slow meditative reading, a Biblical or liturgical passage as Christ's word here and now; asking ourselves, for example, what is He telling us here about Himself, about the Father, about the divine plan for our own salvation and that of our people? How does He ask us to respond to this word of God's love with Him, now in our prayer and also in our life?

1087   Such a form of meditation, especially when the passages chosen are those which the priest is to explain and open out to his people in Sunday Mass, or at a baptism or wedding or funeral, or at a Bible service, will, experience shows, serve to integrate the priest's prayer-life in itself and with his work for his people as "minister of the Word." Any *study* of the liturgical texts and of sacred scripture then serves to enrich and deepen both the priest's own prayer and worship and the sermons in which he opens out God's Word to his people.

The question, obviously, is not one of making Biblical   1088
scholars either of all priests or of the faithful. It is one
simply of restoring that living familiarity with Scripture and,
through it, with Christ, which is our rightful inheritance.

Bibliography   1089

Liturgy and Doctrine, by Charles Davis (New York: Sheed
and Ward), short summary of rediscovered relationship between Scripture, liturgy, doctrine and life.

The Liturgy and the Word of God (Collegeville: Liturgical
Press; paper), a symposium covering all aspects of the subject.

The Psalms as Christian Prayer, by Thomas Worden (New
York: Sheed and Ward), one of the best presentations of the
Scriptural form and basis of Christian piety.

The Family and the Bible, by Mary Reed Newland (New
York: Random House), provides valuable guidelines as to how
to introduce the faithful to the Bible, in its relationship to
the liturgy, to doctrine and to life.

Key to the Psalms, by Mary Perkins Ryan (Note Dame:
Fides), presents key themes, events, figures in the O.T. and
N.T., in reference to the liturgy and Christian living.

The Bible Today (Collegeville: Liturgical Press; magazine).

2. Reading and Praying in the Vernacular

The introduction of the common language into liturgical   1090
rites is an event of numerous and important inplications.
Clearly it was the intention of the Fathers of the Second Vatican Council to provide the people with rites of sacred worship
which would be meaningful and intelligible to them (36, 54,
63, 101, 113). Both those parts of the liturgy which instruct
the faithful and those parts which express their prayer and
devotion are to be spoken or sung in the vernacular language.
This reform in our custom is intended to bring the people into
more effective contact with the sacred scripture and the holy
texts of the liturgy, thereby fostering deeper faith, greater
knowledge, and more sincere prayer.

But these worthy objectives will not automatically be   1091
achieved by the use of the vernacular. Such prayer and read-

ings will have to be done in a more meaningful and appropriate manner than has unfortunately been employed by some priests when reciting Latin texts. To celebrate the liturgy in a manner that is apparently hasty, matter-of-fact, and without attention to the meaning of the words would, of course, be irreverent and improper no matter what the language; however, when the vernacular is used, there is the greatest possibility of scandal. These observations, which must be honestly admitted, are commonly expressed whenever the vernacular is discussed and both clergy and laity are surely anxious not only to avoid the danger but, first of all, to seek the fullest advantages the vernacular can bring. For this reason, the following comments are offered on the manner of speaking the English tongue in liturgical services, in the hope that they might serve as a guide to all. For the purposes of these remarks, there is a basic difference between reading the Word of God and reading other texts.

A. *Reading the Word of God*

1092   All Scripture readings are to be proclamations, not mere recitations. Lectors and priests should approach the public reading of the Bible with full awareness that it is their honored task to render the official proclamation of the revealed Word of God to His assembled holy people. The character of this reading is such that it must convey that special reverence which is due the Sacred Scriptures above all other words.

1093   1. It is of fundamental importance that the reader communicate the fullest meaning of the passage. Without exaggerated emphasis or affectation, he must convey the particular significance of those words, phrases, clauses or sentences which constitute the point being made. Careful phrasing and inflection are necessary to enable the listener to follow every thought and the relationships among them. Patterns of speech must be avoided, and the pattern of thought in the text must be adhered to. The message in all its meaning must be earnestly communicated.

1094   2. The manner of speaking and tone of voice should be clear and firm, never indifferent or uncertain. The reader should not draw attention to himself either by being nervous and awkward or by being obviously conscious of a talent for dramatic reading. It is the message that should be remembered, not the one who reads it. The voice should be reverent without being offensive or overbearing. The pace must be geared to understanding—never hurried, never dragged.

3. By his voice, attitude, and physical bearing, the reader   1095
should convey the dignity and sacredness of the occasion. His role is that of a herald of the Word of God, his function to provide a meaningful encounter with that living Word. Perfection in this mission may not always be achieved, but it must always and seriously be sought.

B. *Praying and Speaking Aloud*

When the celebrant leads the people in prayer, or speaks   1096
to them, or addresses God in their behalf, his manner of speaking will differ somewhat in each case. In every instance, however, he should convey that he sincerely means what he says. This sincerity is crucially important; it makes the difference between a matter-of-fact, ritualized, indifferent celebration and one that is truly an expression of faith and devotion.

1. *Dialogue.* In the greetings and verbal exchange between   1097
celebrant and congregation, all participants should speak their parts with meaning. When the priest says, "The Lord be with you," for example, he must convey that he is really addressing the people, that he sincerely means the greeting, and that he invites response. The tone and inflection of voice must be natural and convincing. At the same time, dialogue should never become extremely informal; all must be aware that the words they speak are part of a sacred rite. The liturgy must always be characterized by dignity and reverence as well as meaningful and sincere speech.

2. *Prayer.* When reading the orations, preface, and the like,   1098
the priest should speak in a manner befitting his sacerdotal role. His tone of voice should be more formal, more reverent; yet he must remember he is speaking to a Person, not merely reciting formulas. Note that this applies no matter which language is used in the prayer; it applies equally to the Canon as

to the Collect or the Lord's Prayer. The latter prayer is gravely abused by a sing-song recitation which pays little attention to the praises and petitions actually contained in the words. The conclusions of prayers, although in set formulas, must never be hurried, or routinely said. Since the affirmative response of the people is expected, the rhythm and tone of the priest should be sufficiently strong to encourage and facilitate the response.

1099   3. *Extent of Liturgical Use of English.* The extent to which it is lawful to use English in the liturgy throughout the dioceses of the United States is determined in the decrees of the National Conference of Bishops, enacted April 2, 1964, and confirmed by the *Consilium for the Implementation of the Constitution on the Sacred Liturgy* in a rescript of May 1, 1964. The following paragraphs summarize and specify what is found in the decrees, which should be consulted for additional details.

(After this summary a 4th section follows, giving directives on the use of the vernacular and the positions of the Faithful at Mass.)—Ed.

Address of Pope Paul VI
to Pastors and Lenten Preachers of Rome
on Promoting the New Liturgy
March 1, 1965

We cannot remain silent about Our satisfaction and Our emotion over this spiritual encounter on the threshold of the holy season of Lent for the year of grace 1965. Your presence around Us is always a cause of consolation and edification. But on rare occasions such as this, We can greet you and see you united. At the same time We can accept the expression of your devotion, your affection, your fidelity, and your persevering, tenacious determination to be co-operators and indeed ministers of Our Roman pastoral office; and We can offer you an expression of Our gratitude, Our esteem, Our trust. Never as on occasions such as the present, do We feel so aware of the seriousness of Our duties and so full of hope that We will not be completely inadequate for them.

You are in very close communion with Us. You bear with Us the burden of the care of souls in this first and elect Apostolic Church. You experience the labors of ministering to it and helping it more than We do. You have full and first claim to be regarded as Our clergy, which means Our confreres, Our sons. You are the priests through whom We want to feel Ourself understood and interpreted, the priests in whom We want to see mirrored and realized that ideal of the priesthood of Christ which stands uppermost in Our thoughts and Our prayers as the main object of His charity and His plan of salvation. You are the shepherds, the teach-

ers, the servants of the people of Rome, whose Christian vocation is connected with the mystery of God's action in
history and involves Our mission as Bishop, as Successor of
the Apostle Peter, as Vicar of Christ. You are beloved and
blessed among all!

1102   So now listen to Us! Or better still, read in Our heart the
many, many things We would like to communicate to you.
We will just go through the main headings.

1103   Our first thought with regard to you concerns your fidelity
to the priestly vocation and ministry: *"hic jam quaeritur
inter dispensatores ut fidelis quis inveniatur."*[1] What this
means is internal adherence to the total and irrevocable
offering of your lives which you have made to the Lord and
to the Church, your holocaust to one love alone, your immolation to the cross of Christ, your imitation of Him as the
only real and lasting model of perfection, your sanctification.
In a word: *"haec est enim voluntas Dei, sanctificatio vestra:
... vocavit nos Deus ... in sanctificationem."*[2]

1104   Our second point concerns the proper outlook and approach to be adopted, with God's blessing and Ours, in
thought, in conduct, in pastoral work, in the guidance of
souls, in preaching, and in social action. We know very well
just how hard it is to determine this at a time like the present, when every position is being shaken by the insidious or
open assaults of an approach which calls everything into
question, exposes everything to criticism, believes that everything can have judgment passed upon it and be changed. Now
then, what We say to you is this. Learn to be open to the
spirit of renewal that is sweeping the world and penetrating
into ecclesiastical regulations too; but, at the same time,
learn to defend yourselves against the dizzy whirl of arbitrary
innovations, of suggestions derived from a current brand of
ideas which are not approved by the Church and not supported by experience. Remember: *ex fructibus eorum!*[3]

1105   If obedience ever had reason to exist in the life of the
Church, if ever it was a source of salvation and merit, then
this seems to Us to be the time for discovering the profound
and salutary motives underlying it, and for offering free,
manly testimony to it that is really worthy of someone who

wants to be a follower of Him who made Himself *"oboediens usque ad mortem."*[4] Have confidence in the guidance of your Superiors. We will repeat it to you once again: *"Oboedite praepositis vestris et subjacete eis. Ipsi enim pervigilant quasi rationem pro animabus vestris reddituri, ut cum gaudio hoc faciatis, et non gementes; hoc enim expedit vobis!"*[5] In other words, rest assured that obedience, as it ought to flourish in every sector of the Church of God, will never be superfluous, or a haughty display of authority; nor will it be illogical or humiliating. It will not be imposed by a command that is despotic and irresponsible—or, as they say today, Constantinian and feudal. Instead it will be ever more clearly derived from a sound and forceful authority that is willed by God and derived from Him, for the transmission of His teachings and the building up of the ecclesial community, for the very providential and complicated exercise of pastoral charity, for the liberation of souls from their doubts and their weaknesses, for the elevation of the sons of God to an awareness of their dignity and to the exercise of their respective responsibilities, for the sanctification of everyone—those who direct, those who obey, and those who observe the sweetness and strength of Catholic conduct.

There are a great many other points too. But right now We cannot and choose not to linger over them. **1106**

Instead, We would like to take advantage of this meeting to make a recommendation to you which fits in with this peculiar moment in the Church's life—the moment for the application of the Council's Constitution on the Sacred Liturgy, which is on the verge of going into effect. A little booklet on this subject will be distributed to you at the end of this ceremony. But you are well acquainted with all this already, for that matter. **1107**

Now then, Our recommendation is this: devote the greatest care, especially during this first year, to knowing, explaining and applying the new norms that the Church intends to use from now on in celebrating divine worship. This is not an easy thing to do; it is a delicate thing. It demands direct and systematic interest. It calls for your personal, patient, loving, truly pastoral help. It means changing many, many **1108** habits that are, from many points of view, respectable and dear. It means upsetting good and devout faithful to offer them new forms of prayer that they won't understand right away; it means winning over many, many people, who pray or don't pray in church as they please, to a personal and collective expression of prayer. It means fostering a more active school of prayer and worship in every assembly of the faithful, introducing into it aspects, gestures, usages, formulas, sentiments that are new; what we might call a religious activism that many people are not used to. In short, it means associating the people of God with the priestly liturgical action. To repeat: this is something difficult and delicate; but it is also necessary, obligatory, providential, revivifying and, We hope, consoling.

1109   Your ministry may never bear such rich external satisfactions and internal consolations as when you begin to note the fruits of the pedagogical and pastoral effort that is being asked of you, and when you actually experience the words of the psalm: *Ecce quam bonum et quam jucundum habitare fratres in unum.*[6] The profound, heartfelt, active unity of your faithful, praying and offering with you, will reveal itself to you in its ever new and mystic beauty and will profoundly reward you for the care and attention you have spent to achieve such results. But be careful! You have to be convinced that this is a great event; that there are very lofty ideas at stake; that there are divine truths, divine realities involved; that the aim is to use this method—the true method, the most authoritative, the most blessed, the most effective one—to reach the heart of modern man and re-enkindle in it the flame of love for God and neighbor, the timid but intoxicating capacity for religious conversation that is genuine, consoling, redeeming. And along with this grand conception of the new liturgy, you must have the art of taking care of details of schedule, arrangement, objects, gestures, movements, times for silence and times for speaking, with all that they demand; and above all—this may well be the most difficult part—details of singing. It will take us years, but we have to begin, over and over again, to persevere in order to succeed in giving the assembly a voice of its own that will be solemn, unanimous, sweet and sublime.

And among the many things that call for preparation, com-   1110
mitment, dignity and propriety, as you know very well, is the Word! The Word has a whole part of the Liturgy of the Mass assigned to it. We are talking about the Word of Sacred Scrip-ture, the divine Word that is to be pronounced and listened to with renewed dignity, with conscious fervor. We are talking about the Word of the Priest, in his function as apostle, prophet, teacher, guide of the People of God. This Word is yours, pastors of souls and Lenten preachers now listening to Us; and We are referring to it right now in order to lend strength and comfort to your ministry, which the sacred Liturgy raises up to its original function as proclaimer of the message of salvation, fills and enriches with biblical content, intimately ties in with sacrificial worship, divests of all rhetorical ornamentation, and strengthens with divine authority.

You certainly remember all that has been said and written   1111
about sacred preaching. Men have discussed the relation-ship that it ought to have with the spiritual and moral life of the one who carries it out. Prayer ought to precede it; he who preaches, St. Augustine teaches, *"sit orator ante-quam dictor."*[7] Sincerity ought to characterize it: *"Sacerdotis Christi mens osque concordent,"*[8] is what St. Jerome said.

Men have also discussed the question of content, which   1112
ought to be truly religious, and aimed not at stirring up admiration, but rather at the instruction and edification of the faithful.

Men have discussed the whole subject, from the excellence   1113
and necessity of the ministry of the word to its varied forms of expression throughout the ages—didactic and hortatory, dogmatic and oratorical. Right now We shall not repeat any of these teachings. If anything, We would like to remind you of the many Masters and the many Saints who have dealt with this ministry. It would make up a body of liter-ature that deserves to be collected and studied.

We will confine Ourself to expressing a wish: that sacred   1114
preachings may be effective. Nowadays the art of making it

effective ought to be one of the most important practical studies in modern pastoral preparation. We are spurred on to this by the example of the speakers we hear talking every day on television. We are encouraged in this direction by the higher educational level of the public. We are obliged to this by the intolerance that men of the present day have for any kind of amateurishness, exaggeration, rhetoric, pseudo-learning, or profane substitutes for the sacred word. We are helped by the present-day demand for words that are plain, simple, to the point, brief and understandable. There still remains the difficulty of expressing divine things in human language, of giving the sacred word that secret power which makes it persuasive and salutary, of making our poor way of talking keen and vital, like a sword, as you find written: *"Vivus est enim sermo Dei et efficax, et penetrabilior omni gladio ancipiti."*[9] Remember, dear pastors and Lenten preachers, that the religious life of our time can depend in great part on the human, and at the same time mysterious, efficacy of sacred preaching. That is why Our exhortation seeks to pay honor to your ministry, to encourage you to dedicate to it not just your voice, but also your mind, your study, your prayer, your suffering and the ardor in your heart. That is why We conclude with a wish that the joy and merit of a truly sacred, truly efficacious, preaching ministry may be reserved for you.

1115   You have come here to hear these things. For you, who are experienced, who have toiled long and hard in the ministry of the word of God, they do not add anything to what you already know and want. But they do add a twofold factor that is new and mysterious. We want to link it to your pastoral eloquence, hoping it gives you power and consolation. We refer to Our mandate and Our blessing. We give you both the one and the other in the very words of Christ: *"Euntes ergo docete . . . Ecce Ego vobiscum sum . . ."*[10]

ECCLESIAE SEMPER
Decree of the Sacred Congregation of Rites
on Concelebration of Mass and
Communion under Both Kinds
March 7, 1965

General Decree

By which the Rites of Concelebrtion and Communion
under Both Kinds are Promulgated

The Church has always been concerned, in arranging and restoring the celebrations of the sacred mysteries, that the rites themselves, which contain the inexhaustble riches of Christ and communicate them to those who are well disposed, should also manifest these riches in the best way possible and thus more easily permeate the minds and lives of the faithful who take part in them.

The Church has made this a particular concern whenever it is a question of celebrating the Eucharist: the Church so prepares and orders the different forms of the Eucharist that they may express the various aspects of the eucharistic sacrifice and teach them to the faithful of Christ. 1117

In every form, however simple, in which the Mass is celebrated, all its characteristics and properties have the force which necessarily belong to the holy sacrifice of the Mass by its very nature. Yet there is particular reason to list the following among these characteristics. 1118

First of all, the unity of the sacrifice of the cross, inasmuch as the many Masses represent only the single sacrifice of 1119

Christ,[1] and from this fact share the nature of the sacrifice as they are the memorial of the bloody immolation achieved upon the cross, the fruits of which are received through this unbloody immolation.

1120 Next to the unity of the priesthood: whereas there are many priests who celebrate Mass, the individual priests are only ministers of Christ, who exercises his priesthood through them and for this purpose, makes the individuals participants in his priesthood in a very special way through the sacrament of order. Thus even when as individuals they offer the sacrifice, they all nevertheless do this in virtue of the same priesthood and act in the person of the High Priest, to whom it belongs to consecrate the sacrament of his body and blood whether through one or through many together.[2]

1121 Finally, the action of the entire people of God appears more clearly. Every Mass, inasmuch as it is the celebration of that sacrament in which the Church lives and grows without cessation,[3] and in which the true nature of the Church itself is preeminently manifested,[4] is, more than all the other liturgical services,[5] the action of the entire holy people of God, acting in a hierarchically ordered manner.

1122 Furthermore, this triple prerogative, which belongs to every Mass is placed before our eyes as it were in a singular manner in the rite by which several priests concelebrate the same Mass.

1123 In this manner of celebrating Mass the several priests, in virtue of the same priesthood and in the person of the High Priest, act together with a single will and a single voice, and together bring about and offer the unique sacrifice by a single sacramental act, and participate in it together.

1124 Therefore this kind of celebration of the sacrifice, in which the faithful all together participate consciously, actively, and in a manner befitting a community, particularly if a bishop presides, is truly the preeminent manifestation of the Church[6] in the unity of the sacrifice and of the priesthood, in the one thanksgiving, around a single altar together with the ministers and the holy people.

1125 It is clear that in this way, through the rite of concelebration, truths of great significance are vividly proposed and taught—truths that pertain to the spiritual and pastoral life of priests and to the Christian formation of the faithful.

For these reasons, much more than for reasons of a merely practical order, different modes and forms of concelebration of the eucharistic mystery have been known from antiquity in the Church. Having evolved in different ways, both in the east and in the west, concelebration has remained in use up to the present time.

For the same reasons it has happened that specialists in the liturgy have undertaken research and offered proposals for the extension of the faculty of concelebrating Mass and for the suitable restoration of this rite.

Lastly, the Second Vatican Council, having thoroughly weighed the matter, extended the faculty of concelebration to various cases and decreed that a new rite of concelebration should be prepared for insertion in the Roman Pontifical and Missal.[7] His Holiness, Pope Paul VI, after the solemn approbation and promulgation of the Constitution on the Sacred Liturgy of the Second Vatican Council, entrusted to the Commission appointed for the Implementation of this Constitution the task of preparing a rite for the concelebration of Mass as soon as possible. After this rite had been repeatedly subjected to the examination of its consultors and members and refined, the Commission, on June 19, 1964, unanimously approved it, and decreed that, if it should please His Holiness, practical experiments should take place in various parts of the world and in different circumstances before the definitive approbation.

Similarly, in obedience to the will of the holy Council, the same Commission for the Implementation of the Constitution on the Sacred Liturgy also prepared the rite of communion under both kinds, determining the cases and the forms in which the Eucharist may be received by the clergy, religious, and laity under both kinds.

For several months many experiments, both with the rite of concelebration and with the rite of communion under both kinds, were carried out throughout the world with the best results, and reports concerning these experiments were sent to the Secretariat of the Commission together with other

1126

1127

1128

1129

1130

observations and proposals. In view of these both rites were edited a final time and presented to His Holiness by His Eminence, Cardinal James Lercaro, President of the Commission.

1131   The Holy Father, after giving due consideration to both rites, with the assistance of the above mentioned Commission and of this Sacred Congregation of Rites, in an audience granted on March 4, 1965, to Cardinal Aredius Mary Larraona, Prefect of the Sacred Congregation of Rites, approved each and every part in a special way and confirmed it by his authority, ordering that it be made public and observed by all beginning on April 15, 1965, Holy Thursday, and carefully inserted in the Roman Pontifical and Missal.

1132   All things to the contrary notwithstanding.

Address of Pope Paul VI
to a General Audience
on Reactions to the Reform
March 17, 1965

Beloved Sons and Daughters! At an audience like this,
our friendly conversation must deal with the subject
of the day: the application of liturgical reform to the
celebration of holy Mass. If the public nature of this meeting
didn't make it impossible, We would like to ask—as We do in
private conversations—about your impressions of this great
new event. It deserves the attention of everyone. We believe,
however, that your reply to Our question would not be very
different from those that We have been receiving these days.

Liturgical reform? You can reduce the replies to two cat-   1134
egories. The first comprises the replies that indicate a certain
confusion, and hence a certain amount of annoyance. Previously, according to these observers, everything was peaceful;
everyone could pray as he wished; we understood all about
the way in which the ceremony was carried on. Now, everything is new, surprising, changed; even the ringing of the bells
at the Sanctus has been done away with. And then those
prayers that one doesn't know where to find; Communion
being received standing up; and Mass ending cut short with a
blessing. Everyone responding, a lot of people moving around,
ceremonies and readings recited out loud. . . . In short, there
is no longer any peace, and we understand less than we did
before; and so on.

We won't offer a criticism of these observations, because   1135
We would have to point out how they reveal very little pene-

tration into the meaning of the religious rites and give evidence not of true devotion and a true sense of the meaning and value of holy Mass, but rather of a certain spiritual laziness that isn't personal effort on understanding and participating in order to better comprehend and carry out the most sacred of religious acts, in which we are invited, and indeed obliged, to join.

1136   We will just repeat what is being said over and over again these days by all priests who are pastors of souls and by all the good teachers of religion. First, it is inevitable that there be a certain amount of confusion and annoyance in the beginning. It is in the very nature of a reform of age-old religious customs that have been piously observed, a reform that is practical—not to mention spiritual—that it should produce a little agitation that will not always be pleasant. But, secondly, a little bit of explanation, a little bit of preparation, a little bit of careful help, will quickly remove the uncertainties and soon produce a feeling and a taste for the new order. For, thirdly, you mustn't believe that after a while people are going to go back to being quiet and devout, or lazy, as they were before.

1137   No, the new order will have to be something different; and it will have to prevent and strike at the passivity of the faithful present at holy Mass. Before, it was enough to attend; now, it is necessary to participate. Before, presence was enough; now, attention and action are demanded. Before, a person could doze and perhaps even chat, but no longer; now, he has to listen and pray.

1138   We hope that the celebrants and the faithful will soon have the new liturgical books, and that these, in their literary and their typographical form, will reflect the dignity of the ones that went before. The assembly is becoming alive and active. Being present means allowing the soul to enter into activity in the form of attention, response, singing, action. The harmony of a community act that is carried out not just with an external gesture, but with an inner movement of the sentiment of faith and devotion, impresses a very special strength and beauty upon the rite. It becomes a chorus, a concert; it turns into the rhythm of an immense wing soaring toward the heights of divine mystery and joy.

The second category of comments reaching Us after the   1139
first celebrations of the new liturgy is marked by enthusiasm
and praise. These people say: at last we can understand the
complicated, mysterious ceremony, and follow it; at last we
really enjoy it; at last the priest is talking to the faithful,
and you can see that he is acting with them and for them.

We have very moving statements from ordinary people,   1140
from children and teen-agers, from critics and observers, from
pious persons who are eager for fervor and for prayer, from
men of long and solid experience and lofty training. They are
positive statements. A very distinguished old gentleman of
great heart, and of a spirituality so deep as to be never fully
satisfied, felt obliged to go to the celebrant after the first
celebration of the new liturgy to tell him quite frankly of
his happiness at having finally taken part in the holy sacrifice
to the full spiritual measure—perhaps for the first time in his
life.

Perhaps this admiration and this kind of holy excitement   1141
will calm down and soon dissolve into a new kind of peaceful habit. What is there that man doesn't get used to? But it is
to be believed that the note of religious intensity that the
new form of the rite calls for, will not grow less; and along
with it the awareness of an obligation to carry out two spiritual
acts simultaneously: one of true, personal participation in the
ceremony, with all the essentially religious qualities that this
implies; the other of communion with the assembly of the
faithful, with the *"ecclesia."* The first of these acts tends
toward love of God; the second, toward love of neighbor. Here
you have the Gospel of charity, which is being made real and
active in the souls of our time. It is really something beautiful,
something new, something great, something full of light and
hope.

But you understand very well, beloved Sons and Daughters,   1142
that this new liturgy, this spiritual rebirth, cannot come about
without your cooperation, without your wholehearted and
serious participation. This compliance on your part is so
important to Us that, as you can see, We have made it the
subject of this talk of Ours. With confidence that you will
really welcome it warmly, We promise you many, many

graces from the Lord, which, with Our Apostolic Blessing, We wish to assure for each of you from this moment on.

The reform of the Liturgy, mandated by the Constitution on the Liturgy at the end of the second session of Vatican II (Fall 1963) began to gather momentum even before the fourth and final session (Fall 1965). Many of the changes were minor and cannot be included here, but among them could be mentioned:

March 25, 1965—Non-clerics allowed to read Passion in Holy Week Liturgy.

April 27, 1965—New Regulations on Preface of Mass.

June 15, 1965—Regulations on liturgical experiments.

September 3, 1965—Pope Paul VI issued his Encyclical Letter Mysterium Fidei *which deals with some aspects of worship. The full text of it can be found in* Official Catholic Teachings: Christ Our Lord.

November 25, 1965—Permission for Saturday evening Mass.

Vatican II closed in December 1965, and the steady work of implementation continued:

January 27, 1966—Decree on Publication of Liturgical Books.

February 14, 1966—Decree on the Reception of Communion by the Sick.

April 17, 1966—Guidelines on Prayer of the Faithful.—Ed.

Address of Pope Paul VI
to the Commission for Implementing the
Constitution on the Sacred Liturgy
October 13, 1966

We greet you with love and respect, honored brothers and dear sons, as you assemble for a plenary meeting. You are a numerous international body, dedicated and learned and cooperating just at the right moment in an undertaking of the greatest importance. You are applying your erudition and your devotion to a reexamination of the Church's liturgical texts, giving them new shape and new substance so that the Church may celebrate the sacred mysteries of true worship of God; by means of these texts she enables believing Christians to share in that worship, to pray publicly as a community and to widen and deepen their spiritual life by drawing on the divine power which makes them holy.

You can understand, then, why We greet you with such respect and pleasure and thank you for coming. You are giving Us an opportunity to associate Ourself and Our own aspirations with the great work you are doing. We must thank you, too, for your efforts. Nothing can serve the Church better in these post-conciliar days; nothing can do more to awaken her love for God, win for her the Holy Spirit's help and enable her to draw men to her, teach them and make them holy.

We often reflect upon your exacting but necessary task, the reexamination of the sacred liturgy in the light of the Ecumenical Council. It is a complex task, which can be mishandled. We would say that it has three aspects. First, you have to investigate the rites and ceremonies which are in fact in use in the Church and you have to examine and suitably remodel them. This operation presents no special difficulties, since the rites and ceremonies in question are well known. Nevertheless, it demands certain qualities of mind: reverence for sacred things, and in particular for the forms of worship the Church uses; respect for tradition, which has handed on a valuable inheritance for us to honor; and understanding of history, which throws light on how the rites now due for revision were composed, on their meaning (either as prayers or as symbols), and on other related matters.

1146 Your inquiry, then, must not be conducted in an excessively radical spirit, as if you were iconoclasts, with a fury to put everything right and leave nothing as it was. No, you must judge maturely, on sound principles, aware that you are dealing with a religious matter that demands respect. The best thing, not the newest fashion, is what we must have in view. And if we are to have innovations, we should prefer those which make available to us the treasures left by the great epochs of Christian piety, rather than those of our own devising. But this does not deny the Church the right to express herself in modern terms, to "sing a new song," if the Holy Spirit's influence really is at work within her to inspire it.[1]

1147 The second aspect of your task demands much discretion. You have to study forms of liturgical expression—words, instrumental music, song, gestures and rite patterns. Thorough research must be done on the biblical origins of the various liturgical acts. The formulae of our prayers must be carefully harmonized with the formulae of our belief, so that our prayers will embody the rich meaning of our faith and at the same time mirror exactly the dogmatic fact they express, giving its various aspects just the right emphasis. The theologians among you will have much here for your erudition to work on; the men of letters will have ample opportunity for craftsmanship. And all of you will find a task that demands intellects on fire with love for Christ and His kingdom.

1148 We are well aware that you come to this task knowing what it means to talk apart with God. There is here a great challenge to your abilities: the success you have will be a practical effect of the life of prayer you lead; but it will also be a function of the artistic talents you bring with you. This will confer on the revisory work you are just beginning the mysterious stamp of beauty; will give it, too, the extra dimension of universality. This, indeed, is a special divine gift, to which God will add another, the quality of permanence and abiding freshness. It is right that the liturgy should be arrayed in such garments.

As you strive to attain majestic language truly worthy of   1149
the liturgy you will not forget, We are sure, the third aspect of your task, one intimately linked with human nature and a primary concern of liturgical scholars today. We mean the need to see that liturgical ceremonies hold no secrets from the great mass of believers, that the people clearly understand their meaning, the form they take, and the actions they entail.[2]

The patterns and the words of religious rites must help   1150
Christians in their daily lives, teach them (for worship has the power to do that), build up their moral and spiritual powers and make them long for union with God. Christians must be able to learn the meaning of the sacred sign and experience its effects in their lives. You members of the Commission, who are about to shape a new liturgy using the treasures handed down to us, need much practical experience and much love to do your task well. In the new liturgy there must be beauty and simplicity, weighty thoughts and clear expression, sound ideas and conciseness, and a happy marriage of traditional and modern forms of expression. That is the lofty task which the Church has assigned to you.

We have said all this, honored brothers and dear sons, to   1151
show you how important We consider the project upon which you are entering with such energy. We are well aware that the results of your endeavors will not be confined to the liturgy. There will be many additional benefits, since your work will have directive force in regard to other wide-ranging reforms begun by the Council's Constitution on the Sacred Liturgy. It will be for Our respected and deserving Congregation of Rites to make rules for the use of the new rites and to promote those which remain unchanged.

1152   Your Commission's function is to watch the progress of the experiments in worship that are taking place now in various sections of the Church. You must check any misguided initiatives that come to your notice and restrain those who take matters into their own hands without authorization; the serenity of public prayer can be disturbed by extravagances and false beliefs can arise. You must forbid harmful practices, but you must also spur on those reluctant to make necessary changes and those who put obstacles in the way. You must encourage sound initiatives; where you see fruitful developments taking place you must give them support, singling out those responsible for special praise.

1153   Your directive authority is of great importance just now; you have Our wholehearted support in your use of it—indeed, We owe you nothing but thanks for the careful watch you are keeping already and the sound decisions you are taking. The desire for a renewal of worship has already brought us the use of local languages and some new liturgical forms. These have come to stay, but any further innovations must first be brought to the notice of the bishops and of this apostolic see and receive their full approval. There must be no initiatives that dishonor divine worship, no obviously profane practices that prevent worshippers giving themselves wholly to prayer, no startling eccentricities that, far from filling a congregation with prayerful spirit, take it aback and so unsettle it that it cannot continue to worship in the calm way its fathers did, and as it has a right to do. Liturgical changes ought to be introduced gradually, in accordance with good teaching method.

1154   We note with pleasure that you are already exercising your supervisory function by means of your valuable little publication, *Notitiae.* But *Notitiae* goes further, and on this We congratulate you again: it makes new liturgical regulations known throughout the Church and publicizes new developments. It thus adds a competitive element to healthy progress and rightly encourages variety in liturgical forms of expression. At the same time it reminds its readers of the need for unity in essentials, which must always be a principal feature of the Church's life of worship.

We are happy to note also how well you have planned your   1155
work, focusing it on just those matters that most need attention. Your wholeheartedness in the task sets a standard for
others and the many excellent results of your endeavors leave
Us in no doubt that more are to come. Now that the Council
has ended, the Church is waiting for measures that will carry
its decrees into effect and give them practical application. She
has reason to rejoice, therefore, in your achievements, since
they obey the Council's wishes (which regulate all your plans)
so implicitly, cover such an important field and make such
speedy progress—allowing, of course, for the difficulty and
complexity of your work and the need for you to be satisfied with nothing less than the best.

Some of the topics you are concerned with—those which   1156
your Cardinal President has singled out for special mention—
are very important and deserve particular consideration, on
Our part as well as yours. One of them is music for worship,
the concern of many liturgists and musicians. This subject
will receive, We are sure, that careful consideration from all
points of view that it requires. Men with pastoral experience
and musicians with their skill will collaborate willingly to
give us what we need. That, at any rate, is Our earnest wish.
The coming Instruction, which will clarify the relationship
between music and liturgy, will make cooperation between
them easier. It will once again, We are sure, unite those two
sublime forms of expression of the human spirit, prayer and
art, in a single work of beauty. The International Congress on
Sacred Music recently held in Chicago gives Us further ground
for confidence that this will come about.

We should like here to remind you of the references made   1157
to music and liturgy by the Ecumenical Council's Constitution on the Sacred Liturgy, and of the high regard it had for
both.[3] The Constitution declared that if the liturgical renewal
is to have those qualities of effectiveness in parish life and fellowship in worship that the Council wants it to have, then a
relationship must be established between the musical art and
singing for worship. This will be done to the extent that, in
their different ways, they become linked to the progressive
unfolding of the religious rites themselves. It is important

that this link should now be made. Both arts, therefore, can break new ground and win new distinction in the field of beauty and worship. As the Constitution says: "The more closely music for worship follows the action of the liturgy itself, the nobler it will be."[4]

1158   The other topic of outstanding importance to which you are to give careful consideration is the Ordinary of the Mass. We have already seen your report on it and know what scholarship and thought have gone into its preparation. You have dealt with the Ordinary of the Mass and also with the composition of the new Missal and the calendar. These are matters of such importance, affecting the whole Church, that We must ask the bishops for their opinion before giving Our approval to what you have proposed.

1159   Continue your researches and your good work, honored brothers and you gentlemen eminent in the liturgical field. You have to encourage you the knowledge that your work is doing a great service to the cause of Christian belief. It is by divine worship, after all, that men profess their belief publicly; by it their faith, individually or communally, is strengthened. Your work is contributing to the proclamation, to the epiphany of Christ, since it is by means of words, the sacraments and the priesthood that the liturgy makes Christ almost visibly present to the minds of believers and makes Him live in them.

1160   You are serving the Church, since the pure and holy speech of the liturgy rises to God, carrying the Church with it so, that she can offer herself to Christ, her head, as His Mystical Body (which indeed she is). She offers herself to Him as the human race He has brought, ready to give Him, in her love, everything from Him. You are serving God's people, since it is from the liturgy (providing that it is clear, simple and a suitable vehicle for His inspiration) that God's people draw wisdom, peace, fellowship and holiness. And finally, you are bringing help to all men of today, since divine worship will make its appeal again in a form corresponding to modern needs. Its mysterious beauty will invite men and women with gentle persuasiveness to rediscover the wonderful land they have lost. Only there is the human spirit at home; only there does it encounter the divine presence in an experience beyond the power of words to describe and without parallel in ordinary earthly life.

Pursue your way, then, with bold confidence. Derive strength from the knowledge that Our trust and good will follow you closely. May our Lord, Christ, show His love for you by enlightening your minds. It is for Him that you have undertaken your task. We represent Him, though unworthily, and give you His blessing.   1161

Sacred Congregation of Rites
Liturgical Experiments
December 29, 1966

For some time now, some newspapers and magazines have been offering their readers news and photographs of liturgical ceremonies—celebrations of the Eucharist in particular—that are alien to Catholic worship. We refer to such unlikely things as "family eucharistic banquets" celebrated in private homes and followed by dinners, and to Masses with arbitrary and unusual rites, vestments and formularies, sometimes accompanied by music of a completely secular and worldly nature, not worthy of a sacred ceremony. All of these expressions of worship, which have been the result of private initiatives, have a fatal tendency to desecrate the liturgy, which is the purest expression of the worship rendered to God by the Church.

1163   It is completely out of place to allege pastoral updating as a motive for this, for updating—and it is useful to repeat this—should take place in an orderly manner and not arbitrarily. All these things are out of step with the letter and the spirit of the Constitution on the Sacred Liturgy issued by the Second Vatican Council. They are contrary to the ecclesial sense of the liturgy and harmful to the unity and dignity of the People of God.

1164   "The desire for a renewal of worship has already brought us the use of local languages and some new liturgical forms," said Pope Paul VI last October 13th. "These have come to stay, but any further innovations must first be brought to the notice of the bishops and of this apostolic see and receive their full approval. There must be no initiatives that dishonor divine worship, no obviously profane practices that prevent worshippers giving themselves wholly to prayer, no startling eccentricities that, far from filling a congregation with prayerful spirit, take it aback and so unsettle it that it cannot continue to worship in the calm way its fathers did, and as it has a right to do."

While we deplore the facts mentioned above and the public-   1165
ity given them, we urgently request local and religious ordinaries to watch over the correct application of the Constitution on the Sacred Liturgy, to call back kindly but firmly those who sponsor such manifestations, however good their intentions, and to repress these abuses when they occur by preventing any undertaking not authorized and guided by the sacred hierarchy. They should also zealously foster the true liturgical renewal desired by the Council, so that the great work of this renewal may be carried out without deviations and may bear those fruits of Christian life which the Church expects of it.

In addition, it must be remembered that it is not permitted   1166
to celebrate Mass in private homes, except in those cases provided for and clearly defined in liturgical legislation.

MUSICAM SACRAM
Instruction of the Sacred Congregation of Rites
on Music in the Sacred Liturgy
March 5, 1967

Sacred music, in those aspects which concern the liturgical renewal was carefully considered by the Second Vatican Ecumenical Council. It explained its role in divine services, issued a number of principles and laws on this subject in the Constitution on the Sacred Liturgy, and devoted to it an entire chapter of the same constitution.

1168   2. The decisions of the Council have already begun to be put into effect in the recently undertaken liturgical renewal. But the new norms concerning the arrangement of the sacred rites and the active participation of the faithful have given rise to several problems regarding sacred music and its ministerial role. These problems appear to be solvable by expounding more fully certain relevant principles of the Constitution on the Sacred Liturgy.

1169   3. Therefore the Commission established to implement the Constitution on the Sacred Liturgy, on the instructions of the Holy Father, has carefully considered these questions and prepared the present instruction. This does not, however, gather together all the legislation on sacred music; it only establishes the principal norms which seem to be more necessary for our own day. It is, as it were, a continuation and complement of the preceding instruction of this Sacred Congregation, prepared by this same Commission on September 26, 1964, for the correct implementation of the Liturgy Constitution.

4. It is to be hoped that pastors of souls, musicians and the   1170
faithful will gladly accept these norms and put them into
practice, uniting their efforts to attain the true purpose of
sacred music, "which is the glory of God and the sanctification of the faithful."[1]

a) By sacred music is understood that music which, being
created for the celebration of divine worship, is endowed
with holiness and goodness of form.[2]

b) The following come under the title of sacred music
here: Gregorian chant; sacred polyphony in its various
forms, both ancient and modern; sacred music for the organ
and other approved instruments; and sacred popular music,
be it liturgical or simply religious.[3]

I

Some General Norms

5. Liturgical worship is given a more noble form when it   1171
is celebrated in song, with the ministers of each degree fulfilling their ministry and the people participating in it.[4] Indeed, through this form, prayer is expressed in a more attrac-
tive way; the mystery of the liturgy, with its hierarchical and
community nature, is more openly shown; the unity of hearts
is more profoundly achieved by the union of voices; minds
are more easily raised to heavenly things by the beauty of
the sacred rites; and the whole celebration more clearly pre-
figures that heavenly liturgy which is enacted in the holy
city of Jerusalem.

Pastors of souls will, therefore, do all they can to achieve   1172
this form of celebration. They will do all they can in order
that assignment of different parts to be performed and duties
to be fulfilled, which characterize sung celebrations, may be
transferred even to celebrations which are not sung, but at
which the people are present. Above all they must take particular care that the necessary and suitable ministers are obtained and to encourage the active participation of the people.

The practical preparation for each liturgical celebration   1173
should be done in a spirit of cooperation by all parties con-

cerned, under the guidance of the rector of the church, whether it be in ritual, pastoral or musical matters.

1174   6. The proper arrangement of a liturgical celebration requires the due assignment and performance of certain functions, by which "each person, minister or layman, who has an office to perform, should do all of, but only, those parts which pertain to his office by the nature of the rite and the norms of the liturgy."[5] This also demands that the meaning and proper nature of each part and of each song be carefully observed. To attain this, those parts especially should be sung which by their very nature require to be sung, using the kind and form of music which is proper to their character.

1175   7. Between the solemn, fuller form of liturgical celebration, in which everything that demands singing is in fact sung, and the simplest form, in which singing is not used, there can be various degrees according to the greater or lesser place allotted to singing. However, in selecting the parts which are to be sung, one should start with those that are by their nature of greater importance, and especially those which are to be sung by the priest or by the ministers, with the people replying, or those which are to be sung by the priest and people together. The other parts may be added gradually according as they are proper to the people alone or to the choir alone.

1176   8. For a liturgical service which is to be celebrated in sung form, whenever one can make a choice between various people, it is desirable that those who are known to be more proficient in singing be given preference. This is especially the case in more solemn liturgical celebrations and in those which either require more difficult singing, or are transmitted by radio or television.[6]

1177   If, however, a choice of this kind cannot be made, and the priest or minister does not possess a voice suitable for the proper execution of the singing, he can render without singing one or more of the more difficult parts which pertain to him, reciting them in a loud and distinct voice. However, this must not be done merely for the convenience of the priest or minister.

9. In selecting the kind of sacred music to be used, wheth-   1178
er it be for the choir or for the people, the capacities of those
who are to sing the music must be taken into account. No
kind of sacred music is prohibited from liturgical actions by
the Church as long as it corresponds to the spirit of the liturgical celebration itself and the nature of its individual
parts,[7] and does not hinder the active participation of the
people.[8]

10. In order that the faithful may actively participate more   1179
willingly and with greater benefit, it is fitting that the format
of the celebration and the degrees of participation in it
should be varied as much as possible, according to the solemnity of the day and the nature of the congregation present.

11. It should be borne in mind that the true solemnity of   1180
liturgical worship depends less on a more ornate form of
singing and a more magnificent ceremonial than on its
worthy and religious celebration, which takes into account
the integrity of the liturgical celebration itself, and the performance of all of its parts according to their own particular
nature. To have a more ornate form of singing and a more
magnificent ceremonial is at times desirable when resources
are available to carry them out properly. On the other hand,
it would be contrary to the true solemnity of the liturgy if
this were to lead to a part of the action being omitted,
changed or improperly performed.

12. It is for the Holy See alone to determine the more im-   1181
portant general principles which are, as it were, the basis of
sacred music, according to the norms handed down, but
especially according to the Constitution on the Sacred
liturgy. Direction in this matter, within the limits laid down,
also belongs to the competent territorial episcopal conferences of various kinds, which have been legitimately constituted, and to the individual bishop.[9]

13. Liturgical services are celebrations of the Church, that   1182
is, of the holy people, united under and directed by the bishop or priest.[10] The priest and his ministers, because of the
sacred order they have received, hold a special place in these
celebrations, as do also—by reason of the ministry they per-

form—the servers, readers, commentators and those in the choir.[11]

1183   14. The priest, acting in the person of Christ, presides over the gathered assembly. Since the prayers which are said or sung aloud by him are proclaimed in the name of the entire holy people and of all present,[12] they should be devoutly listened to by all.

1184   15. The faithful fulfill their liturgical role by means of that full, conscious and active participation which is demanded by the nature of the liturgy itself and which is, by reason of Baptism, the right and duty of the Christian people.[13]

1185   This participation:

a) Above all, should be internal, in the sense that by it the faithful join their minds to what they pronounce or hear, and cooperate with heavenly grace;[14]

b) On the other hand, must be external also, that is, such as to show the internal participation by gestures and bodily attitudes, by acclamations, responses and singing.[15]

1186   The faithful should also be taught to unite themselves interiorly to what the ministers or choir sing, so that by listening to them they may raise their minds to God.

1187   16. One cannot find anything more solemn and more joyful in sacred celebrations than a whole congregation expressing its faith and devotion in song. Therefore, the active participation of the whole people, which is shown in singing, is to be carefully promoted as follows:

a) It should first of all include acclamations, responses to the greetings of the priest and ministers and to the prayers of litany form, and also antiphons and psalms, refrains or repeated responses, hymns and canticles.[16]

b) Through suitable instruction and practices, the people should be gradually led to a fuller—indeed, to a complete— participation in those parts of the singing which pertain to them.

c) Some of the people's song, however, especially if the faithful have not yet been sufficiently instructed, or if musical settings for several voices are used, can be handed over to the choir alone, provided that the people are not excluded from those parts that concern them. But the custom of entrusting to the choir alone the entire singing of the whole Proper and of the whole Ordinary, to the complete exclusion of the people's participation in the singing, is not to be approved.

17. At the proper times, all should observe a reverent silence.[17] Through it the faithful are not only not considered as extraneous or mute spectators at the liturgical service, but are associated more intimately in the mystery that is being celebrated, thanks to that interior disposition which derives from the word of God that they have heard, from the songs and prayers that have been uttered, and from spiritual union with the priest in the parts that he says or sings himself.   1188

18. Among the faithful, special attention must be given to the instruction of members of lay religious societies in sacred singing, so that they may support and promote the participation of the people more effectively.[18] The formation of the whole people in singing should be seriously and patiently undertaken together with liturgical instruction, according to the age, status and way of life of the faithful, and the degree of their religious culture; this should be done even from the first years of education in elementary schools.[19]   1189

19. Because of the liturgical ministry it performs, the choir—or *capella musica* or *schola cantorum*—deserves particular mention.   1190

Its role, by reason of the norms of the Council concerning the liturgical renewal, has become something of yet greater importance and weight. Its duty is, in effect, to ensure the proper performance of the parts which belong to it, according to the different kinds of music sung, and to encourage the active participation of the faithful in the singing.   1191

Therefore: 1192

a) There should be choirs, or *capellae*, or *scholae cantorum*, especially in cathedrals and other major churches, in seminaries and religious houses of studies, and they should be carefully encouraged.

b) It would also be desirable for similar choirs to be set up in smaller churches.

1193   20. Outstanding choirs in basilicas, cathedrals, monasteries and other major churches, which have in the course of centuries earned for themselves high renown by preserving and developing a musical heritage of inestimable value, should be retained for sacred celebrations of a more elaborate kind, according to their own traditional norms, recognized and approved by the ordinary.

1194   However, the directors of these choirs and the rectors of the churches should take care that the people always associate themselves with the singing by performing at least the easier sections of those parts which belong to them.

1195   21. Provision should be made for at least one or two properly trained singers, especially where there is no possibility of establishing even a small choir. The singer will present some simpler musical settings, with the people taking part, and will be able to lead and support the faithful as far as is needed.

1196   The presence of such a singer, even in churches which have a choir, is desirable for those celebrations in which the choir cannot take part but which may fittingly be performed with some solemnity and therefore with singing.

1197   22. According to the customs of each country and other circumstances, the choir can consist of either men and boys, or men or boys only, or men and women, or even, where there is a genuine case for it, of women only.

1198   23. Taking into account the arrangement of each church, the choir should be placed in such a way that:

a) Its nature should be clearly apparent—namely, that it is a part of the whole congregation, and that it fulfills a special role.

b) It is easier for it to fulfill its liturgical function.[20]

c) Each of its members may be able to participate easily in the Mass, that is to say, by sacramental participation.

1199   Whenever the choir also includes women, it should be placed outside the sanctuary.

1200   24. Besides musical formation, suitable liturgical and spiritual formation must also be given to the members of the choir, in such a way that the proper performance of their liturgical role will not only enhance the beauty of the cele-

bration and be an excellent example for the faithful, but will
bring spiritual benefit to the choir members themselves.

25. In order that this technical and spiritual formation   1201
may more easily be obtained, the diocesan, national and
international associations of sacred music should offer their
services, especially those which have been approved and
several times commended by the Holy See.

26. The priest, the sacred ministers and servers, the reader   1202
and those in the choir, and also the commentator, should
perform the parts assigned to them in a way which is intelligible to the people, in order that the people's responses,
when the rite requires it, may be made more easily. It is desirable that the priest and the ministers of every degree
should join their voices to the voice of the whole body of the
faithful in those parts which concern the people.[21]

The Instruction then gives guidelines on the following: 1203

III. Sacred Music in the Celebration of the Mass

IV. The Singing of the Divine Office

*V. Sacred Music in the Celebration of the Sacraments and
Sacramentals, in Special Functions of the Liturgical Year, in
Celebrations of the Word of God, and in Popular Devotions*

*VI. The Language to Be Used in Sung Liturgical Celebrations,
and the Preservation of the Heritage of Sacred Music*

VII. Preparing Melodies for Vernacular Texts

VIII. Sacred Instrumental Music (Ed.)

IX

The Commissions Established for the
Promotion of Sacred Music

68. The diocesan commissions for sacred music are of great   1204
value in promoting sacred music together with pastoral liturgical action in the diocese.

1205   Therefore, they should exist as far as possible in each diocese, and should unite their efforts with those of the liturgical commission.

1206   It often will be commendable for the two commissions to be combined into one, and to consist of persons who are expert in both subjects. In this way progress will be easier.

1207   It is highly recommended that, where it appears to be more effective, several dioceses of the same region should set up a single commission which will establish a common plan of action and concentrate their forces more fruitfully.

1208   69. The liturgical commission, to be set up by the episcopal conference as judged opportune,[22] should also be responsible for sacred music; it should therefore also consist of experts in this field. It is useful, however, for such a commission to confer not only with the diocesan commissions, but also with other societies which may be involved in musical matters in the same region. This also applies to the pastoral liturgical institute mentioned in art. 44 of the Constitution.

1209   In the audience granted on February 9, 1967, to His Eminence Arcadio M. Cardinal Larraona, prefect of the Sacred Congregation of Rites, His Holiness Pope Paul VI approved and confirmed the present instruction by his authority, ordered it to be published and at the same time established that it should come into force on Pentecost Sunday, May 14, 1967.

1210   All things to the contrary notwithstanding.

1211   Rome, Laetare Sunday, the fourth Sunday of Lent, March 5, 1967.

Address of Pope Paul VI
to the Commission for Implementing
the Constitution on the Sacred Liturgy
on Obstacles to Liturgical Renewal
April 19, 1967

With a ready heart We thank Cardinal Lercaro for the noble and deferential words he has addressed to Us on behalf of the group assembled here. Although many things press for Our attention these days, We readily acceded to the request for this audience because We wanted to meet the members of the Commission for Implementing the Constitution on the Sacred Liturgy. It was, after all, set up by Us to re-examine the liturgical books of the Latin rite in the light of the aims and decrees of the recent Council, and to provide Us and Our Sacred Congregation of Rites with judicious help on such an intricate and important matter.

The Commission certainly deserves a renewed vote of confidence and respect from Us, and its members deserve a further word of encouragement. We know the people who belong to this body and We esteem their qualifications. They are people whose knowledge of and regard for the sacred liturgy are well known. We know the heavy work load that must be handled by this Commission, the varied and serious questions it must solve, and the rapid pace it must maintain to accomplish its task in a reasonably short space of time. 1213

We are also well aware of the guiding norms regulating this difficult and delicate job. They are spelled out in section 23 of the Constitution on the Sacred Liturgy. The Commission faithfully adheres to them, but they are worth repeating here: "That sound tradition may be retained, and yet the way re- 1214 main open to legitimate progress, a careful investigation is always to be made into each part of the liturgy which is to be revised. This investigation should be theological, historical, and pastoral. Also the general laws governing the structure and meaning of the liturgy must be studied in conjunction with the experience derived from recent liturgical reforms and from the indults conceded to various places. Finally, there must be no innovations unless the good of the Church genuinely and certainly requires them; and care must be taken that any new forms adopted should in some way grow organically from forms already existing."[1]

1215   The task in which you are engaged is one which provides concrete data and reasoned approaches to this Apostolic See in its lofty task of stimulating and guiding the prayer life of the People of God. We can well understand how this task might provoke various hostile reactions, raise many different issues and give rise to new questions—providing an occasion for interpretations that are illegitimate and impermissible, and for commentaries that are questionable.

1216   It is only natural for innovation to be accompanied by misjudgment and imperfect implementation. Yet, for all this, We feel duty-bound to express Our thanks and overall approval to this Commission. It is a perfect opportunity for Us not only to praise and encourage its laborious work, but also to urge the clergy and the laity to appreciate its merits and insure its effectiveness.

1217   Apropos of all this, We cannot hide the disappointment We have suffered from certain incidents and tendencies that do not at all contribute to the success which the Church expects to achieve from the hard work of the Commission.

1218   The first of these is the unjust and irreverent attack leveled against Cardinal Lercaro, the illustrious president of this Commission, in a recent publication. Obviously We do not agree with it. It does not edify anyone, nor does it help the cause it purports to advance: preserving the Latin language in the sacred liturgy.

1219   The question itself is certainly a worthy one, deserving serious attention. But it cannot be resolved in a way contrary to the great principle confirmed by the Council: liturgical prayer is to be accommodated to the understanding of the people so that it may be comprehended. Nor can it be resolved contrary to the other principle which is called for by man's present societal culture: people can best express their deepest feelings and sentiments in their vernacular language.

Leaving aside the whole question of Latin in the liturgy, which has been hurt rather than helped by the publication mentioned above, We want to express Our regrets to Cardinal Lercaro and register Our support for him. 1220

Another cause of concern and sorrow are the disciplinary irregularities in communal worship that have occurred in various places. They frequently are shaped to suit individual whims and often take forms that are wholly at odds with the precepts now in force in the Church. This greatly upsets many upright Church members. Moreover, these innovations are often interlaced with issues that endanger the peace and good order of the Church, issues that must be rejected. They are also harmful because they set an example that sows confusion in people's minds. In this connection, We would remind you of what the Constitution on the Sacred Liturgy has to say about the regulation of the liturgy: "Regulation of the sacred liturgy depends solely on the authority of the Church."[2] 1221

We are even more anxious, however, to express Our hope that bishops will keep a close watch on such episodes, that they will maintain balance and harmony in the Church's liturgical worship and its religious life. Right now, in this post-conciliar period, these areas are objects of special concern and the most tender care. 1222

We would make the same plea to religious orders, for at present the Church expects them to aid this cause in a special way by their fidelity and example. We also urge the clergy and all the faithful not to give in to unbridled and free-wheeling experimentation, but rather to perfect and execute the rites prescribed by the Church. 1223

This plea is in line with one of the duties of this Commission, which is charged with wisely regulating specific liturgical experiments that seem worthwhile, so that they may be implemented in a responsible and careful way. 1224

1225   An even greater source of sorrow is the inclination of some
to deprive the liturgy of its sacred character—to "desacralize"
it (if we can even call it "liturgy" any more). This necessarily
leads to the desacralization of the Christian religion as well.
This new outlook, whose sordid roots are easy to discern,
would destroy authentic Catholic worship. It leads to doctrinal, disciplinary and pastoral subversions of such magnitude
that We do not hesitate to consider it deviant. We say this with
sadness, not only because it evinces a spirit that runs counter
to canon law and that is too caught up with novelty for its
own sake, but also, and primarily, because it necessarily involves the disintegration of religion.

1226   We fully realize that any given undertaking or teaching can
contain more than a particle of truth, that its sponsors can be
good and learned men. And We are always prepared to consider those aspects of any ecclesial phenomenon that are
worthwhile or worth trying. But We cannot conceal, from
you in particular, the fact that in Our opinion the aforementioned tendency poses the danger of spiritual ruin.

1227   This danger must be repulsed. Individuals, periodicals and
institutions which may be under its spell must be won over
again to the cause of the Church and its support. The norms
and teachings of the Council must be defended.

1228   You have a particular role to play in all this. More than
anyone else, you are called upon to trace out the lineaments
of the sacred liturgy; to delineate its truth, beauty and spiritual
character; to spotlight ever more brightly the Paschal Mystery
imbedded within it. In this way the liturgy will give glory to
God and renew the inner spirit of our distracted but hungering
contemporaries.

1229   We have good reason to hope that, with God's help, this
happy result will come about—if We can judge from the
importance of your work, the seriousness with which you are
approaching it, and the first results of the liturgical renewal.
These results are truly felicitous in some respects, and promise
even better things.

1230   The authentic prayer life of the Church is flourishing once
again on the community level. It is a beautiful thing to see,
and one of the most promising signs of our age. The present

era is a confused and troubled one, yet full of raw vitality. To the person who is inflamed with love for Christ, it offers this most hopeful sign.

So carry on your work calmly and boldly. We can truly say that "God wills it"—for His own glory, for the life of the Church, and for the salvation of the world. And may Our apostolic blessing go with you. 1231

TRES ABHINC ANNOS
Instruction of the Sacred Congregation of Rites
on the Correct Implementation of
the Constitution on the Sacred Liturgy
May 4, 1967

Three years ago, through the instruction *Inter Oecumenici*, issued by this Sacred Congregation of Rites on September 26, 1964, various changes were introduced into the liturgical services. These changes, which came into effect on May 7, 1965, were the first fruits of the general liturgical renewal called for by the conciliar Constitution on the Sacred Liturgy.

1233   The abundant benefits that have begun to be reaped from this are sufficiently shown in many reports from the bishops. It is clear from these reports that the conscious and active participation of the Christian faithful in the sacred liturgy has greatly increased in all parts of the world, particularly with regard to the holy sacrifice of the Mass.

1234   In order to develop this participation and to achieve a greater intelligibility and understanding of the liturgical rites, especially of the Mass, the same bishops have proposed certain other changes. Presented first of all to the Commission for Implementing the Constitution on the Sacred Liturgy, these changes were carefully examined and considered by the Commission and by this Sacred Congregation of Rites.

1235   Although not everything that was proposed can be accepted at present, some things that are recommended by pastoral motives and do not appear to run counter to the future, definitive liturgical reform may well be put into practice immediately. On the one hand they are judged to be useful in the gradual introduction of the liturgical renewal, and on the other they can be applied through rubrical directions which do not demand changes in the liturgical books now in use.

Given this occasion, it seems necessary to recall to everyone's attention that important principle of ecclesiastical discipline which was solemnly confirmed by the Constitution on the Sacred Liturgy, namely: "The regulation of the sacred liturgy depends solely on the authority of the Church. . .Therefore no other person, even if he be a priest, may add, remove or change anything in the liturgy on his own authority."[1]   1236

Ordinaries, both local and religious, will remember their grave duty before the Lord of ensuring that this law, which is of such importance for the Church's life and structures, be fully observed. But all ministers of sacred rites and all the faithful should conform themselves with a willing spirit to this necessary norm.   1237

This is required both for the spiritual good and development of individuals and also for harmonious cooperation in the Lord and mutual good example among the faithful of the same local community. It is demanded moreover by the serious duty of each individual community to work for the good of the Church throughout the world. This is especially true at the present day, when whatever good or evil arises in local communities quickly affects the entire family of God.   1238

All should bear in mind the warning of the Apostle: "For God is not a God of confusion, but of peace."[2]   1239

In order that the liturgical renewal may be more closely realized and make further progress, the following adaptations and changes are laid down.   1240

I

The Choice of Mass Formulas

1. On third class liturgical days outside Lent, either the Mass of the Office of the day or the Mass of the commemoration made at Lauds may be celebrated. In the latter Mass, the color of the Office of the day may be used, according to no. 323 of the Code of Rubrics.   1241

2. The weekday lectionary, if allowed by the conference of bishops in their own territory for Masses celebrated with a   1242

congregation, may also be used in Masses which are celebrated without a congregation; in this case the use of the vernacular is permitted for the readings.

1243   This weekday lectionary may be used on certain second class days which are indicated in the lectionary itself and in all third or fourth class Masses, whether Masses of the season, of a saint, or votive Masses which do not have their own strictly proper readings, that is, readings in which mention is made of the mystery or person being celebrated.

1244   3. On weekdays through the year, when the Mass of the preceding Sunday is used, one of the prayers for particular intentions given in the Missal, or the prayers from one of the votive Masses for particular intentions to be found in the Missal, may be used instead of the Sunday prayers.

II

Orations in the Mass

1245   4. Only one oration is to be said in the Mass. However, according to the rubrics, there may be added before the conclusion of that oration:

a) An oration particular to the rite (Code of Rubrics, No. 447);

—the oration of the votive Mass in the profession of men or women religious, where this Mass has been displaced by the Mass of the day (special rubrics of the Missal);

—The oration of the nuptial Mass where this Mass has been displaced by the Mass of the day (CR, no. 380);

b) the oration in a votive Mass of thanksgiving (CR, no. 382, and special rubrics of the Missal);

—the oration on the anniversaries of the pope and the bishop (CR, nos. 449-450);

—the oration for the anniversary of the priest's own ordination to the priesthood (CR, nos. 451-452).

1246   5. If in the same Mass there are several orations to be said under one conclusion, then only one is in fact added. This should be the one most in keeping with the celebration.

1247   6. In place of the *"oratio imperata"* the bishop may have one or more intentions for special local needs inserted in the

Prayer of the Faithful. Similarly, the competent territorial authority may decree the insertion of intentions in the Prayer of the Faithful. These may be directed to be said for governments and rulers in the various forms that are used in different places, in addition to special intentions for the needs of the entire nation or region.

III

Changes in the Order of the Mass

7. The celebrant genuflects only: 1248

a) when he goes to and comes away from the altar, if the Blessed Sacrament is present in the tabernacle;

b) after the elevation of the host and after the elevation of the chalice;

c) after the doxology at the end of the Canon;

d) at the Communion, before he says *"Panem caelestem accipiam";*

e) after the Communion of the faithful, when any hosts which may be left over have been placed in the tabernacle.

All other genuflections are omitted.   1249

8. The celebrant kisses the altar only at the beginning of   1250
Mass, when he says the prayer *"Oramus te, Domine"*; or when he goes to the altar, if the prayers at the foot of the altar are omitted; and at the end of Mass before he blesses and dismisses the people.

All other kisses of the altar are omitted.   1251

9. At the Offertory, after the offering of the bread and   1252
wine, the celebrant places both the paten (with the host on it) and the chalice on the corporal, omitting the signs of the cross with the paten and with the chalice.

The paten, with the host on it, is left on the corporal both   1253
before and after the Consecration.

10. In Masses celebrated with the people, even when not   1254
concelebrated, the celebrant may recite the Canon aloud, if it seems opportune. In sung Masses those parts of the Canon may be sung which may be sung in a concelebrated Mass.

11. In the Canon, the celebrant: 1255

a) begins the *"Te igitur"* standing upright and with his hands extended;

b) makes one sign of the cross over the offerings: at the words *"benedicas + Haec dona, haec munera, haec sancta sacrificia illibata,"* in the prayer *"Te igitur."* All other signs of the cross over the offerings are omitted.

1256   12. After the Consecration, the celebrant need not join his thumbs and forefingers; if there is any fragment of the host on his fingers, he purifies his fingers over the paten.

1257   13. The rites for the Communion of the priest and the faithful shall be arranged in the following way: after saying, *"Panem caelestem accipiam,"* the celebrant takes the host and, standing facing the people, raises it, saying, "Behold the Lamb of God"; then he adds, "Lord, I am not worthy," three times with the faithful. He next receives the host and drinks from the chalice, omitting the signs of the cross; then he distributes Communion to the faithful in the usual way.

1258   14. The faithful who go to Communion at the Mass of the Chrism on Holy Thursday may receive Communion again at the evening Mass of the same day.

1259   15. Before the postcommunion in Masses celebrated with the people, if it seems opportune, either a period of silence may be observed or a psalm or canticle of praise may be said or sung, for example, Psalm 33 "I Will Bless You, Lord"; Psalm 150 "Praise the Lord in His Sanctuary"; the canticles "Bless the Lord," "You Are Blessed."

1260   16. At the end of the Mass the blessing is given immediately before the dismissal. It is praiseworthy for the priest to recite the *"Placeat"* to himself as he leaves the altar.

1261   In Masses for the dead also, the blessing and dismissal ("The Mass is ended. Go in peace") are given in the usual way, unless the absolution follows immediately; in this case, "Let us bless the Lord" is said, the blessing is omitted, and the celebrant proceeds to give the absolution.

IV

Special Circumstances

1262   17. In the nuptial Mass, the celebrant does not say the prayers "Listen with Favor" and "O God, Your Mighty

Power" between the Lord's Prayer and its embolism, but after the host has been broken and the particle dropped into the chalice, immediately before the *"Agnus Dei."*

If the Mass is celebrated facing the people and it seems   1263
convenient, having put the particle into the chalice the celebrant genuflects, approaches the married couple, and says the prayers mentioned above. He then returns to the altar, genuflects, and continues the Mass in the usual way.

18. A Mass celebrated by a priest who is sick or whose   1264
sight is failing and who has the indult to say a votive Mass, may be arranged as follows:

a) the priest says the prayers and the preface of the votive Mass;

b) another priest, or a deacon, lector, or server shall read the lessons from the Mass of the day or from the weekday lectionary. If there is only a lector or a server, he is granted the faculty to read the Gospel. In this case, the *"Munda cor meum," "Iube domne, benedicere,"* and *"Dominus sit in corde meo"* are omitted; the celebrant says, "The Lord be with you," before the reading of the Gospel and kisses the book at the end;

c) the choir, the people, or even the reader himself may read the Introit, Offertory and Communion antiphons, and the songs between the readings.

V

Variations in the Divine Office

19. Until the general reform of the Divine Office, on first   1265
and second class liturgical days, which have Matins with three Nocturns, it is permissible to say one Nocturn only. The hymn *"Te Deum"* is said at the end of the third reading, in accordance with the rubrics. The rubrics given for the last three days of Holy Week in the Roman Breviary remain unaltered.

20. In individual recitation, the absolution and blessings   1266
before the readings and the conclusion *"Tu autem"* are omitted.

21. When Lauds and Vespers are celebrated together with   1267
the people, a longer Scripture reading may be used in place

of the chapter. It may be taken, for example, from the Matins or the Mass of the day, or from the weekday lectionary, and followed, if convenient, by a short homily. Unless Mass follows immediately, the Prayer of the Faithful may be said before the concluding prayer.

1268   When such additions are made, only three psalms need be said. At Lauds any of the first three psalms may be selected, to be said together with the canticle and the last psalm; at Vespers any three of the five psalms may be selected.

1269   22. When Compline is celebrated together with the people, the Sunday psalms may always be used.

VI

Variations in the Rites for the Dead

1270   23. Violet vestments may be used for the Masses and rites for the dead. However, the conference of bishops may determine another color which is suited to the mentality of the people and does not offend against personal grief, while expressing that Christian hope which is founded on the paschal mystery.

1271   24. At the absolution, the responsory "Deliver me, O Lord" may be replaced with others taken from Matins for the dead, namely, "I believe that my Redeemer lives"; "You who did raise Lazarus"; "Remember me, O God"; "Deliver me, O Lord, from the ways of hell."

VII

Liturgical Vestments

1272   25. The maniple need not be worn at any time.

1273   26. A chasuble may be worn for the *Asperges* before Mass on Sundays, for the blessing and giving of ashes at the beginning of Lent, and for the absolution after Masses for the dead.

1274   27. At concelebrated Masses, each concelebrant must wear those vestments which he is obliged to wear when he is the only celebrant *(Ritus servandus in Concelebratione Missae, no. 12).*

1275   Nevertheless, where there is a serious reason, for example, a large number of concelebrants and a lack of vestments, the concelebrants—always with the exception of the principal celebrant—need not wear a chasuble, but must always wear an alb and stole.

VIII
Use of the Vernacular

28. The competent territorial authority, observing art. 36, § 3 and 4 of the Constitution on the Sacred Liturgy, may decree that in liturgical celebrations with the people present the vernacular may also be used:

 a) in the Canon of the Mass;

 b) in all the rites of Holy Orders;

 c) in the lessons of the Divine Office, even in choral celebration.

 1276

In the audience granted on April 13, 1967, to the undersigned Cardinal Arcadio Maria Larraona, Prefect of the Sacred Congregation of Rites, His Holiness, Pope Paul VI, by his authority approved and confirmed the present instruction in all its parts, ordered that it should be published and carefully observed by all to whom it pertains, beginning June 29, 1967.

 1277

Given at Rome, May 4, 1967, the Feast of the Ascension of our Lord.

 1278

EUCHARISTICUM MYSTERIUM
Instruction of the Sacred Congregation of Rites
on Eucharistic Worship
May 25, 1967

INTRODUCTION

1. *Recent Documents of the Church Concerning the Mystery of the Eucharist*

The mystery of the Eucharist is the true center of the sacred liturgy and indeed of the whole Christian life. Consequently the Church, guided by the Holy Sprit, continually seeks to understand and to live the Eucharist more fully.

1280   In our own day the Second Vatican Council has stressed several important aspects of this mystery.

1281   In the Constitution on the Liturgy the council recalled certain facts about the nature and importance of the Eucharist.[1] It established principles for the reform of the rites of the sacrifice of the Mass so as to encourage the full and active participation of the faithful in the celebration of this mystery.[2] It also extended the practice of concelebration and Communion under both kinds.[3]

1282   In the Constitution on the Church the council showed the close and necessary connection between the Eucharist and the mystery of the Church.[4] Other documents of the council frequently stressed the important role of the Eucharistic Mystery in the life of the faithful.[5] They showed its power to reveal the meaning of man's work, and indeed of all created nature, since in it "natural elements, refined by man, are changed into the glorified Body and Blood."[6]

Pope Pius XII had prepared the way for many of these   1283
statements of the council, especially in the encyclical letter
Mediator Dei,[7] while Pope Paul VI in the encyclical letter
Mysterium Fidei[8] has recalled the importance of certain
aspects of Eucharistic doctrine, of the real presence of Christ
in particular and the worship due to this sacrament even outside the Mass.

2. *The Need to Retain an Overall View of the Teaching Contained in These Documents*

In recent years then, certain aspects of the traditional   1284
teaching on this mystery have been the subject of deeper reflection throughout the Church and have been presented with
new zeal for the greater spiritual benefit of the faithful.
Undertakings and research in various fields, particularly the
liturgical and biblical, have greatly assisted this process.

From the doctrine contained in these documents it is nec-   1285
essary to formulate practical norms which will show the
Christian people how to act in regard to this sacrament so as
to pursue that knowledge and holiness which the council has
set before the Church.

It is important that the mystery of the Eucharist should   1286
shine out before the eyes of the faithful in its true light. It
should be considered in all its different aspects, and the real
relationships which, as the Church teaches, are known to
exist between these various aspects of the mystery should be
so understood by the faithful as to be reflected in their lives.

3. *The Principal Points of Doctrine in These Documents*

Among the doctrinal principles concerning the Eucharist   1287
formulated in these documents of the Church, the following
should be noted as having a bearing upon the attitude of
Christians toward this mystery, and, therefore, as falling
within the scope of this instruction.

a) "The Son of God in the human nature which He united   1288

to Himself redeemed man and transformed him into a new
creation by overcoming death through his own death and
resurrection (cf. *Gal.* 6:15; *II Cor.* 5:17). For by giving His
Spirit He mystically established as His body His brethren
gathered from all nations. In that body the life of Christ is
communicated to those who believe; for through the sacraments they are joined in a mysterious yet real way to the
Christ who suffered and is glorified."⁹

1289   Therefore "Our Saviour at the Last Supper on the night
when He was betrayed instituted the Eucharistic Sacrifice of
His Body and Blood so that He might perpetuate the Sacrifice of the Cross throughout the centuries till His coming. He
thus entrusted to the Church, His beloved Spouse, a memorial
of His death and resurrection: a sacrament of love, a sign of
unity, a bond of charity, a paschal meal in which Christ is
eaten, the mind filled with grace, and a pledge of future glory
given to us."¹⁰

1290   Hence the Mass, the Lord's Supper, is at the same time and
inseparably:

—A sacrifice in which the Sacrifice of the Cross is perpet-
uated;

—A memorial of the death and resurrection of the Lord,
who said "do this in memory of me" (*Luke* 22:19);

—A sacred banquet in which, through the communion of
the Body and Blood of the Lord, the People of God share the
benefits of the Paschal Sacrifice, renew the New Covenant
which God has made with man once for all through the Blood
of Christ, and in faith and hope foreshadow and anticipate
the eschatological banquet in the kingdom of the Father, proclaiming the Lord's death "till His coming."¹¹

1291   b) In the Mass, therefore, the sacrifice and sacred meal belong to the same mystery—so much so that they are linked by
the closest bond.

1292   For in the sacrifice of the Mass our Lord is immolated
when "he begins to be present sacramentally as the spiritual
food of the faithful under the appearances of bread and
wine."¹² It was for this purpose that Christ entrusted this
sacrifice to the Church, that the faithful might share in it
|both spiritually, by faith and charity, and sacramentally,

through the banquet of holy Communion. Participation in the Lord's Supper is always communion with Christ offering Himself for us as a sacrifice to the Father.[13]

c) The celebration of the Eucharist, which takes place at Mass, is the action not only of Christ, but also of the Church. For in it Christ perpetuates in an unbloody manner the sacrifice offered on the cross,[14] offering Himself to the Father for the world's salvation through the ministry of priests.[15] The Church, the spouse and minister of Christ, performs together with Him the role of priest and victim, offers Him to the Father and at the same time makes a total offering of herself together with Him.[16]   **1293**

Thus the Church, especially in the great Eucharistic prayer, together with Christ, gives thanks to the Father in the Holy Spirit for all the blessings which He gives to men in creation and especially in the Paschal Mystery, and prays to Him for the coming of His kingdom.   **1294**

d) Hence no Mass, indeed no liturgical action, is a purely private action, but rather a celebration of the Church as a society composed of different orders and ministries, in which each member acts according to his own order and role.[17]   **1295**

e) The celebration of the Eucharist in the sacrifice of the Mass is the origin and consummation of the worship shown to the Eucharist outside Mass. Not only are the sacred species which remain after Mass derived from the Mass, but they are preserved so that those of the faithful who cannot come to Mass may be united to Christ and His Sacrifice celebrated in the Mass, through sacramental Communion received with the right dispositions.[18]   **1296**

Consequently the Eucharistic sacrifice is the source and the summit of the whole of the Church's worship and of the Christian life.[19] The faithful participate more fully in this sacrament of thanksgiving, propitiation, petition, and praise, not only when they wholeheartedly offer the Sacred Victim, and in it themselves, to the Father with the priest, but also when they receive this same Victim sacramentally.   **1297**

f) There should be no doubt in anyone's mind "that all the faithful ought to show to this most holy sacrament the worship which is due to the true God, as has always been the   **1298** custom of the Catholic Church. Nor is it to be adored any the less because it was instituted by Christ to be eaten."[20] For even in the reserved sacrament He is to be adored[21] because He is substantially present there through that conversion of bread and wine which, as the Council of Trent tells us,[22] is most aptly named transubstantiation.

1299   g) The mystery of the Eucharist should therefore be considered in all its fullness, not only in the celebration of Mass but also in devotion to the sacred species which remain after Mass and are reserved to extend the grace of the sacrifice.[23]

1300   These are the principles from which practical rules are to be drawn to govern devotion due to the sacrament outside Mass and its proper relation to the right ordering of the sacrifice of the Mass according to the mind of the Second Vatican Council and the other documents of the Apostolic See on this subject.[24]

4. *The General Intention of This Instruction*

1301   For this reason the Consilium set up to implement the Constitution on the Liturgy, on the instructions of His Holiness Pope Paul VI, has prepared an instruction setting out such practical rules of this nature as may be suitable for the present situation.

1302   The particular purpose of these rules is not only to emphasize the general principles of how to instruct the people in the Eucharist, but also to make more readily intelligible the signs by which the Eucharist is celebrated as the memorial of the Lord and worshipped as a permanent sacrament in the Church.

1303   For although this sacrament has this supreme and unique feature, that the author of holiness is Himself present in it, nevertheless, in common with the other sacraments, it is the symbol of a sacred reality and the visible form of an invisible grace.[25] Consequently the more intelligible the signs by which it is celebrated and worshipped, the more firmly and effectively it will enter into the minds and lives of the faithful.[26]

PART I

Some General Principles of Particular Importance in the
Catechesis of the People on the Mystery of the Eucharist

5. *What is Required of Pastors Who Are to Give Instruction about This Mystery*

Suitable catechesis is essential if the mystery of the Eucharist is to take deeper root in the minds and lives of the faithful.   1304

To convey this instruction properly, pastors should not only bear in mind the many aspects of the Church's teaching, as contained in the documents of the magisterium, but in their hearts and in their lives they must be open to the spirit of the Church in this matter.[27] Only then will they readily perceive which of the many facets of this mystery best suits the needs of the faithful at any one time.   1305

While recalling all that was said above in no. 3, one should take special note of the following.   1306

6. *The Mystery of the Eucharist as the Center of the Entire Life of the Church*

The catechesis about the Eucharistic Mystery should aim to help the faithful to realize that the celebration of the Eucharist is the true center of the whole Christian life both for the universal Church and for the local congregations of that Church. For "the other sacraments, as indeed every ministry of the Church and every work of the apostolate, are linked with the Eucharist and are directed toward it. For the Eucharist contains the entire spiritual good of the Church, namely Christ Himself, our Passover and living bread, offering through His flesh, living and life-giving in the Spirit, life to men who are thus invited and led on to offer themselves, their labors, and all created things together with Him."[28]   1307

The Eucharist both perfectly signifies and wonderfully effects that sharing in God's life and unity of God's People by which the Church exists.[29] It is the summit of both the   1308 action by which God sanctifies the world in Christ and the worship which men offer to Christ and which through him they offer to the Father in the Spirit.[30] Its celebration "is the supreme means by which the faithful come to express in their lives and to manifest to others the mystery of Christ and the true nature of the Church."[31]

7. *The Mystery of the Eucharist as the Focal Point of the Local Church*

1309   It is through the Eucharist that "the Church continually lives and grows. This Church of Christ is truly present in all legitimate local congregations of the faithful which, united with their pastors, are called churches in the New Testament. These are, each in its own place, the new People, called by God in the Holy Spirit and in all fullness (cf. *I Thess.* 1:5). In them the faithful are gathered by the preaching of Christ's Gospel, and the mystery of the Lord's Supper is celebrated, 'so that through the Body and Blood of the Lord the whole brotherhood is united.'[32] Every gathering around the altar under the sacred ministry of the bishop"[33] or of a priest who takes the place of the bishop[34] "is a sign of that charity and 'unity of the Mystical Body, without which there can be no salvation.'[35] In these communities, though they may often be small and poor or living amongst the 'diaspora,' Christ is present, by whose power the one, holy, catholic, and apostolic Church is united. For 'the partaking of the Body and Blood of Christ has no less an effect than to change us into what we have received'."[36,37]

8. *The Eucharistic Mystery and Christian Unity*

1310   In addition to those things which concern the ecclesial community and the individual faithful, pastors should pay particular attention to that part of her doctrine in which the Church teaches that the memorial of the Lord, celebrated according to His will, signifies and effects the unity of all who believe in Him.[38]

1311   As the Decree on Ecumenism of the Second Vatican Council declares,[39] the faithful should be led to a proper appreciation of the values which are preserved in the Eucharistic tradition according to which our brethren of the other Christian confessions have continued to celebrate the Lord's Supper. For while "they call to mind the death and resurrection of the Lord in the Holy Supper, they profess that it signifies life in communion with Christ and await His coming in glory."[40] But those who have preserved the sacrament of Order, "united with the bishop, have access to God the Father through the Son, the Word incarnate, who suffered and is glorified, by the outpouring of the Holy Spirit, and attain communion with the Blessed Trinity, becoming 'sharers in the divine nature' (*II Peter* 1:4). And so through the celebration of the Lord's Eucharist in these individual churches the Church of God is built up and grows, and their communion is manifested through concelebration."[41]

It is above all in the celebration of the mystery of unity that all Christians should be filled with sorrow at the divisions which separate them. They should therefore pray earnestly to God that all disciples of Christ may daily come closer to a proper understanding of the mystery of the Eucharist according to His mind, and may so celebrate it as to become sharers in the Body of Christ and so become one body (cf. *I Cor.* 10: 17) "linked by the very bonds by which He wishes it to be constituted."[42]   **1312**

9. *The Different Modes of Christ's Presence*

In order that they should achieve a deeper understanding of the mystery of the Eucharist, the faithful should be instructed in the principal ways in which the Lord is present to His Church in liturgical celebrations.[42]   **1313**

He is always present in a body of the faithful gathered in His name (cf. *Matt.* 18:20). He is present too in His Word, for it is He who speaks when the Scriptures are read in the Church.   **1314**

In the sacrifice of the Eucharist He is present both in the person of the minister, "the same now offering through the ministry of the priest who formerly offered himself on the Cross,"[44] and above all under the species of the Eucharist.[45] For in this sacrament Christ is present in a unique way, whole   **1315** and entire, God and man, substantially and permanently. This presence of Christ under the species "is called 'real' not in an exclusive sense, as if the other kinds of presence were not real, but 'par excellence'."[46]

10. *The Connection Between the Liturgy of the Word and the Liturgy of the Eucharist*

1316   Pastors should therefore "carefully teach the faithful to participate in the whole Mass," showing the close connection between the Liturgy of the Word and the celebration of the Lord's Supper, so that they can see clearly how the two constitute a single act of worship.[47] For "the preaching of the Word is necessary for the very administration of the sacraments, inasmuch as they are sacraments of faith, which is born of the Word and fed by it."[48] This is especially true of the celebration of Mass, in which it is the purpose of the Liturgy of the Word to develop the close connection between the preaching and hearing of the Word of God and the Eucharistic Mystery.[49]

1317   When therefore the faithful hear the Word of God, they should realize that the wonders it proclaims culminate in the Paschal Mystery, of which the memorial is sacramentally celebrated in the Mass. In this way the faithful will be nourished by the Word of God which they have received and in a spirit of thanksgiving will be led on to a fruitful participation in the mysteries of salvation. Thus the Church is nourished by the bread of life which she finds at the table both of the Word of God and of the Body of Christ.[50]

11. *The Priesthood Common to All the Faithful and the Ministerial Priesthood in the Celebration of the Eucharist*

1318   The more clearly the faithful understand the place they occupy in the liturgical community and the part they have to play in the eucharistic action, the more conscious and fruitful will be the active participation which is proper to that community.[51]

1319   Catechetical instruction should therefore explain the doctrine of the royal priesthood to which the faithful are consecrated by rebirth and the anointing of the Holy Spirit.[52]

Moreover there should also be further explanation of the role in the celebration of the Eucharist of the ministerial priesthood which differs from the common priesthood of the faithful in essence and not merely in degree.[53] The part played by others who exercise a ministry in the Eucharist should also be explained.[54]

1320

12. *The Nature of Active Participation in the Mass*

It should be made clear that all who gather for the Eucharist constitute that holy people which, together with the ministers, plays its part in the sacred action. It is indeed the priest alone, who, acting in the person of Christ, consecrates the bread and wine, but the role of the faithful in the Eucharist is to recall the passion, resurrection and glorification of the Lord, to give thanks to God, and to offer the immaculate Victim not only through the hands of the priest, but also together with him; and finally, by receiving the Body of the Lord, to perfect that communion with God and among themselves which should be the product of participation in the Sacrifice of the Mass.[55] For the faithful achieve a more perfect participation in the Mass when, with proper disposition, they receive the Body of the Lord sacramentally in the Mass itself, in obedience to his words, "take and eat."[56]

1321

Like the passion of Christ itself, this sacrifice, though offered for all, "has no effect except in those united to the passion of Christ by faith and charity . . . To these it brings a greater or less benefit in proportion to their devotion."[57]

1322

All these things should be explained to the faithful, so that they may take an active part in the celebration of the Mass both by their personal devotion and by joining in the external rites, according to the principles laid down in the Constitution on the Liturgy,[58] which have been further determined by the Instruction *Inter Oecumenici* of Sept. 26, 1964, and the Instruction *Musician Sacram* of March 5, 1967,[59] and through the Instruction *Tres abhinc annos* of May 4, 1967.

1323

13. *The Influence of the Eucharist on the Daily Lives of the Faithful*

1324   What the faithful have received by faith and sacrament in the celebration of the Eucharist should have its effect on their way of life. They should seek to live joyfully and gratefully by the strength of this heavenly food, sharing in the death and resurrection of the Lord. And so everyone who has participated in the Mass should be "eager to do good works, to please God, and to live honestly, devoted to the Church, putting into practice what he has learnt, and growing in piety."[60] He will seek to fill the world with the Spirit of Christ and "in all things, in the very midst of human affairs" to become a witness of Christ.[61]

1325   For no "Christian community can be built up unless it has as its basis and pivot the celebration of the holy Eucharist. It is from this therefore that any attempt to form a community must begin."[62]

14. *Teaching Children About the Mass*

1326   Those who have charge of the religious instruction of children, especially parents, parish priests, and teachers, should be careful when they are introducing them gradually to the mystery of salvation,[63] to give emphasis to instruction on the Mass. Instruction about the Eucharist, while being suited to the age and abilities of the children, should aim to convey the meaning of the Mass through the principal rites and prayers. It should also explain the place of the Mass in participation in the life of the Church.

1327   All this should be borne in mind especially when children are being prepared for First Communion so that the First Communion may be seen as the full incorporation into the body of Christ.

15. *Catechesis about the Mass Should Take the Rites and Prayers as Its Starting Point*

1328   The Council of Trent prescribes that pastors should frequently "either themselves or through others, expound some part of what is read at Mass and, among other things, explain something of the mystery of this sacrament."⁶ ⁵

Pastors should therefore gently lead the faithful to a full   1329
understanding of this mystery of faith by suitable catechesis. This should take as its starting point the mysteries of the liturgical year and the rites and prayers which are part of the celebration. It should clarify their meaning and especially that of the great Eucharistic Prayer, and lead the people to a profound understanding of the mystery which these signify and accomplish.

PART II

The Celebration of the Memorial of the Lord

I. Some General Norms Regarding the Celebration of the Memorial of the Lord in the Community of the Faithful

16. *The Common Unity to Be Shown in the Celebration*

Since through baptism "there is neither Jew nor Greek,   1330
slave nor freeman, male nor female," but all are one in Christ Jesus (cf. *Gal.* 3:28), the assembly which most fully portrays the nature of the Church and its role in the Eucharist is that which gathers together the faithful, men and women, of every age and walk of life.

The unity of this community, having its origin in the one   1331
bread in which all share (cf. *I Cor.* 10:17), is arranged in hierarchical order. For this reason it is necessary that "each person, performing his role as a minister or as one of the faithful, should do all that the nature of the action and the liturgical norms require of him, and only that."⁶ ⁶

The outstanding example of this unity may be seen "in   1332
the full and active participation of the entire people of God . . . in the same Eucharist, in a single prayer, around the one altar where the bishop presides, accompanied by his priests and ministers."⁶ ⁷

17. *The Community Should Not Be Disrupted, nor the Faithful's Attention Diverted*

In liturgical celebrations, the community should not be   1333
disrupted or be distracted from its common purpose. Care

then must be taken not to have two liturgical celebrations at the same time in the same church, since it distracts the people's attention.

1334   This is above all true of the celebration of the Eucharist. That is why that disruption of the congregation is to be assiduously avoided, which, when Mass is celebrated with the people on Sundays and feast days, is caused by the simultaneous celebration of Masses in the same church.

1335   As far as possible it should be avoided on other days as well. The best way of achieving this, is, in accordance with the law, for those priests to concelebrate who want to celebrate Mass at the same time.[68] Likewise, when Mass is being celebrated for the people, in accordance with the public timetable of the church, baptisms, marriages, exhortations, and the common or choral recitation of the Divine Office are to be avoided.

18. *An Awareness of the Local and Universal Church Community Is to Be Fostered*

1336   In the celebration of the Eucharist, a sense of community should be encouraged. Each person will then feel himself united with his brethren in the communion of the Church, local and universal, and even in a way with all men. In the sacrifice of the Mass, in fact, Christ offers Himself for the salvation of the entire world. The congregation of the faithful is both type and sign of the union of the whole human race in Christ its Head.[69]

19. *Welcoming Strangers to the Local Celebration*

1337   When any of the faithful take part in a Eucharistic celebration outside their own parish, they will follow the form of celebration used by the local community.

1338   Pastors should do what they can to help faithful from other areas join with the local community. This is above all necessary in city churches and places where many of the faithful come on vacation. Where there are large numbers of emigrants or people of another language, pastors should provide them at least from time to time with the opportunity of

participating in the Mass in the way to which they are accustomed. "Steps should be taken however to enable the
faithful to say or sing together in Latin those parts of the
Mass which pertain to them."[70]

20. *The Care to Be Taken by Ministers in Celebrating the Liturgy*

To encourage the active participation of the people and to   1339
ensure that the celebrations are carried out as they should be,
it is not sufficient for the ministers to content themselves
with the exact fulfillment of their role according to the liturgical laws. It is also necessary that they should so celebrate
the liturgy that by this very fact they convey an awareness of
the meaning of the sacred actions.

The people have the right to be nourished by the proc-   1340
lamation of the Word of God and by the minister's explanation of it. Priests, then, will not only give a homily whenever it is prescribed or seems suitable but will ensure that
whatever they or the ministers say or sing will be so clear
that the faithful will be able to hear it easily and grasp its
meaning; and they will in fact be spontaneously drawn to
respond and participate.[71] The ministers should undergo a
careful preparation for this, above all in seminaries and religious houses.

21. *The Canon of the Mass*

a) In Masses celebrated with the people, even when not   1341
concelebrated, it is permissible for the celebrant, if it seems
opportune, to say the Canon aloud. In sung Masses *(Missae
in cantu)* it is permissible for him to sing those parts of the
Canon which are at present allowed to be sung in a concelebrated Mass *(Ritus servandus in concelebratione Missae,*
nos. 39, 42) in accordance with the Instruction *Tres abhinc
annos* of May 4, 1967, n. 10.

b) In printing the words of consecration the custom of   1342
printing them in a way different from the rest of the text
should be maintained, in order that they may stand out more
clearly.

22. *The Mass on Radio and Television*

1343   When according to the intention of art. 20 of the Constitution on the Liturgy, the Mass is televised or broadcast, local Ordinaries must see to it that the prayer and participation of the faithful do not suffer. It should be celebrated with such dignity and discretion as to be a model of the celebration of the sacred mystery in accordance with the laws of the liturgical renewal.[72]

23. *Photographs During the Celebration of the Eucharist*

1344   Great care should be taken to ensure that liturgical celebrations, especially the Mass, are not disturbed or interrupted by the taking of photographs. Where there is a good reason for taking them, the greatest discretion should be used, and the norms laid down by the local Ordinary should be observed.

24. *The Importance of the Arrangement of Churches for Well-Ordered Celebrations*

1345   "The house of prayer where the most holy Eucharist is celebrated and preserved should be kept clean and in good order, suitable for prayer and sacred celebrations. It is there too that the faithful gather and find help and comfort in venerating the presence of the Son of God, our Saviour, offered for us on the altar of sacrifice."[73]

1346   Pastors must realize then that the way the church is arranged greatly contributes to a worthy celebration and to the active participation of the people.

1347   For this reason the directives and criteria given in the Instruction *Inter Oecumenici* should be followed regarding: the building of churches and adapting them to the renewed liturgy, the setting up and adorning of altars, the suitable arrangement of the seating for the celebrant and ministers, the correct place from which to give the readings, and the arrangement of the places for the faithful and the choir.

1348   Above all, the main altar should be so placed and constructed that it is always seen to be the sign of Christ Himself, the place at which the saving mysteries are carried out, and the center of the assembly, to which the greatest reverence is due.

In adapting churches care will be taken not to destroy   1349
treasures of sacred art. If in the interests of liturgical renewal a local Ordinary decides, having obtained the advice of experts and—if necessary—the consent of those whom it concerns, to remove some of these works of art from their present position, it should be done with prudence and in such a way that even in their new surroundings they are well located.

Pastors will recall that the material and appearance of vest-   1350
ments greatly contributes to the dignity of liturgical celebrations. "They should strive after noble beauty rather than sumptuous display."[74]

II. Celebrations on Sundays and Weekdays

25. *The Celebration of the Eucharist on Sundays*

Whenever the community gathers to celebrate the Euch-   1351
arist, it announces the death and resurrection of the Lord, in the hope of His glorious return. The supreme manifestation of this is the Sunday assembly. This is the day of the week on which, by apostolic tradition, the Paschal Mystery is celebrated in the Eucharist in a special way.[75]

In order that the faithful may willingly fulfill the precept   1352
to sanctify this day and understand why the Church calls them together to celebrate the Eucharist every Sunday, from the very outset of their Christian formation "Sunday should be presented to them as the primordial feast day,"[76] on which, assembled together, they are to hear the Word of God and take part in the Paschal Mystery.

Moreover, any endeavor that seeks to make Sunday a   1353
genuine "day of joy and rest from work"[77] should be encouraged.

26. *The Celebration of Sunday Around the Bishop and in Parishes*

It is fitting that the sense of ecclesial community, espe-   1354
cially fostered and expressed by the celebration of Sunday

Mass in common, should be encouraged both around the bishop, particularly in the cathedral church, and in the parish assembly, where the pastor takes the place of the bishop.[7][8]

1355   It is important that the active participation of the entire people in the Sunday celebration, which is expressed in singing, should be assiduously promoted. In fact, sung Masses *(Missae in cantu)* should be preferred as far as possible.[7][9]

1356   On Sundays and feast days above all, the celebrations which take place in other churches or oratories should be arranged in connection with the celebrations in the parish church so that they contribute to the general pastoral effort. It is preferable that small religious non-clerical communities and other similar communities, especially those that work in the parish, should take part in the parish Mass on these days.

1357   As regards the time and number of Masses to be celebrated in parishes, the good of the parish community should be kept in mind and the number of Masses should not be so multiplied as to weaken the effectiveness of the pastoral effort; for example: if through the great number of Masses, only small groups of the faithful were to come to each of the Masses in a church that can hold a great number of people. Another example would be if, for the same reason, the priests were so overburdened by their work as to make it difficult for them to fulfill their ministry adequately.

27. *Masses for Particular Groups*

1358   In order to emphasize the value of the unity of the parish community in the celebration of the Eucharist on Sundays and feast days, Masses for particular groups, such as associations and societies, should be held on weekdays if possible. If it is not possible to transfer them to a weekday, one should try to preserve the unity of the parish community by incorporating these particular groups into the parish celebrations on Sundays and feast days.

28. *Anticipating the Sunday and Feast Day Masses on the Previous Evening*

1359   Where permission has been granted by the Apostolic See to fulfill the Sunday obligation on the preceding Saturday

evening, pastors should explain the meaning of this permission carefully to the faithful and should ensure that the
significance of Sunday is not thereby obscured. The purpose of this concession is in fact to enable the Christians of
today to celebrate more easily the day of the resurrection of
the Lord.

All concessions and contrary customs notwithstanding,   1360
when celebrated on Saturday this Mass may be celebrated
only in the evening, at times determined by the local Ordinary.

In these cases the Mass celebrated is that assigned in the   1361
calendar to Sunday, the homily and the prayer of the faithful are not to be omitted.

What has been said above is equally valid for the Mass on   1362
holy days of obligation which for the same reason has been
transferred to the preceding evening.

The Mass celebrated on the evening before Pentecost   1363
Sunday is the present Mass of the Vigil, with the Creed.
Likewise, the Mass celebrated on the evening of Christmas
Eve is the Mass of the Vigil but with white vestments, the
Alleluia and the Preface of the Nativity, as on the feast.
Nevertheless it is not permitted to celebrate the Vigil Mass
of Easter Sunday before dusk on Holy Saturday, certainly
not before sunset. The Mass is always that of the Easter
Vigil, which, by reason of its special significance in the
liturgical year and in the whole Christian life, must be celebrated with the liturgical rites laid down for the Vigil on this
holy night.

The faithful who begin to celebrate the Sunday or holy   1364
day of obligation on the preceding evening may go to Communion at that Mass even if they have already received
Communion in the morning. Those who "have received
Communion during the Mass of the Easter Vigil, or during
the Mass of the Lord's Nativity, may receive Communion
again at the second Easter Mass and at one of the Masses
on Christmas Day."[80] Likewise "the faithful who go to Communion at the Mass of Chrism on Holy Thursday may again
receive Communion at the evening Mass of the same day,"

in accordance with the Instruction *Tres abhinc annos* of May 4, 1967, no. 14.

29. *Masses Celebrated on Weekdays*

1365   The faithful should be invited to go to Mass frequently on weekdays, in fact to go to Mass even daily.

1366   This is particularly recommended on those weekdays which should be celebrated with special care, above all in Lent and Advent, and also on some minor feasts of the Lord and certain feasts of the Blessed Virgin Mary or of saints who are particularly venerated in the universal or local Church.

30. *Mass at Meetings and Gatherings of a Religious Character*

1367   It is very fitting that meetings or congresses which seek to develop the Christian life or apostolate or which seek to promote religious studies, as well as spiritual exercises and retreats of every kind, should be so arranged as to have their climax in the celebration of the Eucharist.

III. The Communion of the Faithful

31. *The Communion of the Faithful during Mass*

1368   Through sacramental Communion the faithful take part more perfectly in the celebration of the Eucharist. It is strongly recommended that they should normally receive it during the Mass and at that point of the celebration which is prescribed by the rite, namely immediately after the Communion of the celebrant.[81]

1369   In order that, even through signs, the Communion may be seen more clearly to be participation in the sacrifice which is being celebrated, care should be taken to enable the faithful to communicate with hosts consecrated during that Mass.[82]

1370   It should belong to the celebrant priest above all to distribute Communion; nor should the Mass continue until the Communion of the faithful is over. Other priests or deacons will help the priest, if need be.[83]

32. *Communion under Both Kinds*

1371   Holy Communion, considered as a sign, has a more complete form when it is received under both kinds. For under this form (leaving intact the principles of the Council of Trent,[84] by which under either species there is received the true sacrament and Christ whole and entire), the sign of the Eucharistic banquet appears more perfectly. Moreover, it shows more clearly how the new and eternal Covenant is ratified in the Blood of the Lord, as it also expresses the relation of the Eucharistic banquet to the eschatological banquet in the Kingdom of the Father (cf. *Matt.* 26: 27-29).

This is why from now on, in accordance with the judgment of the bishops and given the necessary catechesis, Communion from the chalice is permitted in the following cases, which were either already granted by previous legislation[85] or are granted by the present instruction: 1372

1) To newly baptized adults in the Mass which follows their baptism; to confirmed adults in the Mass of their Confirmation; to baptized persons who are received into communion with the Church;   1373

2) To bride and bridegroom in the Mass of their wedding;   1374

3) To newly ordained in the Mass of their ordination;   1375

4) To abbesses in the Mass of their blessing; to virgins in the Mass of their consecration; to professed in the Mass of their first or renewed religious profession, provided that they take or renew their vows during the Mass;   1376

5) To lay missionaries, in the Mass in which they are publicly sent out on their mission, and to all others in the Mass in which they receive an ecclesiastical mission;   1377

6) In the administration of Viaticum, to the sick person and to all who are present when Mass is celebrated in the house of the sick person, in accordance with the existing norms;   1378

7) To deacon, subdeacon, and ministers, who carry out their ministry in a solemn or pontifical Mass;   1379

8) When there is a concelebration: 1380

a) to all who exercise a genuine liturgical function in this concelebration, including lay people and to all seminarians who are present;

b) in their churches, to all members of institutes practicing the evangelical virtues and of other societies in which the members either through religious vows or offering or a promise dedicate themselves to God; and also to all those who normally live in the house of the members of these institutes and societies.

1381   9) To priests who take part in large celebrations, but are not able to celebrate or concelebrate;

1382   10) To all groups which are making retreats or following spiritual exercises, in a Mass which is celebrated during the retreat or exercises for those who are taking part; to all those who are taking part in the meeting of some pastoral commission, in the Mass they celebrate in common;

1383   11) To those listed under nos. 2 and 4, in their jubilee Masses;

1384   12) To the godfather, godmother, parents and spouse of a baptized adult, together with the lay catechists who have prepared him, in the Mass of initiation;

1385   13) To the parents, relatives and special benefactors, who take part in the Mass of a newly ordained priest.

33. *Communion outside Mass*

1386   a) It is necessary to accustom the faithful to receive Communion during the actual celebration of the Eucharist. Even outside Mass, however, priests will not refuse to distribute Communion to those who have good reason to ask for it.[86] By permission of the bishop of the place, according to the norm of the motu proprio *Pastorale Munus,* no. 4,[87] or by permission of the supreme moderator of a religious institute according to the rescript *Cum admotae,* art. 1, no. 1, Communion may be distributed even during the afternoon.

1387   b) When, at the prescribed times, Communion is distributed outside Mass, if it is judged suitable, a short Bible service may precede it, in accordance with the Instruction *Inter Oecumenici,* nos. 37 and 39.

1388   c) If Mass cannot be celebrated because of a lack of priests and Communion is distributed by a minister who has the faculty to do this by indult from the Apostolic See, the rite laid down by the competent authority is to be followed.

34. *The Way of Receiving Communion*

a) In accordance with the custom of the Church, Com-   1389
munion may be received by the faithful either kneeling or
standing. One or the other way is to be chosen, according
to the decision of the episcopal conference, bearing in mind
all the circumstances, above all the number of the faithful
and the arrangement of the churches. The faithful should
willingly adopt the method indicated by their pastors, so that
Communion may truly be a sign of the brotherly union of all
those who share in the same table of the Lord.

b) When the faithful communicate kneeling, no other   1390
sign of reverence toward the Blessed Sacrament is required,
since kneeling is itself a sign of adoration.

When they receive Communion standing, it is strongly   1391
recommended that, coming up in procession, they should
make a sign of reverence before receiving the Blessed Sacrament. This should be done at the right time and place, so
that the order of people going to and from Communion
may not be disrupted.

35. *Communion and the Sacrament of Penance*

The Eucharist should also be presented to the faithful "as   1392
a medicine, by which we are freed from our daily faults and
preserved from mortal sin",[88] they should be shown how to
make use of the penitential parts of the liturgy of the Mass.

"The precept 'let a man examine himself' (*I Cor.* 11:28)   1393
should be called to mind for those who wish to receive Communion. The custom of the Church declares this to be necessary so that no one who is conscious of having committed
mortal sin, even if he believes himself to be contrite, should
approach the holy Eucharist without first making a sacramental confession."[89] "If someone finds himself in a case of
necessity, however, and there is no confessor to whom he can
go, he should first make an act of perfect contrition."[90]

1394   The faithful are to be constantly encouraged to accustom themselves to going to confession outside the celebration of Mass, and especially at the prescribed times. In this way, the sacrament of Penance will be administered calmly and with genuine profit, and will not interfere with active participation in the Mass. Those who receive Communion daily or very frequently should be counseled to go to confession at times suitable to the individual case.

36. *Communion in Circumstances of Particular Solemnity*

1395   It is very fitting that, whenever the faithful are setting out on a new state of life or a new way of working in the vineyard of the Lord, they should take part in the Sacrifice through sacramental Communion in order to dedicate themselves again to God and to renew their covenant with him.

1396   This can well be done, for example: by the assembly of the faithful, when they renew their baptismal vows at the Easter Vigil; by young people, when they do the same in the presence of the Church, in a manner in keeping with their age; by bride and bridegroom, when they are united in the sacrament of marriage; by those who dedicate themselves to God, when they take vows or make their solemn commitment; and by the faithful, when they are to devote themselves to apostolic tasks.

37. *Frequent and Daily Communion*

1397   Since "it is clear that the frequent or daily reception of the Blessed Eucharist increases union with Christ, nourishes the spiritual life more abundantly, strengthens the soul in virtue and gives the communicant a stronger pledge of eternal happiness, parish priests, confessors and preachers will frequently and zealously exhort the Christian people to this holy and salutary practice."[9][1]

38. *Private Prayer After Communion*

1398   On those who receive the Body and Blood of Christ, the gift of the Spirit is poured out abundantly like living water (cf. *John* 7: 37-39), provided that this Body and Blood have

been received sacramentally and spiritually, namely, by that
faith which operates through charity.[92]

But union with Christ, to which the sacrament itself is   1399
directed, is not to be limited to the duration of the celebration of the Eucharist; it is to be prolonged into the entire
Christian life, in such a way that the Christian faithful, con-
templating unceasingly the gift they have received, may make
their life a continual thanksgiving under the guidance of the
Holy Spirit and may produce fruits of greater charity.

In order to remain more easily in this thanksgiving which   1400
is offered to God in an eminent way in the Mass, those who
have been nourished by holy Communion should be encouraged to remain for a while in prayer.[93]

39. *Viaticum*

Communion given as Viaticum should be considered as a   1401
special sign of participation in the mystery celebrated in the
Mass, the mystery of the death of the Lord and His passage
to the Father. By it, strengthened by the Body of Christ, the
Christian is endowed with the pledge of the resurrection in
his passage from this life.

Therefore, the faithful who are in danger of death from any   1402
cause whatever are obliged to receive holy Communion.[94]
Pastors must ensure that the administration of this sacrament
is not delayed, but that the faithful are nourished by it while
still in full possession of their faculties.[95]

Even if the faithful have already communicated on the   1403
same day, it is earnestly recommended that when they are in
danger of death they should again receive Communion.

40. *The Communion of Those Who Are Unable to Come to
   Church*

It is fitting to provide the nourishment of the Eucharist for   1404
those who are prevented from attending its celebration in the
community. They will thus feel themselves united to this
community and sustained by the love of their brethren.

Pastors of souls will take every care to make it possible   1405
for the sick and aged to receive the Eucharist frequently,

even if they are not gravely ill or in danger of death. In fact, if possible, this could be done every day, and should be done in paschal time especially. Communion may be taken to such people at any time of the day.

41. *Communion under the Species of Wine Alone*

1406   In case of necessity, depending on the judgment of the bishop, it is permitted to give the Eucharist under the species of wine alone to those who are unable to receive it under the species of bread.

1407   In this case it is permissible, with the consent of the local Ordinary, to celebrate Mass in the house of the sick person.

1408   If, however, Mass is not celebrated in the presence of the sick person, the Blood of the Lord should be kept in a properly covered chalice and placed in the tabernacle after Mass. It should be taken to the sick person only if contained in a vessel which is closed in such a way as to eliminate all danger of spilling. When the sacrament is administered, that method should be chosen from the ones given in the *Ritus servandus in distributione communionis sub utraque specie* which is most suited to the case. When Communion has been given, should some of the precious Blood still remain, it should be consumed by the minister; he will also carry out the usual ablutions.

IV. The Celebration of the Eucharist in the Life and Ministry of the Bishop and the Priest

42. *The Celebration of the Eucharist in the Life and Ministry of Bishops*

1409   The celebration of the Eucharist expresses in a particular way the public and social nature of the liturgical actions of the Church, "which is the sacrament of unity, namely, a holy people united and ordered under its bishops."[9][6]

1410   In consequence, "the bishop, endowed with the fullness of the sacrament of Order, is the steward of the grace of the supreme priesthood, above all in the Eucharist, which he offers himself or causes to be offered . . . But every legitimate celebration of the Eucharist is regulated by the bishop. For to him is entrusted the task of offering Christian worship to the majesty of God and of directing it according to the Lord's commandments and the Church's laws, further determined for his diocese by his own decisions."[97] The Church is most perfectly displayed in its hierarchic structure in that celebration of the Eucharist at which the bishop presides, surrounded by his priests and ministers, with the active participation of the whole people of God.[98]

43. *Priests Should Take Their Proper Role in the Celebration of the Eucharist*

In the celebration of the Eucharist, priests also are deputed   1411
to perform a specific function by reason of a special sacrament, namely holy Orders. For they too "as ministers of the sacred mysteries, especially in the sacrifice of the Mass . . . act in the person of Christ in a special way."[99] It is, therefore, fitting that, by reason of the sign, they participate in the Eucharist by exercising the order proper to them,[100] by celebrating or concelebrating the Mass and not by limiting themselves to communicating like the laity.

44. *The Daily Celebration of Mass*

"In the mystery of the Eucharistic sacrifice, in which the   1412
priest exercises his highest function, the work of our redemption is continually accomplished. Daily celebration of Mass, therefore, is most earnestly recommended, since, even if the faithful cannot be present, it remains an action of Christ and the Church,"[101] an action in which the priest is always acting for the salvation of the people.

45. *The Laws of the Church Must Be Faithfully Observed in Celebrating Mass*

Especially in the celebration of the Eucharist, no one, not   1413
even a priest, may on his own authority add, omit, or change anything in the Liturgy. Only the supreme authority of the Church, and, according to the provisions of the law, the bishop and the episcopal conferences, may do this.[102] Priests should, therefore, ensure that they so preside over the celebration of the Eucharist that the faithful know that they are

taking part not in a rite established on private initiative,[103] but in the Church's public worship, the regulation of which was entrusted by Christ to the Apostles and their successors.

46. *Pastoral Considerations as the Criterion by Which to Choose Among Different Forms of Celebration*

1414   "Care must be taken not only that in a liturgical action the laws for a valid and licit celebration are observed, but also that the faithful consciously, actively, and fruitfully participate in it."[104] From among the forms of celebration permitted by the law, priests should, therefore, endeavor to choose in each instance those which seem most suited to the needs of the faithful and favorable to their full participation.

47. *Concelebration*

1415   Concelebration of the Eucharist aptly demonstrates the unity of the sacrifice and of the priesthood. Moreover, whenever the faithful take an active part, the unity of the People of God is strikingly manifested,[105] particularly if the bishop presides.[106]

1416   Concelebration both symbolizes and strengthens the brotherly bond of the priesthood, because "by virtue of the ordination to the priesthood which they have in common, all are bound together in an intimate brotherhood."[107]

1417   Therefore, unless it conflicts with the needs of the faithful which must always be consulted with the deepest pastoral concern, and although every priest retains the right to celebrate alone, it is desirable that priests should celebrate the Eucharist in this eminent manner. This applies both to communities of priests and to groups which gather on particular occasions, and also to all similar circumstances. Those who live in community or serve the same church should welcome visiting priests into their concelebration.

1418   The competent superiors should, therefore, facilitate and indeed positively encourage concelebration, whenever pastoral needs or other reasonable motives do not prevent it.

1419   The faculty to concelebrate also applies to the principal Masses in churches and public and semi-public oratories of seminaries, colleges and ecclesiastical institutes, and also of religious orders and societies of clergy living in community without vows. However, where there is a great number of priests, the competent superior may give permission for concelebration to take place even several times on the same day, but at different times or in different sacred places.

48. *The Bread for Concelebration*

If a large host is used for concelebration, as permitted in the *Ritus servandus in concelebratione Missae* no. 17, care must be taken that, in keeping with traditional usage, it should be of such a shape and appearance as befits so great a sacrament.   1420

PART III

The Worship of the Eucharist as a Permanent Sacrament

I. The Reasons for Reserving the Eucharist and Prayer before the Blessed Sacrament

49. *The Reasons for Reserving the Eucharist outside Mass*

"It would be well to recall that the primary and original purpose of reserving the sacred species in church outside Mass is the administration of the Viaticum. Secondary ends are the distribution of Communion outside Mass and the adoration of our Lord Jesus Christ concealed beneath these same species."[108] For "the reservation of the sacred species for the sick . . . led to the praiseworthy custom of adoring the heavenly food which is preserved in churches. This practice of adoration has a valid and firm foundation,"[109] especially since belief in the real presence of the Lord has as its natural consequence the external and public manifestation of that belief.   1421

50. *Prayer before the Blessed Sacrament*

When the faithful adore Christ present in the sacrament, they should remember that this presence derives from the sacrifice and is directed toward both sacramental and spiritual Communion.   1422

1423   In consequence, the devotion which leads the faithful to visit the Blessed Sacrament draws them into an ever deeper participation in the Paschal Mystery. It leads them to respond gratefully to the gift of Him who through His humanity constantly pours divine life into the members of His body.[110] Dwelling with Christ our Lord, they enjoy His intimate friendship and pour out their hearts before Him for themselves and their dear ones, and pray for the peace and salvation of the world. They offer their entire lives with Christ to the Father in the Holy Spirit, and receive in this wonderful exchange and increase of faith, hope and charity. Thus they nourish those right dispositions which enable them with all due devotion to celebrate the memorial of the Lord and receive frequently the bread given us by the Father.

1424   The faithful should therefore strive to worship Christ our Lord in the Blessed Sacrament, in harmony with their way of life. Pastors should exhort them to this, and set them a good example.[111]

51. *The Faithful Should Have Easy Access to Churches*

1425   Pastors should see to it that all churches and public oratories where the Blessed Sacrament is reserved remain open for at least several hours in the morning and evening so that it may be easy for the faithful to pray before the Blessed Sacrament.

II. The Place for the Reservation of the Holy Eucharist

52. *The Tabernacle*

1426   Where reservation of the Blessed Sacrament is permitted according to the provisions of the law, it may be reserved permanently or regularly only on one altar or in one place in the church.[112] Therefore, as a rule, each church should have only one tabernacle, and this tabernacle must be safe and inviolable.[113]

53. *The Blessed Sacrament Chapel*

1427   The place in a church or oratory where the Blessed Sacrament is reserved in the tabernacle should be truly prominent.

It ought to be suitable for private prayer so that the faithful may easily and fruitfully, by private devotion also, continue to honor our Lord in this sacrament.[114] It is therefore recommended that, as far as possible, the tabernacle be placed in a chapel distinct from the middle or central part of the church, above all in those churches where marriages and funerals take place frequently and in places which are much visited for their artistic or historical treasures.

54. *The Tabernacle in the Middle of the Altar or in Some Other Part of the Church*

"The Blessed Sacrament should be reserved in a solid, inviolable tabernacle in the middle of the main altar or on a secondary altar, but in a truly prominent place. Alternatively, according to legitimate customs and in individual cases to be decided by the local Ordinary, it may be placed in some other part of the church which is really worthy and properly equipped.

"Mass may be celebrated facing the people even though there is a tabernacle on the altar, provided this is small yet adequate."[115]

55. *A Tabernacle on an Altar where Mass is Celebrated with a Congregation*

In the celebration of Mass the principal modes of worship by which Christ is present to His Church[116] are gradually revealed. First of all, Christ is seen to be present among the faithful gathered in His name; then in his Word, as the Scriptures are read and explained; in the person of the minister; finally and in a unique way *(modo singulari)* under the species of the Eucharist. Consequently, because of the sign, it is more in keeping with the nature of the celebration that the Eucharistic presence of Christ, which is the fruit of the consecration and should be seen as such, should not be on the altar from the very beginning of Mass through the reservation of the sacred species in the tabernacle.

1428

1429

1430

56. The Tabernacle in the Construction of New Churches and the Adaptation of Existing Churches and Altars

1431   The principles stated in nos. 53 and 55 ought to be kept in mind in the building of new churches.

1432   The adaptation of existing churches and altars may take place only according to the principles laid down in no. 24 of this instruction.

57. The Means of Indicating the Presence of the Blessed Sacrament in the Tabernacle

1433   Care should be taken that the presence of the Blessed Sacrament in the tabernacle is indicated to the faithful by a tabernacle veil or some other suitable means prescribed by the competent authority.

1434   According to the traditional practice, a lamp should burn continually near the tabernacle as a sign of the honor paid to the Lord.[117]

III. Eucharistic Devotions

1435   58. Devotion, both private and public, toward the Sacrament of the Altar even outside Mass, provided it observes the norms laid down by the legitimate authority and those of the present instruction, is highly recommended by the Church, since the Eucharistic sacrifice is the source and summit of the whole Christian life.[118]

1436   In determining the form of such devotions, account should be taken of the regulations of the Second Vatican Council concerning the relationship to be maintained between the liturgy and other, non-liturgical celebrations. Especially important is the rule which states: "The liturgical seasons must be taken into account, and these devotions must harmonize with the liturgy, be in some way derived from it and lead the people toward the liturgy as to something which of its nature is far superior to these devotions."[119]

IV. Eucharistic Processions

1437   59. In processions in which the Blessed Sacrament is solemnly carried through the streets to the singing of hymns, especially on the feast of Corpus Christi, the Christian people give public witness to their faith and devotion toward this sacrament.

However, it is for the local Ordinary to decide whether   1438
such processions are opportune in present-day circumstances. He will also determine the place and form of such processions, so that they may be conducted with dignity and without injury to the reverence due to this sacrament.

V. Exposition of the Blessed Sacrament

60. The exposition of the Blessed Sacrament, for which   1439
either a monstrance or a ciborium may be used, stimulates the faithful to an awareness of the marvelous presence of Christ and is an invitation to spiritual communion with Him. It is therefore an excellent encouragement to offer Him that worship in spirit and truth which is His due.

Care must be taken that during these expositions the   1440
worship given to the Blessed Sacrament should be seen, by signs, in its relation to the Mass. It is thus desirable that when the exposition in question is solemn and prolonged, it should be begun at the end of the Mass in which the host to be exposed has been consecrated. The Mass ends with the *Benedicamus Domino* and the blessing is omitted. In the decoration which accompanies exposition,[120] one must carefully avoid anything which could obscure the desire of Christ in instituting the Eucharist; for He instituted it above all with the purpose of nourishing, healing and sustaining us.[121]

61. *It Is Forbidden to Celebrate Mass before the Blessed Sacrament Exposed*

While the Blessed Sacrament is exposed, the celebration   1441
of Mass in the same area of the church *(eadem aula ecclesiae)* is forbidden, all concessions and contrary customs valid up to the present time, even those worthy of special mention, notwithstanding.

This is because, besides the reasons given in no. 55 of this   1442
instruction, the celebration of the Mystery of the Eucharist includes in a more perfect way that spiritual communion to

which exposition should lead the faithful. Therefore there is no need for this further help.

1443   If exposition of the Blessed Sacrament is prolonged for a day, or for several successive days, it should be interrupted during the celebration of the Mass, unless it is celebrated in a chapel apart from the exposition area and at least some of the faithful remain in adoration.

1444   In places where the interruption of a long-established contrary custom would upset the faithful, the local Ordinary should establish a suitable but not over-long period of time, in order that this norm be explained to the faithful before coming into effect.

62. *How the Rite of Exposition Is to Be Carried Out*

1445   If the exposition is to be only a short one, then the monstrance or ciborium should be placed on the altar table. If exposition is over a longer period, then a throne may be used, placed in a prominent position; care should be taken, however, that it is not too high or far away.

1446   During the exposition everything should be so arranged that the faithful can devote themselves attentively in prayer to Christ our Lord.

1447   To foster personal prayer, there may be readings from the Scriptures together with a homily, or brief exhortations which lead to a better understanding of the Mystery of the Eucharist. It is also good for the faithful to respond to the Word of God in song. It is desirable that there should be periods of silence at suitable times.

1448   At the end of exposition, Benediction with the Blessed Sacrament is given.

1449   If the vernacular is used, instead of singing the *Tantum Ergo* before the blessing, another Eucharisitc hymn may be used, as laid down by the episcopal conference.

63. *Solemn Annual Exposition*

1450   In churches where the Blessed Sacrament is normally reserved, there may be a protracted period of solemn exposition each year, even if not strictly continuous, giving the local community the opportunity to adore and meditate on this mystery more deeply and fervently.

Exposition of this kind should be held only if it is seen   1451
that there will be a reasonable number of the faithful, with the consent of the local Ordinary and according to the law.

64. *Prolonged Exposition*

For any grave and general need, the local Ordinary can   1452
order that there should be prayer before the Blessed Sacrament exposed over a long period, which may be strictly continuous, in those churches where there are large numbers of the faithful.

65. *Interrupting Exposition*

If, because there is not a suitable number of faithful for   1453
the adoration of the Blessed Sacrament, continuous exposition is not possible, it is permissible to replace the Host in the tabernacle, at pre-arranged and publicized times. This should not be done however more than twice in a day, for example, at midday and at night.

This reposition may be carried out in the more simple way   1454
and without singing: the priest dressed in surplice and stole, having adored the Blessed Sacrament for a short time, replaces it in the tabernacle. In the same way, at a set time, the Blessed Sacrament is again exposed; the priest retires after a short period of adoration.

66. *Exposition for Short Periods*

Even brief exposition of the Blessed Sacrament, held in   1455
accordance with the law, should be so arranged that before the blessing with the Blessed Sacrament reasonable time is provided for readings of the Word of God, hymns, prayers, and silent prayers, as circumstances permit.

Local Ordinaries will make certain that these expositions   1456
of the Blessed Sacrament are always and everywhere carried out with due reverence.

Exposition merely for the purpose of giving Benediction   1457
after Mass is forbidden.

VI. Eucharistic Congresses

1458   67. In Eucharistic congresses Christians seek to understand this mystery more deeply through a consideration of its many aspects (cf. above, no. 3). But they should celebrate it in accordance with the norms of the Second Vatican Council and should venerate it through devotions and private prayers, especially by solemn processions, in such a way that all these forms of devotion find their climax in the solemn celebration of Mass.

1459   For the duration of the Eucharistic congress of an entire region, it is fitting that some churches should be reserved for perpetual adoration.

1460   In the audience granted on the 13th of April, 1967, to His Eminence Arcadio M. Cardinal Larraona, Prefect of the Sacred Congregation of Rites, His Holiness Pope Paul VI, by his authority approved and confirmed this instruction, ordered that it should be published, and established that it should come into effect on the feast of the Assumption of the Blessed Virgin Mary, Aug. 15, 1967.

1461   All things to the contrary notwithstanding.

1462   Rome, 25th May, 1967, the Feast of Corpus Christi.

SACRUM DIACONATUS ORDINEM
Motu Proprio of Pope Paul VI
on General Norms for Restoring the
Permanent Diaconate in the Latin Church
June 18, 1967

Beginning already in the early days of the Apostles, the Catholic Church has held in great veneration the sacred order of the diaconate, as the Apostle of the Gentiles himself bears witness. He expressly sends his greeting to the deacons together with the bishops and instructs Timothy[1] which virtues and qualities are to be sought in them in order that they may be regarded as worthy of their ministry.[2]

Furthermore, the Second Ecumenical Vatican Council, following this very ancient tradition, made honorable mention of the diaconate in the Constitution which begins with the words *"Lumen Gentium"* where, after concerning itself with the bishops and the priests, it praised also the third rank of sacred orders, explaining its dignity and enumerating its functions. 1464

Indeed while clearly recognizing on the one hand that "these functions very necessary to the life of the Church could in the present discipline of the Latin Church be carried out in many regions with difficulty," and while on the other hand wishing to make more suitable provision in a matter of such importance wisely decreed that the "diaconate in the future could be restored as a particular and permanent rank of the hierarchy."[3] 1465

Although some functions of the deacons, especially in missionary countries, are in fact accustomed to be entrusted to laymen it is nevertheless "beneficial that those . . . who per- 1466 form a truly diaconal ministry be strengthened by the imposition of hands, a tradition going back to the Apostles, and be more closely joined to the altar so that they may more effectively carry out their ministry through the sacramental grace of the diaconate."[4] Certainly in this way the special nature of this order will be shown most clearly. It is not to be considered as a mere step towards the priesthood, but it is so adorned with its own indelible character and its own special grace so that those who are called to it" can permanently serve the mysteries of Christ and the Church."[5]

1467   Although the restoration of the permanent diaconate is not necessarily to be effected in the whole Latin Church since "it pertains to the competent territorial Episcopal conferences, with the approval of the Supreme Pontiff, to decide whether and where it is timely that deacons of this kind be ordained for the care of souls,"[6] we therefore consider it not only proper but also necessary that specific and precise norms be given to adapt present discipline to the new precepts of the Ecumenical Council and to determine the proper conditions under which not only the ministry of the diaconate will be more advantageously regulated, but the training also of the candidates will be better suited to their different kinds of life, their common obligations and their sacred dignity.

1468   Therefore, in the first place, all that is decreed in the *Code of Canon Law* about the rights and obligations of deacons, whether these rights and obligations be common to all clerics, or proper to deacons—all these, unless some other disposition has been made, we confirm and declare to be in force also for those who will remain permanently in the diaconate. In regard to these we moreover decree the following.

I

1469   1. It is the task of the legitimate assemblies of bishops or episcopal conferences to discuss, with the consent of the Supreme Pontiff, whether and where—in view of the good of the faithful—the diaconate is to be instituted as a proper and permanent rank of the hierarchy.

2. When asking the Apostolic See for approval, the reasons   1470
must be explained which favor the introduction of this new
practice in a region as well as the circumstances which give
well-founded hope of success. Likewise, the manner will
have to be indicated in which the new discipline will be implemented, that is to say, whether it is a matter of conferring
the diaconate on "suitable young men for whom the law of
celibacy must remain intact, or on men of more mature age,
even upon those living in the married state," or on both kinds
of candidates.

3. Once the approval of the Holy See has been obtained, it   1471
is within the powers of each Ordinary, within the sphere of his
own jurisdiction, to approve and ordain the candidates, unless
special cases are concerned which exceed his faculties.

Let the Ordinaries, in drawing up the report on the state of   1472
their diocese, also mention this restored discipline.

II

4. By the law of the Church, confirmed by the Ecumenical   1473
Council itself, young men called to the diaconate are obliged
to observe the law of celibacy.

5. The permanent diaconate may not be conferred before   1474
the completion of the 25th year. Nevertheless, an older age
can be required by the episcopal conferences.

6. Let young men to be trained for the diaconal office be   1475
received in a special institute where they will be put to the
test and will be educated to live a truly evangelical life and
prepared to fulfill usefully their own specific functions.

7. For the foundation of this institute, let the bishops of   1476
the same country, or, if advantageous, of several countries according to the diversity of circumstances, join their efforts.
Let them choose, for its guidance, particularly suitable
superiors and let them establish most accurate norms regarding discipline and the ordering of studies, observing the
following prescriptions.

8. Let only those young men be admitted to training for   1477
the diaconate who have shown a natural inclination of the
spirit to service of the sacred hierarchy and of the Christian

community and who have acquired a sufficiently good store of knowledge in keeping the custom of their people and country.

1478   9. Specific training for the diaconate should be spread over a period of at least three years. The series of subjects, however, should be arranged in such a way that the candidates are orderly and gradually led to carrying out the various functions of the diaconate skillfully and beneficially. Moreover, the whole plan of studies can be so arranged that in the last year special training be given for the various functions which deacons especially will carry out.

1479   10. To this moreover should be added practice and training in teaching the elements of the Christian religion to children and other faithful, in familiarizing the people with sacred chant and in directing it, in reading the sacred books of Scripture at gatherings of the faithful, in addressing and exhorting the people, in administering the sacraments which pertain to them, in visiting the sick, and in general in fulfilling the ministries which can be entrusted to them.

III

1480   11. Older men, whether single or married, can be called to the diaconate. The latter, however, are not to be admitted unless there is certainty not only about the wife's consent, but also about her blameless Christian life and those qualities which will neither impede nor bring dishonor on the husband's ministry.

1481   12. The older age in this case is reached at the completion of the thirty-fifth year. Nevertheless, the age requirement is to be understood in this sense, namely, that no one can be called to the diaconate unless he has gained the high regard of the clergy and the faithful by a long example of truly Christian life, by his unexceptionable conduct, and by his ready disposition to be of service.

1482   13. In the case of married men care must be taken that only those are promoted to the diaconate who while living many years in matrimony have shown that they are ruling well their own household and who have a wife and children leading a truly Christian life and noted for their good reputation.[7]

14. It is to be desired that such deacons be possessed of   1483
no small learning about which we have spoken in numbers
8, 9, 10 above, or that they at least be endowed with that
knowledge which in the judgment of the Episcopal Conference
is necessary for them to carry out their specific functions.
Consequently they are to be admitted for a time in a special
school where they are to learn all that is necessary for worthily
fulfilling the diaconal ministry.

15. Should this be impossible, let the candidate be entrusted   1484
for his education to an outstanding priest who will direct him,
and instruct him and be able to testify to his prudence and
maturity. Care must always and emphatically be taken that
only suitable and skilled men may be admitted to the sacred
order.

16. Once they have received the order of deacon, even   1485
those who have been promoted at a more mature age, cannot
contract marriage by virtue of the traditional discipline of the
Church.

17. Let care be taken that the deacons do not exercise an   1486
art or a profession which in the judgment of the local Ordinary
is unfitting or impedes the fruitful exercise of the sacred office.

IV

18. Any deacon who is not a professed member of a reli-   1487
gious family must be duly enrolled in a diocese.

19. The norms in force with regard to caring for the fitting   1488
sustenance of priests and guaranteeing their social security
are to be observed also in favor of the permanent deacons
taking into consideration also the family of married deacons
and keeping article 21 of this letter in mind.

20. It is the function of the episcopal Conference to issue   1489
definite norms on the proper sustenance of the deacon and
his family if he is married in keeping with the various circumstances of place and time.

21. A deacon who exercises a civil profession must provide   1490
—to the extent in which it is possible—for his own needs
and for those of his family with the proceeds of this profession.

V

1491   22. According to the above-mentioned Constitution of
the Second Vatican Council it pertains to the deacon, to the
extent that he has been authorized by the local Ordinary to
attend such functions:

1) To assist the bishop and the priest during liturgical
actions in all things which the rituals of the different orders
assign to him;

2) To administer baptism solemnly and to supply the
ceremonies which may have been omitted when conferring it
on children or adults;

3) To reserve the Eucharist and to distribute it to himself and to others, to bring it as a Viaticum to the dying and
to impart to the people benediction with the Blessed Sacrament with the sacred ciborium;

4) In the absence of a priest, to assist at and to bless
marriages in the name of Church by delegation from the bishop or pastor observing the rest of the requirements which are
in the Code of Canon Law[8] with Canon 1098 remaining firm
and where what is said in regard to the priest is also to be understood in regard to the deacon;

5) To administer sacramentals and to officiate at funeral and burial services;

6) To read the sacred books of Scripture to the faithful
and to instruct and exhort the people;

7) To preside at the worship and prayers of the people
when a priest is not present;

8) To direct the liturgy of the word, particularly in the
absence of a priest;

9) To carry out, in the name of the hierarchy, the
duties of charity and of administration as well as works of
social assistance;

10) To guide legitimately, in the name of the parish
priest and of the bishop, remote Christian communities;

11) To promote and sustain the apostolic activities of
laymen.

23. All these functions must be carried out in perfect communion with the bishop and with his presbytery, that is to say, under the authority of the bishop and of the priest who are in charge of the care of souls in that place. 1492

24. Deacons, as much as possible, should have their part in pastoral councils. 1493

VI

25. Let the deacons, as those who serve the mysteries of Christ and of the Church, abstain from all vice and endeavor to be always pleasing to God "ready for every good work"[9] for the salvation of men. By reason, therefore, of the order received they must surpass by far all the others in the practice of liturgical life, in the love for prayer, in the divine service, in obedience, in charity, in chastity. 1494

26. It will be the task of the episcopal conference to establish more efficacious norms to nourish the spiritual life of the deacons, both celibate and the married. Let the local Ordinaries, however, see to it that all the deacons: 1495

1) devote themselves assiduously to reading and meditating on the word of God;

2) frequently and if possible every day, participate actively in the sacrifice of the Mass, receive the sacrament of the Most Holy Eucharist and devoutly visit the Sacrament;

3) purify their souls frequently with the sacrament of Penance and, for the purpose of receiving it worthily, examine their conscience each day;

4) venerate and love the Virgin Mary, the Mother of God, with fervent devotion.

27. It is a supremely fitting thing that permanent deacons recite every day at least part of the Divine Office, to be determined by the episcopal conference. 1496

28. Diocesan deacons must, at least every third year, attend spiritual exercises in a religious house or pious institution designated by the Ordinary. 1497

29. Deacons are not to neglect studies, particularly the sacred ones; let them read assiduously the sacred books of the Scripture; let them devote themselves to ecclesiastical studies 1498

in such a way that they can correctly explain Catholic teaching to the rest and become daily more capable of instructing and strengthening the minds of the faithful.

1499   For this purpose, let the deacons be called to meetings to be held at specified times at which problems regarding their life and the sacred ministry are treated.

1500   30. Because of the special character of the ministry entrusted to them they are bound to show reverence and obedience to the bishop; the bishops, however, should in the Lord highly esteem these ministers of the people of God and love them with the love of a father. If for a just cause a deacon lives for a time outside his own diocese he should willingly submit to the supervision and authority of the local Ordinary in those matters which pertain to the duties and functions of the diaconal state.

1501   31. In the matter of wearing apparel the local custom will have to be observed according to the norms set down by the episcopal conference.

VII

1502   32. The institution of the permanent diaconate among the Religious is a right reserved to the Holy See which is exclusively competent to examine and approve the recommendations of the general chapters in the matter.

1503   33. Let the Religious deacons exercise the diaconal ministry under the authority of the bishop and of their own superiors according to the norms in force for religious priests; they are also bound by the laws to which the members of the same Religious family are obliged.

1504   34. A Religious deacon who lives either permanently or for a specified time in a region which lacks a permanent diaconate may not exercise diaconal functions except with the consent of the local Ordinary.

1505   35. The provisions in nos. 32-34 regarding the Religious must be regarded as applying likewise to members of other institutes who profess the evangelical counsels.

VIII

36. Finally as regards the rite to be followed in conferring   1506
the sacred order of the diaconate and those orders which precede the diaconate, let the present discipline be observed until
it is revised by the Holy See.

Finally, after issuing these norms the desire springs spon-   1507
taneously from our heart that deacons in performing their
arduous functions in the modern world follow the examples
which we propose for their imitation; the example of St.
Stephen the protomartyr, who as St. Irenaeus says "was the
first chosen for diaconal service by the Apostles,"[1 1] and of
St. Lawrence of Rome "who was illustrious not only in the
administration of the sacraments but also in the stewardship
of the possessions of the Church."[1 2]

We order, then, that what has been established by us in   1508
this letter, given *"motu proprio"*, be firm and valid, all things
to the contrary notwithstanding.

Given at Rome, at St. Peter's on the feast of St. Ephrem   1509
the Syrian, June 18, 1967 in the fourth year of our pontificate.

The following year saw these further developments:
September 3, 1967 - Graduale Simplex issued;
May 23, 1968 - Decree of the Congregation of Rites on the
            New Eucharistic Prayers & Prefaces;
June 18, 1968 - Constitution approving the new Rites for
            Ordination of Deacons, Priests & Bishops,
            which were published August 15. — Ed.

Consilium for the Implementation of the
Constitution on the Sacred Liturgy
Selection from Instruction on the Translation
of Liturgical Texts
January 25, 1969

The Constitution on the Sacred Liturgy foresees that many Latin texts of the Roman liturgy must be translated into different languages (art. 36). Although many of them have already been translated, the work of translation is not drawing to a close. New texts have been edited or prepared for the renewal of the liturgy. Above all, after sufficient experiment and passage of time, all translation will need review.

1511   2. In accordance with article 36 of the Constitution *Sacrosanctum Concilium* and n. 40 of the Instruction of the Congregation of Rites *Inter Oecumenici,* the work of translation of liturgical texts is thus laid down: It is the duty of the episcopal conferences to decide which texts are to be translated, to prepare or review the translations, to approve them, and "after approval, that is, confirmation by the Holy See" to promulgate them.

1512   When a common language is spoken in several different countries, international commissions should be appointed by the conferences of bishops who speak the same language to make one text for all (Letter of Cardinal Lercaro to the presidents of episcopal conferences, dated October 16, 1964).

1513   3. Although these translations are the responsibility of the competent territorial authority of each country, it seems desirable to observe common principles of procedure, especially for texts of major importance, in order to make confirmation by the Apostolic See easier and to achieve greater unity of practice.

4. The Consilium has therefore thought fit in this decla-   1514
ration to lay down, in common and non-technical terms,
some of the more important theoretical and practical principles for the guidance of all who are called upon to prepare,
to approve, or to confirm liturgical translations.

I

General Principles

5. A liturgical text, inasmuch as it is a ritual sign, is a me-   1515
dium of spoken communication. It is, first of all, a sign perceived by the senses and used by men to communicate with
each other. But to believers who celebrate the sacred rites, a
word is itself a "mystery." By spoken words Christ himself
speaks to his people, and the people, through the Spirit in
the Church, answer their Lord.

6. The purpose of liturgical translation is to proclaim the   1516
message of salvation to believers and to express the prayer
of the Church to the Lord: "Liturgical translations have become . . . the voice of the Church" (address of Paul VI to
participants in the Congress on translations of liturgical
texts, November 10, 1965). To achieve this end, it is not sufficient that a liturgical translation merely reproduce the expressions and ideas of the original text. Rather it must faithfully communicate to a given people, and in their own language, that which the Church by means of this given text
originally intended to communicate to another people in
another time. A faithful translation, therefore, cannot be
judged on the basis of individual words: the total context of
this specific act of communication must be kept in mind, as
well as the literary form proper to the respective language.

7. Thus, in the case of liturgical communication, it is   1517
necessary to take into account not only the message to be
conveyed, but also the speaker, the audience, and the style.
Translations, therefore, must be faithful to the art of communication in all its various aspects, but especially in regard

to the message itself, in regard to the audience for which it is intended, and in regard to the manner of expression.

1518   8. Even if in spoken communication the message cannot be separated from the manner of speaking, the translator should give first consideration to the meaning of the communication.

1519   9. To discover the true meaning of a text, the translator must follow the scientific methods of textual study as used by experts. This part of the translator's task is obvious. A few points may be added with reference to liturgical texts:

1520   10. (a) If need be, a critical text of the passage must first be established so that the translation can be done from the original, or at least from the best available text.

1521   11. (b) Latin terms must be considered in the light of their uses—historical or cultural, Christian or liturgical. For example, the early Christian use of 'devotio' differs from its use in classical or more modern times. The Latin 'oratio' means in English not an oration (one of its senses in classical Latin) but a 'prayer'—and this English word bears different meanings such as prayer of praise or prayer in general or prayer of petition. 'Pius' and 'pietas' are very inadequately rendered in English as 'pious' and 'piety.' In one case the Latin 'salus' may mean 'salvation' in the theological sense; elsewhere it may mean 'safety,' 'health' (physical health or total health), or 'well-being.' 'Sarx-caro' is inadequately rendered in English as 'flesh.' 'Doulos-servus' and 'famula' are inadequately rendered in English by 'slave,' 'servant,' 'handmaid.' The force of an image or metaphor must also be considered, whether it is rare or common, living or worn out.

1522   12. (c) The translator must always keep in mind that the "unit of meaning" is not the individual word but the whole passage. He must therefore be careful that his translation is not so analytical that it exaggerates the importance of particular phrases while it obscures or weakens the meaning of the whole. Thus, in Latin, the piling up of 'ratam, rationabilem, acceptabilem' may increase the sense of invocation. In other tongues, a succession of adjectives may actually weaken the force of the prayer. The same is true of 'beatissima Virgo' or 'beata et gloriosa' or the routine addition of 'sanctus' or 'beatus' to a saint's name, or the too casual use of superlatives. Understatement in English is sometimes the more effective means of emphasis.

13. (d) To keep the correct significance, words and ex-   **1523** pressions must be used in their proper historical, social and ritual meanings. Thus, in prayers for Lent, 'ieiunium' now has the sense of 'lenten observance,' both liturgical and ascetic; the meaning is not confined to abstinence from food. 'Tapeinos-humilis' originally had "class" overtones not present in the English 'humble' or even 'lowly.' Many of the phrases of approach to the Almighty were originally adapted from forms of address to the sovereign in the courts of Byzantium and Rome. It is necessary to study how far an attempt should be made to offer equivalents in modern English for such words as 'quaesumus,' 'dignare,' 'clementissime,' 'maiestas,' and the like.

14. The accuracy and value of a translation can only be   **1524** assessed in terms of the purpose of the communication. To serve the particular congregations who will use it, the following points should be observed in translating:

15. (a) The language chosen should be that in 'common'   **1525** usage, that is, suited to the greater number of the faithful who speak it in everyday use, even "children and persons of small education" (Paul VI in the Allocution cited). However, the language should not be 'common' in the bad sense, but "worthy of expressing the highest realities" (ibid.). Moreover, the correct biblical or Christian meanings of certain words and ideas will always need explanation and instruction. Nevertheless no special literary training should be required of the people; liturgical texts should normally be intelligible to all, even to the less educated. For example, 'temptation' as a translation of 'tentatio' in the Lord's prayer is inaccurate and can only be misleading to people who are not biblical scholars. Similarly, 'scandal' in the ordinary English sense of gossip is a misleading translation of the scriptural 'scandalum.' Besides, liturgical texts must sometimes possess a truly poetic quality, but this does not imply the use of specifically "poetic diction."

1526   16. (b) Certain other principles should be observed so that a translation will be understood by the hearers in the same sense as the revealed truths expressed in the liturgy, viz:

1527   17. (1) When words are taken from the so-called 'sacral' vocabulary now in use, the translator should consider whether the everyday common meaning of these words and phrases bears or can bear a Christian meaning. These phrases may carry a pre-Christian, quasi-Christian, Christian or even anti-Christian meaning. He should also consider whether such words can convey the exact Christian liturgical action and manifestation of faith. Thus in the Greek bible, the word 'hieros' *[sacer]* was often avoided because of its connection with the pagan cults, and instead the rarer word 'hagios' *[sanctus]* was substituted. Another example: The proper meaning of the biblical 'hesed-eleos-misericordia,' is not accurately expressed in English by 'mercy' or 'pity.' Again, the word 'mereri' in classical Latin often signifies 'to be worthy of something.' But in the language of the liturgy it carries a very different meaning from the ancient meaning: "I do something because of which I am worthy of a prize or a reward." In English the word 'to deserve' when used by itself retains the stricter sense. A translation would lead to error if it did not consider this fact, for example, in translating 'Quia quem meruisti portare' in the hymn *Regina caeli* as "because you deserved to bear . . ."

1528   18. (2) It often happens that there is no word in common use that exactly corresponds to the biblical or liturgical sense of the term to be translated, as in the use of the biblical 'justitia.' The nearest suitable word must then be chosen which, through habitual use in various catechetical texts and in prayer, lends itself to take on the biblical and Christian sense intended by the liturgy. Such has been the evolution of the Greek word 'doxa' and the Latin 'gloria' when used to translate the Hebrew 'kabod.' The expression 'hominibus bonae voluntatis' literally translated as 'to men of good will' (or 'good will to men' in order to stress divine favor) will be misleading; no single English word or phrase will completely reflect the original Latin or the Greek which the Latin translates.

Similarly in English there is no exact equivalent for 'mys- | 1529
terium.' In English, 'mystery' means something which cannot
be readily explained or else a type of drama or fiction. Nor
can the word 'venerabilis' (as "in sanctas et venerabiles
manus") be translated as 'venerable,' which nowadays means
'elderly.'

19. (3) In many modern languages a biblical or liturgical | 1530
language must be created by use. This will be achieved rather
by infusing a Christian meaning into common words than by
importing uncommon or technical terms.

20. (c) The prayer of the Church is always the prayer of | 1531
some actual community assembled here and now. It is not
sufficient that a formula handed down from some other
time or region should be translated verbatim, even if accurately, for liturgical use. The formula translated must become
the genuine prayer of the congregation and in it each of its
members should be able to find and express himself.

21. A translation of the liturgy therefore often requires | 1532
cautious adaptation. But cases differ:

22. (a) Sometimes a text can be translated word for word | 1533
and keep the same meaning as the original, for example
'pleni sunt caeli et terra gloria tua.'

23. (b) Sometimes the metaphors must be changed to keep | 1534
the true sense, as in 'locum refrigerii' in northern regions.

24. (c) Sometimes, the meaning of a text can no longer | 1535
be understood, either because it is contrary to modern
Christian ideas (as in 'terrena despicere' or 'ut inimicos
sanctae Ecclesiae humiliare digneris'), or because it has less
relevance today (as in some phrases intended to combat
Arianism), or because it no longer expresses the true original
meaning (as in certain obsolete forms of lenten penance.) In
these cases, so long as the teaching of the Gospel remains
intact, not only must inappropriate expressions be avoided,
but others found which express a corresponding meaning in
modern words. The greatest care must be taken that all translations are not only beautiful and suited to the contemporary
mind, but express true doctrine and authentic Christian
spirituality.

1536   25. A particular form of expression and speech is required for spoken communication. In rendering any liturgical text, the translator must keep in mind the major importance of the spoken or rhetorical style, or what might, by extension of the term, be called the literary genre. On this matter several things should be noted:

1537   26. (1) The literary genre of every liturgical text depends first of all on the nature of the ritual act signified in the words—acclamation or supplication, proclamation or praying, reading or singing. Each action requires its proper form of expression. Moreover a prayer differs as it is to be spoken by one person or by many in unison; whether it is in prose or in verse; spoken or sung. All these considerations affect not only the manner of delivery, but also the choice of words.

1538   27. (2) A liturgical text is a 'linguistic fact' designed for celebration. When it is in written form (as is usually the case), it offers a stylistic problem for translators. Each text must therefore be examined to discover the significant elements proper to the genre, e.g., in Roman prayers the formal structure, *cursus,* dignity, brevity, etc.

1539   28. Among the separate elements are those which are essential and others which are secondary and subsidiary. The essential elements, so far as is possible, should be preserved in translation, sometimes intact, sometimes in equivalent terms. The general structure of the Roman prayers can be retained unchanged; the divine title, the motive of the petition, the petition itself, the conclusion. Others cannot be retained: the oratorical *cursus,* rhetorical prose cadence.

1540   29. It is to be noted that if any particular kind of quality is regarded as essential to a literary genre (e.g., intelligibility or prayers when said aloud) this may take precedence over another quality less significant for communication (e.g., verbal fidelity).

Some particular considerations are then taken up in Part II, and directives for forming committees for translating are given in Part III.

The New Rite of Matrimony came out on March 19, 1969 and the revised Roman Calendar appeared March 21, 1969.

MISSALE ROMANUM
Apostolic Constitution of Pope Paul VI
on the New Roman Missal
April 3, 1969

The Roman Missal, promulgated in 1570 by Our predecessor St. Pius V, by decree of the Council of Trent,[1] has been received by all as one of the numerous and admirable fruits which that holy Council spread throughout the entire Church of Christ. For four centuries, not only has it provided the priests of the Latin rite with norms for the celebration of the Eucharistic Sacrifice, but the saintly heralds of the Gospel have also carried it to almost the entire world. Furthermore, countless holy men have abundantly nourished their piety toward God by its readings from Sacred Scripture or by its prayers, whose general arrangement goes back, in essence, to St. Gregory the Great.

But since that time there has grown and spread among Christian people the liturgical renewal which, according to Pius XII, Our predecessor of honored memory, seems to show the signs of God's providence in the present time, a salvific action of the Holy Spirit in His Church.[2] This renewal has also shown clearly that the formulas of the Roman Missal ought to be revised and enriched. The beginning of this renewal was the work of Our same predecessor, in the restoration of the Paschal vigil and of the Holy Week rite,[3] which formed the first stage of adapting the Roman Missal to the contemporary mentality.

The recent Second Vatican Ecumenical Council, in promulgating the Constitution on the Sacred Liturgy, established

1542

1543

the basis for the general revision of the Roman Missal: in declaring that "both texts and rites should be drawn up so that they express more clearly the holy things which they signify";[4] in ordering that "the rite of the Mass is to be revised in such a way that the intrinsic nature and purpose of its several parts, as well as the connection between them, may be more clearly manifested, and that devout and active participation by the faithful may be more easily achieved";[5] in prescribing that "the treasures of the Bible are to be opened up more lavishly, so that richer fare may be provided for the faithful at the table of God's word";[6] and finally, in ordering that "a new rite for concelebration is to be drawn up and inserted into the Pontifical and into the Roman Missal."[7]

1544   One should not think, however, that this revision of the Roman Missal has been unexpected. The progress accomplished in liturgical studies during the last four centuries has, without a doubt, prepared the way. For instance, after the Council of Trent, the study "of ancient manuscripts of the Vatican Library and of others gathered elsewhere"—as Our predecessor St. Pius V indicates in the apostolic constitution *Quo primum*—aided greatly in the revision of the Roman Missal. Since then, however, more ancient liturgical sources have been discovered and published and, at the same time, liturgical formulas of the Eastern Church have become better known. Accordingly, many wish that such riches, both doctrinal and spiritual, might not be hidden in the darkness of libraries, but might, on the contrary, be brought to light to illuminate and nourish Christian minds and souls.

1545   Let Us now present, in broad lines, the new composition of the Roman Missal. First of all, in a General Instruction which serves as a preface for the book, new regulations are set forth for celebration of the Eucharistic Sacrifice, concerning the rites and functions of each of the participants, and concerning sacred furnishings and places.

1546   The major innovation concerns the Eucharistic Prayer. If in the Roman rite the first part of this prayer, the Preface, has undergone various formulations in the course of the centuries, nevertheless the second part, called "Canon of the Action," assumed an unchangeable form during the 4th and

5th centuries; conversely, the Eastern liturgies allowed for this variety in their anaphoras. In this matter, however, over and above the fact that the Eucharistic Prayer is enriched by a great number of Prefaces, either derived from the ancient tradition of the Roman Church or composed recently, We have decided to add three new Canons to this prayer. In this way, the different aspects of the mystery of salvation will be emphasized and will offer more and more enriching occasions for giving thanks.

However, for pastoral reasons, and in order to facilitate concelebration, We have ordered that the words of the Lord be identical in each formula of the Canon. Thus, in each Eucharistic Prayer, We wish the words to be pronounced thus: over the bread: *"Accipite et manducate ex hoc omnes: Hoc est enim Corpus meum, quod pro vobis tradetur";* over the chalice: *"Accipite et bibite ex eo omnes: Hic est enim calix Sanguinis mei novi et aeterni testamenti, qui pro vobis et pro multis effundetur in remissionem peccatorum. Hoc facite in meam commemorationem."* The words *"Mysterium fidei,"* taken from the context of the words of Christ the Lord, and said by the priest, serve as an introduction to the acclamation of the faithful.   1547

Concerning the rite of the Mass, "the rites are to be simplified, due care being taken to preserve their substance."[8] Also to be omitted are "elements which, with the passage of time, came to be duplicated, or were added with but little advantage,"[9] particularly in the rites of offering the bread and wine, and in those of the breaking of the bread and of communion.   1548

Also, "other elements which have suffered injury through accidents of history are now to be restored according to the pristine norm of the holy Fathers";[10] for example, the homily,[11] the "common prayer" or "prayer of the faithful,"[12] and the penitential rite or act of reconciliation with God and with the brothers, at the beginning of the Mass, where its proper emphasis is restored.   1549

According to the prescription of the Second Vatican Council which directs that "a more notable portion of the Holy Scriptures will be read to the people in the course of   1550 a prescribed number of years,"[13] all of the readings for Sunday are divided into a three-year cycle. In addition, for Sundays and feasts, the readings of the Epistle and Gospel are preceded by a reading from the Old Testament or, during Paschaltide, from the Acts of the Apostles. In this way, the development of the mystery of salvation, shown by the text of Divine Revelation, is more clearly explained. These widely selected biblical readings which give to the faithful on feast days the most important part of Sacred Scripture, are completed by drawing upon the other parts of the Holy Books read on ordinary days.

1551   All this is wisely ordered in such a way that there is developed more and more among the faithful a hunger for the word of God,[14] which, under the guidance of the Holy Spirit, leads the people of the New Covenant to the perfect unity of the Church. In such a case We are strongly confident that priests and faithful will both prepare their hearts more devoutly for the Lord's Supper, meditating more profoundly on Sacred Scripture, and will at the same time nourish themselves more abundantly day by day with the words of the Lord. It will follow, then, that according to the wishes of the Second Vatican Council, Sacred Scripture will be at the same time a perpetual source of spiritual life, an instrument of prime value for transmitting Christian doctrine and, finally, the center of all theology.

1552   In this revision of the Roman Missal, in addition to the three changes mentioned above—namely, the Eucharistic Prayer, the rite for the Mass and the biblical reading—other parts also have been reviewed and considerably modified: the Proper of the Seasons, the Proper of Saints, the Common of Saints, ritual Masses and votive Masses. In all these changes, particular care has been taken with the prayers. Not only has their number been increased so that the new texts might better correspond to new needs, but they have been rendered faithful to the purest of the ancient texts. For each ferial of the principal liturgical seasons—Advent, Christmas, Lent and Easter—a proper prayer has been provided.

1553   Even though the text of the Roman Gradual, at least that which concerns singing, has not been changed, still the responsorial psalm, which St. Augustine and St. Leo the Great often mention, has been restored for a better understanding, and the Introit and Communion antiphons have been adapted for read Masses.

In conclusion, We wish to give the force of law to all that We have set forth concerning the new Roman Missal. In promulgating the official edition of the Roman Missal, Our predecessor St. Pius V presented it as an instrument of liturgical unity and as a witness to the purity of the Church's worship. While leaving room in the new Missal, according to the order of the Second Vatican Council, "for legitimate variations and adaptations,"[15] We hope nevertheless that the Missal will be received by the faithful as an instrument which bears witness to and affirms the common unity of all. Thus, in the great diversity of languages, one unique prayer will rise as an acceptable offering to our Father in heaven, through our High Priest Jesus Christ, in the Holy Spirit.   1554

We order that the prescriptions of this constitution go into effect November 30th of this year, the first Sunday of Advent.   1555

We desire that these statutes and regulations be fixed and in effect now and for the future, despite—if there be any need for this—anything to the contrary that can be found in apostolic constitutions and ordinances issued by Our predecessors, and despite any other regulations, even if worthy of special mention and repeal.   1556

Given at Rome, at St. Peter's, Holy Thursday, April 3rd, in the year 1969, the sixth of Our pontificate.   1557

The new Order of the Mass was published April 6, 1969 and its English translation was approved January 5, 1970.

Revised Rite of Baptism for Children came out on May 15, 1969.

The new Lectionary for the Mass was released May 25, 1969, incorporating much more of the Bible, as Vatican II had directed.

Revised Rite of Funerals appeared May 29, 1969.—Ed.

SACRA RITUUM CONGREGATIO
Apostolic Constitution of Pope Paul VI
on Division of Sacred Congregation of Rites
into Two New Congregations
May 8, 1969

Since its establishment in the year 1588 by Our predecessor of happy memory Sixtus V,[1] the Sacred Congregation of Rites has had a twofold function. First, it controlled and regulated the sacred rites of the Latin Church. Second, it was vested with responsibility for all matters concerning the canonization of saints throughout the whole Church. It is believed that this second function was assigned to the Sacred Congregation of Rites precisely because the purpose of canonization is that the servant of God, enrolled in the calendar of the saints, should be honored with public veneration by the universal Church.

1559   The Sacred Congregation of Rites has discharged this twofold office so prudently during the course of four centuries that it has won for itself outstanding acclaim. As regards the sacred liturgy, let it suffice to mention that—after St. Pius V had published the reformed Roman Breviary and Missal[2]—the Sacred Congregation of Rites, in obedience to the decrees of the sacred Council of Trent,[3] revised and published the other liturgical books. The congregation likewise condensed and restored to their original purity the liturgical formulas and rites which had been corrupted in part during the so-called Middle Ages; and it reduced their excessive variety and brought about a certain liturgical uniformity which was firmly preserved intact thereafter.[4]

1560   In our own time the same sacred congregation, acting under the instructions of Our predecessor St. Pius X, opened the way to a general reform of the liturgy with the revision of the Breviary,[5] which was named after that same holy Pontiff. This was later followed, at the behest of Our predecessor of venerable memory Pius XII, by the reformed Easter Vigil in 1951[6] and by the new Order of Holy Week in 1955.[7] The constitution approved by the Second Vatican Ecumenical Council[8] has been derived, to a certain extent, from these and many other initiatives.

Of no less importance is the work of the said congregation in preparing and expediting the causes of saints. This is clearly evident from the list of saints who, from the year 1588 to the present day, have been enrolled in the calendar of the saints after a detailed examination of their martyrdom or of the heroic degree of their virtues.   1561

Nowadays, however, both the general liturgical renewal decreed by the Second Vatican Council and the revision of the laws governing the causes of saints, in line with the mentality of the present age, appear to demand new studies, attention and care in the treatment of these matters.   1562

Furthermore, careful consideration of the matter clearly reveals that the liturgy is quite distinct from the causes of saints. Each requires different study and training, together with a different method of approach. On this account We Ourself, in the section of the apostolic constitution *Regimini Ecclesiae*[9] dealing with the Sacred Congregation of Rites, ordered that the congregation be divided into two parts or sections, one to deal with divine worship, the other with the causes of saints.   1563

Now, however, after further careful reflection, and having obtained the advice of experts, We have decided to separate the two sections in such a way as to render each of them completely independent.   1564

Wherefore, by Our present apostolic constitution, the existing Sacred Congregation of Rites is replaced by two new congregations, the first to be known as the Sacred Congregation for Divine Worship, and the other as the Sacred Congregation for the Causes of Saints.   1565

(The duties of the two new congregations are then defined in the remainder of the document.)—Ed.

Sacred Congregation for Divine Worship
Instruction on Implementing the
Constitution *Missale Romanum*
October 20, 1969

By his apostolic constitution *Missale Romanum*, April 3, 1969, the Holy Father Pope Paul VI approved the new Roman Missal, reformed in accordance with the requirements of the Second Vatican Council. Three parts of this Missal have already been published, namely: the *Institutio Generalis Missalis Romani*[1] and the *Ordo Missae*,[2] both published by decree of the Sacred Congregation of Rites, April 6, 1969, and the *Ordo lectionum Missae*,[3] published by decree of this sacred congregation, May 25, 1969. The other parts of the Roman Missal will be published in the near future.

1567   In the documents mentioned above, the first Sunday of Advent this year, November 30, 1969, has been designated as the day from which the new rites and texts are to be used. The execution of this part of the reform of the Mass, however, presents a number of serious difficulties: the enormous work involved in preparing the translations of the texts and in publishing the new liturgical books; the need for a thorough and carefully adapted catechesis; the problems of readjustment to the changes among clergy and faithful.

1568   This is why, in response to the requests of many bishops and episcopal conferences, and with the approval of the Holy Father, the Sacred Congregation for Divine Worship has given the following norms for the gradual application of the apostolic constitution *Missale Romanum*. These norms complete those which were published by this same congregation on July 25, 1969.[4]

1. The Latin text of the *Ordo Missae* may be used from November 30, 1969.   1569

2. Episcopal conferences will establish the day on which the vernacular text of this same *Ordo Missae* may begin to be used. It is desirable that the text of the new *Ordo Missae* should be translated as soon as possible and that, when duly approved, it should be brought into use even before the other texts of the Roman Missal have been translated into the vernacular.   1570

3. The translation of the text of the new *Ordo Missae* will be approved, at least temporarily, by the episcopal conference (or by the national liturgical commission and at least by the conference's presiding council). The vernacular texts will be presented to this sacred congregation for confirmation.[5]   1571

                                                                     1572

4. The translation of the text of the *Ordo Missae* should be one and the same for all the countries which use the same language.[6] This also applies to other texts which call for the direct participation of the people.

5. It pertains to the episcopal conferences to approve the new melodies for vernacular texts which are to be sung by the celebrant and ministers.[7]   1573

6. Careful catechesis is required before the texts and rites of the new *Ordo Missae* are introduced. National liturgical institutes and diocesan liturgical commissions will be able to offer the means to achieve this (for example, study sessions, conferences, articles in newspapers and other publications, radio and television broadcasts, etc.). This is necessary if clergy and faithful are to perceive and appreciate the spirit and purpose of the reform.   1574

7. Each episcopal conference will determine the date from which the use of the new *Ordo Missae* is to become obligatory, with the exception of the special cases mentioned in nos. 19-20. This date should be no later than November 28, 1971.   1575

8. It is for the episcopal conference to determine, with the assistance of the competent episcopal commissions and   1576

liturgical centers, those parts of the Mass which the *Institutio Generalis Missalis Romani* leaves to their discretion, namely:

a) the actions and postures of the faithful during the Mass;[8]

b) the gestures by which the altar and the book of the Gospels are to be venerated;[9]

c) the sign of peace;[10]

d) the faculty of using only two readings in the Mass on Sundays and holy days of obligation.[11]

e) the faculty by which women may be allowed to read the biblical readings occurring before the Gospel.[12]

1577   9. The Latin text of the Roman Missal may be used as soon as it is published.

1578   10. Each episcopal conference will decide on what date the vernacular texts of the new Roman Missal may begin to be used. This may be done by stages. When some of the texts have been approved, they could be introduced without waiting for all the texts to be translated. For example, the texts of the Temporal Cycle could be introduced, even if the texts of the Sanctoral Cycle, the Commons, the votive Masses, and the Masses *ad diversa*[13] were not yet ready. The new texts are best introduced at the beginning of liturgical season (for example, Advent, Lent, Eastertide).

1579   11. The translations of the new texts of the Roman Missal will be approved, at least temporarily, by the episcopal conference (or by the national liturgical commission and at least by the conference's presiding council). These vernacular texts will be submitted to this sacred congregation for confirmation.[14]

1580   12. It is for the episcopal conference to prepare a selection of vernacular texts, which may be used as Entrance, Offertory or Communion songs.[15] At the same time as it gives this approval, the episcopal conference will warmly encourage those competent in this field to increase and perfect the selection, taking into account the texts put forward in the new Missal and the special characteristics of each particular language.

1581   13. If the new *Ordo Missae* is used before the new Roman Missal is published, the texts of the antiphons and prayers of the present Missal will be used, bearing in mind the following points:

a) If the Introit antiphon is not sung, it is read once only. The psalm verse and the *Gloria Patri* are not said.[16]

b) If the Offertory antiphon is not sung, it is omitted.[17]

c) The Prayer over the Gifts and the Prayer after Communion will end with the short conclusion.[18]

14. Each episcopal conference will determine the date from which the use of the texts of the new Roman Missal is to become obligatory, with the exception of the cases mentioned in nos. 19-20. This date should be no later than November 28, 1971.   1582

15. Each episcopal conference will determine the day from which the new *Ordo lectionum Missae* may or should be used.   1583

16. While waiting for the translation of the new readings and their confirmation by this sacred congregation, the episcopal conferences may temporarily permit the use of one or more of the duly approved versions of the Sacred Scriptures. In this case, care will be taken to ensure that the precise biblical references are made available to priests (that is, the indications of chapter and verse; the way the reading begins; the way the passages are divided). This is especially important for the readings of the B cycle of Sundays, which begin on November 30, 1969.   1584

17. Until the texts of the new lectionary are ready for use, the readings of the present Roman Missal are retained for each part. The lectionaries already approved for experiment and which are at present in use may continue to be used temporarily, for example, the present ferial lectionaries, the series of readings for such occasions as the celebration of the sacraments, Masses for the dead, certain votive Masses, and so forth.[19]   1585

18. In order to safeguard the liturgical and pastoral importance of the responsorial psalm, the competent national commissions should establish a provisional list of psalms and responses. They should choose from among those at present in use the psalms and responses which best correspond to the texts of the *Ordo lectionum Missae*.[20] These national commissions will warmly encourage those competent in this field to increase and perfect the heritage of texts and melodies that has come down to us, taking into account the texts put   1586

forward in the new lectionary and the special characteristics of each particular language. A similar selection should also be prepared for the Alleluia and other chants before the Gospel.

1587   19. Elderly priests who celebrate Mass without a congregation, and who perhaps experience special difficulty adjusting themselves to the use of the new Order of the Mass, the new texts of the Roman Missal and the new lectionary, may, with the consent of their ordinary, continue to use the rites and texts which are at present in use.

1588   20. Special cases, however, such as priests who are sick or who have other difficulties, should be submitted to this sacred congregation.

1589   His Holiness Pope Paul VI approved the present instruction on October 18, 1969. He ordered that it should be published, and carefully observed by all whom it concerns.

1590   All things to the contrary notwithstanding.

1591   Vatican City, October 20, 1969.

Address of Pope Paul VI
to a General Audience
on the New Mass Rite
November 19, 1969

We should like to call your attention once again to an event that is about to take place in the Latin Catholic Church, and that will become obligatory in Italian dioceses on the First Sunday of Advent, which falls on November 30 this year. That event is the introduction of a new Mass rite into the liturgy. The Mass will be celebrated in a form which is somewhat different from the one we have been accustomed to celebrating these past four centuries, that is, from the days of St. Pius V after the Council of Trent.

The change involves a certain amount of surpise and something out of the ordinary, when we consider that the Mass is the traditional and untouchable expression of our authentic religious worship. We may well ask ourselves: How could such a change ever take place? What does this change consist of? What consequences will this have for those who assist at holy Mass? The answers to these questions, and to similar ones occasioned by this novel event, will be amply provided and reiterated in all the churches, in all religious publications, and in all the schools where Christian doctrine is taught. We urge you to pay attention to these answers, to try and see more clearly and profoundly the stupendous and mysterious notion of the Mass.   1593

But in the meantime, We shall use this brief and elementary discourse to erase from your minds some of the first immedi-   1594

ate difficulties occasioned by this change, by addressing ourselves to the three questions it prompts in our minds.

1595   How could such a change take place? The answer is that it
is due to the express wishes of the recent Ecumenical Council.
The Council says: "The rite of the Mass is to be revised in
such a way that the intrinsic nature and purpose of its several
parts, as well as the connection between them, may be more
clearly manifested, and that devout and active participation
by the faithful may be more easily achieved. For this purpose
the rites are to be simplified, due care being taken to preserve
their substance; elements which, with the passage of time,
came to be duplicated, or were added with but little advantage, are now to be discarded; other elements which have suffered injury through accidents of history are now to be restored according to the pristine norm of the holy Fathers, to
the extent that they may seem useful or necessary."[1]

1596   The reform about to be implemented, then, corresponds
to an authoritative mandate of the Church. It is an act of
obedience, an attempt by the Church to maintain her true
nature. It is a step forward in her authentic tradition. It is a
demonstration of fidelity and vitality to which we all should
render prompt adherence. It is not a whim or a fleeting experiment of an optional nature. It is not some dilettante's
improvisation. It is a law thought out by authoritative
scholars of the sacred liturgy, who studied it long and carefully. We shall do well to accept it with joyous enthusiasm
and to implement it with prompt and unanimous observance.

1597   This reform puts an end to uncertainty, debate and abusive
whims. It recalls us to the oneness of rites and sentiments that
is proper to the Catholic Church, which inherits and continues
the first Christian community that was "of one heart and one
soul."[2] The choral quality of the Church's prayer is one of
the signs of, and forces for, her unity and catholicity. The
coming change is not meant to disturb or break this choral
quality; it is meant to confirm it and make it resound with
new, youthful spirit.

1598   The second question is: What does this change consist of?
As you will see, it involves many new ritual prescriptions
which, in the beginning especially, will call for some attention

and care. Personal devotion and the sense of community will make it easy and pleasant to observe these new prescriptions. But let us be clear on this point: none of the substance of our traditional Mass has been changed. Some might get the wrong impression from a particular ceremony or rubric that has been added, as if this involved or implied an alteration or diminution of the truths that have been acquired once for all and authoritatively sanctioned as part of the Catholic faith. They might think that the correspondence between the law of praying, *lex orandi,* and the law of believing, *lex credendi,* has been compromised as a result.

But that is definitely not the case—first of all, because the **1599** rite and its related rubric are not in themselves a dogmatic definition. They are capable of various theological qualifications, depending on the liturgical context to which they relate. They are gestures and terms relating to a lived and living religious action which involves the ineffable mystery of God's presence; it is an action that is not always carried out in the exact same form, an action that only theological analysis can examine and express in doctrinal formulas that are logically satisfying. It is not the case, secondly, because the Mass of the new rite is and remains the Mass it always was—in some of its aspects even more clearly so than before.

The unity between the Lord's Supper, the sacrifice of the **1600** cross, and the re-presentation of both in the Mass, is inviolably affirmed and celebrated in the new rite, as it was in the old. The Mass is and remains the memorial of the Lord's Last Supper, at which He instituted the sacrifice of the New Testament by changing bread and wine into His Body and Blood and willed, by virtue of the priesthood that He conferred on His Apostles, that it be repeated identically but in a different manner—that is, in an unbloody and sacramental manner—in perpetual memory of Him until His last coming.[3]

In the new rite you will find clearer light shed on the rela- **1601** tionship between the Liturgy of the Word and the properly Eucharistic Liturgy—the latter being the response which realizes and effects the former.[4] You will notice how much emphasis is placed, in the celebration of the Eucharistic sacrifice, on the participation of the assembly of the faithful, who are and fully feel themselves a "Church" at the Mass. You may also see more clearly other wondrous characteristics of our Mass. But do not think that all this is meant to alter the genuine and traditional essence of the Mass. Instead, be wise enough to realize that through this new and diffuse idiom the Church wishes to give greater effectiveness to its liturgical message; to approach each of her children, and the People of God as a whole, in a more direct and pastoral manner.

1602   And so we come to the third question posed above: What consequences will this have for those who assist at holy Mass? The consequences expected, or rather desired, are more intelligent, more satisfying, more real and more sanctifying participation by the faithful in the liturgical mystery—participation, that is, in the hearing of the word of God which lives and resounds through the centuries and the annals of our own souls, and in the mystic reality of Christ's sacramental and propitiatory sacrifice.

1603   So let us not talk about a "new Mass," but rather about a "new era" in the life of the Church. With Our apostolic blessing.

General Instruction of the Roman Missal
Published as Part of the Roman Missal
March 26, 1970

Introduction

When Christ the Lord was about to celebrate the passover meal with his disciples and institute the sacrifice
of his body and blood, he directed them to prepare a
large, furnished room (*Luke* 22:12). The Church has always
taken this command of Christ as bearing on its own responsibility in giving directions concerning the preparation of the
minds of the worshipers and the place, rites, and texts for the
celebration of the holy eucharist. Today, in response to the
decision of the Second Vatican Council, there are new norms
and this new missal, to be used from now on for the Mass of
the Roman rite. These bear witness to the unity and coherence
of the Church's tradition. Although they introduce some new
elements into the celebration, they show the Church's continued concern for the eucharist, its faith, and its unchanging
love of this great mystery.

2. The sacrificial nature of the Mass was solemnly pro-   1605
claimed by the Council of Trent in agreement with the tradition of the universal Church.[1] The Second Vatican Council
reaffirmed this teaching in these significant words: "At the
Last Supper our Savior instituted the eucharistic sacrifice of
his body and blood to perpetuate the sacrifice of the cross
throughout the centuries until he comes again. He entrusted

it to his bride, the Church, as a memorial of his death and resurrection."[2]

1606   This teaching of the council is expressed constantly in the prayers of the Mass. The Leonine Sacramentary states the doctrine concisely: "The work of our redemption is carried out when ever we celebrate the memory of this sacrifice,"[3] and it is properly and carefully presented in the eucharistic prayers. At the anamnesis or memorial, the priest speaks to God in the name of all the people and offers in thanksgiving the holy and living sacrifice, which is the Church's offering, the Victim pleasing to God himself;[4] he prays that the body and blood of Christ may be a sacrifice acceptable to the Father, bringing salvation to the whole world.[5]

1607   In this new missal, then, the Church's rule of prayer corresponds to the Church's enduring rule of faith. It teaches us that the sacrifice of the cross and its sacramental renewal in the Mass are one and the same, differing only in the manner of offering. At the Last Supper Christ the Lord instituted this sacramental renewal and commanded his apostles to do it in memory of him. It is at once a sacrifice of praise and of thanksgiving, a sacrifice that reconciles us to the Father and makes amends to him for the sins of the world.

1608   3. The Church believes that the Lord Jesus is really present among us in a wonderful way under the eucharistic species. The Second Vatican Council[6] and other pronouncements of the Church's magisterium[7] have reaffirmed the same doctrine and the same meaning proposed by the Council of Trent for our belief.[8] At Mass this presence of Christ is proclaimed not only by the words of consecration, by which Christ is made present through transubstantiation, but also by the sense of deep reverence and adoration which are evident in the liturgy of the eucharist. His presence is further recognized by Christians when they honor the eucharist in a special way on Holy Thursday and on Corpus Christi.

1609   4. The distinctive nature of the ministerial priesthood is clear from the prominent place the presbyter occupies and the functions he takes in the rite itself: he offers sacrifice in the person of Christ and presides over the assembly of God's holy people. His priestly role is explained precisely and in greater detail in the preface of the eucharistic prayer at the chrism Mass on Holy Thursday, when the institution of the priesthood is celebrated. That preface describes the responsibilities of the priestly office, explains how the power of the priesthood is conferred by the laying on of hands, and declares it to be the continuation of the power of Christ, the High Priest of the New Testament.

5. The ministerial priesthood throws light on another and important priesthood, namely, the royal priesthood of believers. Their spiritual sacrifice to God is accomplished through the ministry of presbyters, in union with the sacrifice of Christ, our one and only Mediator.[9] The celebration of the eucharist is the action of the whole Church, in which each individual should take his own full part and only his part, as determined by his particular position in the people of God. In this way greater attention is given to some aspects of the eucharistic celebration which have sometimes been overlooked in the course of time. The worshiping community is the people of God, won by Christ with his blood, called together by the Lord, and nourished by his word. It is a people called to offer God the prayers of the entire human family, a people which gives thanks in Christ for the mystery of salvation by offering his sacrifice. It is a people brought together and strengthened in unity by sharing in the body and blood of Christ. This people is holy in origin, but by conscious, active, and fruitful participation in the mystery of the eucharist it constantly grows in holiness.[10]

1610

6. The Second Vatican Council, in setting forth its decrees for the revision of the Order of Mass, directed, among other things, that some rites be restored "to the ancient usage of the holy Fathers,"[11] quoting the apostolic letter *Quo primum* of 1570, in which Saint Pius V promulgated the Tridentine missal. The fact that the same words are used in reference to both Roman missals indicates that, although separated by four centuries, both embrace one and the same tradition. And when the more profound elements of this tradition are considered, it becomes clear how remarkably this new missal complements the older one.

1611

1612   7. The old missal was promulgated in difficult times. There were attacks upon Catholic faith about the sacrificial nature of the Mass, the ministerial priesthood, and the real and permanent presence of Christ under the eucharistic species. Saint Pius V was especially concerned to preserve the recent tradition of the Church then unjustly under attack, and only very slight changes were introduced into the sacred rites. In fact, the missal of 1570 differs very little from the first printed edition of 1474, which in turn faithfully follows the missal used at the time of Pope Innocent III (1198-1216). Manuscripts in the Vatican Library provided some verbal emendations, but did not permit research into the "ancient and approved authors" beyond some liturgical commentators of the Middle Ages.

1613   8. Today, on the other hand, countless writings of scholars have clarified the "usage of the holy Fathers" followed by the revisers of the missal under Saint Pius V. After the Gregorian sacramentary was first published in 1571, many critical studies of other ancient Roman and Ambrosian sacramentaries appeared. Ancient Spanish and Gallican liturgical books also became available, bringing to light many prayers of profound spirituality that had been previously unknown.

1614   Traditions dating back to the first centuries, before the development of the Eastern and Western rites, are also better known today because so many liturgical documents have been discovered.

1615   Progress has been made, moreover, in studying the actual works of the holy Fathers. The teachings of such outstanding saints as Irenaeus, Ambrose, Cyril of Jerusalem, and John Chrysostom have shed light on the theology of the eucharistic mystery in Christian antiquity.

1616   9. The "usage of the holy Fathers" does not require only the preservation of what our immediate ancestors passed on to us. The entire past of the Church and all its customs must be studied profoundly and understood: the Christian communities which flourished among the Semitic, Greek, and Latin peoples differed from one another in the forms of human and social culture by which they professed one common faith. This broader perspective shows us how the Holy

Spirit keeps the people of God faithful in preserving the deposit of faith unchanged, while prayers and rites differ greatly.

10. This new missal bears witness to the Roman Church's   1617
rule of prayer. It guards the deposit of faith handed down by recent councils. At the same time, it marks a major step forward in liturgical tradition.

The Fathers of the Second Vatican Council reaffirmed the   1618
dogmatic statements of the Council of Trent, but they spoke to a far different age in the world's history. They were able, therefore, to bring forward proposals and plans of a pastoral nature which could not have been foreseen four centuries ago.

11. The Council of Trent recognized the great catechetical   1619
value of the celebration of Mass, but was unable to make full use of this value in the actual life to the Church. Many people were demanding that the vernacular be permitted in the eucharistic sacrifice. But the council, judging the conditions of that age, felt bound to answer such demands with a reaffirmation of the Church's traditional teaching. This teaching is that the eucharistic sacrifice is, first and foremost, the action of Christ himself; the unique efficacy of Christ's action is not affected by the manner in which the faithful participate. The council, therefore, stated firmly, but with restraint: "Although the Mass contains much instruction for the faithful, it did not seem expedient to the Fathers that it be celebrated everywhere in the vernacular."[12] The council accordingly condemned the proposition "that the rite of the Roman Church, in which part of the canon and the words of consecration are spoken in a low voice, should be rejected or that the Mass must be celebrated in the vernacular."[13] Although the Council of Trent thus prohibited the use of the vernacular in the Mass, it did direct pastors of souls to substitute appropriate catechesis: "So that the sheep of Christ may not go hungry. . . this holy Synod commands pastors and all who have the care of souls to explain to their people some of the things read at Mass. They are to do this often, personally or through others, during the celebration, especially on Sundays and feast days. They are to explain, among other things, some mystery of this holy sacrifice."[14]

1620   12. The Second Vatican Council was assembled to adapt the Church to the contemporary requirements of its apostolic task. The council therefore examined thoroughly, as had Trent, the educational and pastoral character of the sacred liturgy.[15] Since no Catholic would now deny the lawfulness and efficacy of a sacred rite celebrated in Latin, the council was able to declare that "the use of the mother tongue frequently may be of great advantage to the people" and gave permission for its use.[16] This decision was received everywhere with so much enthusiasm that, under the leadership of the bishops and the Apostolic See, all liturgical celebrations in which the people participate may now be carried out in the vernacular so that the mystery may be more fully understood.

1621   13. The use of the vernacular in the liturgy may certainly be considered most helpful in presenting more clearly the catechesis of the mystery which is celebrated. Nevertheless, the Second Vatican Council also ordered the observance of certain directives, prescribed by the Council of Trent but not obeyed everywhere. These include, for example, the preaching of a homily on Sundays and feast days[17] and permission to interject some explanations into the sacred rites themselves.[18]

1622   Most importantly, the Second Vatican Council strongly urged "that more complete form of participation in the Mass when, after the priest's communion, the faithful receive the Lord's body from the same sacrifice."[19] Thus the council sought to give effect to the recommendation of the Fathers of Trent that for fuller participation in the holy eucharist "the faithful present at each Mass should communicate not only by spiritual desire but also by sacramental communion."[20]

1623   14. Moved by the same spirit of pastoral concern, the Second Vatican Council was able to reconsider the norm laid down by Trent about communion under both kinds. The Church teaches that the full effect of communion is received under the one species of bread; since that doctrine is rarely if ever challenged today, the council gave permission for communion to be received sometimes under both kinds. This clearer form of the sacramental signs offers the faithful "a special opportunity for deepening their appreciation of the mystery in which they share."[2] [1]

15. The Church faithfully fulfills its responsibility as the teacher of truth to guard the "old," that is, the deposit of tradition. At the same time, it fulfills another responsibility, that of examining and prudently introducing the "new" (see Matthew 13:52).

1624

Part of this new missal arranges the prayers of the Church with a clearer relation to the needs of our time. The best examples are in the ritual Masses and the Masses for special intentions. These combine tradition with new ideas. Some prayers remain unchanged from the most ancient tradition of the Church, which successive editions of the Roman missal reflect. Other prayers have been adapted to contemporary needs and conditions. Still others are new compositions, such as the prayers for the Church, for the laity, for blessing of man's labor, the whole community of nations, and for certain contemporary needs. They voice the thoughts and sometimes the words of the recent conciliar documents.

1625

The same awareness of the new state of the world also influenced the changes made in texts from very ancient tradition. It seemed that this cherished treasury of prayers would not be harmed if some phrases were adapted to the language of modern theology and to the current discipline of the Church. Thus some expressions were changed which referred to the value and use of the good things of the earth or which encouraged a particular form of external penance more suited to another age in the history of the Church.

1626

In short, the liturgical norms of the Council of Trent have been completed and perfected in many ways by those of the Second Vatican Council. The council has brought to fulfillment the efforts of the last four hundred years to move the faithful closer to the sacred liturgy, especially the effort of recent times and above all the liturgical movement promoted by Saint Pius X and his successors.

1627

SACRAMENTALI COMMUNIONE
Selection from Instruction of the Sacred Congregation
for Divine Worship
on Communion under Both Kinds
June 29, 1970

The entire tradition of the Church teaches that the faithful participate more perfectly in the Eucharistic celebration through sacramental Communion. By Communion, in fact, the faithful share more fully in the Eucharistic Sacrifice. In this way, they are not limited to sharing in the sacrifice by faith and prayer, nor to merely spiritual communion with Christ offered on the altar, but receive Christ Himself sacramentally, so as to receive more fully the fruits of this most holy sacrifice.

1629   In order that the fullness of the sign in the Eucharistic banquet may be seen more clearly by the faithful,[1] the Second Vatican Ecumenical Council prescribed that in certain cases, to be decided by the Holy See, the faithful could receive Holy Communion under both species. This leaves intact the dogmatic principles recognized in the Council of Trent, which teach that Christ whole and entire, and the true sacrament,[2] are also received under one species alone.[3]

1630   This desire of the Council has gradually been put into effect.[4] The preparation of the faithful has accompanied this gradual development, so that ever more abundant fruits of devotion and spiritual growth should result from this change in Church discipline.

1631   As time has gone on, it has been possible to witness an ever increasing desire that the number of cases in which Communion may be administered under both kinds should be further extended according to the needs of different regions and persons.

Therefore this Sacred Congregation for Divine Worship, taking into account the requests of numerous bishops, and indeed of episcopal conferences, and the requests of superiors of religious families, decrees the following by mandate of the Supreme Pontiff, regarding the faculty for distributing Holy Communion under both species: 1632

1. Communion under both species may be distributed, in accordance with the judgment of the ordinary, in the cases determined by the Holy See, as given in the appendix to this instruction.   1633

2. Moreover, the episcopal conferences may decide to what extent, for what motives and in what conditions ordinaries may allow Communion under both species in other cases which have great importance for the spiritual life of a particular community or group of the faithful.   1634

3. Within these limits, the ordinaries may indicate particular cases. This is on condition, however, that the faculty is not granted indiscriminately, and that such celebrations are clearly specified, together with those points to which particular attention must be paid. This faculty should not be granted on occasions where there are large numbers of communicants. The groups to whom the faculty is conceded should be adequately instructed on the significance of the rite.   1635

4. The ordinary of the place may grant this faculty for all churches and oratories in his territory; the religious ordinary may grant it for houses dependent on him. It is up to these to ensure that the norms given by the Holy See or by the episcopal conference should be observed. Before they grant the faculty, they should be sure that everything will be carried out in a way befitting the holiness of this sacrament.   1636

5. Before the faithful are allowed to receive Communion under both species, they should be adequately instructed on the significance of the rite.   1637

6. In order that Communion under both species may be properly administered, care should be taken to maintain due   1638

reverence and to carry out the rite in accordance with nos. 244-251 of the General Instructions of the Roman Missal.

1639   That method of distribution should be chosen which best ensures that Communion is received with devotion and dignity, and which also avoids the dangers of irreverence. The nature of each liturgical group, and the age, conditions and preparation of those wishing to receive Communion, must also be taken into account.

1640   Among the methods of distribution given by the General Instructions of the Roman Missal, the reception of Communion by drinking from the chalice itself certainly has pre-eminence. However, this method should be chosen only when everything can be carried out in an orderly fashion and without any danger of irreverence toward the Blood of the Lord. If there are other priests present, or deacons or acolytes, they should therefore be asked to help by presenting the chalice.

1641   On the other hand, the method of distribution in which the chalice is passed from one to another does not seem permissible, nor does that in which the communicants approach directly to take the chalice themselves and receive the Blood of the Lord. When the ministers mentioned above are not available, then if the communicants are few in number and Communion is taken directly from the chalice, the same priest should distribute Communion first under the species of bread and then under the species of wine.

1642   Otherwise the rite of Communion under both species by intinction is to be preferred, in order that practical difficulties may be avoided and due reverence be more aptly given to the sacrament. In this way, access to Communion under both species is made easier and safer for the faithful, whatever their age or condition, and at the same time the fullness of sign is preserved.

1643   His Holiness Pope Paul VI confirmed and ratified the present instruction on June 26, 1970, and ordered that it be promulgated.

1644   From the Sacred Congregation for Divine Worship, June 29, 1970.

LITURGICAE INSTAURATIONES
Instruction of the Sacred Congregation
for Divine Worship
on Correct Implementation of
the Constitution on the Sacred Liturgy
September 5, 1970

The reforms which have so far been put into effect in applying the Second Vatican Council's Constitution on the Sacred Liturgy have been concerned above all with the celebration of the Eucharistic mystery. For, in it "the whole spiritual good of the Church is contained. It is Christ Himself, our Passover, the living Bread giving life to men through His flesh, quickened and made vivifying by the Holy Spirit. Men, in turn, are invited and induced to offer themselves, their work and all creation with Christ to God."[1]

In the same way, when the Church assembles to offer the Sacrifice of the Mass according to the renewed form of celebration, it is made manifest that the Mass is the center of the Church's life. Thus the purpose of the reform of the rites is to promote a pastoral action which has its summit and source in the sacred liturgy and to bring to life the Paschal mystery of Christ.[2]

1646

This work of renewal has been carried out, step by step, during the past six years. It has prepared the way for the passage from the former Mass liturgy to the renewed liturgy outlined in detail in the Roman Missal, with the *Ordo Missae* and the General Revision included therein. Now it can be said that a new and promising future lies ahead for pastoral-liturgical action; the way is open to make full use of all the possibilities contained in the new order of Scripture readings

1647

for the Mass and in the abundant variety of forms contained in the Roman Missal.

1648   The wide choice of texts and the flexibility of the rubrics make it possible to adapt the celebration to the circumstances, mentality and preparation of the assembly. Thus there is no need to resort to arbitrary adaptations, which would only weaken the impact of the liturgy. The possibilities offered by the Church's reforms can make the celebration vital, moving and spiritually effective.

1649   The step-by-step introduction of the new liturgical forms has taken into consideration both the overall renewal program and the great variety of local conditions throughout the world. Thus these new forms have been well received by the majority of clergy and laity,[3] although here and there they have met with resistance and impatience.

1650   There were those who, for the sake of conserving ancient tradition, were unwilling to accept these reforms. There were others who, concerned with urgent pastoral needs, felt that they could not wait for the definitive renewal to be promulgated. As a result, some individuals, acting on private initiative, arrived at hasty and sometimes unwise solutions, and made changes, additions or simplifications in the rites which at times went against the basic principles of the liturgy. This only troubled the conscience of the faithful and impeded or made more difficult the progress of genuine renewal.

1651   For these reasons, many bishops, priests and laymen have asked the Apostolic See to intervene; they wanted the Church to use its authority to preserve and increase that fruitful union of minds and hearts that is characteristic of the Christian people in its encounter with God.

1652   This was not possible as long as the Commission [for Implementing the Liturgy Constitution] was engaged in its task of liturgical renewal. But now it can be done on the basis of the final results of this work.

1653   But first of all, the bishops are called upon to exercise their responsibility. It is they whom the Holy Spirit has made leaders in the Church of God;[4] they are "the principal dispensers of the mysteries of God, just as they are the governors, promoters and guardians of the entire liturgical life in the Church committed to them."[5] It is their duty to guide, direct, stimulate and sometimes correct, but always to be shining examples in carrying out the genuine renewal of the liturgy. It must also be their concern that the whole body of the Church can move ahead with one mind, in the unity of charity, on the diocesan, national and international level. This work of the bishops is necessary and especially urgent in this case because of the close relation between liturgy and faith, so that what benefits the one, benefits the other.

With the help of their liturgical commissions, the bishops should be accurately informed about the religious and social condition of the faithful whom they serve; in order to meet their spiritual needs in the best way possible, they should learn to make full use of the possibilities offered by the rites. By thus evaluating the situation in their diocese, they will be able to note what helps and what hinders true renewal and to engage in a wise and prudent work of persuasion and guidance, a work which both recognizes the real needs of the faithful and follows the guidelines laid down in the new liturgical laws.   1654

A well informed bishop will be a great help to the priests who must exercise their ministry in hierarchical fellowship with him;[6] his knowledge will make it easier for them to render him the due obedience that a more perfect expression of divine worship and the sanctification of souls call for.   1655

Thus it is the scope of this document to aid and encourage the bishops in putting fully into effect the liturgical norms, especially those contained in the General Revision of the Roman Missal. In order to restore the orderly and serene celebration of the Eucharist, the center of the Church's life as "a sign of unity, a bond of charity,"[7] the following guidelines should be followed.   1656

1. The recent reforms have simplified liturgical formulas, gestures and actions, according to the principle laid down in the Constitution on the Sacred Liturgy: "The rites should be distinguished by a noble simplicity; they should be short, clear and unencumbered by useless repetitions; they should be accommodated to the minds of the people, and normally should not require much explanation."[8]   1657

1658   But this simplification must not go beyond certain limits, for otherwise the liturgy would be deprived of its sacred signs and of its appeal to the senses. These are necessary to make the mystery of salvation really effective in the Christian community and, by means of catechetical instruction, to make it rightly understood under the visible symbols.

1659   Liturgical reform is not at all synonymous with so-called desacralization, and is not intended as an occasion for what is called secularization. Thus the liturgy must keep a dignified and sacred character.

1660   The effectiveness of liturgical actions does not consist in the continual search for newer rites or simpler forms, but in an ever deeper insight into the word of God and the mystery which is celebrated. The priest will assure the presence of God and His mystery in the celebration by following the rites of the Church rather than his own preferences.

1661   The priest should keep in mind that, by imposing his own personal restoration of sacred rites, he is offending the rights of the faithful and is introducing individualism and idiosyncrasy into celebrations which belong to the whole Church.

1662   The ministry of the priest is the ministry of the Church, and it can be exercised only in obedience, in hierarchical fellowship, and in devotion to the service of God and of his brothers. The hierarchical structure of the liturgy, its sacramental value and the respect due to the community of the faithful require that the priest exercise his liturgical service as a "faithful minister and steward of the mysteries of God."[9] He should not add any rite which is not contained in the liturgical books.

1663   2. Of all the texts proclaimed in the liturgical assembly, the Holy Scriptures are of the greatest value. In the readings, God speaks to His people and Christ, present in His word, announces the good news of the Gospel.[10] Therefore:

1664   a) Full importance must be given to the Liturgy of the Word in the Mass. Other readings, whether from sacred or profane authors of past or present, may never be substituted for the word of God. The purpose of the homily is to explain the readings and make them relevant for the present day.

This is the task of the priest, and the faithful should not add comments or engage in dialogue during the homily.

b) The Liturgy of the Word prepares the assembly and leads them to the celebration of the Eucharist. Thus the two parts of the Mass form one act of worship[11] and may not be celebrated separately, at different times or in different places.   1665

Another liturgical action or part of the Divine Office may be integrated into the Liturgy of the Word; special rules for this will be indicated in the pertinent liturgical books.   1666

3. The liturgical texts composed by the Church also deserve great respect. No one may make changes, substitutions, additions or deletions in them.[12]   1667

a) This rule applies especially to the *Ordo Missae*. The formulas which it contains, in the official translations, may never be altered, not even when Mass is sung. However, some parts of the rite—such as the penitential rite, the Eucharistic prayer, the acclamations of the people, the final blessing—can be chosen from various alternative formulas, as indicated for each rite.   1668

b) The entrance and communion songs can be selected from the Roman Gradual, the simple Gradual, the Roman Missal, and from collections approved by the bishops' conferences. In choosing the songs for Mass, the conferences should consider not only their suitability to the time and circumstances of the celebration, but also the needs of the faithful who will sing them.   1669

c) All means must be used to encourage singing by the people. New forms should be used which are adapted to various mentalities and to modern tastes. The bishops' conferences should indicate selections of songs to be used in Masses for special groups, for example, young people or children; the words, melody and rhythm of these songs, and the instruments used for accompaniment, should correspond to the sacred character of the celebration and place of worship.   1670

The Church does not exclude any kind of sacred music from the liturgy.[13] However, not every type of music, song or instrument is equally capable of stimulating prayer or expressing the mystery of Christ. Music in the celebration must   1671 serve the worship of God, and thus must have qualities of holiness and good form;[14] it must be suited to the liturgical action and the nature of each of its parts; and it must not impede the active participation of the whole assembly,[15] but must direct the attention of mind and heart to the mystery celebrated.

1672   It is the duty of the bishops' conferences to prescribe guidelines for liturgical music or, in the absence of general norms, local bishops may make these for their dioceses.[16] Attention should be given to the choice of musical instruments. These should be few in number, suited to the place and the community; they should foster prayer and should not be too loud.

1673   d) Great freedom of choice is allowed for selecting the orations; especially on ordinary weekdays these may be taken from any one of the 34 Mass formularies, from the Masses for special intentions,[17] or from the votive Masses.

1674   Furthermore, in translating these texts, the bishops' conferences can make use of the special norms given by the Commission; these are contained in the instruction of January 25, 1969, on liturgical translations for use with the people, no. 34.[18]

1675   e) With regard to the readings, besides those indicated for each Sunday, feast and ferial day, a wide choice of readings is given for the celebration of the sacraments and for special circumstances. When Mass is celebrated with special groups, texts which are more suited to the group may be chosen, provided they are taken from some approved lectionary.[19]

1676   f) During the celebration of the Mass, the priest may say a few words to the people: at the beginning, before the readings, the preface, the prayer after Communion, and before the dismissal.[20] But he should abstain from adding comments during the Eucharistic prayer. These words should be brief and to the point, and should be prepared beforehand. If other comments or announcements need to be made, these should be made by the lay leader of the assembly, but he should avoid all exaggeration and limit himself to what is necessary.

g) It is good to add some special intentions for the local   1677
community to the prayers for the Church, the world and the
needy in the universal intercessions or prayer of the faithful.
(Other intentions are not to be inserted in the Roman canon
at the remembrances of the living and the dead.) These intentions should be written down beforehand, in the style of the
prayer of the faithful,[21] and can be read by different members of the assembly.

If the priest knows how to make intelligent use of these   1678
possibilities they give him such a wide range of choice that he
will have no need to resort to private adaptations. Priests
should be taught to prepare their celebration, taking note of
the circumstances and needs of the faithful and acting with
confidence along the lines prescribed by the General Revision
of the Missal.

4. The Eucharistic prayer is the prayer of the priest; of all   1679
the parts of the Mass, it is that which belongs especially to
him alone, because of his office.[22] Thus it is not permitted
to have some part of it read by a minister of lower rank, by
the assembly or by a lay person. This would be against the
hierarchical structure of the liturgy, in which everyone must
take part by doing solely and totally what is required of
him.[23] Thus the priest must say the whole Eucharistic prayer
by himself.

5. The bread used for the celebration of the Eucharist is   1680
wheat bread and, according to the ancient custom of the Latin
Church, is unleavened.[24]

The truth of the sign demands that this bread look like   1681
real food which is broken and shared among brothers. However, it must *always* be made in the traditional form, according to the General Revision of the Missal;[25] this applies both
to the individual hosts for the Communion of the faithful
and to larger altar breads which are broken up into smaller
parts for distribution.

The need for greater truth in the Eucharistic sign is met   1682
more by the color, taste and texture of the bread than by
its shape.

Out of reverence for the Sacrament, great care and atten-   1683
tion should be used in preparing the altar bread; it should

be easy to break and should not be unpleasant for the faithful to eat. Bread which tastes uncooked, or which becomes dry and inedible too quickly, must never be used.

1684   Great reverence must also be used in breaking the consecrated Bread and in receiving the Bread and Wine, both at Communion and in consuming what remains after Communion.[26]

1685   6. Communion under both kinds is the more perfect sacramental expression of the people's participation in the Eucharist.[27] The cases in which this may be done are enumerated in the General Revision of the Roman Missal (no. 242) and in the instruction of the Sacred Congregation for Divine Worship, of June 29, 1970, on Communion under both species. Therefore:

a) Within the limits established by the bishops' conference, ordinaries should not give general permission but should clearly state the cases and celebrations in which it is given. They should avoid occasions when there are large numbers of communicants. The groups should be limited in number, well ordered and homogeneous.

b) The faithful should be given special instruction, so that when they receive Communion under both kinds, they can fully understand its meaning.

c) A priest, deacon or ordained acolyte should be present to offer the chalice to the communicants. In the absence of another minister, the priest should follow the rite given in the General Revision of the Roman Missal, no. 254.

1686   It is best to avoid the practice of passing the chalice from one communicant to another or of having the communicant take the chalice directly from the altar. In these cases Communion should be administered by intinction.

d) The office of administering Communion belongs first to priests, then to deacons and, in some cases, to acolytes. The Holy See can permit the designation of some other worthy person to whom this office may be entrusted. Those who have not been appointed must not distribute Communion or carry the Blessed Sacrament.

1687   The manner of distributing Communion should follow the prescriptions of the General Revision of the Roman Missal (nos. 244-252) and the above-mentioned instruction of June 29, 1970. If permission is given for administering Communion in a different way, the conditions laid down by the Holy See should be observed.

e) Where there is a lack of priests, the bishops may, with permission of the Apostolic See, designate other persons (such as catechists, especially in the missions) to celebrate the Liturgy of the Word and to distribute Holy Communion. They may never say the Eucharistic prayer, but if they find it useful to read the narrative of the Last Supper, they should use it as a reading in the Liturgy of the Word. Thus such liturgical assemblies consist of the celebration of the word, the recitation of the Lord's Prayer and the distribution of Holy Communion according to the prescribed rite.

f) In whatever way Communion is administered, it must be done in a dignified, reverent and orderly manner, with the respect due the Sacrament. Attention must be paid to the nature of each liturgical assembly and to the age, condition and preparation of the communicants.[28]

7. The traditional liturgical norms of the Church prohibit women (single, married, religious) from serving the priest at the altar, even in chapels of women's homes, convents, schools and institutes.   **1688**

However, norms have been published according to which women may: **1689**

a) Proclaim the Scripture readings, except the Gospel. Use should be made of modern technical means, so that they can be easily heard by all. The bishops' conferences can determine the place in the assembly from which women may read the word of God;

b) Say the prayers of the faithful;

c) Play the organ and other instruments which may be used in church; lead the singing of the assembly;

d) Make announcements and give explanatory comments to aid the people's understanding of the rite;

e) Fulfill certain offices of service to the faithful which in some places are usually entrusted to women, such as receiving the faithful at the doors of the church and directing them to their places, guiding them in processions, and collecting their offerings in church.[29]

1690   8. Special care and attention is due the sacred vessels, vestments and church furnishings. Greater freedom is given with regard to their material and design, so that various peoples and artists may have the widest possible scope for applying their talents to divine worship. However, the following should be kept in mind:

a) Things which are used for worship must always be "of high quality, durable, and suited to liturgical use."[30] Thus common or household articles may not be used in the liturgy.

b) Chalices and patens should be consecrated by the bishop before they are used; he will judge whether or not they are suitable for the liturgy.

c) "The vestment common to all ministers of whatever rank is the alb."[31] The practice of wearing only a stole over the monastic cowl or ordinary clerical garb for concelebration is reproved as an abuse. It is never permitted to celebrate Mass or perform other sacred actions, such as the laying on of hands at ordinations or the administering of other sacraments or blessings, while wearing only the stole over street clothes.

d) The bishops' conferences may decide whether or not materials other than those traditionally used may be employed for church furnishings and vestments. They should inform the Apostolic See about their decision.[32]

1691   Bishops' conferences may also propose to the Holy See adaptations in the design of sacred vestments, in conformity with the needs and customs of their regions.[33]

1692   9. The Eucharist is normally celebrated in church.[34] The ordinary, within his own jurisdiction, will decide when there is a real necessity which permits celebration outside the church. In such a case, careful attention should be given to the choice of a place and a table which are fitting for the Eucharistic Sacrifice. As far as possible, dining halls and tables on which meals are eaten should not be used for the celebration.

1693   10. Bishops should give special attention to a permanent arrangement of the church, and especially of the altar and sanctuary, which is suitable for the celebration of the renewed liturgy. In doing this they should follow the norms of the General Revision of the Roman Missal[35] and the Instruction on Worship of the Eucharistic Mystery.[36]

Temporary arrangements made in recent years should be given a final form. Some of these provisory solutions still in use are liturgically and artistically unsatisfactory, and render difficult the worthy celebration of the Mass; the Commission has ordered that they be corrected.[37]   1694

With the help of diocesan committees on liturgy and sacred art, and after consultation, if necessary, with other experts and civil authorities, a detailed study should be made of new building projects, and a review of temporary arrangements in existing churches. All churches should be given a permanent arrangement which takes into account any artistic monuments, adapting them as far as possible to current needs.   1695

11. To make the renewed liturgy understood, a great deal of work still remains to be done in translating accurately and in publishing the new liturgical books. They must be translated completely and must replace all other liturgical books previously in use.   1696

If the bishops' conferences find it necessary and useful to add other formulas or make certain changes, these should first be presented for approval to the Holy See; in printing these additions or changes, they should be distinguished from the official Latin text by some typographical sign.   1697

This work of translation will produce better results if it is done slowly, with the help of many experts, not only theologians and liturgists, but also writers and poets. Thus the vernacular liturgical texts will be works of real literary merit and of enduring quality, whose harmony of style and richness of expression will reflect the profound significance of their content.[38]   1698

In publishing the vernacular liturgical books, the tradition should be kept of not indicating the names of authors and translators. These books are destined for the use of the Christian community, and it is the hierarchy which orders their preparation and publication; to depend in any way on the consent of private individuals would be an offense   1699 against the freedom of authority and the dignity of the liturgy.

1700   12. When liturgical experimentation is seen to be necessary or useful, permission is granted in writing by this sacred congregation alone; the experiments will be made according to clearly defined norms, under the responsibility of the competent local authority.

1701   With regard to the Mass, those faculties which were granted in view of the reform of the rite are no longer in force. With the publication of the new Roman Missal, the norms and form of the Eucharistic celebration are those given in the General Revision and the *Ordo Missae.*

1702   The bishops' conference should decide first on the adaptations already foreseen by the liturgical books and submit their decision to the Holy See for confirmation.

1703   If wider adaptations are necessary, in accordance with no. 40 of the Constitution on the Sacred Liturgy, the bishops should make a detailed study of the culture, traditions and special pastoral needs of their people. If they find there is need for some practical experimentation, this should be done within clearly defined limits. Experiments should be carried out by well prepared groups, under the direction of prudent men especially appointed for the task. Experiments should not be made in large assemblies, nor should they be given publicity. They should be few in number and carried out for periods no longer than a year, after which a report should be made to the Apostolic See. The liturgical changes requested may not be put into effect while awaiting the reply of the Holy See. If changes are to be made in the structure of the rites or in the order of parts as given in the liturgical books, or if completely new actions or texts are to be introduced, a complete outline and program of the modifications should be proposed to the Apostolic See before any experiments are begun.

1704   Such a procedure is required both by the Constitution on the Sacred Liturgy and by the importance of the matter.[39]

1705   13. Finally, it must be remembered that the liturgical renewal is a concern of the whole Church. At pastoral meetings, this renewal should be studied in both its theoretical and its practical aspects as an instrument for the Christian formation of the people, so that the liturgy may become for them a living and meaningful experience.

The present reform, drawing upon an ancient yet living   1706
spiritual tradition, has sought to create a liturgical prayer which is visibly the work of the whole People of God, structured in its variety of orders and ministries.[40] This unity of the whole body of the Church is the guarantee of the liturgy's efficacy and authenticity.

The pastors of the Church should above all consider them-   1707
selves ministers of the community's liturgy. In their generous fidelity to the norms and directives of the Church, and in their spirit of faith, they should be examples for the people. Thus by constantly deepening their own understanding of the liturgical mysteries and by communicating this understanding to the faithful, they will contribute to that growth and progress of the Church which is the fruit of the renewed liturgy, a liturgy which is open to the needs of our times and yet far from every kind of secularism and individualism.

By mandate of Pope Paul VI, the Sacred Congregation for   1708
Divine Worship prepared this instruction; the Supreme Pontiff approved and confirmed it by his authority on September 3 of this year, and ordered that it be published and observed by all.

From the office of the Sacred Congregation for Divine   1709
Worship, September 5, 1970.

This year saw the publication of new rites concerning religious life:
   1) February 2, 1970 - Rites of Religious Profession
   2) May 31, 1970 - Rite of Conservation of Virgins
   3) November 9, 1970 - Rite for Blessing of Abbot or Abbess.—Ed.

LAUDIS CANTICUM
Apostolic Constitution of Pope Paul VI
on the Roman Breviary
November 1, 1970

The hymn of praise, which resounds eternally in the heavenly halls, and which Jesus Christ the High Priest introduced into this land of exile, has always been continued by the Church, in the course of so many centuries, with constancy and faithfulness, in the marvelous variety of its forms.

1711   The Liturgy of the Hours was gradually developed until it became the prayer of the local Church, where at established times and places, with the priest presiding over it, it became a necessary completion, as it were, of the whole divine worship contained in the Eucharistic Sacrifice, to be poured forth and extended at every hour of man's life.

1712   The book of the Divine Office, gradually increased by numerous additions in the course of time, became a suitable instrument for the sacred action for which it is intended. Nevertheless, since considerable modifications in the manner of celebrating the Hours were introduced in different periods, including celebration by the individual, it is not surprising that the book itself, later called the Breviary, has been adapted to various forms, which sometimes required a different composition.

1713   For lack of time, the Council of Trent did not succeed in completing the reform of the Breviary, and entrusted the task to the Apostolic See. The Roman Breviary, promulgated by Our predecessor St. Pius V in 1568, provided in the first place, in accordance with the common ardent desire, for the uniformity of canonical prayer, which no longer existed in the Latin Church at that time.

In the following centuries, various innovations were introduced by the Sovereign Pontiffs Sixtus V, Clement VIII, Urban VIII, Clement XI and others.

1714

In 1911, St. Pius X issued the new Breviary prepared at his request. The ancient custom of reciting the 150 Psalms every week was reestablished, the Psalter was completely rearranged, all repetitions were eliminated, and the possibility was offered of bringing the weekday Psalter and the cycle of biblical readings into line with the Offices of the Saints. Furthermore, the Sunday Office grew in importance and was given a higher ranking so that, in many instances, it took precedence over the feasts of saints.

1715

The whole work of liturgical reform was taken up again by Pius XII. He granted the use, both in private and in public recitation, of a new version of the Psalter drawn up by the Pontifical Biblical Institute, and having established a special commission in 1947, he entrusted the question of the Breviary to it. The bishops of the whole world were consulted on this subject, from the year 1955 on. This diligent work began to yield its fruits with the decree on the simplification of the rubrics of March 23, 1955, and with the norms on the Breviary which John XXIII issued in the Code of Rubrics in 1960.

1716

But though he had only partly provided for the liturgical reform, the same Sovereign Pontiff John XXIII realized that the great principles on which the liturgy was based called for a more thorough study. He entrusted this task to the Second Vatican Ecumenical Council, which he had convened in the meantime. The Council dealt so amply and clearly, so exactly and effectively, with the liturgy in general and with the prayer of the Hours in particular, that nothing similar can be found in the whole history of the Church.

1717

While the Vatican Council was still going on, it was Our care to make provision for implementation of the decrees of the Constitution on the Sacred Liturgy immediately after their promulgation.

1718

1719   For this reason, within the Commission for Implementing the Liturgy Constitution which We had established, a special group was set up which worked very diligently and painstakingly for seven years to prepare the new book for the Liturgy of the Hours, having recourse to the contribution of scholars and experts on liturgical, theological, spiritual and pastoral matters.

1720   After having consulted the Church's entire episcopate and numerous pastors of souls, religious and laymen, the above mentioned commission, as well as the Synod of Bishops which met in 1967, approved the principles and structures of the whole work and of its separate parts.

The New Regulations

1721   It is opportune, therefore, to set forth in detail the new regulations of the Liturgy of the Hours and their motivations.

Details of the restored order follow. Then in closing these remarks are made:

1722   Christian prayer is above all the prayer of the whole human community, which Christ joins to Himself.[1] Everyone takes part in the celebration of this prayer; it is characteristic of the whole body for prayers to be poured forth that represent the voice of Christ's beloved bride, the desires and wishes of the whole Christian people, and supplications and pleas for the needs of all men.

1723   This prayer received its unity from the heart of Christ. Our Redeemer willed, in fact, "that the life begun in His mortal body with His prayers and His sacrifice should continue throughout the centuries in His Mystical Body, which is the Church";[2] thus the prayer of the Church is "the very prayer which Christ Himself, together with His Body, addressed to the Father."[3] It is therefore necessary that as we celebrate the Office we recognize the echo of our voices in the voice of Christ, and His voice in us.[4]

1724   For this characteristic of our prayer to shine forth more clearly, "that warm and living love for Scripture"[5] that is instilled by the Liturgy of the Hours must flourish again in everyone, so that Sacred Scripture will really become the principal source of all Christian prayer. The prayer of the Psalms particularly which accompanies and proclaims the action of God in the history of salvation, must be learned with renewed love by the People of God. This will more easily happen if a deeper knowledge of the Psalms is more diligently promoted among the clergy, in the sense in which they are sung in the sacred liturgy, and this is imparted to the faithful through an appropriate catechesis. A wider reading of Sacred Scripture, not only at Mass but also in the Liturgy of the Hours, will ensure the uninterrupted commemoration of the history of salvation and the efficacious announcement of its continuation in the lives of men.

Since the life of Christ in His Mystical Body also perfects and elevates the personal life of each member of the faithful, any opposition between the prayer of the Church and personal prayer must be rejected; in fact, their mutual relationship must be strengthened and increased. Mental prayer must find a continual nourishment in the readings and in the Psalms. The recitation of the Office must be adapted, as far as possible, to the necessities of ardent personal prayer, owing to the fact—for which provision is made in the general instruction—that those times, modes and forms of celebration must be chosen that are best suited to the spiritual situation of those praying. When the prayer of the Office becomes real personal prayer, then the bonds which unite the liturgy and the entire Christian life are manifested more clearly. The whole life of the faithful, during the individual hours of the day and night, constitutes *leitourgia*, as it were, with which they offer themselves in a service of love to God and to men, adhering to the action of Christ who sanctified the lives of all men by His contact with us and His offering of Himself.   **1725**

The Liturgy of the Hours expresses clearly and confirms effectively this lofty truth, which is inherent in the Christian life.   **1726**

For this reason the prayers of the Hours are proposed to   **1727** all the faithful, even to those who are not obliged by law to recite them.

1728   But let those who have received from the Church the mandate of celebrating the Liturgy of the Hours carry out their duty religiously every day with the complete recitation, as far as possible at the correct time, of the individual Hours; and let them give due importance first of all to morning Lauds and to Vespers.

1729   In celebrating the Divine Office, those who because of Holy Orders bear the sign of Christ the Priest in a particular way, and those who have dedicated themselves with the vows of religious profession to the service of God and the Church in a special manner, should not feel impelled solely by a law they must observe, but rather by recognition of the intrinsic importance of prayer and by its pastoral and ascetic usefulness. It is highly desirable that the public prayer of the Church should spring from a general spiritual renewal and from awareness of the intrinsic need of the whole body of the Church which—in imitation of her Head—cannot be described as anything but a praying Church.

1730   Let praise of God ring out, therefore, more splendidly and beautifully in the Church of our times, by means of the new book of the Liturgy of the Hours which We now establish, approve and promulgated by Our apostolic authority. Let it unite with the praise of the saints and angels resounding in the heavenly mansions and, growing in perfection, let it approach more and more, in the days of this earthly exile, that full praise that is given forever "to him who sits upon the throne, and to the lamb."[6]

1731   We therefore establish that this new book of the Liturgy of the Hours can be used immediately after its publication. It will be the task of episcopal conferences to have editions prepared in the national languages and, after approval or confirmation by the Holy See, to establish the day on which these versions can or must begin to be used, either wholly or in part. From the day when the translations for the celebrations in the vernacular language are to be used, even those who continue to use the Latin language must use solely the revised text of the Liturgy of the Hours.

Those who on account of advanced age or other particular   1732
reasons meet with grave difficulties in the use of the new
Ordo are allowed, with the consent of their ordinary and only in individual recitation, to retain the Roman Breviary
which was formerly in use, in whole or in part.

We wish what We have decreed and ordered to become   1733
effective now and in the future, notwithstanding any contrary constitutions and apostolic regulations promulgated by
Our predecessors and other decrees, even those worthy of
particular mention.

Given in Rome, at St. Peter's on November first, All Saints   1734
Day, of the year 1970, the eighth of Our pontificate.

The revised liturgical rites continued to appear as they
were completed:
December 3, 1970 - Rite for the Blessing of Oils
August 22, 1971 - Rite of Confirmation
January 7, 1972 - Rite for Christian Initiation of Adults
                                                            —Ed.

Secretariat for Promoting Christian Unity
Instruction Concerning Cases when other Christians may
be admitted to Eucharistic Communion in the Catholic Church
June 1, 1972

1. *The Question.*

We are often asked the question: in what circumstances and on what conditions can members of other Churches and ecclesial communities be admitted to eucharistic communion in the Catholic Church?

1736 The question is not a new one. The Second Vatican Council (in the decree on Ecumenism *Unitatis Redintegratio)* and the Directorium Oecumenicum dealt with it.

1737 The pastoral guidance offered here is not intended to change the existing rules but to explain them, bringing out the doctrinal principles on which the rules rest and so making their application easier.

2. *The Eucharist and the mystery of the Church.*

1738 There is a close link between the mystery of the Church and the mystery of the Eucharist.

1739 a) The Eucharist really contains what is the very foundation of the being and unity of the Church: the Body of Christ, offered in sacrifice and given to the faithful as the bread of eternal life. The sacrament of the Body and Blood of Christ, given to the Church so as to constitute the Church, of its nature carries with it:

—the ministerial power which Christ gave to his apostles and to their successors, the bishops along with the priests, to make effective sacramentally His own priestly act—that act by which once and forever He offered Himself to the Father in the Holy Spirit, and gave Himself to His faithful that they might be one in Him;

—the unity of the ministry, which is to be exercised in the name of Christ, Head of the Church, and hence in the hierarchical communion of ministers;

—the faith of the Church, which is expressed in the eucharistic action itself-the faith by which she responds to Christ's gift in its true meaning.

The sacrament of the Eucharist, understood in its entirety with these three elements, signifies an existing unity brought about by Him, the unity of the visible Church of Christ which cannot be lost.   1740

b) "The celebration of Mass, the action of Christ and of the people of God hierarchically ordered, is the center of the whole Christian life, for the universal Church as for the local Church and for each Christian." Celebrating the mystery of Christ in the Mass, the Church celebrates her own mystery and manifests concretely her unity.   1741

The faithful assembled at the altar offer the sacrifice through the hands of the priest acting in the name of Christ, and they represent the community of the people of God united in the profession of one faith. Thus they constitute a sign and a kind of delegation of a wider assembly.   1742

The celebration of Mass is of itself a profession of faith in which the whole Church recognizes and expresses itself. If we consider the marvelous meaning of the eucharistic prayers as well as the riches contained in the other parts of the Mass, whether they are fixed or vary with the liturgical cycle; if at the same time we bear in mind that the liturgy of the word and the eucharistic liturgy make up a single act of worship, then we can see here a striking illustration of the principle *lex orandi lex credendi.* Thus the Mass has a catechetical power which the recent liturgical renewal has emphasized. Again, the Church has in the course of history been careful to introduce into liturgical celebration the main themes of the common faith, the chief fruits of the experience   1743 of that faith. This she has done either by means of new texts or by creating new feasts.

1744   c) The relation between local celebration of the Eucharist and universal ecclesial communion is stressed also by the special mention in the eucharistic prayers of the pope, the local bishop and the other members of the episcopal college.

1745   What has been said here of the Eucharist as center and summit of the Christian life holds for the whole Church and for each of its members, but particularly for those who take an active part in the celebration of Mass and above all for those who receive the Body of Christ. Communion during Mass is indeed the most perfect way of participating in the Eucharist, for it fulfills the Lord's command, "take and eat."

3. *The Eucharist as spiritual food.*

1746   The effect of the Eucharist is also to nourish spiritually those who receive it as what the faith of the Church says it truly is—the body and blood of the Lord given as the food of eternal life (cf. *John* VI, 54-58). For the baptized, the Eucharist is spiritual food, a means by which they are brought to live the life of Christ himself, are incorporated more profoundly in Him and share more intensely in the whole economy of his saving mystery. "He who eats my flesh and drinks my blood abides in me and I in him" (*John* VI, 56).

1747   a) As in the sacrament of full union with Christ and of the perfection of spiritual life, the Eucharist is necessary to every Christian: in our Lord's words, ". . . unless you eat the flesh of the Son of Man and drink his blood, you have no life in you" (*John* VI, 53). Those who live intensely the life of grace feel a compelling need for this spiritual sustenance, and the Church herself encourages daily communion.

1748   b) Yet though it is a spiritual food whose effect is to unite the Christian man to Jesus Christ, the Eucharist is far from being simply a means of satisfying exclusively personal aspirations, however lofty these may be. The union of the faithful with Christ, the head of the mystical body, brings about the union of the faithful themselves with each other. It is on their sharing of the Eucharistic bread that St. Paul bases the union of all the faithful, "Because there is one loaf" (1 *Cor.* X, 17).

By this sacrament "man is incorporated in Christ and united
with His members." By frequent receiving of the Eucharist
the faithful are incorporated more and more in the body of
Christ and share increasingly in the mystery of the Church.

c) Spiritual need of the Eucharist is not therefore merely a   1749
matter of personal spiritual growth: simultaneously, and inseparably, it concerns our entering more deeply into Christ's
Church, "which is his body, the fullness of him who fills all
in all" (*Eph.* I, 23).

4. *General Principles governing admission to communion.*

Where members of the Catholic Church are concerned,   1750
there is a perfect parallel between regarding the Eucharist as
the celebration of the entire ecclesial community united in
one faith and regarding it as sustenance, as a response to the
spiritual needs, personal and ecclesial, of each member. It will
be the same when, in the Lord's good time, all the followers
of Christ are reunited in one and the same Church. But what
are we to say today, when Christians are divided? Any baptized person has a spiritual need for the Eucharist. Those who
are not in full communion with the Catholic Church have recourse to the ministers of their own communities, as their
conscience dictates. But what about those who cannot do
this, and who for that or other reasons come and ask for communion from a Catholic priest?

The Directorium Oecumenicum has already shown how we   1751
must safeguard simultaneously the integrity of ecclesial communion and the good of souls. Behind the Directorium lie
two main governing ideas:

a) The strict relationship between the mystery of the
Church and the mystery of the Eucharist can never be altered,
whatever pastoral measures we may be led to take in given
cases. Of its very nature celebration of the Eucharist signifies
the fullness of profession of faith and the fullness of ecclesial
communion. This principle must not be obscured and must remain our guide in this field.

b) The principle will not be obscured if admission to Catholic eucharistic communion is confined to particular cases of
those Christians who have a faith in the sacrament in con-

formity with that of the Church, who experience a serious spiritual need for the eucharistic sustenance, who for a prolonged period are unable to have recourse to a minister of their own community and who ask for the sacrament of their own accord; all this provided that they have proper dispositions and lead lives worthy of a Christian. This spiritual need should be understood in the sense defined above (No. 3, b and c): a need for an increase in spiritual life and a need for a deeper involvement in the mystery of the Church and of its unity.

1752   Further, even if those conditions are fulfilled, it will be a pastoral responsibility to see that the admission of these other Christians to communion does not endanger or disturb the faith of Catholics.

5. Differences, in view of these principles, between members of the Oriental Churches and other Christians.

1753   The Directorium Oecumenicum gives different directions for the admission to holy communion of separated Eastern Christians, and of others. The reason is that the Eastern Churches, though separated from us, have true sacraments, above all, because of the apostolic succession, the priesthood and the eucharist, which unite them to us by close ties, so that the risk of obscuring the relation between eucharistic communion and ecclesial communion is somewhat reduced. Recently the Holy Father recalled that "between our Church and the venerable Orthodox Churches there exists already an almost total communion, though it is not yet perfect; it results from our joint participation in the mystery of Christ and of His Church.

1754   With Christians who belong to communities whose eucharistic faith differs from that of the Church and which do not have the sacrament of Orders, admitting them to the Eucharist entails the risk of obscuring the essential relation between eucharistic communion and ecclesial communion. This is why the Directorium treats their case differently from that of the Eastern Christians and envisages admission only in exceptional cases of "urgent necessity." In cases of this kind the person concerned is asked to manifest a faith in the Eucharist in conformity with that of the Church, i.e. in the Eucharist as

Christ instituted it and as the Catholic Church hands it on. This is not asked of an Orthodox person because he belongs to a Church whose faith in the Eucharist is conformable to our own.

6. *What Authority decides particular cases?—The meaning of No. 55 of the Directorium Oecumenicum.*

No. 55 of the Directorium allows fairly wide discretionary   1755
power to the episcopal authority in judging whether the necessary conditions are present for these exceptional cases. If cases of the same pattern recur often in a given region, episcopal conferences can give general directions. More often however it falls to the bishop of the diocese to make a decision. He alone will know all the circumstances of particular cases.

Apart from danger of death the Directorium mentions two   1756
examples, people in prison and those suffering persecution, but it then speaks of "other cases of such urgent necessity." Such cases are not confined to situations of suffering and danger. Christians may find themselves in grave spiritual necessity and with no chance of recourse to their own community. For example, in our time, which is one of large-scale movements of population, it can happen much more often than before that non-Catholic Christians are scattered in Catholic regions. They are often deprived of the help of their own communion and unable to get in touch with it except at great trouble and expense. If the conditions set out in the Directorium are verified, they can be admitted to eucharistic communion but it will be for the bishop to consider each case.

The Ordo Cantus Missae, the final product of the musical reform was released on June 24, 1972.—Ed.

IN CELEBRATIONE MISSAE
Declaration of the Congregation
for Divine Worship
on Concelebration
August 7, 1972

I n the celebration of Mass "everyone has the right and duty to take his own part according to the diversity of orders and functions . . . so that in the liturgy the Church may be seen as composed of various orders and ministries."[1] Priests, by reason of their ordination, exercise an office which is properly theirs in the celebration of Mass when, either individually or together with other priests, they celebrate the sacrifice of Christ in the sacramental act and participate in it by communion.[2]

1758   It is therefore fitting for priests to celebrate or concelebrate Mass so that they may participate more fully and in the manner proper to them and not only to communicate like the laity.[3]

1759   Since many petitions have been submitted concerning the correct interpretation of the General Instruction of the Roman Missal,[4] the Sacred Congregation for Divine Worship declares as follows:

1760   1. Members of chapters and members of communities of any religious institute of perfection who are obliged by their office to celebrate for the pastoral good of the faithful may concelebrate the conventual or community Mass on the same day.[5] Eucharistic concelebration in communities is to be greatly esteemed. Concelebration signifies and strengthens the fraternal bond of priests among themselves and with the entire community.[6] In this manner of celebrating the sacrifice, with all participating actively and consciously, in their own proper way, the action of the entire community and the manifestation of the Church are more clearly made visible in the unity of sacrifice and priesthood, in the one act of thanksgiving around the one altar.[7]

2. One who concelebrates at the principal Mass on the occasion of a pastoral visit or a special gathering of priests, for example, at a meeting of a pastoral nature, a congress, or a pilgrimage (as contemplated in the General Instruction, no. 158), may celebrate again for the good of the faithful.   1761

3. The following must be observed: 1762

a) Bishops and competent superiors,[8] should make sure that the concelebration in communities and in priests' residences is done with dignity and true piety. In order to achieve this purpose and the spiritual good of all, the freedom of the concelebrants must be respected and internal and external participation fostered through a genuine and integral ordering of the celebration according to the norms of the General Instruction of the Roman Missal. Care should be taken that each part of the Mass is carried out according to its own nature,[9] the distinction of offices and function is respected, and the role of music and silence is considered.

b) Those priests who celebrate for the people and concelebrate another Mass may not accept another stipend for the concelebrated Mass.

c) Although concelebration is the most important form of eucharistic celebration in communities, even celebration without the participation of the faithful "remains the center of the life of the entire Church and the heart of priestly existence."[10]

Every priest must be afforded the opportunity to celebrate individually,[11] and to foster such freedom everything should be provided which will facilitate this celebration: time, place, server, etc.   1763

On August 7, 1972, this declaration, prepared in consultation with other interested Congregations, was ratified and confirmed by Pope Paul VI, who ordered it to be made public.   1764

From the Congregation for Divine Worship, August 7, 1972.   1765

AD PASCENDUM
Motu Proprio of Pope Paul VI
on the Order of Diaconate
August 15, 1972

For the nurturing and constant growth of the People of God, Christ the Lord instituted in the Church a variety of ministries, which work for the good of the whole body.[1]

1767   From apostolic times the diaconate has had a prominent position among these ministries and has always been held in great honor by the Church. Explicit testimony to this is given by the Apostle St. Paul both in his letter to the Philippians, in which he sends greetings not only to the bishops but also to the deacons,[2] and in a letter to Timothy, in which he explains the qualities and virtues that deacons must have in order to be worthy of their ministry.[3]

1768   Later, when the early Church writers acclaim the dignity of deacons, they do not fail to extol at the same time the spiritual qualities and virtues required for the performance of that ministry, namely, fidelity to Christ, moral integrity and obedience to the bishops.

1769   St. Ignatius of Antioch asserts that the office of deacon is nothing other than "the ministry of Jesus Christ, who was with the Father before all ages and at last appeared."[4] He also observes: "The deacons, who are ministers of the mysteries of Jesus Christ, should please in all every way; for they are not servants of food and drink, but ministers of God's Church."[5]

1770   St. Polycarp of Smyrna exhorts deacons to "be moderate in all things, merciful, diligent, living according to the truth of the Lord, who became the servant of all."[6] Recalling Christ's words, "Whoever wishes to become great among you shall be your servant,"[7] the author of the *Didascalia Apostolorum* addressed the following fraternal exhortation to deacons: "Accordingly, you deacons also should behave in such a way that, if your ministry obliges you to lay down your lives for a brother, you should do so.... If the Lord of heaven and earth served us, and suffered and sustained everything on our behalf, should not this be done all the more by us for our brothers, since we are His imitators and have been given the place of Christ."[8]

Furthermore, when the writers of the first centuries insist   1771 on the importance of the deacons' ministry, they give many examples of the numerous important tasks entrusted to them; and they clearly show how great was their contribution to the apostolate. The deacon is described as "the bishop's ear, mouth, heart and soul."[9] He is at the bishop's disposal in order that he may serve the whole People of God and take care of the sick and the poor;[10] and so he is correctly and rightly called "one who shows love for orphans and the devout and the widowed, one who is fervent in spirit, one who shows love for what is good."[11] Moreover, the deacon is entrusted with the office of bringing the Holy Eucharist to the sick confined to their homes,[12] of conferring Baptism,[13] and of taking pains to preach the Word of God in accordance with the express wish of the bishop.

Accordingly, the diaconate flourished in a wonderful way in   1772 the Church and at the same time gave an outstanding witness of love for Christ and the brethren through the performance of works of charity,[14] the celebration of sacred rites[15] and the fulfillment of pastoral duties.[16]

The exercise of the office of deacon enabled those who were   1773 to become priests to test themselves, to show the merit of their work, and to acquire preparation—all of which were requirements for receiving the dignity of the priesthood and the office of pastor.

As time went on, the discipline concerning this sacred order   1774 was changed. The prohibition against conferring ordination without observing the established sequence of orders was strengthened, and there was a gradual decrease in the number of those who preferred to remain deacons all their lives instead of advancing to a higher order. As a consequence, the permanent diaconate disapppeared almost entirely in the Latin Church.

1775   It is scarcely of importance to recount the decrees of the Council of Trent proposing to restore the sacred orders in accordance with their own nature as ancient functions within the Church;[17] it was much later that the idea matured of restoring this important sacred order as a truly permanent rank. Our predecessor Pius XII alluded briefly to this matter.[18] Finally, the Second Vatican Council supported the wishes and requests that, where this would serve the good of souls, the permanent diaconate be restored as an intermediate order between the higher ranks of the Church's hierarchy and the rest of the People of God, as an expression of the needs and desires of Christian communities, as a driving force for the Church's service or *diakonia* toward the local Christian communities, and as a sign or sacrament of the Lord Christ Himself, "who has come not to be served but to serve."[19]

1776   For this reason, at the Council's third session in October, 1964, the Fathers ratified the principle of renewal of the diaconate. In the 29th article of the Dogmatic Constitution on the Church, which was promulgated the following November, a description is given of the principal characteristics proper to that state: "on a lower level of the hierarchy stand the deacons; they receive the imposition of hands 'not for the priesthood but for the ministry.' Fortified by sacramental grace, in communion with the bishop and his presbyterium, they lend assistance to the People of God in the service of the liturgy, of the word and of charity."[20]

1777   The same constitution made the following declaration about permanency in the rank of deacon: "These duties (of deacons) are very necessary for the life of the Church. But, because of the discipline of the Latin Church prevailing today, they can be fulfilled only with difficulty in many regions. Hence, in time to come, the diaconate could be reinstated as a distinct and permanent rank of the hierarchy."[21]

However, this restoration of the permanent diaconate re-   1778
quired that the Council's instructions be more thoroughly
examined and that there be mature deliberation concerning
the juridical status of both the celibate and the married deacon. Similarly, it was necessary that all aspects of the diaconate of future priests be adapted to contemporary conditions,
so that the period of diaconate would furnish that proof of
life, maturity and aptitude for the priestly ministry which
ancient discipline demanded from candidates for the priesthood.

Thus on June 18, 1967, We issued on Our own initiative the   1779
apostolic letter *Sacrum Diaconatus Ordinem*, establishing suitable canonical norms for the permanent diaconate.[22] On June
17 of the following year, through the apostolic constitution
Pontificalis Romani Recognito,[23] We authorized a new rite
for conferring the sacred orders of diaconate, priesthood and
episcopacy, and at the same time We defined the matter and
the form of the ordination itself.

Now that We are proceeding further and are today promul-   1780
gating the apostolic letter *Ministeria Quaedam*, We deem it
appropriate to issue certain norms concerning the diaconate.
We also want candidates for the diaconate to know what
ministries they are to exercise before sacred ordination, and
when and how they are to assume the responsibilities of celibacy and liturgical prayer.

Since entrance into the clerical state is deferred until the di-   1781
aconate, the rite of first tonsure—by which a layman formerly
became a cleric—no longer exists. But a new rite is introduced,
by which one aspiring to the diaconate or priesthood publicly
manifests his desire to offer himself to God and the Church,
so that he may exercise a sacred order. The Church, accepting
this offering, selects and calls him to prepare himself to receive
a sacred order, and thus he is properly numbered among candidates for the diaconate or priesthood.

It is especially fitting that the ministries of lector and aco-   1782
lyte be entrusted to those who, as candidates for the order of
diaconate or priesthood, desire to devote themselves to God
and the Church in a special way. For the Church, which "does
not cease to take the bread of life from the table of the Word

of God and the Body of Christ and offer it to the faithful,"[24] considers it very opportune that both by study and by gradual exercise of the ministry of the Word and of the Altar candidates for sacred orders should, through intimate contact, understand and reflect upon the dual aspect of the priestly office. In this way the authenticity of the ministry shines forth most effectively. Indeed, the candidates come to sacred orders fully aware of their vocation, fervent in spirit, serving the Lord, constant in prayer and looking on the needs of the saints as their own.[25]

1783   Having weighed well every aspect of the question, having sought the opinion of experts, having consulted with the episcopal conferences and taken their views into account, and having taken counsel with Our honored brothers who are members of the Sacred Congregations competent in this matter, by Our apostolic authority We enact the following norms, derogating—if and insofar as necessary—from provisions of the Code of Canon Law presently in force, and We promulgate these norms with this letter.

The New Norms

1784   I. a) A rite is introduced for admission of candidates to the diaconate and to the priesthood. In order that this admission may be properly made, the free petition of the aspirant, made out and signed in his own hand, is required, as well as a written acceptance from the competent ecclesiastical superior, who is empowered to select for the Church.

1785   b) The competent superior for this acceptance is the ordinary (the bishop and, in clerical institutes of perfection, the major superior). Those can be accepted who give signs of an authentic vocation and, endowed with good moral qualities and free from mental and physical defects, wish to dedicate their lives to the Church's service for the glory of God and the good of souls. It is necessary for those aspiring to the transitional diaconate to have completed at least their 20th year and to have begun their course of theological studies.

1786   c) By virtue of his acceptance, the candidate must take special care with his vocation and foster it. He also acquires a right to the necessary spiritual assistance by which he can develop his vocation and submit unconditionally to the will of God.

II. Candidates for the permanent or transitional diaconate   **1787** and for the priesthood are to receive the ministries of lector and acolyte, unless they have already done so, and are to exercise them for a fitting time, in order to be better disposed for the future service of the Word and of the Altar.

Dispensation from reception of these ministries by such   **1788** candidates is reserved to the Holy See.

III. The liturgical rites by which admission of candidates   **1789** for the diaconate and the priesthood takes place and the above-mentioned ministries are conferred, should be performed by the ordinary of the aspirants (the bishop and, in clerical institutes of perfection, the major superior).

IV. The intervals established by the Holy See or by the   **1790** episcopal conferences between conferral—during the course of theological studies—of the ministry of lector and that of acolyte, and between the ministry of acolyte and the order of deacon, must be observed.

V. Before ordination, candidates for the diaconate shall   **1791** give to the ordinary (the bishop and, in clerical institutes of perfection, the major superior) a declaration made out and signed in their own hand, testifying that they are about to receive the sacred order freely and of their own accord.

VI. The special consecration of celibacy observed for the   **1792** sake of the kingdom of heaven, and its obligation for candidates to the priesthood and for unmarried candidates to the diaconate, are in fact linked with the diaconate. The public commitment to holy celibacy before God and the Church is to be celebrated in a particular rite, even by religious, and is to precede ordination to the diaconate. Celibacy accepted in this way is a diriment impediment to marriage.

In accordance with traditional Church discipline, a married   **1793** deacon who has lost his wife cannot enter a new marriage.[26]

VII. a) Deacons called to the priesthood are not to be or-   **1794** dained until they have completed the course of studies prescribed by the norms of the Apostolic See.

1795   b) With regard to the course of theological studies preceding the ordination of permanent deacons, the episcopal conferences, taking into consideration the local situation, will issue suitable norms and submit them to the Sacred Congregation for Catholic Education for approval.

1796   VIII. In accordance with norms 29-30 of the General Instruction on the Liturgy of the Hours:

a) Deacons called to the priesthood are bound by their sacred ordination to the obligation of celebrating the Liturgy of the Hours.

b) It is most fitting that permanent deacons recite daily at least a part of the Liturgy of the Hours, to be determined by the episcopal conference.

1797   IX. Entrance into the clerical state and incardination into a diocese are brought about by ordination to the diaconate.

1798   X. The rite for admission of candidates to the diaconate and priesthood, and for the special consecration of holy celibacy, will soon be published by the competent department of the Roman Curia.

Transitional Norms

1799   Candidates for the Sacrament of Orders who have already received first tonsure before the promulgation of this letter retain all the duties, rights and privileges of clerics. Those who have been promoted to the order of subdiaconate are held to the obligations they have taken on regarding both celibacy and the Liturgy of the Hours. But they must renew their public commitment to celibacy before God and the Church by the new special rite preceding ordination to the diaconate.

1800   We order that what We have decreed in this letter that We have issued on Our own initiative be regarded as established and ratified, notwithstanding any measure to the contrary, and is to take effect on January 1, 1973.

1801   Given at Rome, at St. Peter's, August 15th, the Solemnity of the Blessed Virgin Mary, in the year 1972, the tenth of Our pontificate.

MINISTERIA QUAEDAM
Motu Proprio of Pope Paul VI
on the Ministries of Lector and Acolyte
August 15, 1972

Even in the earliest times certain ministries were established by the Church for the purpose of suitably giving worship to God and for offering service to the People of God according to their needs. By these ministries the performance of duties of a liturgical and charitable nature appropriate to varying circumstances was entrusted to the faithful. Conferral of these functions often took place in a special rite in which, after God's blessing had been implored, the individual was appointed to a special class or rank for the fulfillment of some ecclesiastical duty.

Some of these functions, which were more closely connected with the liturgical action, slowly came to be considered as preparatory institutions for the reception of sacred orders, so that the offices of porter, lector, exorcist and acolyte were called minor orders in the Latin Church in relation to the sub-diaconate, diaconate and priesthood, which were called major orders. Generally, though not everywhere, these minor orders were reserved to those who received them on their way to the priesthood. 1803

Nevertheless, since the minor orders have not always been the same, and many tasks connected with them have also been performed by the laity, as at present, it seems fitting to reexamine this practice and to adapt it to contemporary needs, so that what is obsolete in these offices may be removed, what is useful may be retained, what is necessary may 1804 be defined, and at the same time what is required of candidates for Holy Orders may be determined.

1805   While the Second Vatican Council was in preparation, many pastors of the Church requested that the minor orders and subdiaconate be reexamined. Although the Council decreed nothing about this for the Latin Church, it did enunciate certain principles for resolving the question. There is no doubt that the norms laid down by the Council regarding the general and orderly renewal of the liturgy[1] also include those areas which concern ministries in the liturgical assembly, so that from the very arrangement of the celebration the Church clearly appears structured in different orders and ministries.[2] Thus the Second Vatican Council decreed that "in liturgical celebrations each person, minister or layman, who has an office to perform, should do all of, but only, those parts which pertain to his office by the nature of the rite and the norms of liturgy."[3]

1806   There is a close connection between this statement and an earlier one in the same constitution: "Mother Church earnestly desires that all the faithful should be led to that full, conscious, and active participation, in liturgical celebrations which is demanded by the very nature of the liturgy. Such participation by the Christian people as 'a chosen race, a royal priesthood, a holy nation, a purchased people' (1 *Pt* 2, 9; see 2, 4-5) is their right and duty by reason of their baptism. In the restoration and promotion of the sacred liturgy, this full and active participation by all the people is the aim to be considered before all else; for it is the primary and indispensable source from which the faithful are to derive the true Christian spirit; and therefore pastors of souls must zealously strive to achieve it, by means of the necessary instruction, in all their pastoral work."[4]

1807   Among the specific functions to be preserved and adapted to contemporary needs, there are some which are especially connected with the ministries of the Word and of the Altar and which, in the Latin Church, are called the offices of lector, acolyte and subdeacon. It is fitting that these be preserved and adapted in such a way that from now on the two offices of lector and acolyte should include the functions of the subdiaconate.

There is nothing to prevent episcopal conferences from requesting the Apostolic See to permit other offices besides these common to the Latin Church, if they judge the establishment of such offices in their region to be necessary or very useful because of special reasons. These include, for example, the offices of porter, exorcist and catechist,[5] as well as others conferred upon those dedicated to works of charity, where this service has not been given to deacons.   1808

In accordance with the real situation and with the contemporary outlook, the above-mentioned ministries shall no longer be called minor orders; their conferral will not be called "ordination," but "installation"; moreover, only those who have received the diaconate will be properly known as clerics. Thus the distinction will be more apparent between clergy and laity, between what is proper and reserved to the clergy and what can be entrusted to the laity; thus their mutual relationship will appear more clearly, insofar as "the common priesthood of the faithful and the ministerial or hierarchical priesthood, while they differ in essence and not only in degree, are nevertheless interrelated. Each of them shares in its own special way in the one priesthood of Christ."[6]   1809

Having weighed well every aspect of the question, having sought the opinion of experts, having consulted with the episcopal conferences and taken their views into account, and having taken counsel together with Our esteemed brothers who are members of the Sacred Congregations competent in this matter, by Our apostolic authority We enact the following norms, derogating—if and insofar as necessary—from provisions of the Code of Canon Law presently in force, and We promulgate them with this letter.   1810

I. First tonsure is no longer conferred; entrance into the clerical state is joined to the diaconate.   1811

II. Those orders hitherto called minor orders are henceforth to be called "ministries."   1812

III. Ministries may be committed to lay Christians; hence they are no longer to be considered as reserved to candidates for the Sacrament of Orders.   1813

1814   IV. Two ministries adapted to present-day needs are to be preserved in the whole Latin Church, namely, those of lector and acolyte. The functions heretofore committed to the subdeacon are entrusted to the lector and the acolyte; consequently, the major order of the subdiaconate no longer exists in the Latin Church. There is nothing, however, to prevent the acolyte being also called a subdeacon in some places, if the episcopal conference so decides.

1815   V. The lector is appointed for his own special function, that of reading the Word of God in the liturgical assembly. Accordingly, he is to read the lessons from Sacred Scripture, except for the Gospel, in the Mass and other sacred celebrations; he is to recite the psalm between the readings when there is no psalmist; in the absence of a deacon or cantor, he is to present the intentions for the Prayer of the Faithful; he is to direct the singing and the participation of the faithful; he is to prepare the faithful for the worthy reception of the sacraments. He can also, insofar as necessary, attend to preparing other members of the faithful who are temporarily appointed to read the Sacred Scripture in liturgical celebrations. In order that he may more fittingly and perfectly fulfill these functions, he should meditate assiduously on Sacred Scripture.

1816   The lector should be familiar with the office he has undertaken and should make every effort and employ suitable means to acquire that increasingly warm, vital love[7] and knowledge of the Scriptures that will make him a more perfect disciple of the Lord.

1817   VI. The acolyte is appointed to aid the deacon and to minister to the priest. It is therefore his duty to serve at the altar and to assist the deacon and priest in liturgical celebrations, especially in the celebration of Mass. He is also to distribute Holy Communion as an extraordinary minister when the ministers referred to in canon 845 of the Code of Canon Law are not available or are prevented by ill health, age or another pastoral ministry from performing this function, or when the number of those approaching the Sacred Table is so great that the celebration of Mass would be unduly prolonged.

In the same extraordinary circumstances the acolyte can   1818
be entrusted with exposing the Blessed Sacrament for public
adoration by the faithful and he can replace it afterwards,
but he cannot bless the people. He can also, as necessary,
take care of instructing other faithful who are temporarily
appointed to assist the priest or deacon in liturgical celebrations by carrying the missal, cross, candles, and so forth,
or by performing other such duties. He will carry out these
functions more worthily if he participates in the Holy Eucharist with increasingly fervent piety, receives nourishment from
it and deepens his knowledge of it.

Especially destined as he is for the service of the altar, the   1819
acolyte should learn about all matters concerning public divine worship and strive to grasp their inner spiritual meaning;
in that way he will be able daily to offer himself entirely to
God, to be an example to all by his seriousness and reverence
in the sacred precincts, and to have a sincere love for the
Mystical Body of Christ, that is, the People of God, and especially for the weak and the sick.

VII. In accordance with the venerable tradition of the   1820
Church, installation in the ministries of lector and acolyte
is reserved to men.

VIII. The following are requirements for admission to the   1821
ministries:

a) presentation of a petition freely made out and signed by
the aspirant to the ordinary (the bishop and, in clerical institutes of perfection, the major superior), who has the power
to decide on its acceptance;

b) a suitable age and specific qualities to be determined by
the episcopal conference;

c) a firm desire to give faithful service to God and the Christian people.

IX. The ministries are conferred by the ordinary (the bishop   1822
and, in clerical institutes of perfection, the major superior) according to the liturgical rite *"De Institutione Lectoris"* and
"De Institutione Acolythi," being revised by the Apostolic See.

X. Intervals determined by the Holy See or the episcopal   1823
conferences shall be observed between the conferral of the

ministry of lector and that of acolyte whenever more than one of these is conferred on the same person.

1824   XI. Candidates for the diaconate and priesthood are to receive the ministries of lector and acolyte, unless they have already done so, and are to exercise them for a suitable period, in order to be better disposed for the future service of the Word and of the Altar. Dispensation of such candidates from undertaking these ministries is reserved to the Holy See.

1825   XII. The conferral of ministries does not imply the right to maintenance or salary from the Church.

1826   XIII. The installation rite for lectors and acolytes is to be published soon by the competent department of the Roman Curia.

1827   These norms shall come into effect on January 1, 1973.

1828   We order that what We have decreed in this letter that is issued on Our own initiative, be established and ratified, notwithstanding anything to the contrary.

1829   Given at Rome, at St. Peter's, August 15th, the Solemnity of the Assumption of the Blessed Virgin Mary, in the year 1972, the tenth of Our pontificate.

The new Rite for the conferral of these ministries came out on December 3, 1972. The English version was approved July 30, 1973.—Ed.

SACRAM UNCTIONEM INFIRMORUM
Apostolic Constitution of Pope Paul VI
on the Anointing of the Sick
November 30, 1972

The Catholic Church professes and teaches that the sacred Anointing of the Sick is one of the seven Sacraments of the New Testament; that it was instituted by Christ; and that it is "alluded to in Mark (*Mk*. 6, 13), and recommended and promulgated to the faithful by James the Apostle and brother of the Lord. 'Is any one among you sick?' he asks. 'Let him bring in the presbyters of the Church, and let them pray over him, anointing him with oil in the name of the Lord. And the prayer of faith will save the sick man, and the Lord will raise him up, and if he be in sins, they shall be forgiven him' (*Jas*. 5, 14-15)."[1]

From ancient times, evidences of the Anointing of the Sick are found in the Church's tradition, particularly her liturgical tradition, in both the East and the West. Especially worthy of note in this regard are the letter which Our predecessor Innocent I addressed to Decentius, Bishop of Gubbio,[2] and the venerable prayer used for blessing the oil for the sick, "Send forth, O Lord, your Holy Spirit, the Paraclete," which was inserted in the Eucharistic Prayer[3] and is still preserved in the Roman Pontifical.[4]   1831

In the course of the centuries, the parts of the body of the sick person to be anointed with holy oil were more explicitly defined in the liturgical tradition, in diverse ways, and various prayer formulas were added to accompany the anointings; these formulas are contained in the liturgical books of various   1832

Churches. During the Middle Ages, in the Roman Church, the custom prevailed of anointing the sick on the five senses, using the formula, "May the Lord forgive you by this holy anointing and His most loving mercy whatever sins you have committed," adapted to each sense.[5]

1833   In addition, the doctrine concerning the sacred anointing is expounded in the documents of ecumenical councils, namely, the Council of Florence and, in particular, the Council of Trent and the Second Vatican Council.

1834   After the Council of Florence had described the essential elements of the Anointing of the Sick,[6] the Council of Trent declared its divine institution and explained what is given in the Epistle of St. James concerning the sacred anointing, especially with regard to the reality and effects of the sacrament:

1835   "This reality is, in fact, the grace of the Holy Spirit, whose anointing takes away sins, if any still remain to be taken away, and the remnants of sin; it also relieves and strengthens the soul of the sick person, arousing in him a great confidence in the divine mercy, whereby being thus sustained he more easily bears the trials and labors of his sickness, more easily resists the temptations of the devil 'lying in wait' (*Gn.* 3, 15), and sometimes regains bodily health, if this is expedient for the health of the soul."[7]

1836   The same Council also declared that in these words of the Apostle it is stated with sufficient clarity that "this anointing is to be administered to the sick, especially those who are in such a condition that they appear to have reached the end of their life; for this reason it is also called the sacrament of the dying."[8] Finally, the Council declared that the priest is the proper minister of the sacrament.[9]

1837   The Second Vatican Council adds the following: " 'Extreme Unction,' which may also and more fittingly be called 'Anointing of the Sick,' is not a sacrament only for those who are at the point of death. Hence, as soon as any one of the faithful begins to be in danger of death from sickness or old age, the fitting time for him to receive this sacrament has certainly already arrived."[10] The fact that the use of this sacrament concerns the whole Church is shown by these words: "By the

sacred anointing of the sick and by the priests' prayer the
whole Church commends the sick to the suffering, glorified
Lord so that He may relieve and save them (see *Jas.* 5, 14-16);
and it urges them to contribute to the welfare of the People
of God by freely associating themselves with Christ's passion
and death (see *Rom.* 8, 17; *Col.* 1, 24; 2 *Tm.* 2, 11-12; 1 *Pt.*
4, 13)."[11]

All these elements had to be taken into consideration in   **1838**
revising the rite of sacred anointing, in order better to adapt
to present-day conditions those elements which were subject
to change.[12] We deemed it fitting to modify the sacramental
formula in such a way that, in view of the words of St. James,
the effects of the sacrament might be better expressed. Moreover, since olive oil, which hitherto had been prescribed for
the valid administration of the sacrament, is unobtainable or
difficult to obtain in some parts of the world, We decreed, at
the request of numerous bishops, that in future, according to
the circumstances, oil of another sort may also be used, provided it is obtained from plants, since this more closely resembles olive oil. Concerning the number of anointings and the
parts of the body to be anointed, it has seemed to Us opportune to proceed to a simplification of the rite.

Therefore, since this revision touches in certain points upon   **1839**
the sacramental rite itself, by Our apostolic authority We
establish that the following is to be observed for the future in
the Latin Rite:

The Sacrament of the Anointing of the Sick Is Administered   **1840**
to Those Dangerously Ill by Anointing Them on the Forehead
and Hands with Properly Blessed Olive Oil or, if Opportune,
with Another Vegetable Oil, and Saying Once Only the Following Words: *"Per istam sanctam unctionem et suam piissi-
mam misericordiam adjuvet te Dominus gratia Spiritus Sancti,
ut a peccatis liberatum te salvet atque propitius allevet."*

In case of necessity, however, it is sufficient that a single   **1841**
anointing be given on the forehead or, because of the particular condition of the sick person, on another more suitable part
of the body, the whole formula being pronounced. This sacrament may be repeated if the sick person, having once received

the anointing, recovers and then again falls sick; or if, in the course of the same illness, the danger become more acute.

1842   Having established and declared these elements concerning the essential rite of the Sacrament of the Anointing of the Sick, We also approve, by Our apostolic authority, the Order for the Anointing of the Sick and for Their Pastoral Care, as revised by the Sacred Congregation for Divine Worship. At the same time We revoke, where necessary, or abrogate the prescriptions of the Code of Canon Law or other laws hitherto in force; other prescriptions and laws which are neither abrogated nor changed by the above mentioned Order remain valid and in force.

1843   The Latin edition of the Order containing the new rite will enter into force as soon as it is published. The vernacular editions, prepared by the episcopal conferences and ratified by the Apostolic See, will come into force on a day to be prescribed by the individual conferences. The old Order can be used until December 31, 1973. From January 1, 1974, however, only the new Order is to be used by all those whom it concerns.

1844   We desire that these decrees and prescriptions of Ours shall be fully effective in the Latin Rite now and in the future, notwithstanding, insofar as necessary, the apostolic constitutions and directives issued by Our predecessors and other prescriptions, even if worthy of special mention.

1845   Given in Rome, at St. Peter's, on the 30th day of November, in the year 1972, the tenth of Our pontificate.

The new Rite for the Anointing of the Sick appeared on January 18, 1973. The English version was approved December 28, 1973.—Ed.

IMMENSAE CARITATIS
Selection from Instruction of the Sacred Congregation
for the Discipline of the Sacraments
on Facilitating Communion
January 29, 1973

C hrist the Lord has left to the Church, His spouse, a testament of His immense love. This wonderful gift of the Eucharist, which is the greatest gift of all, demands that such an important mystery be increasingly better known and its saving power more fully shared. Moved by pastoral zeal and concern, the Church has on more than one occasion issued suitable laws and documents, with the intention of fostering devotion to the Eucharist—the summit and center of Christian worship.

Present-day conditions demand, however, that there be greater access to Holy Communion, without any violation of the supreme reverence due such a sacrament,[1] so that the faithful, by sharing more fully in the fruits of the Sacrifice of the Mass, may devote themselves more readily and effectively to God and to the good of the Church and of their fellow men.

1847

First of all, provision must be made lest reception of Holy Communion become impossible or difficult owing to an insufficient number of ministers. Provision must also be made lest the sick be deprived of very great spiritual consolation by being impeded from receiving Holy Communion because they may be unable to observe the law of fast, even though this law is already very moderate. Finally, it seems appropriate to determine in what circumstances the faithful who ask to re-

1848

ceive sacramental Communion a second time on the same day
may properly be permitted to do so.

1849   After study of the recommendations of certain episcopal
conferences, the following norms are issued in regard to:

1. Extraordinary ministers for the distribution of Holy
Communion;
2. A more extensive faculty for receiving Holy Communion twice in the same day;
3. Mitigation of the Eucharistic fast for the sick and elderly;
4. The piety and reverence due the Blessed Sacrament
whenever the Eucharist is placed in the hand of the communicant.

*Specific regulations are then given on these items; and the
document closes with the following:*

1850   Let the greatest diligence and care be taken particularly
with regard to fragments which perhaps break off the hosts.
This applies to the minister and to the recipient whenever
the sacred Host is placed in the hands of the communicant.

1851   Before initiating the practice of giving Holy Communion
in the hand, a suitable instruction and catechesis of Catholic
doctrine is necessary concerning both the real and permanent
presence of Christ under the Eucharistic species and the reverence due this Sacrament.[2]

1852   The faithful must be taught that Jesus Christ is Lord and
Savior, and that the same worship and adoration given to
God is owed to Him present under the sacramental signs.
Therefore let the faithful be counseled not to omit a sincere
and fitting thanksgiving after the Eucharistic banquet, according to each one's particular ability, state and duties.[3] In order
that participation in this heavenly table may be altogether
worthy and profitable, the value and effects deriving from it
for both the individual and the community must be pointed
out to the faithful in such a way that their familiar attitude
reveals reverence, fosters intimate love for the Father of the
household who gives us "our daily bread,"[4] and leads to a

living relationship with Christ, of whose flesh and blood we partake.[5]

The Supreme Pontiff Paul VI has approved and sanctioned   1853
this instruction by his authority and has directed that it be published, decreeing that it enter into force on the day of publication.

Given at Rome, from the Sacred Congregation for the Dis-   1854
cipline of the Sacraments, January 29, 1973.

EUCHARISTIAE PARTICIPATIONEM
Letter from the Sacred Congregation for Divine Worship
to the Presidents of the National Conferences of Bishops
on Eucharistic Prayers
April 27, 1973

The reform of the sacred liturgy, and especially the reorganization of the Roman Missal recently completed in accordance with the requirements of Vatican Council II,[1] are intended above all to facilitate intelligent, devout, active participation by the faithful in the Eucharist.[2]

1856 A notable feature of this new Roman Missal, published by authority of Pope Paul VI, is undoubtedly the wealth of texts from which a choice may often be made, whether in the case of readings from Holy Writ or in that of the chants, prayers and acclamations of the whole community, or again in regard to the "presidential" prayers, not excluding the Eucharistic Prayer itself, for in addition to the venerable traditional Roman Canon, three new texts have been brought into use.[3]

1857 2. The reason for providing this ample variety of texts and the purpose intended by the revision of the prayer forms to be used are of a pastoral nature, namely, in order to bring about unity and diversity of liturgical prayer. By using these texts as set forth in the Roman Missal, various groups of the faithful who gather to celebrate the Eucharist are able to sense that they form part of the one Church, praying with one faith and one prayer. At the same time they possess an appropriate means, especially when the vernacular is used, to proclaim in many ways the one mystery of Christ; and it becomes easier for individual faithful to raise their hearts to the

Lord in prayer and thanksgiving,[4] and to share in the celebration with greater spiritual results.

3. Although several years have passed since the promulgation   1858
of the new Roman Missal, it has not yet been fully introduced
everywhere for celebration with the people, because its
translation into the vernacular of so many nations has been
an enormous work requiring a considerable period of time.[5]
Moreover, the opportunity thus provided for increasing pastoral effectiveness is often not known, nor is sufficient thought
given, in arranging the Mass, to the spiritual good of the congregation.[6]

4. Meanwhile, many have expressed a desire to adapt the   1859
Eucharistic celebration still further by the composition of
new prayer forms, including even new Eucharistic Prayers.
They say that the choice provided by the present "presidential" prayers and the four Eucharistic Prayers in the Order of
the Mass still does not fully meet the many requirements of
various groups, regions and peoples. This Sacred Congregation
has received many requests to approve, or grant the faculty
of approving and bringing into use, new texts for prayers and
Eucharistic Prayers more in line with modern thinking and
speech.

Moreover, during recent years many authors of various   1860
languages and countries have published Eucharistic Prayers
which they had composed for the sake of study. In spite of
the limitations prescribed by Vatican Council II[7] and episcopal prohibitions, some priests have used privately composed
texts often in their celebration of Mass.

5. Consequently this Sacred Congregtion, by mandate of   1861
the Supreme Pontiff and after consulting experts from various
parts of the world, has carefully studied the question of the
composition of new Eucharistic Prayers and of giving episcopal conferences the faculty for approving them, together with
related questions and their consequences. The conclusions of
this study were submitted to the members of this Sacred Congregation in plenary session, to the judgment of the other
Sacred Congregations concerned, and finally to the Supreme
Pontiff.

1862   After mature consideration of the whole matter, it does not seem advisable at this juncture to grant episcopal conferences the general faculty of composing or approving new Eucharistic Prayers. On the contrary, it seems more opportune to call attention to the pressing need for fuller instruction on the nature and reality of the Eucharistic Prayer.[8] Since this prayer is the center of the celebration, it must also be the center of a more profound instruction. It also seems necessary to provide priests with more detailed information on the possibilities they have for encouraging full participation of the faithful by using the current liturgical regulations and the prayer forms of the Roman Missal.

1863   6. Therefore the four Eucharistic Prayers contained in the revised Roman Missal remain in force, and no other Eucharistic Prayers composed without permission or approval of the Apostolic See may be used. Episcopal conferences and individual bishops are earnestly asked to present pertinent reasons to the priests in order to bring them wisely to the observance of the one practice of the Roman Church, to the benefit of the Church itself and in furtherance of the proper arrangement of liturgical functions.

1864   The Apostolic See is motivated by the pastoral desire for unity in reserving to itself the right to regulate such an important matter as the order of the Eucharistic Prayers. Within the unity of the Roman rite it will not refuse to consider legitimate requests and will readily consider such requests from episcopal conferences for drawing up new Eucharistic Prayers for particular circumstances and introducing them into the liturgy. But the Holy See will prescribe the norms to be followed in each case.

1865   7. After making known this decision, it seems useful to offer some considerations which may clarify its meaning and facilitate its execution. Some of these have to do with the nature and importance of the Eucharistic Prayer in liturgical—and especially Roman—tradition; others concern what can be done to accommodate the celebration to individual congregations without in any way altering the text of the Eucharistic Prayer.

8. By its very nature the Eucharistic Prayer is the "center   1866
of the entire celebration," and "a prayer of thanksgiving and
sanctification" whose purpose is "that the whole congregation
of the faithful may unite itself with Christ in proclaiming
the wondrous things of God and in offering the sacrifice."[9]
This prayer is offered by the ministering priest, who interprets
God's voice as it is addressed to the people, and the people's
voice as they lift their souls to God. The priest alone should
be heard, while the congregation gathered to celebrate the
sacred liturgy remains devoutly silent.

Over and above its catechetical nature, which strives to   1867
highlight the specific characteristics of the particular celebration, there is in this prayer an element of thanksgiving for the
universal mystery of salvation or for some particular aspect
of this mystery which the liturgy is celebrating, according to
the day, feast, rite or season.[10]

For this reason, in order that those participating in the Eu-   1868
charist may better render thanks to God and bless Him, the
new Roman Missal already contains "a great number of Prefaces, either derived from the ancient tradition of the Roman
Church or composed recently. In this way, the different aspects of the mystery of salvation will be emphasized and will
offer more and more enriching occasions for giving thanks."[11]

For the same reason, the priest presiding at the Eucharist   1869
enjoys the faculty of introducing the Eucharistic Prayer to
the people with a brief reminder[12] of the motives for thanksgiving, in words suited to the congregation at the particular
time. In this way those present can perceive that their own life
is part and parcel of salvation history and so gain ampler
benefits from the Eucharistic celebration.

9. Again, so far as the purpose of the Eucharistic Prayer is   1870
concerned, as well as its make-up and structure, the aspect of
petition or intercession is to be considered secondary. In the
revised liturgy this aspect is developed especially in the general
intercessions whereby, in a freer form and one more suited to
the circumstances, supplications are made for the Church and
for mankind. Nonetheless, the new liturgical books also offer
a variety of forms of intercession to be inserted into the dif-

ferent Eucharistic Prayers, according to the structure of each. They are to be used in particular celebrations, and above all in ritual Masses.[13] In this way the reason for any particular celebration is clearly defined, and the offering of this prayer in communion with the whole Church is signified.[14]

1871   10. Besides the variations noted above, which are intended to bring about a closer connection between the thanksgiving and the intercessions, the Roman tradition also has other special formulas for use *infra actionem* on the principal solemnities of the liturgical year, whereby the memorial of the mystery of Christ that is being celebrated is made more manifest.[15]

1872   It is evident from this that ancient tradition was concerned with maintaining the unchangeable character of the text, while not excluding appropriate variations. If the faithful, hearing the same text again and again, unite themselves more readily with the priest celebrant in prayer, nevertheless some variations, though only a few in number, prove acceptable and useful; they foster attention, encourage devotion and lend a special quality to the prayer.

1873   Nor is there any reason why episcopal conferences should not make similar provision for their own areas in regard to the points mentioned above (nos. 8-10), and request approval from the Holy See. The same holds true for a bishop in regard to the Proper for his diocese, and for the competent authority in regard to the Proper for a religious family.

1874   11. The ecclesial dimension of the Eucharistic celebration is to be highly esteemed. For while such a celebration "expresses and brings about the unity of the faithful who form one body in Christ,"[16] "the celebration of Mass is of itself a profession of faith in which the whole Church recognizes and expresses itself."[17] All this is abundantly apparent in the Eucharistic Prayer itself; there it is not just an individual person or a local community, but "the one and only Catholic Church," existing in any number of individual Churches,[18] that addresses itself to God.

1875   Whenever Eucharistic Prayers are introduced without approval by competent Church authority, unrest and dissensions frequently arise among priests and within congregations, even though the Eucharist should be "a sign of unity" and "a bond of charity."[19] Indeed, many people complain of the overly subjective character of such texts. Those taking part in the celebration have a right that the Eucharistic Prayer, which they ratify by their "Amen," should not be mingled with or wholly imbued with the personal preferences of the one who composes the text or uses it.

Hence it is obviously necessary that only those texts of the Eucharistic Prayer are to be used which, having been approved by lawful Church authority, clearly and fully manifest ecclesial sense.   1876

12. Due to the very nature of the Eucharistic Prayer, a more precise adaptation of the celebration for various congregations and circumstances, and a fuller expression of the catechetical content, cannot be always or conveniently effected in it; they should be inserted, however, in those parts and formulas of the liturgical action which lend themselves to variation or require it.   1877

13. First of all, those who prepare or preside at the celebrations are reminded of the faculty granted by the General Instruction on the Roman Missal,[20] by which they can, in certain cases, choose Masses and also texts for the various parts of the Mass, such as the readings, prayers and chants, so that they correspond "as far as possible to the needs, spiritual preparation and capacity of the participants."[21] Nor should it be forgotten that other documents published since the promulgation of the General Instruction offer norms and suggestions for enlivening celebrations and adapting them to pastoral needs.[22]   1878

14. Among the possibilities for further adaptation which are left to the individual celebrant, it is well to keep in mind the admonitions, homily and general intercessions.   1879

First, there are the admonitions, by which the faithful are brought to a deeper understanding of the meaning of the sacred action or any of its parts. Of special importance are those admonitions which the priest himself is invited by the General Instruction on the Roman Missal to compose and deliver; he may introduce the faithful to the Mass of the day before the celebration begins, to the Liturgy of the Word be-   1880 fore the readings, or to the Eucharistic Prayer before the Preface; he may summarize the entire sacred action before the dismissal.[2 3]

1881   Then again, importance is to be given to those admonitions prescribed in the Order of the Mass for certain rites, which are to be introduced either before the penitential act or before the Lord's Prayer. Naturally, these admonitions need not be given word for word as set out in the Missal; it may well be advisable, at least in certain instances, to adapt them somewhat to the actual circumstances of the particular gathering. Nevertheless, the special nature of all admonitions should be heeded, so that they do not turn into sermons or homilies; care must be taken to be brief and to avoid tedious verbosity.

1882   15. In addition to the admonitions, the homily must be kept in mind. It is "part of the liturgy itself,"[2 4] and explains the Word of God proclaimed in the liturgical assembly for the faithful there present, in a manner suited to their capacity and way of life, and relative to the circumstances of the celebration.

1883   16. Finally, considerable importance is to be attached to the general intercessions with which the congregation responds to the Word of God as it has been explained and received. To be effective, the petitions offered up for various needs throughout the world should be suited to the congregation, bringing to bear in their composition that wise freedom consistent with the nature of this prayer.

1884   17. In addition to the selection of its various elements, a truly living and communal celebration requires that the one presiding and the others who have some particular function to perform should give thought to the various forms of verbal communication with the congregation, namely, the readings, homily admonitions, introductions and the like.[2 5]

1885   In reciting prayers, especially the Eucharistic Prayer, the priest must avoid not only a dry, monotonous style of reading but an overly subjective and emotional manner of speaking and acting as well. As he presides over the function, he must be careful in reading, singing or acting to help the participants form a true community, celebrating and living the memorial of the Lord.

18. In order to ensure a fuller impact of the Word and greater spiritual fruit, due regard must be given—as many people desire—to the sacred silence which is to be observed at stated times as part of the liturgical actions;[26] in this way each individual, according to temperament and his experience at the moment, makes some self-examination or meditates briefly on what he has just heard, or praises God and prays to Him in his heart.[27]   **1886**

19. In view of all this, it is earnestly hoped that pastors of souls will take great care to instruct the faithful, rather than to introduce novelties into texts and rites of the sacred action. This will enable the people to understand better the nature, structure and elements of the celebration, especially the Eucharistic Prayer, and to participate more fully and more knowledgeably in the celebration itself. The power and effectiveness of the sacred liturgy does not consist merely in the newness and variety of its elements, but in a deeper communion with the mystery of salvation made present and operative in the liturgical action. In this way alone are the faithful, in their profession of one faith and outpouring of one prayer, enabled to work out their salvation and to be in communion with their brethren.   **1887**

The Supreme Pontiff Paul VI, on April 18, 1973, approved and confirmed this circular letter prepared by the Sacred Congregation, and ordered its publication.   **1888**

From the offices of the Sacred Congregation for Divine Worship, April 27, 1973.   **1889**

Two further documents dealing with the Eucharist followed soon after:
May 24, 1973-Declaration on First Confession and First Communion.
June 21, 1973-On Uses of the Eucharist outside of Mass.
—Ed.

PUEROS BAPTIZATOS
Sacred Congregation for Divine Worship
Selection from Directory for Masses with Children
November 1, 1973

Introduction

The Church has a duty to be specially concerned about the welfare of children who have been baptized but not yet fully initiated by the Sacraments of Confirmation and the Eucharist, or who have only recently made their first Communion. They are growing up in a world which can hardly be described as conducive to their spiritual welfare,[1] and many parents make light of the obligations they assumed at the baptism of their children of giving them a Christian upbringing.

1891   2.   The Church is the place where children should receive their Christian education, but there is a problem here. Liturgical, and especially Eucharistic celebrations, which of their very nature have an educative value,[2] are scarcely fully effective where children are concerned. The Mass may be in their own language, but the words and symbols used are not those which they can understand.

1892   There are, of course, many things in their day-to-day life which children do not always understand, and this does not make them uninterested. So one does not have to insist that every detail of the liturgy be made completely comprehensible to them. All the same, it must surely be spiritually harmful to them to have the experience of going to church for years without ever understanding properly what is going on.

Recent psychology has proved the profound influence that the religious experience of infancy and early childhood has on the religious development of the individual.[3]

3. The Church, whose Master "took the little children in   1893
his arms and blessed them" (*Mk* 10, 16), cannot be content to leave such children to their own devices. The Second Vatican Council's Constitution on the Sacred Liturgy spoke of the need to adapt the liturgy to various groups.[4] Shortly after the Council, therefore, and especially at the first Synod of Bishops in Rome in 1967, very careful consideration was given to the question of helping children to take part in the liturgy. On that occasion the president of the Commission for Implementing the Constitution on the Sacred Liturgy said in his address that there could be no question "of composing a special rite, but rather of restricting, abbreviating or omitting certain elements, and of choosing suitable texts."[5]

4. The General Instruction in the 1969 revision of the Ro-   1894
man Missal set out in detail all the regulations concerning the celebration of the Eucharist with the people. Thereupon this Congregation, in response to repeated requests from all over the Catholic world, commenced work on preparing a special Directory for Children's Masses to serve as a kind of supplement to the General Instruction. Specialists in the field, men and women from nearly every country, cooperated in this work.

5. In this Directory, as in the General Instruction, certain   1895
adaptations are reserved to conferences of bishops or to individual bishops.[6]

When such conferences consider particular adaptations   1896
(which cannot be included in a general directory) necessary for children's Masses in their own territory, they should, in accordance with article 40 of the Constitution on the Sacred Liturgy, apply to the Holy See for permission to introduce them.

6. This Directory is concerned with children who have   1897
not yet reached the age of "pre-adolescence." It does not specifically mention physically or mentally handicapped children, for whom of course a greater degree of adaptation

is often necessary.[7] All the same, the general principles which follow can also be made applicable to them.

1898   7. Chapter I of this Directory (nos. 8-15) lays down the basic principles and discusses the various ways of helping children to understand the Mass. Chapter II (nos. 16-19) deals briefly with adult Masses in which children also participate. Chapter III (nos. 20-54) deals more extensively with children's Masses in which some adults are also taking part.

Note: The details of adaptation then follow as outlined, after which the document concludes as follows:

1899   55. Everything contained in this Directory is intended to help children to meet Christ with joy in the celebration of the Eucharist and to stand with Him in the Father's presence.[8] Formed by a conscious and active participation in the Eucharistic sacrifice and meal, they must daily learn to become better witnesses to Christ among their friends and peers, at home and outside the home, by living the faith "which operates through charity" (*Gal* 5, 6).

1900   This Directory, prepared by the Sacred Congregation for Divine Worship, was approved, confirmed and ordered to be promulgated by Pope Paul VI on October 22, 1973.

1901   Issued by the Sacred Congregation for Divine Worship on November 1, 1973, the feast of All Saints.

1902   By special mandate of the Supreme Pontiff.

Sacred Congregation for Divine Worship
Selection from the Decree and Rite of Penance
December 2, 1973

DECREE

Reconciliation between God and men was brought about by our Lord Jesus Christ in the mystery of his death and resurrection (see *Romans* 5:10). The Lord entrusted the ministry of reconciliation to the Church in the person of the apostles (see *2 Corinthians* 5:18ff). The Church carries this ministry out by bringing the good news of salvation to men and by baptizing them in water and the Holy Spirit (see *Matthew* 28:19).

Because of human weakness, Christians "turn aside from [their] early love" (see *Revelation* 2:4) and even break off their friendship with God by sinning. The Lord, therefore, instituted a special sacrament of penance for the pardon of sins committed after baptism (see *John* 20:21-23), and the Church has faithfully celebrated the sacrament throughout the centuries—in varying ways, but retaining its essential elements. 1904

The Second Vatican Council decreed that "the rite and formulas of penance are to be revised in such a way that they may more clearly express the nature and effects of this sacrament."[1] In view of this the Congregation for Divine Worship has carefully prepared the new Rite of Penance so that the celebration of the sacrament may be more fully understood by the faithful. 1905

1906   In this new rite, besides the *Rite for Reconciliation of Individual Penitents,* a *Rite for Reconciliation of Several Penitents* has been drawn up to emphasize the relation of the sacrament to the community. This rite places individual confession and absolution in the context of a celebration of the word of God. Furthermore, for special occasions a *Rite for Reconciliation of Several Penitents with General Confession and Absolution* has been composed in accordance with the Pastoral Norms on General Sacramental Absolution, issued by the Congregation for the Doctrine of the Faith on June 16, 1972.[2]

1907   The Church is solicitous in calling the faithful to continual conversion and renewal. It desires that the baptized who have sinned should acknowledge their sins against God and their neighbor and have heartfelt repentance for them, and it tries to prepare them to celebrate the sacrament of penance. For this reason the Church urges the faithful to attend penitential celebrations from time to time. This Congregation has therefore made regulations for such celebrations and has proposed examples or specimens which episcopal conferences may adapt to the needs of their own regions.

1908   Accordingly Pope Paul VI has by his authority approved the *Rite of Penance* prepared by the Congregation for Divine Worship and ordered it to be published. It is to replace the pertinent sections of the *Roman Ritual* now in use. The rite in its Latin original is to come into force as soon as it is published, but vernacular versions will be effective from the day determined by the episcopal conferences, after they have approved the translation and received confirmation from the Apostolic See.

1909   Anything to the contrary notwithstanding.

1910   From the office of the Congregation for Divine Worship, December 2, 1973, the First Sunday of Advent.

By special mandate of the Pope

RITE OF PENANCE

Introduction

I. The Mystery of Reconciliation in the History of Salvation

The Father has shown forth his mercy by reconciling the   1911
world to himself in Christ and by making peace for all things
on earth and in heaven by the blood of Christ on the cross.[1]
The Son of God made man lived among men in order to free
them from the slavery of sin[2] and to call them out of darkness into his wonderful light.[3] He therefore began his work
on earth by preaching repentance and saying: "Turn away
from sin and believe the good news" (*Mark* 1:15).

This invitation to repentance, which had often been sound-   1912
ed by the prophets, prepared the hearts of men for the coming
of the Kingdom of God through the voice of John the Baptist
who came "preaching a baptism of repentance for the forgiveness of sins" (*Mark* 1:4).

Jesus, however, not only exhorted men to repentance so   1913
that they should abandon their sins and turn wholeheartedly
to the Lord,[4] but he also welcomed sinners and reconciled
them with the Father.[5] Moreover, by healing the sick he signified his power to forgive sin.[6] Finally, he himself died for
our sins and rose again for our justification.[7] Therefore, on
the night he was betrayed and began his saving passion,[8] he
instituted the sacrifice of the new covenant in his blood for
the forgiveness of sins.[9] After his resurrection he sent the
Holy Spirit upon the apostles, empowering them to forgive
or retain sins[10] and sending them forth to all peoples to
preach repentance and the forgiveness of sins in his name.[11]

The Lord said to Peter, "I will give you the keys of the   1914
kingdom of heaven, and whatever you bind on earth will be
bound in heaven" (*Matthew* 16:19). In obedience to this
command, on the day of Pentecost Peter preached the forgiveness of sins by baptism: "Repent and let every one of
you be baptized in the name of Jesus Christ for the forgiveness of your sins" (*Acts* 2:38).[12] Since then the Church has

never failed to call men from sin to conversion and by the celebration of penance to show the victory of Christ over sin.

1915   2. This victory is first brought to light in baptism where our fallen nature is crucified with Christ so that the body of sin may be destroyed and we may no longer be slaves to sin, but rise with Christ and live for God.[13] For this reason the Church proclaims its faith in "the one baptism for the forgiveness of sins."

1916   In the sacrifice of the Mass the passion of Christ is made present; his body given for us and his blood shed for the forgiveness of sins are offered to God again by the Church for the salvation of the world. In the eucharist Christ is present and is offered as "the sacrifice which has made our peace"[14] with God and in order that "we may be brought together in unity"[15] by his Holy Spirit.

1917   Furthermore our Savior Jesus Christ, when he gave to his apostles and their successors power to forgive sins, instituted in his Church the sacrament of penance. Thus the faithful who fall into sin after baptism may be reconciled with God and renewed in grace.[16] The Church "possesses both water and tears: the water of baptism, the tears of penance."[17]

II. The Reconciliation of Penitents in the Church's Life

The Church Is Holy but Always in Need of Purification

1918   3. Christ "loved the Church and gave himself up for her to make her holy" (*Ephesians* 5:25-26), and he united the Church to himself as his bride.[18] He filled her with his divine gifts,[19] because she is his body and fulness, and through her he spreads truth and grace to all.

1919   The members of the Church, however, are exposed to temptation and unfortunately often fall into sin. As a result, "while Christ, 'holy, innocent, and unstained' (*Hebrews* 7:26), did not know sin (2 *Corinthians* 5:21) but came only to atone for the sins of the people (see *Hebrews* 2:17), the Church, which includes within itself sinners and is at the same time holy and always in need of purification, constantly pursues repentance and renewal."[20]

Penance in the Church's Life and Liturgy

4. The people of God accomplishes and perfects this con-   1920
tinual repentance in many different ways. It shares in the sufferings of Christ[21] by enduring its own difficulties, carries
out works of mercy and charity,[22] and adopts ever more fully
the outlook of the Gospel message. Thus the people of God
becomes in the world a sign of conversion to God. All this
the Church expresses in its life and celebrates in the liturgy
when the faithful confess that they are sinners and ask pardon of God and of their brothers and sisters. This happens in
penitential services, in the proclamation of the word of God,
in prayer, and in the penitential aspects of the eucharistic
celebration.[23]

In the sacrament of penance the faithful "obtain from the   1921
mercy of God pardon for their sins against him; at the same
time they are reconciled with the Church which they wounded
by their sins and which works for their conversion by charity,
example, and prayer."[24]

Reconciliation with God and with the Church

5. Since every sin is an offense against God which disrupts   1922
our friendship with him, "the ultimate purpose of penance is
that we should love God deeply and commit ourselves completely to him."[25] Therefore, the sinner who by the grace of
a merciful God embraces the way of penance comes back to
the Father who "first loved us" (*1 John* 4:19), to Christ who
gave himself up for us,[26] and to the Holy Spirit who has
been poured out on us abundantly.[27]

"By the hidden and loving mystery of God's design men   1923
are joined together in the bonds of supernatural solidarity,
so much so that the sin of one harms the others just as the
holiness of one benefits the others."[28] Penance always entails reconciliation with our brothers and sisters who are
always harmed by our sins.

In fact, men frequently join together to commit injustice.   1924
It is thus only fitting that they should help each other in doing penance so that freed from sin by the grace of Christ they

may work with all men of good will for justice and peace in the world.

The Sacrament of Penance and Its Parts

1925   6. The follower of Christ who has sinned but who has been moved by the Holy Spirit to come to the sacrament of penance should above all be converted to God with his whole heart. This inner conversion of heart embraces sorrow for sin and the intent to lead a new life. It is expressed through confession made to the Church, due satisfaction, and amendment of life. God grants pardon for sin through the Church, which works by the ministry of priests.[29]

A. Contrition

1926   The most important act of the penitent is contrition, which is "heartfelt sorrow and aversion for the sin committed along with the intention of sinning no more."[30] "We can only approach the Kingdom of Christ by *metanoia*. This is a profound change of the whole person by which one begins to consider, judge, and arrange his life according to the holiness and love of God, made manifest in his Son in the last days and given to us in abundance" (see *Hebrews* 1:2, *Colossians* 1:19 and *passim*)[31] The genuineness of penance depends on this heartfelt contrition. For conversion should affect a person from within so that it may progressively enlighten him and render him continually more like Christ.

B. Confession

1927   The sacrament of penance includes the confession of sins, which comes from true knowledge of self before God and from contrition for those sins. However, this inner examination of heart and the exterior accusation should be made in the light of God's mercy. Confession requires in the penitent the will to open his heart to the minister of God, and in the minister a spiritual judgment by which, acting in the person of Christ, he pronounces his decision of forgiveness or retention of sins in accord with the power of the keys.[32]

C. Act of Penance (Satisfaction)

1928   True conversion is completed by acts of penance or satisfaction for the sins committed, by amendment of conduct, and also by the reparation of injury.[33] The kind and extent of the satisfaction should be suited to the personal condition of each penitent so that each one may restore the order which he disturbed and through the corresponding remedy be cured of the sickness from which he suffered. Therefore, it is necessary that the act of penance really be a remedy for sin and a help to renewal of life. Thus the penitent, "forgetting the things which are behind him" (*Philippians* 3:13), again becomes part of the mystery of salvation and turns himself toward the future.

D. Absolution

Through the sign of absolution God grants pardon to the   1929
sinner who in sacramental confession manifests his change of heart to the Church's minister, and thus the sacrament of penance is completed. In God's design the humanity and loving kindness of our Savior have visibly appeared to us,[34] and God uses visible signs to give salvation and to renew the broken covenant.

In the sacrament of penance the Father receives the repen-   1930
tant son who comes back to him, Christ places the lost sheep on his shoulders and brings it back to the sheepfold, and the Holy Spirit sanctifies this temple of God again or lives more fully within it. This is finally expressed in a renewed and more fervent sharing of the Lord's table, and there is great joy at the banquet of God's Church over the son who has returned from afar.[35]

The Necessity and Benefit of the Sacrament

7. Just as the wound of sin is varied and multiple in the life   1931
of individuals and of the community, so too the healing which penance provides is varied. Those who by grave sin have withdrawn from the communion of love with God are called back in the sacrament of penance to the life they have lost. And those who through daily weakness fall into venial sins draw strength from a repeated celebration of penance to gain the full freedom of the children of God.

a) To obtain the saving remedy of the sacrament of penance, according to the plan of our merciful God, the faithful must confess to a priest each and every grave sin which they remember upon examination of their conscience.[36]

b) Moreover, frequent and careful celebration of this sacrament is also very useful as a remedy for venial sins. This is not a mere ritual repetition or psychological exercise, but a serious striving to perfect the grace of baptism so that, as we bear in our body the death of Jesus Christ, his life may be seen in us ever more clearly.[37] In confession of this kind, penitents who accuse themselves of venial faults should try to conform more closely to Christ and to follow the voice of the Spirit more attentively.

1932   In order that this sacrament of healing may truly achieve its purpose among Christ's faithful, it must take root in their whole lives and move them to more fervent service of God and neighbor.

1933   The celebration of this sacrament is thus always an act in which the Church proclaims its faith, gives thanks to God for the freedom with which Christ has made us free,[38] and offers its life as a spiritual sacrifice in praise of God's glory, as it hastens to meet the Lord Jesus.

III. Offices and Ministries in the Reconciliation of Penitents

The Community in the Celebration of Penance

1934   8. The whole Church, as a priestly people, acts in different ways in the work of reconciliation which has been entrusted to it by the Lord. Not only does the Church call sinners to repentance by preaching the word of God, but it also intercedes for them and helps penitents with maternal care and solicitude to acknowledge and admit their sins and so obtain the mercy of God who alone can forgive sins. Furthermore, the Church becomes the instrument of the conversion and absolution of the penitent through the ministry entrusted by Christ to the apostles and their successors.[39]

1935   9. The Minister of the Sacrament of Penance

a) The Church exercises the ministry of the sacrament of penance through bishops and presbyters. By preaching God's word they call the faithful to conversion; in the name of

Christ and by the power of the Holy Spirit they declare and grant the forgiveness of sins.

In the exercise of this ministry presbyters act in communion with the bishop and share in his power and office of regulating the penitential discipline.[40]   **1936**

b) The competent minister of the sacrament of penance is a priest who has the faculty to absolve in accordance with canon law. All priests, however, even though not approved to hear confessions, absolve validly and licitly all penitents who are in danger of death.

10. The Pastoral Exercise of This Ministry   **1937**

a) In order to fulfill his ministry properly and faithfully the confessor should understand the disorders of souls and apply the appropriate remedies to them. He should fulfill his office of judge wisely and should acquire the knowledge and prudence necessary for this task by serious study, guided by the teaching authority of the Church and especially by fervent prayer to God. Discernment of spirits is a deep knowledge of God's action in the hearts of men; it is a gift of the Spirit as well as the fruit of charity.[41]

b) The confessor should always be ready and willing to hear the confessions of the faithful when they make a reasonable request of him.[42]

c) By receiving the repentant sinner and leading him to the light of the truth the confessor fulfills a paternal function: he reveals the heart of the Father and shows the image of Christ the Good Shepherd. He should keep in mind that he has been entrusted with the ministry of Christ, who mercifully accomplished the saving work of man's redemption and who is present by his power in the sacraments.[43]

d) As the minister of God the confessor comes to know the secrets of another's conscience, and he is bound to keep the sacramental seal of confession absolutely inviolate.

The Penitent

11. The acts of the penitent in the celebration of the sacra-   **1938**
ment are of the greatest importance.

1939   When with proper dispositions he approaches this saving remedy instituted by Christ and confesses his sins, he shares by his actions in the sacrament itself; the sacrament is completed when the words of absolution are spoken by the minister in the name of Christ.

1940   Thus the faithful Christian, as he experiences and proclaims the mercy of God in his life, celebrates with the priest the liturgy by which the Church continually renews itself.

(Chapter IV then outlines details of celebration of the Sacrament of Penance and Chapter V describes Penitential Celebrations. The final Chapter [VI] deals with regional adaptations.)—Ed.

Selection from Address of Pope Paul VI
to the Secret Consistory
on the Present State of the Church
June 27, 1977

*O*n *June 27, 1977, Pope Paul VI held one of the solemn gatherings known as a consistory, and, during it, four new cardinals were created. Part of the ceremony was "secret," that is attended only by the new cardinals and all the other cardinals present in Rome that day. The following address was delivered by the Pope on this occasion.*

Toward the close of this speech, Paul VI refers to Archbishop Marcel Lefebvre and his traditionalist movement with its seminary at Econe, Switzerland, and to the ordinations conferred there by the Archbishop.   1942

Liturgical Renewal

The Pope's attention is drawn today, once more, to a par-   1943
ticular point of the church's life: the indisputably beneficial
fruits of the liturgical reform. Since the promulgation of the
conciliar constitution, *Sacrosanctum Concilium,* great progress
has taken place, progress that responds to the premises laid
down by the liturgical movement of the last part of the 19th
century and that has fulfilled that movement's deep aspirations for which so many churchmen and scholars have worked
and prayed.

The new Rite of the Mass, promulgated by us after long   1944
and painstaking preparation by the competent bodies and into which there have been introduced side-by-side with the
Roman Canon, which remains substantially unchanged,

other eucharistic prayers, has borne blessed fruits. These include a greater participation in the liturgical action, a more lively awareness of the sacred action, a greater and wider knowledge of the inexhaustible treasures of Sacred Scripture and an increase of a sense of community in the church.

1945   The course of these recent years shows that we were on the right path. But unfortunately, in spite of the vast preponderance of the healthy and good forces of the clergy and the faithful, abuses have been committed and liberties have been taken in applying the liturgical reform. The time has now come definitely to leave aside divisive ferments, which are equally pernicious on both sides, and to apply fully, in accordance with the correct criteria that inspired it, the reform approved by us in application of the wishes of the council.

1946   As for those who, in the name of a misunderstood creative freedom, have caused so much damage to the church with their improvisations, banalities and frivolities, and even certain deplorable profanations, we strongly call upon them to keep to the established norm: if this norm is not respected, grave damage could be done to the very essence of dogma, not to speak of ecclesiastical discipline, according to the golden rule, *lex orandi, lex credendi.* We call for absolute fidelity in order to safeguard the *regula fidei.* We are certain that, in this work, we are supported by the untiring, circumspect and paternal action of the bishops, who are responsible for Catholic faith and prayer in the individual dioceses.

1947   But with equal right we address ourself to those who take up an unbending attitude of nonacceptance in the name of a tradition that proves to be more a banner for contumacious insubordination than a sign of authentic fidelity. We call upon them to accept, as is their strict duty, the voice of the Pope and of the bishops, to understand the beneficial meaning of the modifications made to the sacred rites in incidental matters (modifications which represent a true continuity, and, indeed, often recall the old in adapting to the new), and not to remain obstinately closed in their incomprehensible preconceptions. In the name of God, we exhort them: "We beseech you on behalf of Christ, be reconciled to God" (2 *Cor.* 5:20).

The Unity of the Church

These recommendations, which spring from our heart, are   1948
intended to emphasize the deeply felt need for that unity of
the church of which we have spoken at the beginning of this
address.

We mean, above all, *unity in charity.* On the eve of the   1949
Holy Year, we launched a pressing appeal for reconciliation
within the church (cf. apostolic exhortation, *Paterna cum
Benevolentia,* Dec. 8, 1974: *AAS* 67, 1975, pp. 5-23). We
think it necessary to insist anew on this appeal, since, it seems
to us, the flock tends at times to be divided, and the church's
members undergo the worldly temptation to oppose one
another.

Now it is in the ardor with which they seek unity that the   1950
true disciples of Christ are recognized; it is in the harmony of
fraternal sentiments, inspired by humility, mutual respect,
benevolence and understanding, that the Christian communities reflect the true face of the church. On the other hand,
the spectacle of divisions damages the credibility of the Christian.

We therefore address ourself to all our sons and daughters,   1951
that there may be banished from within the ecclesial community those sources of corrosive criticism, division of minds,
insubordination to authority and mutual suspicion that have
occasionally succeeded in paralyzing abundant spiritual energies and in holding up the church's conquering advance on
behalf of the kingdom of God. We desire that everyone should
feel at ease in the ecclesial family, without exercising exclusion
or isolation harmful to unity in charity; and we desire that
there should not be sought the dominance of some to the
detriment of others. "United, heart and soul" (*Acts* 4:32),
like the Christians of the first mother community in Jerusalem, under the aegis of Peter, we must work, pray, suffer
and strive in order to bear witness to the risen Christ, "to the
ends of the earth" (*Acts* 1:8).

But Christ has wished that this unity in charity should   1952
never be separated from *unity in truth,* without which the

former could become linked to an indefensible pluralism or a fatal indifferentism. The *regula fidei* to which we have already referred demands this perfect consistency in fidelity to the word of God, without any obscuring of the clear source of truth, which flows from the Most Blessed Trinity and is communicated to humanity by Christ, the Son of God and Son of Man, the cornerstone on which the church is founded. Nor must there be any interruption of the continuity that has passed down that revelation through the centuries with unaltered fidelity and has drawn forth the treasures hidden within it, in continuous deepening, but *eodem sensu eademque sententia* (St. Vincent of Lerins, *Commonitorium*, 23).

1953   But the question arises: According to the very teaching of Christ and the unchangeable constitution of the church, who is responsible for judging fidelity to the deposit of faith, the conformity of a doctrine or rule of conduct to the living tradition of the church? It is the authentic magisterium, which comes from the apostolic see and the body of bishops in communion with that see. Ever since the beginning, this has always been the touchstone of truth, be it a matter of faith or morals, sacramental discipline or the more important orientations of pastoral action for the proclamation of the Gospel in the world.

1954   Today it is very necessary to remember this, since certain interpretations of doctrine imperil the faith of believers who are not sufficiently mature or instructed. As we have already said, when we dealt with abuses in the liturgy, we are certain that the bishops are unceasingly vigilant on this point. And we warmly urge everyone—bishops, priests, religious and laity—to work with one mind for unity in truth.

1955   And, with a heart full of sadness, we express again the suffering which the coming unlawful ordinations cause us—ordinations which our brother in the episcopate is preparing to confer wrongfully, as he has done in the past. We firmly deplore these ordinations. In this way, he is emphasizing his personal opposition to the church and his activity of division and rebellion in matters of extreme gravity, notwithstanding our own patient exhortations and the suspension he has incurred formally forbidding him to persist in his designs contrary to the canonical norm.

Young people are thus being placed outside of the church's   1956
authentic ministry, which, by the sacred law of the church,
they will be forbidden to exercise. The faithful who will
follow them are led astray in a posture of confusion if not in
downright rebellion greatly harmful to themselves and to
ecclesial communion. Whatever may be the pretexts, this constitutes a wound to the church, one of those which St. Paul
condemned so severely.

We ask this brother of ours to be mindful of the breach he   1957
is producing, the disorientation which he is causing, the division which he is introducing with the gravest responsibility.
Our predecessors, to whose discipline he presumes to appeal,
would not have tolerated a disobedience as obstinate as it
is pernicious for so long a period as we have so patiently done.
We ask you to pray with us to the Holy Spirit that He may
enlighten consciences.

Christ wanted His church to be one, holy, catholic and   1958
apostolic. But, if unity is broken by one side or another,
a shadow is thrown over the entire ecclesial reality in its
constituent marks. For unity Christ prayed (cf. *Jn.* 17:20-
26); for unity, He gave His life: "Jesus was to die . . . to
gather together in unity the scattered children of God" *(Jn.*
11:51 ff.). Unity was His gift to the church at the beginning
of her life, so that before the world and for the world she
might be a united witness to the word of God and to His
salvation.

This unity which the Catholic Church guards intact is what   1959
we earnestly commend to all our brothers and sons and
daughters. As we approach the Solemnity of the Holy Apostles Peter and Paul, columns of the church for which they
gave their lives, we entrust to them the protection of this
unity; for this we call upon the intercession of Mary, mother
of the church. And, in asking the generous, conscious and
active cooperation of all our brothers and sons and daughters,
we impart in support of firm and worthy intentions our special apostolic blessing.

Letter from Cardinal Villot
to a Latin American Liturgical Conference
on the Influence of the Liturgical Movement
July 21, 1977

To his excellency, Romeu Alberti, bishop of Apucarana,
President of the Department of Liturgy of the Latin
American Episcopal Conference:

1961   Your Excellency:

The Conference of the Liturgical Commissions of Latin America, which the Department of Liturgy of the Latin American Episcopal Conference has convened at Caracas,
is a very important event in the development of the liturgical and ecclesial life of the continent. That is why the
Holy Father has asked Cardinal Robert James Knox, Prefect
of the Sacred Congregation for the Sacraments and Divine Worship, to bring his words of encouragement for
the work of the meeting and his good wishes for its success.

1962   The liturgical movement is a powerful force for renewal
and is extremely influential in the life of the Church. Pope
Pius XII called it a sign of the Spirit's action in the Church.
Since the Second Vatican Council the movement has become
a sign of hope and of the ever vigorous youthfulness that
flows from the mystery of Christ which is celebrated in the
liturgy and from which the Church is continually reborn and
renewed.

1963   The liturgical movement is also an important source of life
for the Latin American Church which is today fervently dedicated to the work of evangelization and human progress. The

Church is endeavoring to help men discover their dignity and their faith and to live these in a more authentic way.

In this task the liturgy is the summit toward which pastoral work should tend, as being the way of full participation in the Christian mystery of salvation. At the same time, the liturgy is the source which sustains men's energies along the difficult road.

I. From Reform to Renewal

The liturgical reform and its implementation in the ecclesial communities of Latin America have been the object of intense and determined work which has been carried on despite the lack of means and personel.

At least for some, however, the reform has meant a purely external change. They have not grasped with sufficient depth the spiritual life-giving content which the liturgical reform seeks to bring to faith and to the development of the various ecclesial communities. In these cases, there has not been a serious preparation of those involved in pastoral work. Other pressing needs have arisen in the life of the community and have limited, to some extent at least, the energies applied to the liturgical reform.

Where necessary, we must begin anew. Where the effort has already begun, it must be intensified. All must move forward and pass from reform to renewal, from ritual change to the perception and assimilation of the content of the reform.

In the process there will also be a renewal of consciences and of commitment to Christian life, for these spring from the experience of the mystery of Christ in the liturgy and from an increasingly close incorporation into the Church.

A. The Task of True Renewal

The first and most important work to be done is to help the community discover in the liturgical celebration the mystery of salvation in all its dimensions. That mystery is not simply a past event, nor simply a reality captured in a sacrament and presented in the liturgical celebration. No, it is

1964

1965

1966

1967

1968

1969

directly and concretely related to the life of modern man.

1970   Contemporary history, with all its vicissitudes, as lived and endured by the Church and mankind, is taken up by the liturgy, united to the salvation God has wrought and effectively transformed into a history of salvation through the preaching and representation of the divine action. Unless man's history and its relation to the liturgy are seen in this light, the liturgy is in danger of being separated from life and changed into something purely ritual or esthetic or even into a way of escape from present reality.

1971   If men are to attain to such a deeper understanding of the mystery, so that it will become a source of renewal for the liturgical reform itself, an effort must be made to help the participating community to understand the various signs which are part of the celebration.

1972   This means, in the first place, understanding the value of the assembly—the gathering of God's people for the celebration—as an expressive sign and an act of faith on the part of the Church. By means of the liturgical assembly the Church manifests itself to the world and testifies to its presence as a kingly, prophetic and priestly people whose aim is the worship of God and the renewal of the world.

1973   It also means understanding the sign-value of God's word which is proclaimed by the assembly and continues God's saving action in the history of mankind in every age. This word constantly renews the marvelous signs of God. Though past now, these signs continue to give meaning and salvific effect to the history of contemporary man.

1974   Another sign to be understood aright is the sacraments. These are acts of the Church which enable the men of today to enter into contact with the saving humanity of Christ and with his mystery. This mystery is made present by faith, prayer and the action of the Church as guided and supported by the Holy Spirit. As for the Eucharist in particular, it must be understood as being not only a sacrament but a true sacrifice.

1975   Still another point to be grasped is the sign-value of the gestures, postures and actions which are part of the sacramental action. These are not simply rituals in the purely external sense but expressions of the faith of the Christian community.

To be properly understood, finally, is the commitment which the celebration presupposes in the life of individuals and community. A celebration is not authentic or truly effective unless it leads to a continual conversion whereby the faith and fraternal love which are proclaimed, heard, prayed about and experienced in the celebration take form in a life truly new. 1976

Unless pastoral action succeeds in making the Christian community understand and revive these values in its life, the liturgical reform will remain a matter simply of external changes which rouse curiosity but quickly prove ineffective. The reform will not be the source of a genuine renewal of the Church's life. 1977

B. Role of the Liturgical Commissions

The attainment of these goals depends on the national and diocesan liturgical commissions which must orient their activity in this direction. It also depends on the priests and other ministers and agents of pastoral action who must help the celebrating community to understand the real point and content of the celebration. 1978

There is need, then, of helping priests and faithful to get a better grasp of true content of the liturgy. They must move from ideas and criteria which are imprecise and hackneyed to an authentic vision of the experienced reality of Christ's mystery which is operative in the sacraments of the Church for the Christian fulfillment of man. If this line of thought is pursued, it will be easy to make people also understand that because of its very nature and purpose the liturgy is not a fad which may in time fade into the background of the Church's life. 1979

The liturgy will always be of primordial importance even though circumstances may require urgent attention to other aspects of the Church's life and work, such as catechesis or efforts in behalf of human progress. It is easy to show that even in these circumstances the liturgy continues to be the 1980 summit toward which all these other activities tend as to their full realization.

1981   In order that the celebrating community may, in its concrete real-life situations, grasp the profound and life-giving reality of the mystery, the liturgical commissions must help the priests and various other ministers to make the celebrant vitally relevant. This means taking prudent advantage of the options given in the liturgical books for preparing, organizing and carrying out celebrations which relate to the lives and capacities of the participants. There must be a timely choice of the means used to promote participation, so that this may be truly conscious, active and devout or, in other words, spiritually fruitful.

1982   When the liturgical, celebration is carried out in the light of these principles, it will prove to be an authentic agent for the proclamation and incarnation of God's salvation in the reality of each celebrating community for not only will it make use of the community's language and some elements of its culture, it will also, and above all, take into account the community's concerns and aspirations. It will be the expression of the community's faith, not as an abstraction but as a force for the renewal of each individual, of the community as a whole, as of the world in which it lives.

1983   In short, a renewed liturgy will give new energy to the life of the Church and its commitment to service.

II. The Liturgy and Evangelization

1984   The pastoral undertakings of the entire Church are focused at the present time on the problem of evangelization. This is clear from the work of the episcopal conferences, of the Synod of Bishops and of the General Meeting of the Latin American Episcopal Conference which will take place in 1978. These undertakings are important for the countries that are receiving the message of salvation for the first time.

1985   They may, however, be even more important for the traditionally Christian countries of Latin America, which are being called to live in a more conscious and deliberate way the faith they received from their forefathers by making it a source of personal commitment and the commitment of others.

It is clear that the liturgy plays an extremely important part **1986** in the work of evangelization. This is because the mystery of salvation which is proclaimed finds in the liturgy its supreme realization and also because from a pastoral viewpoint the liturgy provides a privileged place, as well as a sure and effective basis, for evangelization. Evangelization and liturgy, or—to use the current phrase—evangelization and sacramentalization, are not mutually exclusive but, on the contrary, mutually complementary.

Any celebration would be incomplete and ineffective with- **1987** out the evangelization which precedes and prepares for it. Equally incomplete would be an evangelization which did not lead quite naturally to the celebration of the sacraments.

A sacrament, being a sacrament of faith, requires a prior **1988** evangelization which rouses the faith of the person who will receive the sacrament so that he will understand, experience and translate into real life that which he celebrates.

A sacrament, in turn, like liturgical celebrations generally, **1989** becomes an effective means of evangelization when, through pastoral efforts, the community is brought to understand the value of the signs, gestures, words and elements of the celebration and when evangelization endeavors to take as its starting point the rites and texts, the content of the mystery and the cycle of celebrations, thus linking the work of formation with the life of the liturgical action.

In this way, the repetition of the action and the recurrence **1990** of the liturgical and sacramental celebration will help gradually to complete the evangelization and formation of the Christian community, to penetrate ever more deeply into the content of the formulas and rites, and to experience them as an expression of faith, even prior to experiencing them as prayer formulas of the Church. The recurrence helps the evangelizers see to it that the message received in the liturgy through word and sacramental action is applied to life.

From this profound union of evangelization and liturgy **1991** there will also come an eagerness for the renewal of the celebration itself. This cannot fail to have a strong influence on the life of the Church. If a celebration is to be evangelizing, it must be constantly renewed not only in its externals but also, and above all, in its spirit and in the way in which it is carried out.

1992   The Church, that is, the local celebrating community, will thus not be simply a passive recipient of evangelization. On the contrary, it will profit by the inherent dynamism flowing from the preaching and sacramental enactment of the mystery of salvation. It will build itself up and grow. It will feel impelled to communicate to the world the salvation God is offering

1993   This missionary impulse will certainly be beneficial for the character and various structures of the ecclesial communities as they realize they are committed to being, in their entirety, influential centers for mission, renewal and progress rather than, and prior to, being centers for ritual.

1994   For this reason it is desirable that there be ongoing effective collaboration among the departments and commissions which are working, at various levels of commitment and responsibility, in the areas of catechetics, liturgy, education and human progress. In this way it will be possible to make a common and integrated effort which will bring out more clearly the correlation of the work being done in all these sectors and will produce a joint pastoral result.

1995   It is worth pointing out that this common work should derive light and guidance from that which is the main treasure of the liturgy: I mean the mystery of salvation as an idea and force which will create a convergence and thus unify all pastoral action.

III. Liturgy and Some Particular Problems of the Latin American Church

1996   The renewal of the Church which should result from a properly applied liturgical reform will also take into account the situations peculiar to the Church of the Latin American continent. These situations spring from a historical life which reflects a rich past and they can contribute in turn to a new enrichment. Consequently, they are reasons for great hope. Thus, when the renewal takes concrete shape on this continent, the result will not be a useless kind of differentiation which is a mere curiosity but rather something new and special which shows the richness yielded by plurality in unity.

In this regard, we would like to point out certain aspects   1997
of religious life on the continent which must be taken into
account in the liturgical renewal.

a) One of the characteristics of the Latin American people   1998
is a type of religion often called "popular." Sometimes,
"popular" refers, in this context, to an uninstructed and in-
completely formed faith. At other times, it refers to a faith
that finds expression in forms which are unconnected with
the liturgy or which reflect the cultural and religious traditions of the past.

Despite its imperfections, this set of manifestations of   1999
faith constitute an authentic value and it would be a mistake
to try to eliminate it from the life of the people, especially
the more simple, without providing an adequate substitute.
On the contrary, it should be studied, understood, appreciated and purified of all that is incorrect. It should be made
the basis for a beneficial evangelization and enriched with
elements from the liturgy which will help it to develop and
lead to an authentic liturgy which is intelligent and prudently adapted to particular situations.

These same forms of popular faith and devotion frequently   2000
arise as substitutes for a liturgy which is too remote from the
understanding and speech of the faithful. When properly
purified, these forms can and should even become the basis
for a liturgy which is prudently adapted to particular situations, groups of individuals and stages in the maturing and
deepening of faith.

b) The Christian faith and life of many communities have   2001
been preserved and developed (and in some cases are being
preserved and developed even in our day) thanks to the gifts
of ministry which the Spirit of the Lord is constantly bestowing on the Church. It is necessary, of course, to promote and
foster vocations to the priestly and deaconal ministries. However, the discovery and implementation of new forms of ministry, including a liturgical life not reserved to ministers in the
narrow sense of this term and including also other aspects of
the religious and human life of communities (especially those

communities that are without a priest), is another objective which should greatly concern the Latin American Church.

2002   In the past, these lay ministers were devoted almost exclusively to the prayer life of the community. They contributed to the preservation of the faith through religious practices which were often devotional in character. Today, however, these same ministers have before them a much wider field of action, even with regard to the liturgy.

2003   These ministries must be encouraged and cultivated; those who exercise them must receive a proper formation. Such ministries are a gift from the Spirit and a source of hope for the future of the ecclesial communities.

2004   c) The special situation of the Latin American Church frequently gives rise to smaller groups or communities within the traditional communities. No one can fail to see how important these smaller communities are as the fruit of a Christian commitment which is usually mediated by the liturgical celebration.

2005   At the pastoral level, these smaller communities must evidently not be allowed to become a divisive force within the ecclesial communities by turning into self-centered groups. They must instead be vital, conscious nuclei which are effective in forming a Church which has greater influence on the human situation in which it finds itself. As far as the liturgy is concerned, here again these smaller communities can be a real force for renewal if they assimilate the authentic values of the reform and turn these into a source of life and if they communicate these values to their brothers by helping in and inspiring the celebrations of the wider local community.

2006   It is, therefore, indispensable that the celebrations of these groups not be arbitrary or unduly affected but represent rather a deeper and more committed grasp of the mystery which should feed a more intense spiritual life in themselves and, thereby, in the entire local community.

2007   d) The presence of the varied cultures with which the Latin American continent is so richly endowed raises the problem of adapting them to the liturgy of the Roman Rite. In some cases, the cultures are autochthonous and still marked by a certain purity of tradition. In other cases, the cultures have arisen from the fusion of native elements with others imported from the old world and from countries with a different tradition.

There is no question here of simply creating a new liturgy   2008
or of novelty for novelty's sake. Neither is there question of following an impulse to archeologize and revive elements which have gone out of use. A discerning pastoral sensitivity, based on a secure faith which is profoundly lived by the Christian community, together with close cooperation between the bishops of the Church and persons competent in the various sciences,will show the way of making use of valid elements in the authentic local traditions.

Then the liturgy, in keeping, with the prudent advice given   2009
by the Second Vatican Council, will be able to find clearer expression in the language, mentality and life of the various local Churches while also respecting the essential unity of faith and maintaining a profound communion of love with all.

e) Finally, the Holy Father exhorts the bishops of the   2010
Latin American Church to continue their fervent efforts to guide, organize, direct and promote the liturgy throughout the continent. The organizations within the Latin American Episcopal Conference providentially make possible a fruitful coordination of pastoral efforts and can even supply when local efforts fail.

The various national and regional organizations can and   2011
must intensify their efforts (which have already produced consoling results) to give new life to the faith and prayer of the people of God. Let the bishops guide their fellow-workers and be an example and inspiration to them, by showing how the liturgy can, when its possibilities are prudently exploited and when it has its proper place in the overall pastoral plan, be a vital force for the accomplishment of the Church's mission.

These are the desires the Holy Father cherishes in connec-   2012
tion with the work of this Conference of the National Liturgical Commissions. He invokes upon the participants the graces and light of the Spirit, and imparts the Apostolic Blessing to your Excellency, to your collaborators in organizing the Conference and to the participants.

References

SACRA TRINDENTINA: Decree on Frequent and Daily Reception of Holy Communion, December 20, 1905.

1   Sess. XXII, cap. 6.

2   *John* 6:59.

3   St. Augustine, Serm. 57 in St. Matthew, *De Orat. Dom.*, n. 7.

4   Sess. XIII, cap. 2.

5   *Acts* 2:42.

6   Part II, cap. 4, n. 60.

QUAM SINGULARI: Decree of the Sacred Congregation of the Discipline of the Sacraments on First Communion, August 8, 1910.

1   *Mark* 10:13-16.

2   *Matt.* 18:3-5.

3   Sess. XXI *de Communione*, c. 4.

4   Sess. XIII *de Eucharistia*, c. 8, can. 9.

5   Sess. XIII *de Eucharistia*, c. 2.

6   *Summ. Theo.* III, q. 80, art 9, ad 3.

7   In St. Thom. art. 9, dub. 6.

8   In St. Thomas. III, disput. 214, c. 4, no. 43.

9   III, tit. 14, c. 2, sec. 5.

10   Sess. XXI, chap. IV.

11   P. 11, *De Sacr. Euchar.* no. 63.

MYSTICI CORPORIS: Selection from Encyclical Letter of Pope Pius XII on the Mystical Body of Christ and Our Union in It with Christ, June 29, 1943.

1   Cf. *Col.* I, 24.

2   *Acts,* XX, 28.

3   Cf. I *Peter,* IV, 13.

4   Cf. *Eph.,* II, 21–22; I *Peter,* II, 5.

5   Cf. *John,* XV, 5.

6   Cf. St. Thos., III, q. 64, a. 3.

7   *Eph.,* IV, 7.

8   *Eph.,* IV, 16; cf. *Col.,* II, 19.

9   *Mal.,* I. 11.

10   Cf. *Didache,* IX, 4.

11   Cf. *Rom.,* VIII, 35.

12   St. Thoms., III, q. 30, a. 1, c.

13   *John,* II, 11.

14   *Col.,* I, 24.

15   Cf. *Vesper humn of the Office of the Sacred Heart.*

16   Cf. Pius X, *Ad Diem Illum: A.S.S.,* XXXVI, p. 453.

MEDIATOR DEI, Encyclical Letter of Pope Pius XII on the Sacred Liturgy, November 30, 1947.

1   *Tim.* 2:5.

2   Cf. *Heb.* 4:14.

3   Cf. *Heb.* 9:14.

4   Cf. *Mal.* 1:11.

5   Cf. Council of Trent Sess. 22, c. 1.

6   Cf. *ibid.,* c. 2.

7   Encyclical Letter *Caritate Christi,* May 3, 1932.

8   Cf. Apostolic Letter (Motu Proprio) *In cotidianis precibus,* March 24, 1945.

9   1 *Cor.* 10:17.

10   Saint Thomas, *Summa Theologica,* II^a II^{ae}, q. 31, art. 1.

1^1 Cf. Book of *Leviticus.*

12   Cf. *Heb.* 10:1.

13   *John,* 1:14.

14   *Heb.* 10:5-7.

15   *Ibid.* 10:10.

16   *John,* 1:9.

17   *Heb.* 10:39.

18   Cf. 1 *John,* 2:1.

19   Cf. 1 *Tim.* 3:15.

20   Cf. Boniface IX, *Ab origine mundi,* October 7, 1391; Callistus III, *Summus Pontifex,* January 1, 1456; Pius II, *Triumphans Pastor,* April 22, 1459; Innocent XI, *Triumphans Pastor,* October 3, 1678.

21   *Eph.* 2:19-22.

22   *Matt.* 18:20.

23   *Acts,* 2:42.

24   *Col.* 3:16.

25   Saint Augustine, *Epist.* 130, *ad Problam,* 18.

26   Roman Missal, Preface for Christmas.

27   Giovanni Cardinal Bona, *De divina psalmodia,* c. 19, par. 3, 1.

28   Roman Missal, Secret for Thursday after the Second Sunday of Lent.

29   Cf. *Mark,* 7:6 and *Isaias,* 29:13.

30   1 *Cor.* 11:28.

31   Roman Missal, Ash Wednesday; Prayer after the imposition of ashes.

32   *De praedestinatione sactorum,* 31.

33   Cf. Saint Thomas, *Summa Theologica,* II^a II^{ae}, q. 82, art. 1.

34   Cf. 1 *Cor.* 3:23.

35   *Heb.* 10:19-24.

36   Cf. 2 *Cor.* 6:1.

37   Cf. Code of Canon Law, can. 125, 126, 565, 571, 595, 1367.

38   *Col.* 3:11.

39   Cf. *Gal.* 4:19.

40   *John,* 20:21.

41   *Luke,* 10:16.

42   *Mark,* 16:15-16.

43   Roman Pontifical, Ordination of a priest: anointing of hands.

44   *Enchiridion,* c. 3.

45   *De gratia Dei* "Indiculus."

46   Saint Augustine, *Epist.* 130, *ad Problam,* 18.

47   Cf. Constitution *Divini cultus,* December 20, 1928.

48   Constitution *Immensa,* January 22, 1588.

49   Code of Canon Law, can. 253.

50   Cf. Code of Canon Law, can. 1257.

51   Cf. Code of Canon Law, can. 1261.

52   Cf. *Matt.* 28:20.

53   Cf. Pius VI, Constitution *Auctorem fidei,* August 28, 1794, nn.
31-34, 39, 62, 66, 69-74.

54   Cf. *John,* 21:15-17.

55   *Acts,* 20:28.

56   *Ps.* 109:4.

57   *John,* 13:1.

58   Council of Trent, Sess. 22, c. 1.

59   *Ibid.,* c. 2.

60   Cf. Saint Thomas, *Summa Theologica,* III^a, q. 22, art. 4.

61   Saint John Chrysostom, *In Joann. Hom.,* 86:4.

62   *Rom.* 6:9.

63   Cf. Roman Missal, Preface.

64   Cf. *Ibid.,* Canon.

65   *Mark,* 14:23.

66   Roman Missal, Preface.

67   *1 John,* 2:2.

68   Roman Missal, Canon of the Mass.

69   Saint Augustine, *De Trinit.,* Book XIII, c. 19.

70   *Heb.* 5:7.

71   Cf. Sess. 22, c. 1.

72   Cf. *Heb.* 10:14.

73   Saint Augustine, *Enarr. in Ps.* 147, n. 16.

74   *Gal.* 2:19-20.

75   Encyclical Letter, *Mystici Corporis,* June 29, 1943.

76   Roman Missal, Secret of the Ninth Sunday after Pentecost.

77   Cf. Sess. 22, c. 2. and can. 4.

78   Cf. *Gal.* 6:14.

79   *Mal.* 1:11.

80   *Phil.* 2:5.

81   *Gal.* 2:19.

82   Cf. Council of Trent, Sess. 23, c. 4.

83   Cf. Saint Robert Bellarmine, *De Missa,* 2, c. 4.

84   *De Sacro Altaris Mysterio,* 3:6.

85   *De Missa,* 1, c. 27.

86   Roman Missal, Ordinary of the Mass.

87   *Ibid.,* Canon of the Mass.

88   Roman Missal, Canon of the Mass.

89   *1 Peter,* 2:5.

90   *Rom.* 12:1.

91   Roman Missal, Canon of the Mass.

92   Roman Pontifical, Ordination of a priest.

93   *Ibid.,* Consecration of an altar, Preface.

94   Cf. Council of Trent, Sess. 22, c. 5.

95   *Gal.* 2:19-20.

96   Cf. *Serm.* 272.

97   Cf. *1 Cor.* 12:27.

98   Cf. *Eph.* 5:30.

99   Cf. Saint Robert Bellarmine, *De Missa,* 2, c. 8.

100   Cf. *De Civitate Dei,* Book 10, c. 6.

101   Roman Missal, Canon of the Mass.

102   Cf. *1 Tim.* 2:5.

103 Encyclical Letter *Certiores effecti,* November 13, 1742, par. 1.

104 Council of Trent, Sess. 22, can. 8.

105 *1 Cor.* 11:24.

106 Roman Missal, Collect for Feast of Corpus Christi.

107 Sess. 22, c. 6.

108 Encyclical Letter *Certiores effecti,* par. 3.

109 Cf. *Luke,* 14:23.

110 *1 Cor.* 10:17.

11! Cf. Saint Ignatius Martyr, *Ad Eph.* 20.

112 Roman Missal, Canon of the Mass.

113 *Eph.* 5:20.

114 Roman Missal, Postcommunion for Sunday within the Octave of Ascension.

115 *Ibid.,* Postcommunion for First Sunday after Pentecost.

116 Code of Canon Law, can. 810.

117 Book IV, c. 12.

118 *Dan.* 3:57.

119 Cf. *John* 16:23.

120 Roman Missal, Secret for Mass of the Most Blessed Trinity.

121 *John,* 15:4.

122 Council of Trent, Sess. 13, can. 1.

123 Second Council of Constantinople, *Anath, de trib. Capit.,* can. 9; compare Council of Ephesus, *Anath. Cyrill.* can. 8. Cf. Council of Trent, Sess. 13, can. 6; Pius VI Constitution *Auctorem fidei,* n. 61.

124 Cf. *Enarr. in Ps.* 98:9.

125 *Apoc.* 5:12, cp. 7:10.

126 Cf. Council of Trent, Sess. 13, c. 5 and can. 6.

127 *In I ad Cor.,* 24:4.

128 Cf. *I Peter,* 1:19.

129 *Matt.* 11:28.

130 Cf. Roman Missal, Collect for Mass for the Dedication of a Church.

131. Roman Missal, Sequence *Lauda Sion* in Mass for Feast of Corpus Christi.

132 *Luke,* 18:1.

133   *Heb.* 13:15.

134   Cf. *Acts,* 2:1-15.

135   *Ibid.,* 10:9.

136   *Ibid.,* 3:1.

137   *Ibid.,* 16:25.

138   *Rom.* 8:26.

139   Saint Augustine, *Enarr. in Ps.* 85, n. 1.

140   Saint Benedict, *Regula Monachorum,* c. 19.

141   *Heb.* 7:25.

142   *Explicatio in Psalterium,* Preface. Text as found in Migne, Patres Patini, 70:10. But some are of the opinion that part of this passage should not be attributed to Cassiodorus.

143   Saint Ambrose, *Enarr. in Ps.* 1, n. 9.

144   *Exod.* 31:15.

145   *Confessions,* Book 9, c. 6.

146   Saint Augustine, *De Civitate Dei,* Book 8, c. 17.

147   *Col.* 3:1-2.

148   Saint Augustine, *Enarr. in Ps.* 123, n. 2.

149   *Heb.* 13:8.

150   Saint Thomas, *Summa Theologica,* III^a, q. 49 and q. 62, art. 5.

151   Cf. *Acts,* 10:38.

152   *Eph.* 4:13.

153   Roman Missal, Collect for Third Mass of Several Martyrs outside Paschaltide.

154   Saint Bede the Veerable, *Hom. subd.* 70 for Feast of All Saints.

155   Roman Missal, Collect for Mass of Saint John Damascene.

156   Saint Bernard, *Sermon 2 for Feast of All Saints*.

157   *Luke,* 1:28.

158   "Salve Regina."

159   Saint Bernard, *In Nativ. B.M.V.,* 7.

160   *Heb.* 10:22.

161   *Ibid.,* 10:21.

162   *Ibid.,* 6:19.

163   Cf. Code of Canon Law, Can. 125.

164   Cf. *John,* 14:2.

165   *John,* 3:8.

166   Cf. *James,* 1:17.

167   *Eph.* 1:4.

168   Cf. Apostolic Letter (Motu Proprio) *Tra le sollecitudini,* November 22, 1903.

169   *Ps.* 68:10; *John,* 2:17.

170   Supreme Sacred Congregation of the Holy Office, Decree of May 26, 1937.

171   Cf. Pius X, Apostolic Letter (Motu Proprio) *Tre le sellecitudini.*

172   Cf. Pius X, *loc. cit.;* Pius XI, Constitution *Divini cultus,* 2, 5.

173   Pius XI, Constitution *Divini cultus,* 9.

174   Saint Augustine, *Serm.* 336, n. 1.

175   Roman Missal, Preface.

176   Saint Ambrose, *Hexameron,* 3:5, 23.

177   Cf. *Acts,* 4:32.

178   Code of Canon Law, can. 1178.

179   Pius XI, Constitution *Divini cultus.*

180   Cf. Saint Augustine, *Tract. 26 in John* 13.

181   Cf. *Matt.* 13:24-25.

182   Encyclical letter *Mystici Corporis.*

183   *Joel,* 2:15-16.

184   I *Thess.* 5:19.

185   *Ibid.,* 5:21.

186   *Heb.* 13:17.

187   I *Cor.* 14:33.

188   *Apos.* 5:13.

CHRISTUS DOMINUS: Apostolic Constitution of Pope Pius XII on Eucharistic Fast, January 6, 1953.

1   I *Cor.* 11:23.

2   See *Lk.* 22:20.

3   I *Cor.* 11:24.

4   *Mt.* 26:28.

5   See I *Cor.* 11:24-25.

6   See the hymn *Lauda Sion* in the Roman Missal.

7   See Benedict XIV, *De Synodo Diocesana*, 6, ch. 8, no. 10.

8   Conc. Hippo., canon 28; Mansi 3, 923.

9   Conc. Carth. III, ch. 29; Mansi 3, 885.

10   See. St. Augustine, *Ep. LIV ad Ian.*, ch. 6; *PL* 33, 203.

11   See I *Cor.* 12:21ff.

12   St. Augustine, *loc. cit.*

13   Conc. Tolet. VII, ch. 29; Mansi 10, 768.

14   Conc. Bracar. III, canon 10; Mansi 9, 841.

15   Conc. Matiscon. II, canon 6; Mansi 9, 952.

16   Conc. Constant., sess. 13; Mansi 27, 727.

17   Decree of S.C. Conc., *Sacra Tridentina Synodus*, December 20, 1905, *AAS* 38, 400; *Fontes* 6, no. 4326, 828.

18   Decree of S.C. Sacr., *Quam singulari*, August 8, 1910; *AAS* 2, 577, *Fontes* 5, no. 2103, 80.

19   Canon 863; see canon 854, § 5.

20   *Mt.* 28:19.

21   *Mk* 10:14.

22   Cant 2:16; 6:2.

23   *AAS* 39, 603; *Fontes* 6, no. 4331, 843.

24   *AAS* 15, 151.

25   St. Thomas, *Opuse, LVII,* Office of the Feast of Corpus Christi, lect. IV, *Opera Omnia*, Rome, 1570, vol. XVII.

26   I *Cor.* 10:17.

27   The day of promulgation was January 16, 1953.

MUSICAE SACRAE DISCIPLINA, Encyclical Letter of Pope Pius XII on Sacred Music, December 25, 1955.

1   Motu Proprio, *Fra le sollecitudini dell'ufficio pastorale (Among the Cares of the Pastoral Office), Acta* Pii X, I, 77.

2   Cf. *Gen.* 1, 26.

3   *Epis.* 161, *De origine animae hominis (On the Origin of Man's Soul),* 1, 2; *P.L.* XXXIII, 725.

4   Cf. *Ex.* 15, 1-20.

5   II *Sam.* 6, 5.

6   Cf. I *Para.* 23, 5; 25, 2-31.

7   *Eph.* 5, 18ff; cf. *Col.* 3, 16.

8   I *Cor.* 14, 26.

9   Pliny, *Epis.* X, 96-97.

10   Tertullian, *De anima (On the Soul)*, ch. 9; *P.L. II* 701; and *Apol.* 39; *P.L.* 1, 540.

11   Council of Trent, Session XXII: *Decretum de observandis et evitandis in celebratione Missae (Decree on What Should Be Observed and Avoided in the Celebration of Mass).*

12   Cf. Encyclical Letter of Benedict XIV *Annus Qui*, Complete Works (Prati edition, vol. 17, 1, page 16).

13   Cf. Apostolic Letter *Bonum est confiteri Domino (It is Good to Trust in the Lord)*, August 2, 1828; *Cf. Bullarium Romanum*, Prati edition, ex Typ. Aldina, IX, 139ff.

14   Cf. *Acta Pii X*, I 75-87; *Acta Sanctae Sedis*, XXXVI (1903-1904) 329-39; 387-95.

15   Cf. *A.A.S., XXI.* 33 ff.

16   Cf. *A.A.S.*, XXXIX, 521-95.

17   St. Augustine, *Confessions*, Book X, chap. 33, MPL, XXXII, 799ff.

18   *Acta Pii X*, loc. cit., 78.

19   Letter to Card. Respighi, *Acta Pii X*, loc. cit., 68-74, see 73ff.; *Acta Sanctae Sedis*, XXXVI (1903-04), 325-29, 395-98, see 398.

20   Pius XI, Apostolic Constitution. *Divini cultus (On Divine Worship)*, *A.A.S.*, XXI (1929), 33ff.

21   *Code of Canon Law*, Can. 5.

22   Council of Trent, Session XXII, *De Sacrificio Missae*, C. VIII.

23   *Acta Pii X*, loc. cit., 80.

24   *A.A.S.*, XXXIX (1947), 590.

25   *Apoc.* 5, 13.

26   Decrees of the Sacred Congregation of Rites, No's. 3964, 4201, 4231.

27   St. Cyprian, *Letter to Donatus* (Letter 1, n. 16) *PL*, IV, 227.

Address of Pope Pius XII to the International Congress on Pastoral Liturgy on the Liturgical Movement, September 22, 1956.

1   *Acta Ap. Sedis*, a. 5, 1913, pp. 449-451.

2   *Acta Ap. Sedis*, a. 39, 1947, pp. 522-595.

3   *Acta Ap. Sedis*, a. 47, 1955, pp. 838-847.

4   *Acta Ap. Sedis*, a. 48, 1956, pp. 5-25.

5   *Acta Ap. Sedis*, a. 39, 1947, pp. 528-529.

6   I *Cor.* 3, 23.

7   I *Peter* 5, 2.

8   *Acta Ap. Sedis*, a. 39, 1947, p. 544.

9   *Acta Ap. Sedis*, a. 46, 1954, pp. 313-317; 666-677.

10   *Acta Ap. Sedis*, a. 46, 1954, pp. 668-670.

11   *Conc. Trid.*, Sess. XXII, cap. 2.

12   *Acta Ap. Sedis*, 1. c., p. 668.

13   *Acta Ap. Sedis*, 1. c., p. 669.

14   Cf. *Conc. Trid.*, Sess. XIII, ch. 4 and 3.

15   *Acta Ap. Sedis*, a. 37, 1945, pp. 131-132.

16   *Mt.* 1, 21.

17   *John,* 1, 29.

18   *John,* 3, 14-15.

19   *Luke,* 12, 50.

20   I *Cor.*, 11, 23-25.

21   Cf. *John,* 21, 7.

22   Cf. *Catech. Rom.*, pars II, cap. IV, n. 43, sq.

23   *Acta Ap. Sedis*, a. 19, 1927, pag. 289.

24   *Conc. Trid.*, Sessio XIII, can. 6.

25   *Conc. Trid.*, 1. c., can. 7.

26   *Acta Ap. Sedis*, a. 44, 1952, pp. 542-546.

27   *Acta Ap. Sedis*, 1. c., p. 544.

28   *John,* 1, 1-3.

29   I *Cor.*, 15, 28.

Vatican II, SACROSANCTUM CONCILIUM: Constitution on the Sacred Liturgy, December 4, 1963.

1   Secret of the ninth Sunday after Pentecost.

2   Cf. *Heb.* 13, 14.

3. Cf. *Eph.* 2, 21-22.

4   Cf. *Eph.* 4, 13.

5   Cf. *Is.* 11, 12.

6   Cf. *John* 11, 52.

7   Cf. *John* 10, 16.

8   *1 Tim.* 2, 4.

9   *Heb.* 1, 1.

10 Cf. *Is.* 61, 1; *Luke* 4, 18.

11 St. Ignatius of Antioch, *To the Ephesians,* 7, 2.

12 Cf. *1 Tim.* 2, 5.

13 *Sacramentarium Veronense,* ed. C. Mohlberg, n. 1265, p. 162.

14 Easter Preface of the Roman Missal.

15 Cf. Prayer after the second lesson for Holy Saturday, as it was in the Roman Missal before the restoration of Holy Week.

16 Cf. *Mark* 16, 15.

17 Cf. *Acts* 26, 18.

18 Cf. *Rom.* 6, 4; *Eph.* 2, 6; *Col.* 3, 1; *2 Tim.* 2, 11.

19 *Rom.* 8, 15.

20 Cf. *John* 4, 23.

21 Cf. *1 Cor.* 11, 26.

22 *Acts* 2, 41-47.

23 *Luke* 24, 27.

24 Council of Trent, Session XIII, October 11, 1551, decree *On the Holy Eucharist,* c. 5.

25 *2 Cor.* 9, 15.

26 *Eph.* 1, 12.

27 Council of Trent, Session XXIII, September 17, 1562 doctrine *On the Holy Sacrifice of the Mass, c. 2.*

28 Cf. St. Augustine, *In Ioannis Evangelium Tractatus VI,* chap. I, n. 7; *PL* 35, 1428.

29   *Matt.* 18, 20.

30   Cf. *Apoc.* 21, 2; *Col.* 3, 1; *Heb.* 8, 2.

31   Cf. *Phil.* 3, 20; *Col.* 3, 4.

32   *Rom.* 10, 14-15.

33   Cf. *John* 17, 3; *Luke* 24, 27; *Acts* 2, 38.

34   Cf. *Matt.* 28, 20.

35   Postcommunion for Paschal Vigil and Easter Sunday Masses.

36   Collect of the Mass for Tuesday of Easter Week.

37   Cf. *2 Cor.* 6, 1.

38   Cf. *Matt.* 6, 6.

39   Cf *1 Thess.* 5, 17.

40   Cf. *2 Cor.* 4, 10-11.

41   Secret for Monday of Pentecost Week.

42   *1 Pet.* 2, 9; cf. 2, 4-5.

43   St. Cyprian, *On the Unity of the Catholic Church*, 7; cf. Letter 66, n. 8, 3.

44   Cf. Council of Trent, Session XXII, September 17, 1562, doctrine *On the Holy Sacrifice of the Mass.* c. 8.

45   *Rom.* 15, 4.

46   Cf. St. Ignatius of Antioch, *To the Magnesians,* 7; *To the Phillipians,* 4; *To the Smyrnians,* 8.

47   Cf. St. Augustine, *In Ioannis Evangelium Tractatus XXVI*, chap. VI, n. 13; *PL* 35, 1613.

48   Roman Breviary, feast of Corpus Christi, Second Vespers, antiphon to the Magnificat.

49   Cf. St. Cyril of Alexandria, *Commentary on the Gospel of John*, book XI, chap. XI-XII; *PL* 74, 557-564.

50   Cf. *1 Tim.* 2, 1-2.

51   Council of Trent, Session XXI, July 16, 1562, *Doctrine on Communion under Both Species,* chap. 1-3.

52   Council of Trent, Session XXIV, November 11, 1563, *On Reform,* chap. I; cf. Roman Ritual title VIII, chap. II, n. 6.

53   *1 Thess.* 5, 17.

54   *John* 15, 5.

55   *Acts* 6, 4.

56   *1 Pet.* 1, 3.

57   Cf. *Eph.* 5, 19; *Col.* 3, 16.

Address of Pope Paul VI to Pastors and Lenten Preachers of Rome on Promoting the New Liturgy, March 1, 1965.

1   *Cor* 4, 1.

2   *1 Thes* 4, 3-7.

3   By their fruits!"

4   *Phil* 2, 8.

5   *Heb* 13, 17.

6   *Ps* 132, 1.

7   *De doctrina christiana, PL* 34, 103.

8   *Epistle* 52, 7; *PL* 22, 533.

9   *Heb* 4, 12.

10   *Mt* 28, 19-20.

ECCLESIAE SEMPER: Decree of the Sacred Congregation of Rites on Concelebration of Mass and Communion under Both Kinds, March 7, 1965.

1   Cf. Council of Trent, sess. XXII, cap. I.

2   Cf. St. Thomas Aq., S. Th. III, a. 3, ad 2-3.

3   Cf. Vatican Council II, Const. on the Church, art. 26.

4   Cf. Vatican Council II, Const. on the Liturgy, art. 2 and 41.

5   Cf. *ibid.*, art. 26.

6   Cf. *ibid.*, art. 41.

7   Cf. *ibid.*, art. 57 and 58.

Address of Pope Paul VI to the Commission for Implementing the Constitution on the Sacred Liturgy, October 13, 1966.

1   Cf. *Constitution on the Sacred Liturgy,* no. 23.

2   Cf. *ibid.*, nos. 11, 14, etc.

3   Nos. 39, 44, 112, 114, 115, 116, 120, 121.

4   No. 112.

MUSICAM SACRAM: Instruction of the Sacred Congregation of Rites on Music in the Sacred Liturgy, March 5, 1967.

1   *Constitution on the Sacred Liturgy,* no. 112.

2   Cf. St. Pius X, Motu proprio *Tra le sollecitudini,* no. 2: *ASS* (1903-1904), 332.

3   Cf. Instruction of the Sacred Cong. of Rites, Sept. 3, 1958, no. 4.

4   *Constitution on the Sacred Liturgy,* no. 113.

5   Ibid., no. 28.

6   Cf. Instruction of the Sacred Cong. of Rites, Sept. 3, 1958, no. 95.

7   Cf. *Constitution on the Sacred Liturgy,* no. 116.

8   Ibid., no. 28.

9   Ibid., no. 22.

10   Cf. *Constitution on the Sacred Liturgy,* no. 26 and nos. 41-42; *Dogmatic Constitution on the Church,* no. 28.

11   Cf. *Constitution on the Sacred Liturgy,* no. 29.

12   Ibid., no. 33.

13   Ibid., no. 14.

14   Ibid., no. 11.

15   Ibid., no. 30.

16   Ibid.

17   Cf. *Constitution on the Sacred Liturgy,* no. 30.

18   Cf. Instruction of the Sacred Cong. of Rites, Sept. 26, 1964, nos. 19 and 59.

19   Cf. *Constitution on the Sacred Liturgy,* no. 19; Instruction of the Sacred Cong. of Rites, Sept. 3, 1958, nos. 106-108.

20   Cf. Instruction of the Sacred Cong. of Rites, Sept. 26, 1964, no. 97.

21   Ibid., no. 48*b*.

22   Cf. *Constitution on the Sacred Liturgy,* no. 44.

Address of Pope Paul VI to the Commission for Implementing the Constitution on the Sacred Liturgy on Obstacles to Liturgical Renewal, April 19, 1967.

1   *Constitution on the Sacred Liturgy*, no. 23.

2   *Ibid.*, no. 22.

EUCHARISTICUM MYSTERIUM: Instruction of the Sacred Congregation of Rites on Eucharistic Worship, May 25, 1967.

1   Cf. Vat. Council II, Const. on Liturgy, *Sacrosanctum Concilium*, nn. 1, 41, 47—*AAS* 56 (1964), pp. 97-98, 111, 113.

2   Cf. *Ibid.*, nn. 48-54, 56—*AAS* 56 (1964), pp. 113-115.

3   Cf. *Ibid.*, nn. 55, 57—*AAS* 56 (1964), pp. 115-116.

4   Cf. Const. on the Church, *Lumen Gentium*, nn. 3, 7, 11, 26, 28, 50—*AAS* 57 (1965), pp. 6, 9-11, 15-16, 31-32, 33-36, 55-57.

5   Cf. Decree on Ecumenism, *Unitatis Redintegratio*, 2, 15—*AAS* 57 (1965), pp. 91-92, 101-102; Decree on the Bishops' Pastoral Office in the Church, *Christus Dominus*, nn. 15, 30—*AAS* 58 (1966), pp. 679-680, 688-689; Decree on the Ministry and Life of Priests, *Presbyterorum Ordinis*, nn. 2, 5-8, 13-14, 18; *AAS* 58 (1966), pp. 991-993, 997-1005, 1011-1014, 1018-1019.

6   Cf. Const. on the Church in the Modern World, *Gaudium et Spes*, n. 38—*AAS* 58 (1966), pp. 1055-1056.

7   *AAS* 39 (1947), pp. 547-572; cf. Address to those who took part in the International Conference on Pastoral Liturgy held at Assisi, 22. ix. 1956; *AAS* 48 (1956), pp. 715-724.

8   *AAS* 57 (1965), pp. 753-774.

9   Vat. II Const. on the Church, *Lumen Gentium*, n. 7—*AAS* 57 (1965), p. 9.

10   Vat. II Const. on Liturgy, *Sacrosanctum Concilium*, n. 47—*AAS* 56 (1964), p. 113.

11   Cf. Vat. II Const. on Liturgy, *Sacrosanctum Concilium*, nn. 6, 10, 47, 106—*AAS* 56 (1964), pp. 100, 102, 113, 126; Decree on the Ministry and Life of Priests, *Presbyterorum Ordinis*, n. 4—*AAS* 58 (1956), pp. 995-997.

12   Paul VI, Encyc. Lett., *Mysterium Fidei—AAS* 57 (1965), p. 763.

13   Cf. Pius XII, Encyc. Lett., *Mediator Dei—AAS* 39 (1947), pp. 564-566.

14   Cf. Vat. II Const. on Liturgy, *Sacrosanctum Concilium*, n. 47—
AAS 56 (1964), p. 113.

15   Cf. Council of Trent, Session XXII, Decree on the Mass, Chap.
I—*Denz.* 938 (1741).

16   Cf. Vat. II Const. on the Church, *Lumen Gentium*, n. 11—*AAS*
57 (1965), pp. 15-16; Const. on Liturgy, *Sacrosanctum Concilium*, nn.
47-48—*AAS* 56 (1964), p. 113; Decree on the Ministry and Life of
Priests, *Presbyterorum Ordinis*, nn. 2, 5—*AAS* 58 (1966), pp. 991-3,
997-9; Pius XII, Encyc. Lett., *Mediator Dei, AAS* 39 (1947), p. 552;
Paul VI, Encyc. Lett., *Mysterium Fidei—AAS* 57 (1965), p. 761.

17   Cf. Vat. II Const. on Liturgy, *Sacrosanctum Concilium*, nn.
26-28—*AAS* 56 (1964), p. 107; and below n. 44.

18   Cf. below n. 49.

19   Cf. Vat. II Const. on the Church, *Lumen Gentium*, n. 11—*AAS*
57 (1965), pp. 15-16; Const. on Liturgy, *Sacrosanctum Concilium*, n.
41—*AAS* 56 (1964), p. 111; Decree on Ministry and Life of Priests,
Presbyterorum Ordinis, nn. 2, 5, 6—*AAS* 58 (1966), pp. 991-3, 997-9,
999-1001; Decree on Ecumenism, *Unitatis Redintegratio*, n. 15—*AAS*
57 (1965), pp. 101-2.

20   Council of Trent, Session XIII, Decree on the Eucharist, Chap.
V—*Denz.* 878 (1643).

21   Paul VI, Encyc. Lett., *Mysterium Fidei—AAS* 57 (1965), pp.
769-70; Pius XII, Encyc. Lett., *Mediator Dei—AAS* 39 (1947), p. 569.

22   Cf. Session XIII, Decree on the Eucharist, Chap. 4—*Denz.* 877
(1642); can. 2—*Denz.* 884 (1642).

23   Cf. The above-mentioned documents in so far as they deal with
the sacrifice of the Mass; besides the following which deal with both
aspects of the mystery: the Decree on the Ministry and Life of Priests,
Presbyterorum Ordinis, nn. 5, 18—*AAS* 58 (1966), pp. 997-9, 1018-9;
Paul VI, Encyc. Lett., *Mysterium Fidei—AAS* 57 (1965), p. 754; Pius
XII, Encyc. Lett., *Mediator Dei—AAS* 39 (1947), pp. 547-572; the
address to those who took part in the International Conference on
Pastoral Liturgy, held at Assisi on 22. ix. 1956—*AAS* 48 (1956), pp.
715-723.

24   Cf. Paul VI, Encyc. Lett., *Mysterium Fidei—AAS* 57 (1965), pp.
769-772; Pius XII, Encyc. Lett., *Mediator Dei—AAS* 39 (1947), pp.
547-572; S.C.R., Instruction *De Musica Sacra*, 3. ix. 1958—*AAS* 50
(1958), pp. 630-663; Instruction *Inter Oecumenici*, 26. ix. 1964—
AAS 56 (1964), pp. 877-900.

25   Cf. Council of Trent, Session XIII, Decree on the Eucharist,
Chap.3—*Denz.* 876 (1639). Cf. also St. Thomas Aquinas, *Summa
Theol.* III, q. 60, a. 1.

26 Cf. Vat. II Const. on Liturgy, *Sacrosanctum Concilium*, nn. 33, 59—*AAS* 56 (1964), pp. 108-109, 116.

27 Cf. *Ibid.*, nn. 14, 17-18—*AAS* 56 (1964), pp. 104, 105.

28 Vat. II Decree on the Ministry and Life of Priests, Presbyterorum Ordinis, n. 5—*AAS* 58 (1966), p. 997.

29 Vat. II Const. on the Church, *Lumen Gentium*, n. 11—*AAS* 57 (1965), pp. 15-16; Decree on Ecumenism, *Unitatis Redintegratio*, nn. 2, 15—*AAS* 57 (1965), pp. 91-92, 101-102.

30 Cf. Vat. II Const. on Liturgy, *Sacrosanctum Concilium*, n. 10—*AAS* 56 (1964), p. 102.

31 *Ibid.*, n. 2—*AAS* 56 (1964), pp. 97-98; cf. also n. 41—*AAS* 56 (1964), p. 111.

32 Mozarabic Prayer—*PL* 96, 759 B.

33 Vat. II Const. on the Church, *Lumen Gentium*, n. 26—*AAS* 57 (1965), p. 31.

34 Cf. Vat. II Const. on Liturgy, *Sacrosanctum Concilium*, n. 42—*AAS* 56 (1964), pp. 111-112.

35 Cf. St. Thomas Aquinas, *Summa Theol.* III, q. 73, a. 3.

36 St. Leo the Great, *Serm.* 63, 7: *PL* 54, 357 C.

37 Vat. II Const. on the Church, *Lumen Gentium*, n. 26—*AAS* 57 (1965), pp. 31-32.

38 Cf. Vat. II Const. on the Church, *Lumen Gentium*, nn. 3, 7, 11, 26—*AAS* 57 (1965), pp. 6, 9-11, 15-16, 31-32; Decree on Ecumenism, *Unitatis Redintegratio*, n. 2—*AAS* 57 (1965), pp. 91-92.

39 Cf. *Ibid.*, nn. 15, 22—*AAS* 57 (1965), pp. 101-102, 105-106.

40 *Ibid.*, n. 22—*AAS* 57 (1965), p. 106.

41 *Ibid.*, n. 15—*AAS* 57 (1965), p. 102.

42 Paul VI, Encyc. Lett., *Mysterium Fidei*—*AAS* 57 (1965), p. 773.

43 Cf. Vat. II Const. on Liturgy, *Sacrosanctum Concilium*, n. 7—*AAS* 56 (1964), pp. 100-101.

44 Council of Trent, Session XXII, Decree on the Mass, Chap. II—*Denz.* 940 (1743).

45 Cf. Vat. II Const. on Liturgy, *Sacrosanctum Concilium*, n. 7—*AAS* 56 (1964), pp. 100-101.

46 Paul VI, Encyc. Lett. *Mysterium Fidei*—*AAS* 57 (1965), p. 764.

47 Cf. Vat. II Const. on Liturgy, *Sacrosanctum Concilium*, n. 56—*AAS* 56 (1964), p. 115.

48   Vat. II Decree on the Ministry and Life of Priests, *Presbyterorum Ordinis*, n. 4—*AAS* 58 (1966), pp. 995-7.

49   Cf. *Ibid.*, n. 4—*AAS* 58 (1966), pp. 995-7; Cf. also n. 3 of this instruction.

50   Cf. Vat. II Const. on Divine Revelation, *Dei Verbum*, n. 21—*AAS* 58 (1966), pp. 87-8.

51   Cf. Vat. II Const. on Liturgy, *Sacrosanctum Concilium*, nn. 14, 26, 30, 38—*AAS* 56 (1964), pp. 104, 107, 108 110.

52   Cf. Vat. II Const. on the Church, *Lumen Gentium*, n. 10—*AAS* 57 (1965), pp. 14-15; Decree on the Ministry and Life of Priests, *Presbyterorum Ordinis*, n. 2—*AAS* 58 (1966), pp. 991-3; Paul VI Encyc. Lett., *Mysterium Fidei*—*AAS* 57 (1965), p. 761.

53   Cf. Vat. II *Lumen Gentium*, n. 10—*AAS* 57 (1965), pp. 14-15; Decree on Ministry and Life of Priests, *Presbyterorum Ordinis*, nn. 2, 5—*AAS* 58 (1966), pp. 991-3, 997-9.

54   Cf. Vat. II Const. on Liturgy, *Sacrosanctum Concilium*, nn. 28-9—*AAS* 56 (1964), pp. 107-8.

55   Cf. *Ibid.*, nn. 48, 106—*AAS* 56 (1964), pp. 113, 126.

56   Cf. *Ibid.*, n. 55—*AAS* 56 (1964), p. 115.

57   St. Thomas Aquinas, *Summa Theol.* III, q. 79, a. 7, ad. 2.

58   Cf. Vat. II Const. on Liturgy, *Sacrosanctum Concilium*, nn. 26-32—*AAS* 56 (1964), pp. 107-8.

59   Cf. S.R.C. Instruction *Musicam Sacram*, 5. iii. 1967—*AAS* 59 (1967), pp. 300-320.

60   Hippolytus, *Traditio Apostolica*, 21—ed. B. Botty, 1963, pp. 58-9; cf. Vat. II Const. on Liturgy, *Sacrosanctum Concilium*, nn. 9, 10—*AAS* 56 (1964), pp. 101-2; Decree on the Apostolate of the Laity, *Apostolicam actuositatem*, n. 3—*AAS* 58 (1966), pp. 839-40; Decree on the Church's missionary activity, *Ad Gentes divinitus*, n. 39—*AAS* 58 (1966), 986-7; Decree on Ministry and Life of Priests, *Presbyterorum Ordinis*, n. 5—*AAS* 58 (1966), pp. 997-9.

61   Vat. II Past. Const. on Church in the Modern World, *Gaudium et Spes*, n. 43—*AAS* 58 (1966), p. 1063.

62   Cf. Conc. Vatican II, Decree on the Ministry and Life of Priests, *Presbyterorum Ordinis*, n. 6.

63   Vat. II Decl. on Christian Education, *Gravissimum educationis*, n.2—*AAS* 58 (1966), pp. 730-1.

64   Vat. II Decree on Ministry and Life of Priests, *Presbyterorum Ordinis*, n. 5—*AAS* 58 (1966), pp. 997-8.

65 Session XXII, Decree on the Mass, Chap. 8—*Denz.* 946 (1749).

66 Vat. II Const. on Liturgy, *Sacrosanctum Concilium*, n. 28—*AAS* 56 (1964), p. 107.

67 *Ibid.*, n. 41—*AAS* 56 (1964), p. 111; cf. Const. on the Church, *Lumen Gentium*, n. 26—*AAS* 57 (1965), pp. 31-32.

68 Cf. n. 47 of this instruction.

69 Cf. Vat. II Const. on the Church, *Lumen Gentium*, n. 3—*AAS* 57 (1965), p. 6.

70 Vat. II Const. on Liturgy, *Sacrosanctum Concilium*, n. 54—*AAS* 56 (1965), p. 115.

71 Cf. *Ibid.*, n. 11—*AAS* 56 (1964), pp. 102-3.

72 Cf. S.R.C. Instruction *Musicam Sacram*, 5. iii. 1967. nn. 6, 8, 11—*AAS* 59 (1967), pp. 302-3.

73 Vat. II Decree on Ministry and Life of Priests, *Presbyterorum Ordinis*, n. 5—*AAS* 58 (1966), p. 998.

74 Vat. II Const. on Liturgy, *Sacrosanctum Concilium*, n. 124—*AAS* 56 (1964), p. 131.

75 Cf. *Ibid.*, nn. 6, 106—*AAS* 56 (1964), pp. 100, 126.

76 *Ibid.*, n. 106—*AAS* 56 (1964), p. 126.

77 *Ibid.*

78 Vat. II Const. on Liturgy, *Sacrosanctum Concilium*, nn. 41-2—*AAS* 56 (1964), pp. 111-2; Const. on the Church, *Lumen Gentium*, n. 28—*AAS* 57 (1965), pp. 33-36; Decree on Ministry and Life of Priests, *Presbyterorum Ordinis*, n. 5—*AAS* 58 (1966), pp. 997-9.

79 Cf. S.C.R. Instruction *Musicam Sacram*, 5. iii. 1967, nn. 16, 27—*AAS* 59 (1967), pp. 305, 308.

80 S.C.R. Instruction *Inter Oecumenici*, 26. ix. 1964, n. 60—*AAS* 56 (1964), p. 891.

81 Vat. II Const. on Liturgy, *Sacrosanctum Concilium*, n. 55—*AAS* 56 (1964), p. 115.

82 Cf. *Ibid.*, n. 55—*AAS* (1964), p. 115; *Missale Romanum, Ritus servandus in celebratione Missae*, 27. vi. 1965, n. 7.

83 Cf. S.C.R., Rubrics on the Breviary and *Missale Romanum*, 26. vii. 1960, n. 502—*AAS* 52 (1960), p. 680.

84 Cf. Session XXI, Decree on Eucharistic Communion, Chaps. 1-3—*Denz.* 930-2 (1726-9).

85 *Ritus servandus in distributione communionis sub utraque specie* 7. iii. 1965, n. 1.

86   Cf. Pius XII Encyc. Lett., *Mediator Dei—AAS* 39 (1947).

87   Cf. *AAS* 56 (1964), p. 7—*AAS* 59 (1967), p. 374.

88   Council of Trent, Session XIII Decree on the Eucharist, Chap. 2—*Denz.* 875 (1638); cf. also Session XXII, Decree on the Mass, Chaps. 1-2—*Denz.* 938 (1740), 940 (1743).

89   Council of Trent, Session XIII, Decree on the Eucharist, Chap. 7—*Denz.* 880 (1646-7).

90   C.I.C., can. 859.

91   S.C. of the Council, Decree on the daily reception of Communion, 20. xii. 1905, n. 6—*AAS* 38 (1905-1906), pp. 401 Seq; Pius XII, Encyc. Lett., *Mediator Dei—AAS* 39 (1947), p. 565.

92   Cf. Council of Trent Session XIII, Decree on the Eucharist Chap. 8—*Denz.* 881 (1648).

93   Cf. Pius XII Encyc. Lett., *Mediator Dei—AAS* 39 (1947), p. 566.

94   Cf. C.I.C., can. 864, 1.

95   Cf. C.I.C., can. 865.

96   Vat. II Const. on Liturgy, *Sacrosanctum Concilium*, n. 26—*AAS* 56 (1964), p. 107.

97   Vat. II Const. on the Church, *Lumen Gentium*, n. 26—*AAS* 57 (1965), pp. 31-32.

98   Vat. II Const. on Liturgy, *Sacrosanctum Concilium*, n. 41—*AAS* 56 (1964), p. 111.

99   Vat. II Decree on the Ministry and Life of Priests, *Presbyterorum Ordinis*, n. 13—*AAS* 58 (1966), 1011; cf. Const. on the Church, *Lumen Gentium*, n. 28—*AAS* 57 (1965), pp. 33-6.

100   Vat. II Const. on Liturgy, *Sacrosanctum Concilium*, n. 28—*AAS* 56 (1964), p. 107.

101   Vat. II Decree on the Ministry and Life of Priests, *Presbyterorum Ordinis*, n. 13—*AAS* 58 (1966), pp. 1011-1012; cf. Paul VI, Encyc. Lett., *Mysterium Fidei—AAS* 57 (1965), p. 762.

102   Vat. II Const. on Liturgy, *Sacrosanctum Concilium*, n. 22, Para. 3—*AAS* 56 (1964), p. 106.

103   Cf. St. Thomas Aquinas, *Summa Theol.* II-II, q. 93, a. 1.

104   Vat. II Const. on Liturgy, *Sacrosanctum Concilium*, n. 11—*AAS* 56 (1964), pp. 102-103; cf. also n. 48, *ibid.*, p. 113.

105   Vat. II Const. on Liturgy, *Sacrosanctum Concilium*, n. 57—*AAS* 56 (1964), pp. 115-116; S.C.R., General Decree, *Ecclesiae Semper*, 7 iii. 1965—*AAS* 57 (1965), pp. 410-12.

106   Vat. II Const. on Liturgy, *Sacrosanctum Concilium*, n. 41–*AAS* 56 (1964), p. 111; Const. on the Church, *Lumen Gentium*, n. 28–*AAS* 57 (1965), pp. 33-36–Decree on the Ministry and Life of Priests, *Presbyterorum Ordinis*, n. 7–*AAS* 58 (1966), 1001-1003.

107   Vat. II Const. on the Church, *Lumen Gentium*, n. 28–*AAS* 57 (1965), p. 35; cf. Decree on the Ministry and Life of Priests, *Presbyterorum Ordinis*, n. 8–*AAS* 58 (1966), pp. 1003-5.

108   S.C. of Sacraments, Instruction *Quam Plurimum*, 1. x. 1949–*AAS* 41 (1949), pp. 509-10; cf. Council of Trent, Session XIII, Decree on Eucharist, Chap. 6–*Denz.* 879 (1645); St. Pius X, Decree *Sacra Tridentina Synodus*, 20. xii. 1905–*Denz.* 1981 (3375).

109   Pius XII, Encyc. Lett., *Mediator Dei–AAS* 39 (1947), p. 569.

110   Vat. II Decree on the Ministry and Life of Priests, *Presbyterorum Ordinis*, n. 5–*AAS* 58 (1956), pp. 997-9.

111   Cf. *Ibid.*, n. 18–*AAS* (1966), pp. 1018-9.

112   Cf. C.I.C., can. 1268, Para. 1.

113   Cf. S.C. Rites, Instruction *Inter Oecumenici*, Sept. 26, 1964, n. 95; S.C. Sacraments, Instruction *Nullo unquam tempore*, May 28, 1938, n. 4; *AAS* 30 (1938) pp. 199-200.

114   Cf. Conc. Vatican II, Decree on the Ministry and Life of Priests, *Presbyterorum Ordinis*, n. 18; Paul VI, Enc. *Mysterium Fidei: AAS* 57 (1965), p. 771.

115   S.C. Rites, Instruction *Inter Oecumenici*, Sept. 26, 1964, n. 95.

116   Cf. *Ibid.*, n. 9.

117   Cf. Code of Canon Law, can. 1271.

118   Cf. Conc. Vatican II, Dogmatic Constitution on the Church, *Lumen Gentium*, n. 11.

119   Conc. Vatican II, Constitution on Liturgy, *Sacrosanctum Concilium*, n. 13.

120   Cf. *Ibid.*, n. 62.

121   Cf. S. Pius X, Decree *Sacra Tridentina Synodus*, Dec. 20, 1905: *Denz.* 1981 (3375).

SACRUM DIACONATUS ORDINEM: Motu Proprio of Pope Paul VI on General Norms for Restoring the Permanent Diaconate in the Latin Church, June 18, 1967.

1   Cf. *Phil.* 1:1.

2   Cf. 1 *Tim.* 3:8-13.

3   Cf. *AAS* 57 (1965) p. 36 n. 29.

4   Cf. Second Vatican Council, Decree: *Ad gentes,* n. 16; *AAS* 58 (1966) p. 967.

5   Cf. *AAS* 57 (1965) p. 46.

6   *Ibid.* p. 36.

7   Cf. 1 *Tim.* 3:10-12.

8   Cf. canons 1095 § 2, and 1096.

9   Cf. 2 *Tim.* 2:21.

10   Canon Law of the Eastern Church. *Concerning Persons* canon 87. *AAS* 49 (1957) p. 462.

11   *Adversus haereses* 4.15.1, *PG* 7; 1013.

12   St. Leo the Great, *Sermon* 85, *PL* 54:436.

MISSALE ROMANUM: Apostolic Constitution of Pope Paul VI on the New Roman Missal, April 3, 1969.

1   See Apost. const. *Quo primum,* July 13, 1570.

2   See Pius XII, Discourse to participants in the First International Congress on Pastoral Liturgy at Assisi, Sept. 22, 1956: *AAS* 48 (1956), 712.

3   See Sacred Congr. of Rites, Decree *Dominicae Resurrectionis,* Feb. 9, 1951: *AAS* 43 (1951), 128 ff.; Decree *Maxima Redemptionis nostrae mysteria,* Nov. 16, 1955; *AAS* 47 (1955), 838 ff.

4   *Constitution on the Sacred Liturgy,* no. 21: *AAS* 56 (1964), 106.

5   Ibid., no. 50: *AAS* 56 (1964), 114.

6   Ibid., no. 51: *AAS* 56 (1964), 114.

7   Ibid., no. 58: *AAS* 56 (1964), 115.

8   Ibid., no. 50: *AAS* 56 (1964), 114.

9   Ibid.

10   See ibid.

11   See ibid., no. 52: *AAS* 56 (1964), 114.

12   See ibid., no. 53: *AAS* 56 (1964), 114.

13   Ibid., no. 51: *AAS* 56 (1964), 114.

14   See *Am* 8, 11.

15   *Constitution on the Sacred Liturgy,* no. 38: *AAS* 56 (1964), 110.

SACRA RITUUM CONGREGATIO: Apostolic Constitution of Pope Paul VI on Division of Sacred Congregation of Rites into Two New Congregations, May 8, 1969.

1   See apost. const, in the form of a Bull, *Immensa aeterni Dei:* in the *Bullarium Romanum* VIII, Turin, ed. 1863, p. 989.

2   See *Canones et Decreta Sacrosancti Oecumenical et Generalis Councilii Tridentini,* sess. XXII, XXIV, XXV.

3   See apost. const. *Quo primum,* July 13, 1570.

4   The five volumes of *Authentic Decrees* published by this Sacred Commission on the liturgy are an eloquent testimony to the work it accomplished.

5   See apost. const. *Divino afflatu,* Nov. 1, 1911: *AAS* 3 (1911), 633-638.

6   See Sacred Congr. of Rites, decree *Dominicae Resurrectionis: AAS* 43 (1951), 128 ff.

7   See Sacred Congr. of Rites, decree *Maxima Redemptionis nostrae mysteria: AAS* 47 (1955), 838 ff.

8   See *Constitution on the Sacred Liturgy: AAS* 56 (1964), 97-138.

9   See nos. 58-64: *AAS* 59 (1967), 904-908.

Sacred Congregation for Divine Worship Instruction on Implementing the Constitution *Missale Romanum,* October 20, 1969.

1   General Revision of the Roman Missal (instruction on the use of the Missal in the future).—Ed.

2   Order for Mass (description of the prayers to be used and rubrics to be carried out in the course of the Mass).——Ed.

3   Order of the readings for Mass (list of the Scripture readings to be used at Mass).——Ed.

4   *De editionibus apparandis et de usu novi Ordinis lectionum Missae: AAS* 61 (1969), 548-549.

5   See *Declaratio circa interpretationes textuum liturgicorum "ad interim" paratas: Notitiae* 5 (1969), p. 68.

6   See Letter to presidents of episcopal conferences, Oct. 16, 1969: *Notitiae* 1 (1965), p. 195; Instruction *De popularibus interpretationibus conficiendis,* Jan. 25, 1969, nos. 41-42: *Notitiae* 5 (1969), pp. 11-12.

7   See *Instruction on Putting into Effect the Constitution on the Sacred Liturgy*, Sept. 26, 1964, no. 42; *Instruction on Music in the Sacred Liturgy*, Mar. 5, 1967, no. 57.

8   See *IG*, no. 21.

9   See *IG*, no. 232.

10   See *IG*, no. 56b.

11   See *IG*, no. 318.

12   See *IG*, no. 66.

13   Variant Masses (Masses for special occasions or special intentions, for example, peace).——Ed.

14   See above, no. 3.

15   *IG*, nos. 26, 50, 56e.

16   See *IG*, no. 26.

17   See *IG*, no. 50.

18   See *IG*, no. 32.

19   See Instruction *De editionibus apparandis et de usu novi Ordinis lectionum Missae*, July 25, 1969, nos. 4-5.

20   See also the Common texts for the singing of the responsorial psalm in this same *Ordo*, nos. 174-175.

Address of Pope Paul VI to a General Audience on the New Mass Rite, November 19, 1969.

1   *Constitution on the Sacred Liturgy*, no. 50.

2   *Acts* 4, 32.

3   See De la Taille, *Mysterium Fidei*, Elucid. IX.

4   See Bouyer.

5   In the person of Christ. See St. Ignatius, *ad Eph. IV*.

6   1 *Cor* 14, 19.

7   *PL* 38, 228, *Serm.* 37; see also *Serm.* 299, p. 1371.

8   No. 19.

9   Zundel.

General Instruction of the Roman Missal, Published as Part of the Roman Missal, March 26, 1970.

1   See Session XXII, September 17, 1562.

2   Vatican Council II, Constitution on the Sacred Liturgy, *Sacrosanctum Concilium* [=L], no. 47; see Dogmatic Constitution on the Church, *Lumen gentium* [=E], nos. 3, 28; Decree on the Ministry and Life of Priests, *Presbyterorum Ordinis* [=P], nos. 2, 4, 5.

3   *Sacramentarium Veronense,* ed. Mohlberg, no. 93.

4   See Eucharistic Prayer III.

5   See Eucharistic Prayer IV.

6   See l 7, 47; P 5, 18.

7   See Pius Xii, encyclical letter *Humani generis: AAS* 42 (1950) 570-571; Paul VI, encyclical letter *Mysterium Fidei: AAS* 57 (1965) 762-769; Solemn of Rites [=SRC], instruction *Eucharisticum mysterium* [=EM], May 25, 1967, nos. 3f, 9: *AAS* 59 (1967) 543, 547.

8   See Session XIII, October 11, 1551.

9   See P 2.

10   See L 11.

11   L 50.

12   Session XXII, Teaching on the Holy Sacrifice of the Mass, chapter 8.

13   *Ibid.,* chapter 9.

14   *Ibid.,* chapter 8.

15   See L 33.

16   L 36.

17   See L 52.

18   See L 35, 3.

19   L 55.

20   Session XXII, Teaching on the Holy Sacrifice of the Mass, chapter 6.

21   See L 55.

SACRAMENTALI COMMUNIONE: Selection from Instruction of the Sacred Congregation for Divine Worship on Communion under Both Kinds, June 29, 1970.

1   See *Institutio generalis Missalis romani,* no. 240.

2   See Council of Trent, sess. XXI, *Decr. de Communione Eucharistica,* chap. 1-3: Denz. 929-932 and (1725-1729).

3   See *Constitution on the Sacred Liturgy,* no. 55.

4   S. Congr. of Rites, general decree promulgating the rite of con-celebration and of Communion under both species, *Ecclesiae semper,* Mar. 7, 1965: *AAS* 57 (1965), 411-412; Instruction on Worship of the Eucharistic Mystery, *Eucharisticum Mysterium,* May 25, 1967, no. 32: *AAS* 59 (1967), 558-559; *Institutio generalis Missalis romani,* nos. 76, 242.

LITURGICAE INSTAURATIONES: Instruction of the Sacred Congregation for Divine Worship on Correct Implementation of the Constitution on the Sacred Liturgy, September 5, 1970.

1   Vat. Coun. II, *Decree on the Priestly Ministry and Life,* no. 5: *AAS* 58 (1966), 997.

2   See S. Congr. of Rites, Instruction on Putting into Effect the Constitution on the Sacred Liturgy, Sept. 26, 1964, nos. 5-6: *AAS* 56 (1964), 878.

3   See Pope Paul VI, Address to General Audience, Aug. 20, 1969; *L'Osservatore Romano,* Aug. 21, 1969.

4   See *Acts* 20, 28.

5   Vat. Coun. II, *Decree on the Pastoral Office of Bishops in the Church,* no. 15: *AAS* 58 (1966), 679-680; *Constitution on the Sacred Liturgy,* no. 22: *AAS* 56 (1964), 106.

6   See *Decree on the Priestly Ministry and Life,* no. 15: *AAS* 58 (1966), 1014-1015.

7   *Constitution on the Sacred Liturgy,* no. 47: *AAS* 56 (1964), 113.

8   Ibid., no. 34: *AAS* 56 (1964), 109.

9   See 1 *Cor.* 4, 1.

10   See *Constitution on the Sacred Liturgy,* nos. 7, 33: *AAS* 56 (1964), 100-101, 108.

11   See ibid., no. 56: *AAS* 56 (1964), 115.

12   See ibid., no. 22, § 3: *AAS* 56 (1964).

13   See S. Congr. of Rites, Instruction on Music in the Sacred Liturgy, Mar. 5, 1967, no. 9: *AAS* 59 (1967), 303; *Constitution on the Sacred Liturgy,* no. 116: *AAS* 56 (1964), 131.

14   See S. Congr. of Rites Instruction on Music in the Sacred Liturgy, no. 4: *AAS* 59 (1967), 301.

15 See *Constitution on the Sacred Liturgy*, nos. 119-120: *AAS* 56 (1964), 130.

16 See S. Congr. of Rites, Instruction on Music in the Sacred Liturgy, no. 9: *AAS* 59 (1967), 303.

17 See *Institutio generalis Missalis romani*, no. 323.

18 See *Notitae* 5 (1969), pp. 9-10; see also nos. 21-24; ibid., pp. 7-8.

19 See S. Congr. for Divine Worship, Instruction on Masses for Special Occasions, *Actio pastoralis*, May 15, 1969, no. 6*e*: *AAS* 61 (1969), 809.

20 See *Institutio generalis Missalis romani*, no. 11.

21 See ibid., nos. 45-46.

22 See ibid., no. 10.

23 See *Constitution on the Sacred Liturgy*, no. 28: *AAS* 56 (1964), 107.

24 See *Institutio generalis Missalis romani*, no. 282.

25 See ibid., no. 283.

26 See S. Congr. of Rites, Instruction on Worship of the Eucharistic Mystery, May 25, 1967, no. 48: *AAS* 59 (1967), 566.

27 See *Institutio generalis Missalis romani*, no. 240.

28 See S. Congr. for Divine Worship, Instruction on Communion under Both Species, June 29, 1970, no. 6: *AAS* 62 (1970), 665.

29 See *Institutio generalis Missalis romani*, no. 68.

30 See ibid., no. 288.

31 See ibid., no. 298.

32 See *Constitution on the Sacred Liturgy*, no. 128: *AAS* 56 (1964), 132-133.

33 See *Institutio generalis Missalis romani*, no. 304.

34 See ibid., no. 260.

35 See nos. 153-280.

36 See nos. 52-57: *AAS* 59 (1967), 567-569.

37 See Letter of Cardinal Giacomo Lercaro, president of the Commission for Implementing the Constitution on the Sacred Liturgy, to the presidents of episcopal conferences, June 30, 1965: *Notitiae* 1 (1965), 261-262.

38 Pope Paul VI, Address to the Italian liturgical commissions, Feb. 7, 1969: *L'Osservatore Romano*, Reb. 8, 1969.

39 See no. 40: *AAS* 56 (1964), 111.

40 See *Institutio generalis Missalis romani*, no. 58.

LAUDIS CANTICUM: Apostolic Constitution of Pope Paul VI on the Roman Breviary, November 1, 1970.

1   See Vat. Coun. II, *Constitution on the Sacred Liturgy,* no. 83: *AAS* 56 (1964), 121.

2   Pius XII, encyc. *Mediator Dei,* Nov. 20, 1947, no. 2: *AAS* 39 (1947), 522.

3   Vat. Coun. II, *Constitution on the Sacred Liturgy,* no. 84: *AAS* 56 (1964), 121.

4   See St. Augustine, *Enarrationes in ps. 85,* no. 1.

5   Vat. Coun. II, *Constitution on the Sacred Liturgy,* no. 24: *AAS* 56 (1964), 106-107.

6   See *Ap* 5, 13.

IN CELEBRATIONE MISSAE: Declaration of the Congregation for Divine Worship on Concelebration, August 7, 1972.

1   General Instruction of the Roman Missal [=IG], no. 58. See Vatican Council II, Constitution on the Liturgy, *Sacro sanctum Concilium* [=L], no. 28: AAS 56, 1964, p. 107.

2   See`Congregation of Rites, *Ecclesiae semper* (March 7, 1965): AAS 57, 1965, pp. 410-411.

3   See Congregation of Rites, *Eucharisticum mysterium* (May 25, 1967) no. 43: AAS 59, 1967, p. 564.

4   Ibid. Nos. 76, 158.

5   See IG no. 76.

6   See Vatican Council II, *Lumen Gentium,* no. 28: AAS 57, 1965, p. 53; *Presbyterorum ordinis,* no. 8: AAS 58, 1966, pp. 1003-1005.

7   *Ecclesiae semper, op. cit; Eucharisticum mysterium, op. cit.,* no. 47.

8   IG no. 155.

9   See Congregation of Rites, *Musicam Sacram* (March 5, 1967) no. 6: AAS 59, 1967, p. 302.

10   See Synod of Bishops, *De sacerdotio ministeriale,* part two, no. 4: AAS 63, 1971, p. 914.

11   *Eucharisticum mysterium, op. cit.* no. 47.

AD PASCENDUM: Motu Proprio of Pope Paul VI on the Order of Diaconate, August 15, 1972.

1   See Vat. Coun. II, *Dogmatic Constitution on the Church*, no. 18: *AAS* 57 (1965).

2   See *Phil.* 1, 1.

3   See I *Tim.* 3, 8-13.

4   *Ad Magnesios*, VI, 1: *Patres Apostolici*, ed. F.X. Funk, I, Tübingen (1901), p. 235.

5   *Ad Trallianos*, II, 3: *Patres Apostolici*, ed. F. X. Funk, I, Tübingen (1901), p. 245.

6   *Epist. ad Philippenses*, V, 2: *Patres Apostolici*, ed. F. X. Funk, I, Tübingen (1901), pp. 301-303.

7   *Mt.* 20, 26-27.

8   *Didascalia Apostolorum*, III, 13, 2-4: *Didascalia et Constitutiones Apostolorum*, ed. F. X. Funk, I, Paderborn (1906), p. 214.

9   *Didascalia Apostolorum*, II, 44, 4: ed. F. X. Funk, I, Paderborn (1906), p. 138.

10   See *Traditio Aposotlica*, 39 and 34: *La Tradition Apostolique de Saint Hippolyte. Essai de reconstitution* by B. Botte, Münster (1963), pp. 87 and 81.

11   *Testamentum D. N. Jesu Christi*, I, 38: ed. and tr. into Latin by I.E. Rahmani, Mainz (1899), p. 93.

12   See St. Justin, *Apologia* I, 65, 6 and 67, 5: St. Justin, *Apologiae duae*: ed. G. Rauschen, Bonn (1911), pp. 107 and 111.

13   See Tertullian, *De Baptismo*, XVII, 1: *Corpus Christianorum*, I, *Tertulliani Opera*, part I, Turnholt (1954), p. 291.

14   See *Didascalia Apostolorum*, II, 31, 2: ed F. X. Funk, I, Paderborn (1906), p. 112; see *Testamentum D. N. Jesu Christi*, I, 31: ed. and tr. into Latin by I. E. Rahmani, Mainz (1899), p. 75.

15   See *Didascalia Apostolorum* II, 57, 6; 58, 1: ed. F. X. Funk, I, Paderborn (1906), pp. 162 and 166.

16   See St. Cyprian, *Epistolae* XV and SVI: ed. G. Hartel, Vienna (1871), pp. 513-520; see St. Augustine, *De catechizandis rudibus*, I, cap. I, 1 : *PL* 40, 309-310.

17   Session XXIII, capp. I-IV: *Mansi*, XXXIII, coll. 138-140.

18   Address to participants in 2nd International Congress of the Lay Apostolate, Oct. 5, 1957: *AAS* 49 (1957), 925.

19 *Mt.* 20, 28.

20 *AAS* 57 (1965), 36.

21 *Ibid.*

22 *AAS* 59 (1967), 697-704.

23 *AAS* 60 (1968), 369-373.

24 See Vat. Coun. II, *Dogmatic Constitution on Divine Revelation*, no. 21: *AAS* 58 (1966), 827.

25 See *Rom.* 12, 11-13.

26 See Paul VI, apost. letter *Sacrum Diaconatus Ordinem*, no. 16: *AAS* 59 (1967), 701.

MINISTERIA QUAEDAM: Motu Proprio of Pope Paul VI on the Ministries of Lector and Acolyte, August 15, 1972.

1 See Vat. Coun. II, *Constitution on the Sacred Liturgy*, no. 62: *AAS* 56 (1964), 117; see also no. 21: loc. cit., 105-106.

2 See Ordo Missae, *Institutio Generalis Missalis Romani*, no. 58, definitive edition (1969), p. 29.

3 Vat. Coun. II, *Constitution on the Sacred Liturgy*, no. 28: *AAS* 56 (1964), 107.

4 Ibid., no. 14: loc. cit., 104.

5 See Vat. Coun. II, *Decree on the Missionary Activity of the Church*, no. 15: *AAS* 58 (1966), 965; ibid., no. 17: loc. cit., 967-968.

6 Vat. Coun. II, *Dogmatic Constitution on the Church*, no. 10: *AAS* 57 (1965), 14.

SACRAM UNCTIONEM INFIRMORUM: Apoltolic Constitution of Pope Paul VI on the Anointing of the Sick, November 30, 1972.

1 Council of Trent, sess. XIV, *De extr. unct.*, chap. I (see *ibid.*, canon I): *CT* VII, 1, 355-356; *DS* 1695, 1716.

2 Ep. *Si Instituta Ecclesiastica*, chap. 8: *PL* 20, 559-561; *DS* 216.

3 *Liber Sacramentorum Romanae Ecclesiae Ordinis Anni Circuli*, ed. L. C. Mohlberg *(Rerum Ecclesiasticarum Documenta, Fontes*, IV), Rome (1960), p. 61; *Le Sacramentaire Grégorien*, ed. J. Deshusses *(Spicilegium Friburgense*, 16), Fribourg (1971), p. 172; see *La Tradition Apostolique de St. Hippolyte*, ed. B. Botte *(Liturgiewissenschaftliche Quellen und Forschungen*, 39), Münster in W. (1963), pp. 18-19; *Le*

Grand Echologe du Monastère Blanc, ed. E. Lanne (*Patrologia Orientalis*, XXVIII, 2), Paris (1958), pp. 392-395.

4   See *Pontificale Romanum: Ordo benedicendi Oleum Catechu-menorum et Infirmorum et conficiendi Chrisma*, Vatican City (1971), pp. 11-12.

5   See M. Andrieu, *Le Pontifical Romain au Moyen-Age*, vol. 1, *Le Pontifical Romain du XLLe siècle (Studi e Testi*, 86), Vatican City (1938), pp. 267-268; vol. 2, *Le Pontifical de la Curie Romaine au XIIIe siècle (Studi e Testi*, 87), Vatican City (1940), pp. 491-492.

6   *Decr. pro Armeniis*, G. Hofmann, *Conc. Florent.*, I/II, p. 130; *DS* 1324 f.

7   Council of Trent, sess. XIV, *De extr. unct.*, chap. 2: *CT* VII, 356; *DS* 1696.

8   *Ibid.*, chap. 3: *CT, ibid.; DS* 1698.

9   *Ibid.*, chap. 3, canon 4: *CT, ibid.; DS* 1697-1719.

10   Vat. Coun. II, *Constitution on the Sacred Liturgy*, no. 73: *AAS* 56 (1964), 118-119.

11   Vat. Coun. II, *Dogmatic Constitution on the Church*, no. 11: *AAS* 57 (1965), 15.

12   See Vat. Coun. II, *Constitution on the Sacred Liturgy*, no. 1: *AAS* 56 (1964), 97.

IMMENSAE CARITATIS: Selection from Instruction of the Sacred Congregation for the Discipline of the Sacraments on Facilitating Communion, January 29, 1973.

1   See Council of Trent, sess. 13, *Decretum de SS. Eucharistiae Sacramento*, chap. 7; DS 880 (1646-1647): "If it is not fitting for one to approach any sacred functions except in a state of holiness, then certainly to the extent that the holiness and godliness of this heavenly Sacrament is more and more known to the Christian, he must take all the more care that he does not come to receive it without great reverence and holiness, especially because of the Apostle's fearful words, which we read: 'He who eats and drinks unworthily, without distinguishing the body of the Lord, eats and drinks judgment to himself' (1 *Cor* 11, 29). Thus one who intends to receive Holy Communion should recall the following precept: 'But let a man prove himself' (1 *Cor* 11, 28), Church custom declares that proving oneself is necessary, so that no one who is aware of having committed mortal sin, though considering himself contrite, will approach the Holy Eucharist without having first made a sacramental confession. This holy Synod declares

that this must be observed perpetually by all Christians, even by priests, wr ose auty it is to celebrate Mass, as long as there are confessors avail-ao e. If, in case of urgent necessity, a priest will have celebrated without previous confession, he is to make a confession as soon as possible." S. Congr. of the Council, decree *Sacra Tridentina Synodus,* Dec. 20, 1905: *ASS* 38 (1905-1906), 400-406; S. Congr. for the Doctrine of the Faith, *Norms for the Imparting of General Absolution,* June 16, 1972, norm I: *AAS* 64 (1972), 511.

2   See Vat. Coun. II, *Constitution on the Sacred Liturgy,* no. 7: *AAS* 56 (1964), 100-101; S. Congr. of Rites, *Instruction on Worship of the Eucharistic Mystery,* May 25, 1967, no. 9: *AAS* 59 (1967), 547; S. Congr. for divine Worship, Instruction *Memoriale Domini,* in which we read: "Let any danger whatsoever be avoided that a lack of reverence or false opinions about the Most Holy Eucharist might creep into souls": *AAS* 61 (1969), 545.

3   Paul VI, Address to International Committee for Eucharistic Congresses:*AAS* 64 (1972), 287.

4   See *Lk* 11, 3.

5   See *Heb* 2, 14.

EUCHARISTIAE PARTICIPATIONEM: Letter from the Sacred Congregation for Divine Worship to the Presidents of the National Conferences of Bishops on Eucharistic Prayers, April 27, 1973.

1   See Paul VI, Apost. const. *Missale Romanum,* Apr. 3, 1969: *AAS* 61 (1969), 217-222.

2   See Vat. Coun. II, *Constitution on the Sacred Liturgy,* no. 48: *AAS* 56 (1964), 113.

3   See Paul VI, Apost. const. *Missale Romanum,* Apr. 3, 1969: *AAS* 61 (1969), 219.

4   See *General Instruction on the Roman Missal,* no. 54.

5   As regards the principles governing translations, see Commission for Implementing the Constitution on the Sacred Liturgy, *Instruction sur la traduction des textes liturgiques pour la célébration avec le peuple,* Jan. 25, 1969: *Notitiae* 5 (1969), 3-12.

6   See *General Instruction on the Roman Missal,* no. 313.

7   See Vat. Coun. II, *Constitution on the Sacred Liturgy,* no. 22, § 3: *AAS* 56 (1964), 106.

8   See Cardinal Benno Gut, Letter to Presidents of Episcopal Conferences, June 2, 1968: *Notitiae* 4 (1968), 146-148; *Indications pour faciliter la catéchèse des anaphores de la Messe: ibid.,* 148-155

9   *General Instruction on the Roman Missal*, no. 54.

10   See *ibid.*, no. 55a.

11   Paul VI, Apost. const. *Missale Romanum*, Apr. 3, 1969: *AAS* 61 1969), 219.

12   See *General Instruction on the Roman Missal*, no. 11.

13   In regard to Eucharistic Prayer I, or the Roman Canon, besides the faculty of introducing names in the *Memento* for godparents in Masses for the initiation of adults into the Church, and the formulas for the *Hanc igitur* in Masses from the Easter vigil to the second Sunday of Easter, for adult Baptisms, for Confirmation, for ordination, marriages, profession, for the consecration of virgins; in regard to Eucharistic Prayers II, III and IV, see Embolisms for adult converts, newly professed religious and consecrated virgins.

14   See *General Instruction on the Roman Missal*, no. 55g.

15   See proper *Communicantes* for Christmas and its octave, for Epiphany, from the Mass of the Paschal vigil until the second Sunday of Easter, for Ascension and for Pentecost.

16   Vat. Coun. II, *Dogmatic Constitution on the Church*, no. 3: *AAS* 57 (1965), 6.

17   Secretariat for Promoting Christian Unity, *Instruction on the Eucharist and Non-Catholic Christians*, June 1, 1972, no. 2b: *AAS* 64 (1972), 520.

18   See Vat. Coun. II, *Dogmatic Constitution on the Church*, no. 23: *AAS* 57, 27.

19   Augustine, *In Joannis Evangelium Tractatus* 26, 13: *CCL* 36, 266; see Vat. Coun. II, *Constitution on the Sacred Liturgy*, no. 47: *AAS* 56 (1964), 113.

20   See *General Instruction on the Roman Missal*, nos. 314-324.

21   *Ibid.*, no. 313.

22   See. S. Congr. for Divine Worship, Instruction *Actio Pastoralis*, May 15, 1969: *AAS* 61 (1969), 806-811; Instruction *Memoriale Domini*, May 29, 1969: *AAS* 61 (1969), 541-547; *Instruction on Holy Communion under Both Species*, June 29, 1970: *AAS* 62 (1970), 664-667.

23   See *General Instruction on the Roman Missal*, no. 11.

24   Vat. Coun. II, *Constitution on the Sacred Liturgy*, no. 52: *AAS* 56 (1964), 114.

25   See *General Instruction on the Roman Missal*, no. 18.

26   See Vat. Coun. II, *Constitution on the Sacred Liturgy*, no. 30: *AAS* 56 (1964), 108; S. Congr. of Rites, *Instruction on Music in the Sacred Liturgy*, Mar. 5, 1967, no. 17: *AAS* 59 (1967), 305.

27   See *General Instruction on the Roman Missal*, no. 23.

PUEROS BAPTIZATOS: Sacred Congregation for Divine Worship Selection from Directory for Masses with Children, November 1, 1973.

1   See S. Congr. for the Clergy, *General Catechetical Directory*, no. 5: *AAS* 64 (1972), 101-102.

2   See Vat. Coun. II, *Constitution on the Sacred Liturgy*, no. 33.

3   See. S. Congr. for the Clergy, *General Catecheticl Directory*, no. 78: *AAS* 64 (1972), 146-147.

4   See Vat. Coun. II, *Constitution on the Sacred Liturgy*, no. 38; see also S. Congr. for Divine Worship, Instruction *Actio Pastoralis*, May 15, 1969: *AAS* 61 (1969), 806-811.

5   On the Liturgy in the first Synod of Bishops: *Notitae* 3 (1967), p. 368.

6   See Vat. Coun. II, *Constitution on the Sacred Liturgy*, nos. 42 and 106; See *General Instruction on the Roman Missal*, no. 23; See S. Congr. of Rites, *Instruction on Worship of the Eucharistic Mystery*, May 25, 1967, no. 38: *AAS* 59 (1967), 562.

7   See *Ordo Missae* with deaf and dumb children in Germany, June 26, 1970, approved and confirmed by this Congregation (Prot. no. 1546/70).

8   See Roman Missal, eucharistic Prayer II.

Sacred Congregation for Divine Worship: Selection from the Decree and Rite of Penance, December 2, 1973.

1   *2 Corinthians* 5:18ff; *Colossians* 1:20.

2   *John* 8:34-36.

3   *1 Peter* 2:9.

4   *Luke* 15.

5   *Luke* 5:20, 27-32; 7:48.

6   *Matthew* 9:2-8.

7   *Romans* 4:25.

8   Roman Missal, Eucharistic Prayer III.

9   *Matthew* 26:28.

10   *John* 20:19-23.

11   *Luke* 24:47.

12   *Acts* 3:19, 26; 17:30.

13   *Romans* 6:4-10.

14   Roman Missal, Eucharistic Prayer III.

15   Roman Missal, Eucharistic Prayer II.

16   Council of Trent, Session XIV, *De sacramento Paenitentiae*, Chapter I: Denz.-Schön. 1668 and 1670: can. 1; Denz.-Schön. 1701.

17   St. Ambrose, Letter 41:12: PL 16, 1116.

18   *Revelation* 19:7.

19   *Ephesians* 1:22-23; Second Vatican Council, constitution *Lumen Gentium*, no. 7: *AAS* 57 (1965) 9-11.

20   Second Vatican Council, constitution, *Lumen gentium*, no. 8: *ibid.*, 12.

21   *1 Peter* 4:13.

22   *1 Peter* 4:8.

23   Council of Trent, Session XIV, *De sacramento Paenitentiae:* Denz.-Schön. 1638, 1740, 1743; Congregation of Rites, instruction *Eucharisticum mysterium*, May 25, 1967, no. 35: *AAS* 59 (1967) 560-561; Roman Missal, *General Instruction*, nos. 29, 30, 56 a. b. g.

24   Second Vatican Council, constitution *Lumen gentium*, no. 11: *AAS* 57 (1965) 15-16.

25   Paul VI, Apostolic Constitution *Paenitemini*, February 17, 1966: *AAS* 58 (1966) 179; Second Vatican Council, constitution *Lumen gentium*, no. 11: *AAS* 57 (1965) 15-16.

26   *Galatians* 2:20, *Ephesians* 5:25.

27   *Titus* 3:6.

28   Paul VI, Apostolic Constitution *Indulgentiarum doctrina*, January 1, 1967, no. 4: *AAS* 59 (1967) 9; see Pius XII, encyclical *Mystici Corporis*, June 29, 1943: *AAS* 35 (1943) 213.

29   Council of Trent, Session XIV, *De sacramento Paenitentiae*, Chapter I: Denz.-Schön. 1673-1675.

30   *Ibid.*, Chapter 4: Denz.-Schön. 1676.

31   Paul VI, Apostolic Constitution *Paenitemini*, February 17, 1966: *AAS* 58 (1966) 179.

32   Council of Trent, Session XIV, *De sacramento Paenitentiae*, Chapter 5: Denz.-Schön. 1679.

33   Council of Trent, Session XIV, *De sacramento Paenitentiae*, Chapter 8: Denz.-Schön. 1679-1692; Paul VI, Apostolic Constitution *Indulgentiarum doctrina*, January 1, 1967, nos. 2-3: *AAS* 59 (1967) 6-8.

34   *Titus* 3:4-5.

35   *Luke* 15:7, 10, 32.

36   Council of Trent, Session XIV, *De sacramento Paenitentiae*, can. 7-8: Denz.-Schön. 1707-1708.

37   *2 Corinthians* 4:10.

38   *Galatians* 4:31.

39   *Matthew* 18:18; *John* 20:23.

40   Second Vatican Council, constitution *Lumen gentium*, no. 26: *AAS* 57 (1965) 31-32.

41   *Philippians* 1:9-10.

42   Congregation for the Doctrine of the Faith, *Normae pastorales circa absolutionem sacramentalem generali modo impertiendam*, June 16, 1972, No. XII: *AAS* 64 (1972) 514.

43   Second Vatican Council, constitution *Sacrosanctum Concilium*, no. 7: *AAS* 56 (1965) 100-101.